THE
THIRD REICH
IN HISTORY AND
MEMORY

Also by Richard J. Evans

The Feminist Movement in Germany 1894–1933
The Feminists
Comrades and Sisters
Death in Hamburg
Rethinking German History
In Hitler's Shadow
Proletarians and Politics
Rituals of Retribution
Rereading German History
In Defence of History
Tales from the German Underworld
Telling Lies About Hitler
The Coming of the Third Reich
The Third Reich in Power
The Third Reich at War
Cosmopolitan Islanders
Altered Pasts

THE
THIRD REICH IN
HISTORY AND
MEMORY

RICHARD J. EVANS

OXFORD
UNIVERSITY PRESS

OXFORD
UNIVERSITY PRESS

Oxford University Press is a department of the
University of Oxford. It furthers the University's objective
of excellence in research, scholarship, and education
by publishing worldwide.

Oxford   New York

Auckland   Cape Town   Dar es Salaam   Hong Kong   Karachi
Kuala Lumpur   Madrid   Melbourne   Mexico City   Nairobi
New Delhi   Shanghai   Taipei   Toronto

With offices in

Argentina   Austria   Brazil   Chile   Czech Republic   France   Greece
Guatemala   Hungary   Italy   Japan   Poland   Portugal   Singapore
South Korea   Switzerland   Thailand   Turkey   Ukraine   Vietnam

Oxford is a registered trade mark of Oxford University Press
in the UK and certain other countries.

Published in the United States of America by
Oxford University Press
198 Madison Avenue, New York, NY 10016

Library of Congress Cataloging-in-Publication Data
Evans, Richard J.
The Third Reich in history and memory / Richard J. Evans.
pages   cm
"First published in Great Britain by Little, Brown Book Group."
Includes bibliographical references and index.
ISBN 978-0-19-022839-2 (hardback : alkaline paper)
1. National socialism.   2. Hitler, Adolf, 1889–1945.   3. World War, 1939–1945—
Influence.   4. Germany—Economic policy—1933–1945.   5. Germany—Politics and
government—1933–1945.   6. Germany—Politics and government—1945.   7. Germany—
History—1933–1945—Historiography.   8. Collective memory—History—21st
century.   9. War and society—History.   10. Political culture—History.   I. Title.
DD256.48E93 2015
943.086—dc23   2014038585

9 8 7 6 5 4 3 2 1
Printed in the United States of America
on acid-free paper

CONTENTS

PREFACE

Over the past fifteen years or so, since the end of the twentieth century, our understanding of Nazi Germany has been transformed in a variety of ways. This collection of previously published essays offers both a report on this transformation and a critical commentary on it. There have been several major changes in perspective that have informed research and writing. The first of these is the 'global turn' in historical studies that has accompanied the globalisation processes in society, culture and the economy since the late twentieth century. Often seen against the long-term background of modern German history since the era of Bismarck's unification of the country in the nineteenth century, the Third Reich is now increasingly also viewed in a broader international, even global context, as part of the age of imperialism, its drive for domination building on a broader tradition of the German quest for empire. The neglected role of food supplies and food shortages in the Second World War can only be understood on a global level. Nazi policies in Eastern Europe drew heavily on Hitler's image of the American colonisation of the Great Plains. Companies like Krupp and Volkswagen were not merely or at times mainly German enterprises, they operated on a global scale. Several of the essays in this volume look at the dividends this new perspective has brought, and point up, too, some of its limitations.

This is linked to a shift of perception in historical studies that has increasingly placed the nation-state in a broader, transnational context, looking not only at how it related to other nation-states but also how it was affected by wider developments. Nazism, for example, appears in recent work as an ideology drawing on sources from many countries from Russia to France, Italy to Turkey, rather than being the culmination of exclusively German intellectual traditions, as used to be the case. Increasingly, historians have come to see the Nazi extermination of the Jews not as a unique historical event but as a genocide with parallels and similarities in other countries and at other times. Here again, a change of perspective has brought dividends, but it is also increasingly running up against problems of interpretation that some of the essays in this book seek to identify.

This applies even more to a third area of recent research, the work carried out on Nazi society. Over the past decade and a half, Nazi Germany has come to appear to growing numbers of historians as a political system that rested not on police terror and coercion but on popular approval and consent. Several of the essays in this book take stock of this work and argue that for all the advances in understanding it has brought, the time has come to remember that Nazi Germany actually was a dictatorship in which civil rights and freedoms were suppressed and opponents of the regime were not tolerated. Repression was carried out not just against social outsiders but also against huge swathes of the working classes and their political representatives. Prominent Jews in the Weimar Republic, notably Walther Rathenau, were not despised, marginal figures but enjoyed huge popular support and admiration, expressed in the national outpouring of grief on his death. Nazism, it should not be forgotten, was a tiny fringe movement until the very end of the 1920s. The regime had to work hard to get popular support once it came to power in 1933, and violence played as important a role as propaganda. Hitler and the propagation of his image to the German people were vital in winning people over, but recent research has advanced considerably our knowledge of the man behind the image, and this, too, is an essential part of understanding the Third Reich.

Perhaps the most remarkable change that has come about in

historical work on Nazi Germany since the late twentieth century, however, has been the increasing intertwining of history and memory. It is now almost impossible to write about the Third Reich in the years of its existence, 1933–45, without also thinking about how its memory survived, often in complex and surprising ways, in the post-war years. The essays in this book examine how prominent industrial firms and individual businessmen who became involved, sometimes very heavily indeed, in the crimes of Nazism, tried to suppress the memory of their involvement after the war. Often the transformation of memory took on strange forms, as in the appropriation by Mexicans of the Volkswagen Beetle, originally the Nazi 'Strength-through-Joy Car', as a national icon in the late twentieth century. Sometimes, however, the growing need to confront the misdeeds of Nazism and expose the complicity and guilt of those who participated in them has led to crude and sweeping condemnation where historians should be making careful distinctions. The discovery of a wealthy businessman's concealment of his activities in the Third Reich has led to massive exaggerations about his implication in the worst crimes of the regime; the revelation, after decades of careful cover-ups, of the role professional diplomats played in the development of Nazi foreign policy has led to unsupported accusations that they actually drove on the extermination of the Jews rather than merely facilitating it (bad enough in itself, but not the same thing, and a thesis that implicitly lets the real guilty parties off the hook).

Nazi Germany found its climax and fulfilment and also experienced its eventual downfall in the Second World War, and here, too, there has been a change of perspective since the late twentieth century. The war's global scope and connections have now been recognised; there were not two separate wars, in East and West, but, rather, one war with multiple connections between the various theatres. Military history, as this volume shows, can be illuminating in itself, but also needs to be situated in a larger economic and cultural context. Wherever we look, whether at decision-making at the top, or at the inventiveness and enterprise of second-rank figures, wider contextual factors remained vital.

Finally, in recent years research has focused increasingly on post-war Germany, where the subterranean continuities with the Nazi era have become steadily more apparent. The 'ethnic cleansing' of millions of undesirable citizens did not end with the Nazis but continued well into the years after the fall of the Third Reich, though this time directed against Germans rather than being perpetrated by them. Urban planners developed utopias that found expression in the Nazis' idea of the de-urbanised city but also shared many of their assumptions with visions of the city in other parts of the world. And the growing campaign for the restitution of artworks looted by the Nazis or stolen from their original, often Jewish owners, addresses a problem that did not begin with the Third Reich and did not end with its demise. Here again, the long-term perspective helps us understand the problem at hand, which is also a problem of global dimensions. The extension of historical research into the postwar era has further strengthened the close mutual relations between history and memory. The essays collected here show, among other things, that memory needs to be subjected to the close scrutiny of history if it is to stand up, while history's implications for the collective cultural memory of Nazism in the present need to be spelled out with precision as well as with passion.

The following chapters, all written in the last fifteen years, reflect these major shifts in perception of Nazi Germany, a fact that prompted me to bring them together in a single volume, that, it is to be hoped, adds up to more than the sum of its parts. Most of them are extended book reviews that use a new study of one or other aspect of the Third Reich as a starting point for wider reflections, and for this reason there is inevitably a certain amount of overlap and repetition; I have tried to reduce it to a minimum, but sometimes it has been impossible to avoid. Only where some original research is involved, as in Chapters 6 and 7, or where the article originally appeared in an academic journal, as in Chapter 17, have I provided endnote references; in three of the chapters – 14, 17 and 24 – I have added a brief

Afterword responding to points made by critics on the chapter's first publication, or pointing the reader to further literature discussed in the text. For permission to reprint, I am grateful to the editors of the journals and magazines where these essays first appeared; full details are provided in the Acknowledgements on page 441. And I am especially indebted to Victoria Harris for assembling the chapters from very disparate sources, and to Christine L. Corton for reading the proofs with a professional eye.

RICHARD J. EVANS
Cambridge
March 2014

PART I

REPUBLIC AND REICH

1. BLUEPRINT FOR GENOCIDE?

Dotted around the world there are still a few reminders of the fact that, between the 1880s and the First World War, Germany, like other major European powers, possessed an overseas colonial empire. If you go to Windhoek in Namibia, you can still pick up a copy of the *Allgemeine Zeitung*, a newspaper which caters for the remaining German-speaking residents of the town. If you fancy a trip to the Namibian seaside you can go to the coastal town of Lüderitz, passing ruined railway stations with their names still in Gothic letters, and spend time on Agate Beach enjoying the surf and keeping an eye out for penguins. In Tanzania, you can stay in the lakeside town of Wiedhafen. If you're a businessman wanting to bulk-buy palm oil in Cameroon, the Woermann plantations are still the place to go. In eastern Ghana, German-style buildings that once belonged to the colony of Togo are now advertised as a tourist attraction.

Similarly, in the Pacific you can sail round the Bismarck Archipelago and visit Ritter Island (though there's not much left: a volcanic eruption blew most of it to bits in 1888). Further east, if you visit a bookshop in Samoa you can pick up the works of the leading local poet, Momoe von Reiche. In Chinese restaurants almost anywhere in the world you can order a German-style Tsingtao beer, first produced in China in 1903 by the Germania brewery in the German-run town of the same name (now transliterated as Qingdao). In Qingdao itself you may come across the imposing Romanesque-revival edifice of St

Michael's Cathedral, which looks as if it belongs in a city somewhere in north Germany a century or so ago. In a sense, it does.

All in all, it's not much compared to the extensive remains, physical, cultural and political, left by larger and longer-lasting European overseas empires, which together covered most of the world's land surface at one time or another. The German empire lasted a mere three decades and was broken up at the end of the First World War, its constituent parts redistributed among Britain, France, Belgium, Australia and South Africa. Small in surface area compared to the British, ephemeral in duration, the former empire still attracted attention in the interwar years, when colonial propagandists lobbied to get it back, but even the Nazis paid it little serious attention, preferring to go for conquests in Europe instead, at least to begin with.

For many years, such historical writing as there was on the subject – the work of the Anglo-German economic historian William Otto Henderson was the outstanding instance – tended to focus on refuting the allegations of violence and brutality that had led to the empire's dismantling and redistribution at the Paris Peace Conference in 1919. By the 1960s these arguments were no longer very relevant. However, the situation was transformed by the work of Helmut Bley, who in *South-West Africa under German Rule 1894–1914* (1968) reconstructed the horrifying story of the German war against the Herero and Nama tribes in Namibia in 1904–7.

The story told by Bley isn't complicated. The mounting pace of land seizures by the colonial government in the early 1900s led to attacks on German farmers, resulting in around 150 settler deaths and the dispatch of 14,000 troops from Berlin under General Lothar von Trotha, a hard-line Prussian army officer with previous colonial experience. 'I know,' he said, 'that African tribes yield only to violence. To exercise this violence with crass terrorism and even with gruesomeness was and is my policy.' After defeating a Herero force at Waterberg, he announced that any Herero 'found inside the German frontier, with or without a gun or cattle' would be executed. Herero cattle herders caught in the action were killed on the spot; women and children were driven into the desert and left to starve. The Chief of the General Staff in Berlin, Alfred von Schlieffen, in thrall, like all Prussian officers, to the supposedly Clausewitzian doctrine that the aim of a war must be the total annihilation of the enemy force, praised Trotha's campaign as 'brilliant', especially his use of the desert to complete what the General Staff's official publication, *Der Kampf*, called, approvingly, 'the extermination of the Herero nation'.

But voices were raised in criticism, too; Chancellor Bernhard von Bülow described the action disapprovingly as un-Christian and warned it would damage Germany's reputation abroad. Social Democratic and Catholic Centre Party politicians were outspoken in their condemnation. The civilian governor of the colony, Theodor Leutwein, elbowed aside by the military because of his policy of compromise with the Hereros, protested about the action to Bülow and declared the extermination a 'grave mistake'. He was dismissed for his pains, but his view that the Hereros should instead be recruited as labourers won sufficient adherents to bring about the arrest of the remainder of the tribe, mostly women and children, along with the members of the Nama, and their incarceration in 'concentration camps' (the first official German use of the term).

Here, however, their fate was no better. At the worst of the camps, on the rocky terrain of Shark Island off the Namibian coast, the prisoners were used as forced labour, fed on minimal rations, exposed to bitter winds without adequate clothing and beaten with leather whips if they failed to work hard enough. Every day, bodies were taken to the beach and left for the tide to carry them out into the shark-infested waters. Even the South African press complained about the 'horrible cruelty' of the camp regime. The camps also became sites of scientific investigation, as the anthropologist Eugen Fischer, later a leading 'racial hygienist' under the Third Reich, descended on the town of Rehoboth to study its mixed-race inhabitants (he called them the 'Rehoboth bastards'). He and his colleagues obtained skulls for craniometric studies of different races; up to three hundred of them eventually found their way to Germany.

Fischer concluded that mixed-race offspring (of Boers or German settlers and black Africans) were inferior to the former but superior to the latter, and decided they were suitable as a kind of non-commissioned officer class in the police, postal service and other arms of the state. As a useful if inferior race, they should be protected, unlike the Herero and the Nama. The law, however, followed Trotha's belief that Africans were subhuman and his almost pathological fear that racial mixing would spread disease. In 1905, racial intermarriage was banned by law, and two years later all existing marriages between Germans and Africans were annulled. These measures introduced the term *Rassenschande*, or 'racial defilement', into German legal terminology – it was to resurface thirty years later, in the Nuremberg Laws. The official status ascribed to the German settlers was different from that of the rest of the population, allowing Herero men to be conscripted for forced labour and compelling them to wear identification tags (another measure later applied by the Nazis).

The Herero population, estimated to be 80,000 before the war, was reduced to 15,000 by the end, while up to 10,000 out of a total of 20,000 Nama were exterminated. Of some 17,000 Africans incarcerated in the concentration camps, only half survived. Given Trotha's racial beliefs, there can be no doubt that this was what would later come to be called a genocide. Its exposure by Bley raised in urgent form the question of continuity between the Kaiser's Germany and Hitler's. Other colonial regimes were brutal, most notably Belgian rule in the Congo, and did not hesitate to use mass murder to suppress uprisings or establish control, from the French in Algeria in the 1870s to the Italians in Ethiopia in the 1930s. Racial discrimination, expropriation and labour conscription were far from uniquely German.

But only the Germans introduced concentration camps, named them as such and deliberately created conditions so harsh that their purpose was clearly as much to exterminate their inmates as it was to force them to work. (It would be left to the Nazis to devise the chilling term 'extermination through labour', but the effect was the same.)

Only the Germans mounted an explicit attempt to exterminate an entire colonised people on racial grounds. Only the Germans legally banned racial intermarriage in their colonies, as they did not only in South-West Africa but also in East Africa (1906) and Samoa (1912). Only the Germans subsequently mounted a campaign of racial extermination on a global scale which encompassed not only Europe's Jews but also, potentially, the Jewish inhabitants of the rest of the world. Was there a connection between the two?

For decades after the publication of Bley's book, this question remained, perhaps surprisingly, unaddressed. The critical historians of the 1970s and 1980s who turned their attention to continuities between Imperial Germany and the Third Reich concentrated on the domestic roots of Nazism, on Hitler's rule in Germany and on the Holocaust. The anti-imperialism of the left, fuelled by the Vietnam War, and perhaps part of the background to Bley's work, subsided as American troops left and Europe's remaining colonies were given their independence. In West Germany the legacy of colonialism in everyday life began to vanish with growing economic modernity. Even the grocery shops selling *Kolonialwaren* – coffee, tea, spices, rice and similar dry goods from overseas – that could still be seen in German towns in the early 1970s were now largely renamed or disguised; few who buy their coffee at an Edeka store today, for example, realise that the name stands for *Einkaufsgenossenschaft der Kolonialwarenhändler* (consumer cooperative of colonial goods traders). After the 1970s, Germany's former colonies seemed an irrelevance and were largely forgotten.

In the 1990s interest began to revive with the emergence of post-colonial studies. As historians now put racism and racial ideology instead of totalitarianism and class exploitation at the centre of their explanations of National Socialism, the history of the German colonising experience no longer seemed so very irrelevant. The renewal of interest was signalled by the publication in 1996 of a revised, English-language edition of Bley's now classic work, as *Namibia under German Rule*. Monographs and articles began to appear on colonialist discourse in Germany, on the colonial origins of racial science and on representations of colonial subjects in literature. The growing interest in cultural memory led to studies of postcolonial memories and commemorations in Germany. Sebastian Conrad's *German Colonialism: A Short History* (2012) sums up this new literature and places it in the context of globalisation, which has led to a revival of interest in the empire. With its many excellent illustrations and maps, its annotated critical bibliography and its acute awareness of historiographical trends, it is a model of its kind, providing an essential guide to the subject and intelligent pointers for further research.

The origins of German colonialism, as Conrad notes, lay partly in German history, where colonial dreams and fantasies served as a blank screen on to which nationalists could project an image of German unity before it was finally achieved. As the composer Richard Wagner declared in 1848, 'we will sail in ships across the sea and here and there set up a new Germany ... We will do better than the Spanish, for whom the New World became a cleric-ridden slaughterhouse, and differently from the English, for whom it became a treasure-trove. We will do it in a wonderful, German way.' Far more important, however, was the global context of German capitalism, centred on autonomous trading states like Hamburg. Leading Hamburg merchants in the 1870s were said to have visited 'every town on the Mississippi' and to have stayed 'twenty times in London' but never once been to Berlin. Building on the rapid growth of German industry and economic power, Hamburg's merchants traded in many coastal areas of Africa and other uncolonised parts of the globe, and maintained 279 consulates in cities across the world. German scientists, explorers and missionaries, such as Gerhard Rohlfs, the first European to traverse Africa from north to south (often wearing Muslim dress), won a popular following back at home for their exploits.

Bismarck was unenthusiastic ('As long as I remain chancellor,' he said in 1881, 'we will not become involved in colonialism'), but in 1884 he triggered the 'scramble for Africa' by declaring protectorates over a number of areas in which German economic interests were involved, backing similar moves by the French in an attempt to divert their energies from avenging their loss of Alsace-Lorraine in the Franco-Prussian War. Perhaps he also wanted to placate mercantile interests represented by the powerful National Liberal Party, whose support he needed in forthcoming national elections. A scramble for territory had in any case become almost inevitable after Anglo-French rivalry in North Africa reached a critical point in 1881–2. Whatever the reason, as the scramble extended from Africa across the globe, Germany amassed an empire that eventually became the fourth largest after the British, French and Dutch.

The eclectic group of territories claimed by the Germans included the sparsely populated arid region of present-day Namibia, where German cattle ranchers quickly established themselves, and where the mining of copper and diamonds from 1907 onwards brought some profit to private enterprise; the malarial coastal areas of Cameroon, where the mercantile interests of the Woermann family from Hamburg were dominant (rubber and palm oil were produced by German-run plantations inland); Togo, where trade, again in palm oil, was controlled largely by local Afro-Brazilian elites on the coast; the populous colony of German East Africa (present-day Tanzania minus Zanzibar, but including Rwanda and Burundi), where German settlers established cotton and sisal plantations; New Guinea and Samoa and associated Pacific islands, where German settlers were few and mercantile interests prevailed; and the Chinese treaty port of Jiaozhou, leased for ninety-nine years in 1897 and run by the German naval ministry, which adopted an energetic policy of modernisation and improvement, providing the town of Qingdao with electric streetlights and a university at which Chinese students could imbibe German science and scholarship.

Bismarck's vision of protectorates run by private enterprise without the involvement of the state, along the lines of the old East India Company's administration of the subcontinent, did not last long. Violent clashes with African societies resisting growing exploitation by German merchants and settlers soon brought in formal rule by German bureaucrats, backed by military force. This only made things worse, as the state began to use violence to protect planters and settlers who had clashed with indigenous farmers and traders, provoking resistance on a larger scale. The genocidal war in South-West Africa was the most dramatic instance, but violence was a constant feature of German rule. In East Africa, for instance, continual military clashes, many of them triggered by the unscrupulous colonial adventurer Carl Peters, drew the imperial government in Berlin to take over the colony's administration in 1891; but armed conflict continued, with sixty-one major 'penal expeditions' launched in the following six years. In 1905, conflict over land seizures, tax rises and forced labour requirements led to the Maji-Maji uprising, in which some 80,000 Africans died at the hands of the military. In contrast to the situation in South-West Africa, this was not seen as a racial war by the Germans, and indeed many of the casualties were inflicted by African troops in German uniform, but the death toll was immense, with more than 200,000 Africans perishing from the famine caused by the destruction of rebel fields and villages.

Violence, including public beatings of Africans, was a part of everyday life in the German colonies: the officially recorded number of beatings in Cameroon, certainly an underestimate, rose from 315 in 1900 to 4,800 in 1913. African chiefs in Cameroon took their case to the Reichstag, but the governor's subsequent dismissal had more to do with the objections of traders and missionaries to his policy of granting big land concessions to the planters than with his undoubted brutality. The situation reached a crisis point near the end of German rule, when a former paramount chief was publicly executed for objecting to racial segregation measures in Douala, the main town. The continuing fragility of German control was evident. Given their small numbers in comparison to the Africans – fewer than two thousand settlers and officials in Cameroon – the Germans could hope to establish only 'islands of power' in their colonies. Nowhere did Africans wholly accept German sovereignty. Their effective exclusion from the political and public spheres of the colonies doomed German rule to appear alien to them.

Indeed, it frequently prompted Africans to combine in resistance; after the Maji-Maji uprising, the governor of East Africa conceded that what began as a locally limited rebellion by a few 'half-savage tribes' eventually turned 'into a kind of national struggle against foreign rule'. Sometimes German policies could create new identities, as in Rwanda, where colonial officers armed with ethnographic manuals turned loose social differentiations between Hutu and Tutsi into fixed racial identities that then became the basis for legal distinctions. The result was what some historians have described as an 'ethnogenesis' that laid the foundations for the genocidal massacres in 1994.

It was also possible for scientific experiments to be carried out in the colonies that would have been impossible in Germany. The Nobel Prize-winning bacteriologist Robert Koch had no difficulty injecting a thousand East Africans suffering from sleeping sickness with dangerously high doses of arsenic every day in the search for a cure, with predictably high death rates among the subjects. Indeed, ideas of racial differentiation and hereditary 'inferiority' were given a huge boost by eugenic investigations by scientists such as Eugen Fischer and helped generate and popularise the racial ideas later put into practice by the Nazis. Shows like the Berlin Colonial Exhibition of 1896, alongside the presentation of an African village in Hagenbeck's Tierpark, a privately run zoo in Hamburg, played their part in building a popular sense of racial superiority among Germans.

Some saw the colonies as laboratories of modernity, where new towns and cities could be built without regard to the rights of existing landowners, where racial science could be employed to create a new social order in place of outmoded European hierarchies of status, and where new model communities could be founded on the traditional patriarchal principles currently being undermined by an increasingly vociferous feminist movement back home. The vocabulary and purposes of colonial missionary work were re-imported into Germany as the Protestant 'Inner Mission' set out to rescue the destitute and 'work-shy' from the 'dark continent' of poverty and ignorance in the slums of major cities. In 1913, a new law defining

German citizenship on the basis of ethnic descent rather than residence (as was usual in the rest of Europe) drew directly on racial doctrines hammered out in the colonies. German nationalists began to think of Poles and 'Slavs' as racially inferior, and to abandon talk of Germany's 'civilising mission' in Eastern Europe, as the belief that Poles could be turned into useful Germans began to give way to the conviction that their racial character, like that of the Africans, put them beyond redemption.

Does all this mean that there was a direct line from the colonial empire to the Holocaust? For all the obvious similarities between the Herero and Nama genocide and the extermination of Europe's Jews less than forty years later, there were also significant differences. Although there undoubtedly were concentration camps in South-West Africa, they were not like Treblinka, devoted solely to killing members of a racial minority. The Jews appeared to the Nazis as a global threat; Africans, like Slavs, were a local obstacle to be subjugated or removed to make way for German settlers. Colonial experience, particularly in the field of race, infused the ideology of National Socialism, but the personal continuities were few, despite the examples of Hermann Göring's father, the first governor of South-West Africa, or Franz Ritter von Epp, who served with Trotha in the Herero war and later became Nazi governor of Bavaria, or Viktor Boettcher, deputy governor of Cameroon and later the senior state official in a Nazi-occupied part of Poland.

Trotha's genocidal war was an exception in German colonial history, and it owed more to the military and racial doctrines of its author than to the wider characteristics of German colonialism. There was no equivalent in Eastern Europe between 1939 and 1945 of the self-proclaimed mission of modernisation and civilisation enshrined in the educational, economic and religious policies adopted in the final phase of German colonial rule. It took the brutalising influence of the First World War – itself part of colonialism's impact on Europe – to make political violence an endemic feature of life in Germany in the 1920s and 1930s and to turn men like Boettcher into Nazis. German colonialism does seem to have been more systematically racist in conception and more brutally violent in operation than that of other European nations, but this does not mean it inspired the Holocaust.

Nevertheless, the Herero war, far more than any other aspect of colonialism, has entered the public memory of present-day Germany as a significant parallel to and precursor of the Holocaust. It has led to impassioned debates about how best it should be commemorated. Nowhere have such arguments been more keenly debated than in the trading port of Bremen, where, in a small park behind the main railway station, there is a ten-metre-high brick elephant; commuters and tourists walk past it every day. Put up towards the end of the Weimar Republic, the stylised monument was conceived as a memorial to and a reminder of the history of German colonialism. Terracotta tiles were set into the plinth, each bearing the name of one of the former colonies. Speeches delivered to vast crowds gathered in the park for the statue's inauguration on 6 July 1932 celebrated the achievements of colonialism and demanded the restoration of the lost colonies.

Improbably, the elephant survived the Second World War unscathed, although the various inscriptions around the plinth were quickly removed after 1945. By the fiftieth anniversary of its construction in 1982, it had become an embarrassment, especially in view of the continuing rule of the South African apartheid regime over Namibia. In 1988, the local youth wing of the trade union IGM put up a sign next to the plinth: 'For Human Rights, Against Apartheid'. Two years later, the elephant was officially declared an 'anti-colonial monument' in defiance of its original purpose, obvious though that was. When Namibia gained its independence, Bremen's mayor staged an official celebration around the elephant, and in 1996 Sam Nujoma, the Namibian president, unveiled a new plaque inscribed 'In Memory of the Victims of German Colonial Rule in Namibia 1884–1914' on a state visit to Germany. The elephant is now cared for by an officially recognised society dedicated to tolerance, creativity and multiculturalism. A bronze plaque reminds visitors of the monument's past; nearby a small memorial to the Herero and Nama has been built as a kind of 'anti-monument'.

2. IMAGINING EMPIRE

A few decades ago, historians searching for the longer-term roots of Nazism's theory and practice looked to the ruptures and discontinuities in German history: the failed revolution of 1848; the blockage of democratic politics after unification in 1871; the continued dominance of aristocratic elites over a socially and politically supine middle class; the entrenched power of the traditionally authoritarian and belligerent Prussian military tradition – in short, everything, they argued, that had come by the outbreak of the First World War to distinguish Germany from other major European powers and set it on a 'special path' to modernity that ended not in the creation of a democratic political system and open society to go with an industrial economy, but in the rise and triumph of the Third Reich.

Such arguments were discredited by the 1990s, as it became clear that imperial Germany's middle classes had been far from supine, its political culture was active and engaged, and its aristocratic elites had lost most of their power by the outbreak of the First World War. The 1848 revolution was shown to have transformed German political culture, not to have restored the old regime. Comparisons with other countries revealed similar deficits of social mobility and openness in Britain, tendencies to authoritarianism in France, military domination in Austria and more besides. But if there was no domestic 'special path' from unification to the rise of the Third Reich, where should historians look instead?

Over the last few years, the answer, it has become increasingly clear, can be found only by expanding our vision and viewing German history not in a domestic context or even a European one, but in the context of global and above all colonial developments in the Victorian era and after. This view of German history is perhaps possible only at a time when we have become acutely aware of globalisation as a contemporary phenomenon, but it has thrown up many vital new interpretations and generated a growing quantity of significant research that links Germany's relation to the world in the nineteenth century with its attempt under the Nazis to dominate it. Now this research has been brought together in *Nazi Empire* (2010), a powerful and persuasive new synthesis by Shelley Baranowski, previously known for more specialised studies, notably an excellent book on the Nazi leisure organisation 'Strength through Joy'.

Baranowski's story begins in the mid-1880s, when Bismarck reluctantly agreed to the establishment of colonial protectorates in order to win the support of National Liberals and Free Conservatives in the Reichstag. Bismarck was wary of the financial and political commitment involved in full colonisation, but he was soon outflanked by imperialist enthusiasts, merchants and adventurers, and by 1890, when he was forced out of office, Germany had a fully fledged overseas empire. It was, admittedly, not much to write home about. The 'scramble for Africa' had left the Reich with little more than leftovers after the British and the French had taken their share: Namibia, Cameroon, Tanganyika, Togo; elsewhere in the world, New Guinea and assorted Pacific islands such as Nauru and the Bismarck Archipelago. A younger generation of nationalists, who did not share Bismarck's sense of the precariousness of the newly created Reich, complained it was an empire on the level of the (late nineteenth-century) Spanish or Portuguese empires, hardly worthy of a major European power.

Moreover, the colonies Germany did possess proved in more than one instance peculiarly difficult to run. The colonial regime responded with policies of extreme harshness. Prussian military doctrine held that the complete destruction of enemy forces was the prime objective of war, but in the colonies this became enmeshed with racism and a fear of guerrilla attacks to create a genocidal mentality that responded to unrest and uprisings with a policy of total annihilation, by methods that included deliberate starvation through the destruction of crops and villages, leading to more than 200,000 deaths in the German colony of Tanganyika during the Maji-Maji uprising. Even more notoriously, in Namibia, the Hereros and Nama were driven into the desert without supplies, their waterholes poisoned, their cattle sequestered; they died of disease and malnutrition. Victory was followed by an apartheid regime with laws and regulations forbidding racial mixing and reducing the Africans to the status of poorly paid labourers.

Already, however, German policy had begun to move towards the acquisition of new colonies. Where were they to come from? With Kaiser Wilhelm II's assumption of a leading role in policy-making, Germany began the construction of a large battle fleet in 1898. By focusing on heavy battleships rather than light, mobile cruisers, the navy's creator, Admiral von Tirpitz, was adopting the high-risk strategy of working towards, or at least threatening, a Trafalgar-style confrontation in the North Sea that would defeat or cripple the British, whose domination of the seas was regarded as the major obstacle to German imperial glory, and force them to agree to an expansion of the German overseas empire. Germany now adopted an aggressive 'world policy', aiming to boost the status of its empire and gain a 'place in the sun' comparable to that of other European powers. Soon, uncontrollable imperialist enthusiasms were bubbling up from the steamy undergrowth of pressure-group politics.

These focused on Europe as much as overseas. A large chunk of Poland, annexed in the eighteenth century, belonged to Germany, and the government began to encourage ethnic Germans to settle in areas dominated by Polish-speakers, but although 130,000 moved there in the imperial period, that was by no means enough to replace the 940,000 ethnic Germans who migrated west between 1886 and 1905 in search of a better life. Dissatisfied with this situation, radical nationalists began to demand a war in the east that would conquer the Slavs and rescue the millions of imperilled German-speakers who lived in Eastern Europe from 'Russification' or 'Magyarisation' by incorporating them into a hugely expanded Reich. The influential Pan-German League went even further, pressing the government to contemplate the annexation of Holland, Flanders, Switzerland, Luxembourg, Romania and the Habsburg Empire, all of which they thought of as 'German' lands, and to couple this with the removal of civil rights from Germany's tiny Jewish minority. Once German domination of Europe had been achieved, the expansion of the overseas empire would inevitably follow.

Under such influences, Social Darwinism gained increasing currency in government circles, propagating a view of international relations as determined by a struggle between races – Germanic, Slavic, Latin – for survival and ultimately domination. A large colonial empire was obviously Germany's due. Nevertheless, colonial ideology continued to be opposed by the two largest political parties, the Marxist-oriented Social Democrats and the Catholic Centre, who vehemently condemned German colonial atrocities in 1905–6. In 1913, these parties, together with left-wing liberals, managed to block the introduction of anti-miscegenation measures in Germany on grounds of the sanctity of marriage (for the Catholics) and the universality of human rights (for the socialists and liberals). Even so, the resulting Citizenship Law, uniquely among European nations, defined citizenship not by residence but by 'community of descent'.

When war threatened in 1914, the pressure from the Pan-Germans made it (at the very least) easier for the government to get involved, while the Social Darwinist convictions of some of the major actors weakened the will to find a peaceful way out of the crisis. Once war had broken out, the government formulated a secret programme that aimed for major territorial acquisitions and the economic and military subjugation of most of Europe, as well as the seizure of the French and Portuguese possessions in sub-Saharan Africa. These aims went far beyond those of the British and French; hardliners in the leadership, driven by the military stalemate in the west, Allied control of the seas and growing food shortages at home, demanded even more far-reaching annexations.

Meanwhile, German rule in the occupied areas of Europe became ever harsher at the same time as the military tightened its grip on Germany itself. After the Bolshevik Revolution in 1917 and the effective capitulation of the Russians at Brest-Litovsk in March 1918, more than a million square miles and fifty million people, together with most of Russia's coal, iron and oil deposits and half its industry, were lost to Germany and its Turkish ally. A million German troops helped impose a ruthless military dictatorship in the occupied areas, which stretched from Estonia in the north through huge swathes of Belarus and Ukraine to the north-eastern hinterland of the Black Sea in the south. Along with economic exploitation and the brutal suppression of nationalist movements came the imposition of a new racial order in which the inhabitants of the region were explicitly treated as second-class citizens, foreshadowing the regime that would be imposed by the Nazis a quarter of a century later.

In the peace settlement that followed defeat in 1918, Germany lost all its overseas colonies, 13 per cent of its territory in Europe (including Alsace-Lorraine to France, and industrial areas in the east to the newly created state of Poland), and almost all its military equipment. Its armed forces were restricted to 100,000 men, and the government had to agree to the payment over subsequent decades of large sums of money in reparations for the economic damage caused by the war. These terms caused general disbelief and then outrage; after all, the war had ended while German troops were still on foreign soil, and military defeat had been far from total. Moreover – a fact often overlooked by historians – British and French troops occupied the Rhineland for most of the 1920s, providing a constant reminder of Germany's subjugation to foreign powers. In 1923, when the Germans fell behind with reparation payments, the French sent an expeditionary force into the industrial region of the Ruhr to seize key resources, causing further resentment

Yet did this amount, as Baranowski claims, to the 'colonisation' of Germany by the Allies? German propaganda attacks on the occupation of the Ruhr focused heavily on the racial defilement symbolised by

France's use of troops from its African colonies. But by the mid-1920s the violent clashes between revolutionary and counter-revolutionary forces that had brought machine guns and tanks on to the streets of Germany's major cities in the immediate aftermath of the war had subsided and the economy had stabilised. The negotiating skills of Gustav Stresemann, the long-serving Foreign Minister, brought readmission into the international community, the renegotiation of reparations and the removal of the occupying troops. There is little evidence of any widespread feeling among Germans that the country had been 'colonised'; only among extreme antisemites was there a conviction that the Weimar Republic was controlled by an international Jewish conspiracy, but even here the language of colonisation can rarely be found, and it must also be remembered that the Nazi Party did so poorly in the elections of 1928, winning less than 3 per cent of the vote, that it soft-pedalled its violent antisemitism in subsequent elections. The anti-Jewish disturbances of the postwar years were both less widespread and less representative of public opinion than Baranowski implies.

Only once the Depression of the early 1930s had bankrupted banks and businesses and put more than a third of the workforce out of a job did the Nazis win mass support; and only when they were brought into power as the conservative elites' coalition partners – the elites were seeking popular legitimacy for their plans to destroy Weimar democracy – did they unveil their visceral antisemitism once more and begin to implement it in a series of decrees and laws backed by stormtrooper violence against Nazism's opponents, above all on the left. By this time, the idea of a German empire had come to be dominated not by overseas colonies, which had been the concern only of small and impotent minority pressure groups during the Weimar years, but by the vision of a European empire, one that built on the experiences of the First World War but went far beyond them.

Still, memory of Germany's overseas empire remained and was even revived by the Nazis. How far did the colonial experience influence the policy of extermination under Hitler? Baranowski addresses this central question in a subtle and balanced way, avoiding some of the excesses of the most vehement historical exponents of the continuity thesis but retaining some of its central elements even so. In the first half of 1933 the Nazis set up hundreds of concentration camps, into which they drove more than 100,000 of their political opponents, using them for forced labour and treating them so brutally that many hundreds died. But these bore little resemblance to the camps in which the Hereros had been starved to death in Namibia, and in any case the idea of concentrating civilian populations in prison camps was by no means a German invention: it dated back at least as far as US campaigns against Native Americans in the 1830s.

The Nazis did see their camps as a kind of counter-insurgency tool, but their primary purpose was to intimidate and 're-educate' opponents of the regime, who were brutalised until they agreed not to mount any further resistance. Almost all the inmates had been released by 1934, by which time the task of repression had been turned over to the regular police, the courts and the state prison system. If there was a colonial precedent, then, as Baranowski remarks, it had been totally transformed and owed far more to the political polarisation of Europe after the Bolshevik Revolution – at roughly the same time, similar institutions emerged in the Soviet Union, owing nothing at all to colonial precedents.

There was no parallel in the Soviet Union, however, to the racial policies adopted by the Nazis. How much did the Nazis' imposition of 'racial hygiene', the laws against intermarriage and sexual relations between Jews and non-Jews, and the forcible sterilisation of up to 400,000 'hereditarily inferior' Germans, owe to Germany's colonial experience? As Baranowski persuasively argues, there were striking precedents in the anti-miscegenation laws passed in pre-1914 Namibia, the segregationist response to colonial insurrection and the more extreme policies advocated by the Pan-Germans during the debates over the Citizenship Law of 1913. 'Imperialism,' she remarks, 'linked the two bourgeois phobias of socialism and racial mixing, in which workers were imagined much like "natives".' Germany's decolonisation in 1919 eliminated the previous distinction between colonial and domestic law and boosted fears of 'alien races' such as Jews and Gypsies polluting the German race at home. The concepts were the same; only the practice was radicalised.

There were personal continuities, too, in many different areas, including medicine, eugenics and racial anthropology – the anthropologist Eugen Fischer used his research on mixed-race groups in German South-West Africa before the First World War to argue against racial mixing during the Third Reich, when medical scientists who had trained in his institute, such as the Auschwitz doctor Josef Mengele, played a major role in implementing eugenic policies. Yet in the end these continuities were less important than the discontinuities that Baranowski enumerates. Arguing persuasively against the trend of much recent historical opinion, she insists repeatedly on the centrality of terror and violence to the Nazi seizure and practice of power, which marked a crucial rupture with Weimar's administration of welfare and policing. The crushing of the labour movement, the arrest or exile of Jewish and liberal public health and welfare officials, and, she might have added, the destruction of the free press and news media, removed the major obstacles to the deployment of eugenicist policies by the state, while the rapid growth of the racially obsessed SS under Himmler pushed on the central implementation of policies such as the mass sterilisation of the allegedly mentally ill and handicapped on a scale unrivalled in any other country. Uniquely, too, this policy, coupled with the exclusion of Jews from economic and social life on racial grounds, was designed to pave the way for a war of imperialist expansion in the east, and during the war itself was transformed into a campaign of mass murder in which 200,000 mentally ill and disabled Germans were killed by Nazi doctors.

The symbiosis of racial policy and war became even clearer from 1939 onwards. Building on recent scholarship, Baranowski shows in detail how the invasion of Poland was designed from the outset to destroy the Polish nation, executing Poles and Jews in scores of thousands, displacing them from their homes, expropriating their property or – in the case of the Poles – shipping them off to Germany as forced labour. The Germans all but eliminated any distinction between combatants and civilians, abandoning any attempt to follow the laws and conventions of war to which – with rare exceptions – they adhered in the west. SS and army troops alike regarded the Poles as savages, the Jews as a lower species of being. All this was repeated on a larger scale following the invasion of the Soviet Union in June 1941, reflecting not only prejudices against Slavs and 'eastern Jews' widespread even in the working class before 1914 but also the practices common among European conquerors of colonial territories since the Spanish invasion of the Americas in the sixteenth century.

Yet, as Baranowski points out, 'the mass expulsion or killing of native populations' in the colonial setting of the nineteenth century 'often followed frontier conflicts on the ground between European settlers and indigenous peoples over land and resources'. Administrations in the imperial metropoles often tried to restrain settlers greedy for land and labour, though they generally ended up tolerating and eventually endorsing their rapacity. Even the genocidal decision in the Namibian war was taken locally, by a military commander who brushed aside the reservations of the colonial governor and his superiors in Berlin, and colonial atrocities frequently aroused fierce criticism at home. The Nazis, by contrast, launched their war of racial subjugation and extermination in the east without the slightest provocation and in the absence of any doubts or criticisms, except on the part of a handful of conservative army officers. Moreover, throughout the war they coordinated and directed operations from the centre, acting on directions from Hitler himself. This is not to deny that there were disputes within the Nazi elite over the implementation of ethnic cleansing and annihilation. But the basic direction of policy was clear, culminating in the General Plan for the East, the extermination by starvation and disease of at least thirty million and possibly as many as forty-five million Slavs and the resettlement of most of Eastern Europe by German colonists. Here indeed, as Baranowski puts it, was the 'Nazi place in the sun'.

German plans for Africa, revived in the 1930s as Hitler took up once more the demand for the return of former colonies, envisaged no such policy of genocide; rather, they differed little in essence from conventional European paradigms of colonial development. The 'natives' were to be separated out from European settler society, to be sure, but German administrators were to educate, feed and improve the health of indigenous Africans, developing the colonial economies to aid the supply of raw materials and foodstuffs for the metropole. This was partly because the Nazis did not see African countries as a major source of German settlement, but also because their inhabitants posed no threat of the kind they imagined was constituted by the Slavs and, above all, the Jews. The destruction of the Slavs and Jews was linked in Nazi policy to the purification of the German race itself, as it was not in the colonial situation. Indeed, SS units even roamed Eastern Europe in search of 'racially valuable' blond, blue-eyed children, kidnapping tens of thousands of them and arranging their adoption by German parents under new identities – a policy unthinkable in colonial Africa. Finally, Nazi policy in Eastern Europe was driven at least in part by the immediate imperatives of ensuring an adequate food supply for Germany itself, whose agriculture was in no way able to feed the Reich and its armies. Once more, therefore, the Nazis radicalised earlier imperialist practices or departed from them in significant respects, rather than simply continuing them.

How can the Nazi extermination of the Jews be fitted into the colonial paradigm? Certainly, prewar radical nationalists incorporated antisemitism into their vision of international relations as a Darwinian struggle for survival and supremacy between races. The policies of segregation, deportation and expropriation to which Germany's and then Europe's Jews were subjected all had their precedents in the colonies. But the deliberate scouring of a whole continent and potentially – as suggested by the minutes of the conference held at Wannsee to discuss the implementation of the 'Final Solution of the Jewish Question in Europe' – the entire surface of the globe for Jews to be carried off to assembly-line extermination in gas chambers or killing pits had no precedent.

Baranowski sensibly calls into question the arguments of some historians that the mass murders committed by German colonial administrators and military commanders before 1914 were not only comparable to the later Nazi genocide, but even created a genocidal mentality that led directly to the 'Final Solution'. As she points out, other European powers engaged in similar policies, all of which, including those of the Germans, were designed above all to destroy the economic independence of conquered populations and turn them into a docile labour force or, in areas deemed suitable, clear them out to make way for settlement. Something like this was what the Nazis planned in Eastern Europe, and at some points in the process Nazi administrators did use Jewish labour for the war economy as well, but in the long run this was, as they put it, just a slower form of 'annihilation through labour', *Vernichtung durch Arbeit*. While the General Plan for the East undoubtedly envisaged the genocidal elimination of tens of millions of Slavs, it was driven by ideological imperatives fundamentally different from those of the 'Final Solution', which designated the Jews as 'the world-enemy', the *Weltfeind*, not a regional obstacle posed by savages but a world conspiracy mounted by a cunning and ruthless enemy designed to destroy the German nation entirely.

These arguments will be discussed and debated for a long time to come. Although Baranowski set out to write a textbook, she has produced something much more important: a skilful and carefully nuanced synthesis of some of the most productive ideas to have emerged in the debate about the origins of Nazism and Nazi extremism in the past few years. Reflecting current concerns, these focus not so much on how or why the Nazis came to power, as on what they did once they had achieved it, above all during the war. From this point of view, they are addressing a rather different set of questions from those posed by the old 'special path' thesis. Baranowski's book nonetheless puts them clearly on the map, debates their pros and cons with subtlety and sophistication, and should be read by anyone interested in the calamitous and ultimately exterminatory path taken by German history in the twentieth century.

3. THE DEFEAT OF 1918

In November 1918, after more than four years in the trenches, Adolf Hitler was in hospital away from the front, temporarily blinded by a gas attack. As he was recovering, he was told of Germany's surrender and the overthrow of the Kaiser. 'Again,' he later wrote, 'everything went black before my eyes.' He went on:

> And so it had all been in vain. In vain all the sacrifices and privations; in vain the hunger and thirst of months which were often endless; in vain the hours in which, with mortal fear clutching at our hearts, we nevertheless did our duty; and in vain the death of two million ... Was it for this that these boys of 17 sank into the earth of Flanders? Was this the meaning of the sacrifice which the German mother made to the fatherland when with sore heart she let her best-loved boys march off, never to see them again?

Like many others in Germany, Hitler struggled to find an explanation for Germany's apparently sudden collapse. How could it all have gone so wrong, so quickly?

Defeat was all the more puzzling since only a few months before, in spring 1918, victory seemed within the Kaiser's grasp. After years of stalemate, the war took a sudden turn in Germany's favour. Early in 1917 the Germans decided to wage unrestricted submarine warfare – attacking civilian vessels – and U-boats were sinking a monthly average of more than half a million tons of shipping bringing supplies to Britain. The Americans had entered the war as a result, but it was taking a long time for them to mobilise. Allied troops were war-weary, and widespread mutinies in the French army, involving up to 40,000 men, were a stark reminder of the fragility of morale. In October 1917, German reinforcements enabled the Austro-Hungarian army to win a major victory at Caporetto: 265,000 Italians surrendered and 400,000 fled in confusion, while the pursuing forces advanced fifty miles in just over two days.

Most important of all, the October Revolution and the disintegration of the tsarist army took Russia out of the war. This enabled the Germans to redeploy huge numbers of troops – their forces on the Western Front increased from 3.25 million to more than four million men by April 1918. Paul von Hindenburg, a stolid general who effectively replaced the Kaiser as the figurehead of the German war effort after being brought out of retirement to win spectacular victories on the Eastern Front early in the war, and Quartermaster-General Erich Ludendorff, the real driving force behind those victories, decided to capitalise on Germany's strong position by launching a final, overwhelming attack on the Allied armies in the west.

Operation Michael, as it was named, deployed new and highly effective artillery tactics: enemy guns and command posts were targeted before a 'creeping barrage' that moved ahead of the advancing infantry was laid down, forcing the defenders to stay under cover until the Germans were almost upon them. With a superiority of more than two to one in men and guns, the Germans launched their attack on 21 March, firing more than three million rounds in the first day. Allied command posts some thirty miles behind the front were badly hit, along with gun positions, in the largest artillery bombardment of the war. As the German infantry swarmed over the Allied trenches, their advance concealed in a number of places by thick fog, the British and French were forced back along a fifty-mile front. The losses on both sides were the heaviest of any single day in the war. On 9 April, a second major German attack further north was equally successful and was followed by an advance on Paris, creating panic in the city. In a relatively short space of time, the long stalemate on the Western Front had been broken. The Allied military leadership was traumatised, and by the end of June, Hindenburg and Ludendorff were celebrating a series of stunning victories. Yet little more than three months after that, the German leaders were suing for peace. How did this happen?

A first explanation has to do with military intelligence. Both sides in 1914–18 used traditional methods: gathering intelligence from POWs and from captured documents and equipment, keeping careful watch on the enemy front line and sending spies out to gather information behind it. They also employed aerial reconnaissance and intercepted telephone and, increasingly, radio messages, decrypting them if necessary. Though they had not anticipated the spring offensive, the Allies were well prepared for the final German attack on 15 July. But the Germans never established an effective espionage network behind Allied lines, could not decrypt Allied signals and easily fell prey to deceptions and feints.

Second, the war in the air was now being won by the Allies. It extended far beyond the front line. In 1916, anti-aircraft fire led the Germans to abandon Zeppelin raids on London, but they now developed large bombers such as the Gothas and, most remarkably, the Giant, a monster with a 138-foot wingspan which was so solidly built that none was ever shot down. These caused considerable damage in 1917, and forced up to a quarter of a million Londoners to take shelter in the Underground every night. In May 1918, forty-three German bombers attacked London; but this was their last major raid. The shortage of raw materials in Germany had become so serious that new planes could not be built in sufficient numbers, and those that were built were shoddily constructed and often broke down. By the summer the Allies were producing many more planes than the Germans: only eighteen of the costly Giants were ever built. Meanwhile, the British and French had begun to launch bombing raids on the Rhineland, though they were on too small a scale to be really effective, especially since the Germans organised effective countermeasures. In the last year of the war, the British dropped 665 tons of bombs, a high proportion of which missed their targets. The real importance of the air war was at the front, in Italy as well as France and Belgium. By mid-1918 the Allies' air superiority was preventing German reconnaissance planes from finding out very much about their preparations for attack, while they themselves were gaining accurate information about enemy dispositions.

There was also a shift in the balance of power where the gas war was concerned. Few of the statistics David Stevenson gives in *With Our Backs to the Wall* (London, 2011), his book about the conduct of the war in 1918, are as striking as those involving poison gas. The Germans released 52,000 tons of gas on the Western Front, twice as much as the French and three and a half times as much as the British, killing or wounding 300,000 soldiers with the loss of only 70,000 to gas attacks from the other side. In 1918, the Germans produced nearly twenty million gas shells: half or more of the shells fired in Operation Michael were chemical. By the late spring, however, the British had developed an effective gas mask, while their own new fast-acting Livens Projectors – a mortar-like weapon that launched large drums filled with chemicals – caused widespread fear among German troops, whose masks proved useless against them, and were in any case not being produced in sufficient numbers because of a shortage of rubber. The Allies were mass-manufacturing gas, and knowledge of this was one more factor in prompting the Germans to sue for peace.

By the summer of 1918 the Allies had also changed their offensive tactics, using artillery not to obliterate but to neutralise pinpointed enemy positions and cut barbed-wire entanglements, laying down a curtain of fire behind the front line to stop reinforcements and deploying mobile units to surprise and outflank enemy positions. By this time tanks were also being used in large numbers, but they could move only at walking pace and ran out of petrol after sixteen miles. Here the Germans were very far behind, failing to produce enough tanks till it was too late. Although tanks often broke down and could easily be destroyed by artillery fire, they caused panic among German troops;

in 1919 Ludendorff gave the prospect of facing thousands of them as a major reason for having sought an armistice.

Economically, the Allies eventually proved stronger than the combined productive might of Germany and Austria-Hungary, and their allies Turkey and Bulgaria. The French produced huge quantities of armaments, supplying the American Expeditionary Force with most of what it needed, while the British could draw on the resources of the empire as well as on their own manufacturing base. It was the Americans, however, who had by far the largest economy, and US supplies of food, steel, munitions and equipment were crucial in keeping the Allies going in the final phase.

The best chance for the Germans lay in destroying American shipping in the Atlantic as it brought men and supplies to Europe. The British tried many methods of protecting shipping from U-boats, including arming merchant vessels or breaking up their outlines with geometrically patterned 'dazzle painting'. But the most effective by far was the convoy system: ships sailing in groups and accompanied by spotter-balloons and destroyers armed with depth charges were difficult to sink without incurring serious risk. U-boats in this period were not true submarines – they had no air supply and could remain below the surface only for quite short periods – and were relatively easy to spot and sink. In the end, there were simply not enough of them to win a decisive victory. Too many broke down or were damaged and had to limp back to port for repairs; nor were there enough trained personnel to man them. Plans for an enormous increase in construction came too late to make a difference.

The German government diverted as many resources as it could to arms and arms-related industries, neglecting agriculture and food supplies. The Allied blockade cut off essential agricultural imports, and by 1918 the death rate among women in Germany was nearly a quarter higher than its prewar level, with women weakened by poor nutrition succumbing to pneumonia and tuberculosis. Rations were below the minimum needed to survive, and a huge black market developed, while food riots led by women and children convulsed the major cities in the winter of 1915–16. The next winter, generally known in Germany as the 'turnip winter' because of the failure of the potato crop, was even worse. Malnourishment led to declining productivity in war-related industries. More than half a million German civilians are reckoned to have died from malnutrition and related diseases during the war.

Conditions were even worse in Austria-Hungary, where soldiers were not only weak from hunger when the Italians launched their final, successful attack in 1918, but arrived at the front in their underwear and had to take uniforms from the bodies of those killed in front of them. Bulgaria was in the worst situation of all, with mass starvation averted only by American grain deliveries after the armistice. It was this that caused Hitler to decide that conquest of Europe's 'bread basket' in Ukraine would be a central war aim for the Nazis. Germans did not starve in the Second World War as they had in the First: millions of Eastern Europeans were made to starve instead.

Malnutrition and disease affected the quality of new recruits in the final phase of the war. Hitler recalled that in August and September 1918, 'the reinforcements coming from home rapidly grew worse and worse, so that their arrival meant, not a reinforcement but a weakening of our fighting strength. Especially the young reinforcements were mostly worthless. It was often hard to believe that these were sons of the same nation which had once sent its youth out to the battle for Ypres.' The German spring offensive had cost too many lives. In April 1918 alone, 54,000 soldiers were reported killed or missing, and 445,000 had to be taken off duty, wounded or sick. By July, the number of men in the field was 883,000 lower than in March and most units were below strength. One of the few major gaps in Stevenson's account is his failure to deal adequately with the role of the medical services: trench fever, typhus, gas gangrene and many other, often fatal infections grew more common as the war went on, and must have worsened combat effectiveness and morale. It would have been interesting to have an estimate of which side dealt with this better.

In the early stages of the war, eighteen-to-twenty-year-olds made up

10 per cent of German fatalities; by 1918, the figure was nearly 25 per cent. Inexperienced and poorly trained, they were demoralised by the spring offensive's failure. Things were made worse by the miserable rations, described graphically in Erich Maria Remarque's novel *All Quiet on the Western Front*. From May onwards, discipline began to break down, and from July huge numbers began to desert or surrender – 340,000 in all, nearly as many as were lost to enemy action or disease in the same period. Their spirits were dampened not least by millions of propaganda leaflets dropped over German lines from Allied balloons or planes, offering good food and comfortable quarters to anyone who gave himself up. By contrast, as they first stopped the German advance in its tracks, then turned it back, the Allied forces began to experience a fresh optimism, boosted during the summer by the arrival of large numbers of American troops. By November, the Central Powers were outnumbered by the Allies on the Western Front by a factor of nearly two to one.

It was this growing disparity in numbers, in addition to the potential deployment of a vast army of tanks, which most worried Ludendorff and prompted him to launch the spring offensive. Stevenson regards this decision as the cardinal error of the war, along with the declaration of unrestricted submarine warfare just over a year earlier. In the First World War, attack was seldom the best means of defence. With bolder and more sophisticated leadership, the Reich might have stopped the Americans entering the conflict. But Kaiser Wilhelm II was too erratic to provide this, and at the crisis of the war the generals had pushed aside the civilian leadership and taken over themselves. Stevenson speculates that even after America's entry, Germany might have been able to make a separate peace by accepting Wilson's Fourteen Points, and forced the Allies to come to terms by sitting tight on the Western Front with troops transferred from the victorious East. Alternatively, if they were set on attacking, they might have done better to turn their firepower against British supply lines in north-west France instead of mounting a full-frontal assault in the centre. But even in 1918 Ludendorff was still pursuing the mirage of total victory.

Stevenson puts the blame for these failures on Germany's tendency to allow 'excessive influence for formidable technicians consumed by hubris, inadequately restrained by politicians whose judgements, if also deficient, were generally superior, but who could not depend on the emperor'. But Ludendorff was not just a technician: he was a highly political general. He loathed democracy and regarded the socialists – the largest political grouping in Germany, even if they were by now divided – as traitors. His section chief on the General Staff, the artillery expert Max Bauer, spent his spare time writing a rambling tract arguing for polygamy, and portraying war as the supreme expression of the masculine urge to rule the world through what he called 'detumescence'. Ludendorff was a modern general, but this went together with an equally modern form of politics that could fairly be called proto-fascist.

In August 1918, during a surprise Allied attack at Amiens, German troops, according to Allied observers, 'surrendered freely and in large numbers without any serious fighting'. Ludendorff, as Stevenson notes, began to fear that if this continued 'the army would become unreliable for domestic repression'. He was 'attracted by the plan to broaden the government, shifting blame onto those who had agitated so long against the war effort'. This would be only a temporary expedient, of course: as soon as peace had been signed, the old regime would return to power. In October, a quasi-democratic government led by the liberal Max von Baden and supported by the majority parties in the Reichstag was put into office. Ludendorff declared his keenness to continue with the submarine war, but the new government forced his resignation by threatening to resign itself – a neat reversal of the tactic by which he had got what he wanted from previous administrations. Armistice negotiations duly began.

When it became known that Germany was suing for peace, its army disintegrated: soldiers simply started going home. In Kiel, the naval command ordered the fleet to sail out to rescue its honour, severely compromised by having spent most of the war in harbour, with a final assault on the Royal Navy. Not surprisingly, the sailors rebelled, arrested their officers and began to form workers' and sailors' councils. The German revolution had begun. Within a short time it led to the abdication of the Kaiser and the formation of a revolutionary council which after a few months ushered in the democratic Weimar Republic. The new regime was, as Ludendorff had hoped, obliged to sign the Treaty of Versailles, which was widely regarded as a national humiliation. Shortly afterwards, in March 1920, the old regime tried to make a comeback, with heavily armed troops and reactionary politicians and bureaucrats taking over Berlin, only to be defeated ignominiously by a general strike. In 1923, Ludendorff took part in the equally unsuccessful Beer Hall putsch, led by Adolf Hitler and his infant Nazi Party.

In the Allied countries there was general rejoicing at the victory. This had been, it was thought, the war that would end all wars. Those in the know were not so sure. On the day the armistice was signed, the French leader Georges Clemenceau's daughter said to him: 'Tell me, Papa, that you are happy.' 'I cannot say it,' Clemenceau replied, 'because I am not. *It will all be useless.*' And so it was.

David Stevenson's account of these events is absorbing and authoritative. Yet this is also a bloodless book. There are few quotations, and the biographical sketches Stevenson provides read as if they had been taken from official obituaries. Nevertheless, the way people experienced the war was vitally important. As Hitler lay in his hospital bed, struggling to find an explanation for Germany's defeat – according to his account in *Mein Kampf* – he experienced a blinding flash of revelation: Germany had not really been defeated at all. Instead, its victorious armies had been stabbed in the back by Jewish revolutionaries on the home front. Strikes and demonstrations, fomented by traitors, had undermined and finally destroyed the war effort. 'There is no making pacts with Jews; there can only be the hard either-or,' he concluded. 'I, for my part, decided to go into politics.'

Like much else in *Mein Kampf,* this statement smoothed over a more complex situation, and there were to be many twists and turns before he emerged the following year as a far-right politician. But long before he came to power, Hitler had made it his mission to refight the First World War, this time with a different ending. The 'spirit of 1914', the mythical national community of all Germans in support of the Fatherland, would be recreated in the Third Reich; and the enemies of Germany, the Jews, would be destroyed. And next time, Germany would carry on fighting till the very end.

4. WALTHER RATHENAU

On the morning of 24 June 1922, the German Foreign Minister Walther Rathenau set off for work from his villa in the leafy Berlin suburb of Grünewald, as he usually did when he was in the German capital. The weather was fine, so he instructed his chauffeur to use the black open-top limousine. The Minister sat, alone, in the back. He took no security precautions, used the same route every day, and had dismissed the police protection he had earlier been offered. As the car slowed down to negotiate a bend just before joining the main road, another, larger vehicle, an open-top tourer, came out of a side street and overtook it. Two men were sitting in the back, clad somewhat oddly in long leather coats and leather driving helmets that left only their faces open to the elements.

Drawing level, the vehicle slowed down alongside the coupé, pushing it across the road. As the Minister looked up, alarmed, one of the other car's passengers leaned forward, picked up a long-barrelled machine-pistol, cradled it in his armpit and opened fire. A rapid series of shots rang out. Bringing his car to a halt, Rathenau's chauffeur began shouting for help. At the same moment there followed a loud explosion as the other leather-clad assassin lobbed a hand grenade into the back of the limousine, causing it to spring into the air. A passing nurse came upon the scene and cradled the dying Foreign Minister in her arms as the chauffeur began to drive to the nearest police station, but could do nothing.

The assassins, Erwin Kern and Hermann Fischer, drove into a side street, removed their leather gear, disposed of the machine-pistol and calmly walked away as police cars sped past them on their way to the scene of the crime. Soon the police mounted the largest manhunt Germany had ever seen. 'Wanted' posters appeared all over the country, and police forces everywhere were issued with eyewitness descriptions of the men. The two assassins made their way to Saaleck Castle in Saxony, where the custodian was a sympathiser, but the police tracked them down, and in a shootout Kern was killed, while Fischer committed suicide. Both of them were in their mid-twenties. The driver, Ernst Techow, was only twenty-one. His parents turned him in; in court, he claimed he had acted under duress, and he received a relatively mild prison sentence. In the meantime, Rathenau's mother had written an emotional letter of forgiveness to Techow's mother, prompting strong feelings of guilt in the young man. On his release in 1927 he joined the French Foreign Legion, and during the Second World War he is said to have expiated his crime by saving Jews in Marseilles from deportation to Auschwitz.

Police inquiries soon established that the three young men were part of a much wider conspiracy involving others as young as sixteen. All of them were from good families. The conspirators included the sons of a general, a senior police officer and a member of Berlin's town council, now deceased. All of them belonged to extreme right-wing nationalist organisations, and several had served in the notorious 6,000-strong Free Corps brigade led by former naval captain Hermann Erhardt that had taken part in the bloody suppression of the Munich Soviet in 1919 and the right-wing Kapp putsch that had occupied Berlin briefly in a botched attempt to overthrow the Republic the following year.

Following its enforced dissolution, a number of its members had gone underground, formed a secret resistance group called the 'Organisation Consul' and carried out a number of murders, including that of Matthias Erzberger, a prominent signatory of the Treaty of Versailles. One of the men involved in providing logistical support for the assassination, the nineteen-year-old bank clerk Ernst von Salomon, wrote a best-selling novel vindicating the Free Corps and the Organisation Consul after his release from prison in 1927: entitled *Die Geächteten* ('The Despised Ones'), it delivered an unapologetic glorification of the violent and extreme nationalism from which these young men drew their inspiration.

The killing sent a shock wave through the fledgling Weimar Republic. In the subsequent Reichstag debate, Reich Chancellor Wirth caused uproar by accusing the right-wing press of inciting the murder, and, pointing to the nationalist benches, declaring: 'There stands the enemy who drips his poison into the wounds of a people – there stands the enemy – and there is no doubt about it: this enemy stands on the right!' At the government's direction, flags were flown at half-mast on official buildings, while the trade unions staged mass demonstrations in protest against the murder, and Reich President Ebert immediately issued a Decree for the Protection of the Republic, confirmed in a modified form by a law steered through the Reichstag on 21 July. It was a key moment in the history of the Weimar Republic. It brought to an end a long series of similar assassination attempts, including an acid attack on the Social Democrat Philipp Scheidemann, whose proclamation from the balcony of the Reichstag on 9 November 1918 had established the Republic (the acid had become diluted, and most of it hit his beard anyway), and an assault with an iron bar on the popular muck-raking journalist Maximilian Harden, a friend of Rathenau's (which he also survived, but only just). It also brought to an end the short existence of the Organisation Consul.

The murder was a central episode in the Republic's turbulent history. Why had the Foreign Minister aroused such hatred that people wanted him dead? The immediate cause was his negotiation of the Treaty of Rapallo, signed on 16 April 1922. This brought together the Soviet Union and the Weimar Republic, two newly established, insecure states shunned by the international community, in a mutual agreement to normalise diplomatic relations, renounce territorial claims and begin economic cooperation. The Soviets promised not to demand financial reparations for war damage. The Treaty of Brest-Litovsk, in which the Kaiser's government had forced the nascent Soviet government to cede huge swathes of territory to Germany early in 1918, was formally repudiated.

In a way characteristic of the paradoxes of Weimar, Rapallo had been backed by Reich Chancellor Wirth not least because it promised to strengthen ties that had already formed between the Red Army and the German Reichswehr, through which the latter was circumventing the restrictions on arms and equipment imposed by the Treaty of Versailles – for example, by backing the construction of combat aircraft by a Junkers factory based in Russia. The ultimate victim of the German-Soviet rapprochement was to be Poland. 'Poland must be eliminated,' Wirth said privately, adding that 'Rapallo should be supplemented ... as military problems too ought to be settled with special reference to Poland'.

This background to the treaty was hidden from the ultra-rightists of the Organisation Consul, who saw in it an act of compromise with Bolshevism and a craven abandonment of Germany's aims in the First World War. The day before the murder, the right-wing nationalist Karl Helfferich had furiously denounced Rapallo in the Reichstag, blaming the Foreign Minister personally for his policy of détente and accusing him of lack of patriotism in his refusal to repudiate the Treaty of Versailles. In fact, the young conspirators had laid their plans long before, but the chorus of condemnation of Rapallo by the right-wing press and politicians almost certainly influenced their decision to target its main German author. In their witness statements, and in the depiction of the plot by Ernst von Salomon, the ideology of the young conspirators came across as vague, immature and confused. Rathenau, said Kern, as depicted in *Die Geächteten*, 'might pursue what the chattering classes call a policy of fulfilment [of Versailles]. We are fighting for higher things ... We are not fighting so that the people can be happy, we are fighting to force the people into its trajectory of fate'.

Salomon insisted to the end of his days that Rathenau had been killed because he had pursued a policy of negotiation instead of confrontation with the Soviet Union. But in the trial, the accused had urged 'the exclusion of Jews' from public office through a violent 'internal war'. Antisemites such as these young men believed that Jews were traitors to Germany – a belief held among others by the nascent Nazi Party and its leader Adolf Hitler, whose stormtrooper movement included many former members of the Erhardt Brigade when it was launched in 1921. Such men objected vehemently to the fact that the German Foreign Minister was a Jew, and saw this as a central reason for what they regarded as his treachery to the national cause.

Rathenau himself was proud of his Jewish identity, even though he withdrew formally from the Jewish religious community in Berlin relatively early in his life. He believed that Jews, while not abandoning their identity in a misguided search for assimilation with the majority Christian society, should none the less do their best fully to participate in German culture and institutions. What he wanted was not the total disappearance of Jewish identity in Germany, but the absorption of German culture by Germany's Jews so that they could encounter their fellow Germans on equal terms while still remaining fundamentally Jewish. Yet this, too, was unrealistic. Antisemitism was becoming more rather than less widespread in the Kaiser's time, and shifting from a religious to a racial basis. Extreme parties were emerging, still on the fringes of politics but with the potential, as the Weimar Republic was to demonstrate, to move to the centre, that wanted the civil equality of the Jews, granted in 1871, to be reversed.

Rathenau's self-identification as a Jew, however convoluted, was one reason among many why he attracted the hostility of antisemites. It is justification enough for the inclusion of *Walther Rathenau: Weimar's Fallen Statesman*, by the leading Israeli historian of German antisemitism, Shulamit Volkov, in Yale University Press's *Jewish Lives* series. Volkov has been able to make good use of the unpublished correspondence and writings in his private papers, discovered in the KGB Special Archive in Moscow after the fall of the Soviet Union and currently in the process of editing and publication. This is now by far the best and most sophisticated life of Rathenau in English.

In discussing Rathenau's Jewishness, to be sure, Volkov goes too far in underscoring the social cohesion and isolation of Germany's Jewish community in this period; the Jewish community was in fact dissolving gradually into the larger culture of Germany by the end of the century. The process of assimilation was accelerating fast, with thirty-five Jewish-Christian marriages for every one hundred purely Jewish marriages in Berlin by the outbreak of the First World War, compared with only nine around 1880, and no fewer than seventy-three per hundred in Hamburg. Twenty-thousand German Jews were baptised between 1880 and 1920. In a community numbering little more than half a million, these numbers were significant. Rathenau's ambivalent thoughts on Jewish identity, written in 1897, were in large part a reaction to these changes, as they were to the rise of racial antisemitism.

His complex sense of Jewish identity was only one of several aspects of Rathenau's character that fascinated contemporaries and have continued to preoccupy historians ever since. Much ink has been spilled trying to explain why he never married. In a sensitive and perceptive analysis of the question, Volkov comes to the conclusion that while he was almost certainly heterosexual, and fell in love with at least three women during his life, Rathenau was emotionally repressed and socially awkward, and found it difficult to achieve intimacy. Moreover, he was something of a workaholic: his achievements covered not one area of human activity, but several.

Rathenau first came to prominence as a writer. He attracted the attention of contemporary intellectuals not least because Maximilian Harden, whose magazine *Die Zukunft* published his early essays, introduced him into Berlin's intellectual and artistic milieu, where he frequented literary salons and met men like Hugo von Hoffmansthal, Frank Wedekind and Stefan Zweig. Born in 1867, Rathenau had become a well-known writer by the First World War, publishing two volumes of essays by 1908, on subjects ranging from economics to morality. In articles on modern art he rejected what he saw as the unacceptable modernism of the French Impressionists and advocated the revival of a German art that would express the fundamental characteristics of the German soul. Such views, expressed on some occasions in pseudo-Nietzschean aphorisms that seem merely pretentious to the modern reader, none the less won him a wide readership among the German intelligentsia of the day, though they also aroused the ire of Hoffmansthal, who condemned their 'pedantry, pretention, snobbery' and above all the 'stale and crafty Germannness' that he said was expressed so often by Jews.

Yet what fascinated many people about Rathenau was the fact that he was not solely a writer or aesthete, but, on the contrary, spent most of his time as a successful businessman. His father was Emil Rathenau, the founder of the General Electricity Company (*Allgemeine Elektrizitäts-Gesellschaft*, or AEG), one of Germany's largest companies and a major supplier of electrical power. Walther Rathenau went into his father's business, pioneering technical innovations and rapidly climbing up the AEG hierarchy, sitting on the supervisory board, steering the company through a series of mergers and acquisitions, surviving bruising rivalries with other industrialists such as Hugo Stinnes, and taking on a leading role in the firm by the eve of the First World War.

By this time, Rathenau's wealth had enabled him to buy a small eighteenth-century Prussian royal palace at Freienwalde, and construct a neo-classical villa to his own designs in Berlin. Count Harry Kessler, a close acquaintance, found the villa tasteless and snobbish, full of 'dead *Bildung*, petty sentimentality, and stunted eroticism'. The novelist Joseph Roth, by contrast, remarked of Rathenau that 'he lived wonderfully, among great books and rare objects, amid beautiful paintings and colours'. Rathenau became notorious, by contrast, for the frugality of his dinners, where, complained the writer Franz Blei, one could expect nothing more than 'fish, lamb cutlets and dumplings ... a tiny glass of champagne, never refilled by the servant ... [and] a bottomless pot of black coffee, intended to keep the guests awake till the early morning' while Rathenau monopolised the conversation by delivering speeches 'like a preacher or a rabbi, never less than a quarter of an hour', as Kessler complained. People found him pompous and opinionated. He was, critics later mocked, 'a prophet in a tuxedo', 'Jesus in a frock-coat', 'Jehovah at the coffee-table'. He quarrelled with one friend after another, breaking with Harden over the latter's furious public condemnation of the Kaiser and his entourage, and over his own relationship, probably never consummated, with the married Lily Deutsch. He alienated Kessler with his self-important monologues and his social pretensions, or so Kessler claimed.

It was the liberal Jewish banker Bernhard Dernburg, appointed Colonial Secretary after the scandal of the German genocide of the Hereros in South-West Africa, who brought Rathenau into politics by inviting him on a fact-finding tour of Germany's African colonies. Rathenau bluntly condemned the genocide as 'the greatest atrocity that has ever been brought about by German military policy'. This won him the respect of Reich Chancellor Bülow, who had himself heavily criticised the conduct of the German army in South-West Africa. Rathenau's essays began to treat political topics, taking a moderate liberal approach, for example, to the question of the reform of the Prussian three-class voting system. He attacked the domination of Prussian politics by the landed and bureaucratic aristocracy, whom he blamed for the exclusion of Jews from elite positions in army and state. He advocated the political advancement of the industrial and financial middle classes, where prejudice against Jews, he thought, was unimportant. Only then could Germany become fully modern. Published in 1912 as *Critique of the Times*, these essays went through seven editions in the first year and turned Rathenau into a political as well as a literary sensation.

Yet he did not take the plunge into serious politics, preferring to continue with his business and with his writings, which included a vaporous and little-read philosophical treatise *On the Mechanism of the Spirit*, a set of patriotic poems, a further attack on the backwardness of the Prussian state and a plea for European economic unity. It was the outbreak of war in 1914 that brought him a political role. He was put in charge of the procurement of raw materials after the Allied blockade cut Germany off from its foreign sources of supply. Rathenau worked hard at this job, and achieved an astonishing degree of success, but privately he remained critical of the Prussian state (run by 'adventurers, fools and pedants') and sceptical about the benefits the war might bring for Germany: 'On the day that the Kaiser and his paladins on their white chargers ride victorious through the Brandenburg Gate, history will have lost all meaning,' he wrote. Published in 1919, the aphorism was widely used as evidence for his defeatism by his enemies. Yet at the same time, as his influence within the AEG increased after his father's death in 1915, he boosted aircraft and munitions production until it constituted 45 per cent of the firm's total turnover.

By this time, however, Rathenau had resigned from the Office of Raw Materials, hoping for a higher political position. But this was to elude him, at least for the time being. His experiences in the war procurement office had led him to believe that the economy had to be centrally directed, and he supported the Hindenburg Programme, which tried, unsuccessfully, to achieve this aim. Rathenau believed that victory over Britain was the highest priority for Germany, and backed the forced transportation of Belgian workers to Germany to aid in war production, an action entirely contrary to international law. Yet he opposed the introduction of unrestricted submarine warfare and wanted a peace without annexations. Thus he found himself increasingly marginalised as the political situation in Germany polarised.

The growing atmosphere of rabid antisemitism among German conservatives prompted Rathenau to identify himself far more clearly than before with the Jewish mainstream in Germany and condemn Christian antisemites as lacking the true Christian spirit. 'I see the beginning of the worst internal strife at the moment when the external strife comes to an end,' he wrote prophetically in 1917. Deprived of political engagement, he turned to writing again, putting a case for a modern state in the postwar era to come, economically centralised but based on spiritual values, in his best-selling book *In Days to Come*.

Many found the contrast between his own great personal wealth and his condemnation of materialism hard to swallow. His insistence, repeated in another best-selling book, *The New Economy*, on the need for tight state controls over industry, alienated his fellow businessmen such as the influential Stinnes. And his advocacy of limited and cautious parliamentary reform was overtaken by events as the war was lost, the Kaiser was forced to abdicate and the socialists came to power.

Rathenau was one of many Germans outraged by the terms of the 1918 armistice and the Treaty of Versailles. Initially, indeed, when Germany's military leader Erich von Ludendorff called for a ceasefire, Rathenau urged the people to rise up and carry on fighting until better peace terms were obtained. By now he had made enemies on all sides: the left, the right, businessmen, the working class, Jews, antisemites. When he published a small tract on *The Kaiser* in 1919, he alienated not only supporters of the ousted monarch but also the political spokesmen of the aristocracy and the middle class, both of whom he blamed for the disasters of the Kaiser's reign. It was some time before he came round to Harden's view that it was necessary first for the peace terms to be fulfilled before Germany earned the international trust necessary for their agreed revision.

While he worked hard at managing AEG in the inflationary economic climate of the postwar era, Rathenau continued to pour out a stream of political writings, urging a new, more responsible political culture in place of the violently polarised extremisms of the left and right that characterised the founding period of the Weimar Republic. This brought him close to the moderate liberals of the Democratic Party, and he began to find a new outlet as a 'passionate, even charismatic' political orator, as Volkov notes. Thus it was, following the failure of the Kapp putsch (which Volkov misdates to March 1919 instead of March 1920), that Rathenau came to be engaged as a government adviser on socialisation and then on negotiations with the Allies about reparations. Here he again clashed with Stinnes, who was determined to fend off demands for the state control of industry and reduce deliveries of coal to the French to a minimum.

Rathenau's realisation that it was necessary, rather, to win the trust of the French brought him close to Joseph Wirth, then Finance Minister, who was soon relying on him to help steer Germany through the economic minefield of reparations negotiations. When Wirth became Reich Chancellor, he immediately appointed him Minister of Reconstruction, and on 2 June 1921, speaking in the Reichstag, Rathenau formally announced the government's commitment to a policy of 'fulfilment' of the terms of the Treaty of Versailles, including the payment of reparations in both money and kind. His talks with the British and French reached a series of sensible compromises and notably improved relations. Confident, well-prepared, skilful, eloquent, and increasingly influential in politics and diplomacy, Rathenau, as Volkov remarks, 'had finally come into his own'.

On 21 January 1922 Wirth, hitherto his own Foreign Minister, appointed Rathenau to the post. By this time Rathenau had started to become disillusioned with 'fulfilment', however, and began to look for another way forward. Rapallo was the result. His aims in negotiating the treaty were in fact very limited; alarmed by signs of a rapprochement between the Western Allies and the Soviets, he pushed for an agreement with Moscow not least in order to close off any possibility that Lenin's government would add its own voice to the Anglo-French demand for reparations. But the sensation caused by the treaty simply made his enemies more bitter still. As the attacks on him became more shrill, he grew increasingly apprehensive about the possibility of assassination. 'If my dead body,' he remarked, 'were to be a stone in the bridge leading to understanding with France, then my life would not have been lived in vain.'

It was not to be so. If Rathenau's murder brought defenders of the republic together in the short run, it did not, as Volkov claims, force the other side to choose less violent tactics in the crusade to bring it down. In fact, its consequences were far more ambivalent. The original stipulations of Ebert's decree for the protection of the Republic, promulgated the day after the assassination, set a dangerous precedent, to be used later by the Nazis. The decree prescribed the death penalty for anyone convicted of conspiring to kill a member of the government, and set up a special State Court to try such cases, packing it with judges sympathetic to the government's stance and appointed personally by the President. This was to find expression in the notorious People's Court of the Nazi era.

After Ebert's death and the election of the conservative Paul von Hindenburg as Reich President, the State Court was taken over by the reactionary, German-nationalist judges who dominated the legal system of the Republic. They took an increasingly lenient view of political crimes committed in the name of Germany, undermining the Republic's public legitimacy. In the shorter term, the assassination of the Foreign Minister caused a run on the mark and accelerated the currency depreciation that was already taking a grip on Germany, leading to the hyper-inflation of the following year, the collapse of the economy, the French invasion of the Ruhr and Hitler's attempted putsch in Bavaria. The putsch was defeated, but paramilitary violence did not disappear, and within a few years it reached a scale that the Republic was wholly unable to control. Rathenau's policy of 'fulfilment' was taken up, more successfully, by Gustav Stresemann, but that, too, did not last. Within eight years of Rathenau's death, Weimar democracy had been replaced by authoritarian rule; by 1933 it had been replaced by the Nazi dictatorship, in which many of those who had advocated his assassination found their own kind of fulfilment.

5. BERLIN IN THE TWENTIES

For liberals and leftists in Germany, Berlin has always represented the dark side of German history: capital of the military state of Prussia, it became the grandiose centre and symbol of the Reich founded by Bismarck in 1871, always culturally stuffy, conservative, dull, backward, dominated by civil servants and soldiers. No wonder, when they established a democratic republic following the revolution that overthrew the Kaiser after Germany's defeat in the First World War, the victorious liberals and Social Democrats sought to distance themselves symbolically from it by holding the Constituent Assembly in the provincial town of Weimar, for ever associated with the name of Germany's greatest poets and writers, Goethe and Schiller. Weimar was, of course, far from the revolutionary turbulence and street fighting that was raging across the capital in the early months of 1920, but it was also far from its associations with a past they wanted to reject.

It took a while for Berlin to lose these associations. Before the First World War, modernist culture had flourished elsewhere, above all in the Bavarian capital Munich, in south Germany, with artists like Vassily Kandinsky, Alexei von Jawlensky, Franz Marc and August Macke pioneering abstract and semi-abstract paintings in the group they dubbed *Der Blaue Reiter*, 'the blue rider', and with radical clubs and cabarets, little socialist or anarchist magazines, and left-wing writers and playwrights flourishing in Schwabing, the bohemian quarter of the town, Munich's equivalent of Paris's Left Bank. Schwabing's radicals achieved brief political prominence with the collapse of the Bavarian monarchy at the end of the war, when the journalist Kurt Eisner became head of government, looking every inch the bohemian with his long, bushy beard and broad-brimmed floppy hat. When Eisner was assassinated by a right-wing fanatic, a group of figures from the ultra-left cultural milieu including Ernst Toller, Erich Mühsam, Gustav Landauer and B. Traven (later author of *The Treasure of the Sierra Madre*) established a short-lived revolutionary council, brusquely elbowed aside by hard-line Communists.

Their regime did not last long either. In the spring of 1919 the legitimate Social Democratic government, which had abandoned Munich to the revolutionaries, gathered large numbers of heavily armed Free Corps troops who marched on the Bavarian capital and put the Communist regime down in a bloodbath. A year later, on 13 March 1920, a similar backlash happened in Berlin, when the local Free Corps and a group of right-wing former military and civil servants of the Kaiser tried to oust the national government and install a military dictatorship in the Kapp putsch (named after its leader Wolfgang Kapp). But the outcome was dramatically different from that of the counter-revolution in Munich. Workers and trade unionists brought Berlin to a halt with a general strike, the putschists lost their nerve and democratic rule was restored. In Munich, where the atmosphere was far more conservative, the Social Democratic government was pushed out of office under threat of military action, giving way to a right-wing cabinet led by Gustav Ritter von Kahr. Kahr was backed by the Munich police and army and silently supported by the Catholic conservative political mainstream, the Bavarian People's Party. He turned Munich into a 'centre of order', allowing far-right groups to flourish. One of them was the Nazi Party, led by Adolf Hitler, who later repaid the favour by having Kahr murdered during the 'Night of the Long Knives' in 1934.

Cultural radicalism, banished from Munich by the counter-revolutionary clampdown, relocated to Berlin. Throughout the 1920s the national capital became a byword for artistic experimentation, anti-authoritarianism, radicalism and hedonism of every variety. It became a magnet for foreigners looking for urban adventure, celebrated by Christopher Isherwood in his novels *Mr Norris Changes Trains* and *Goodbye to Berlin*, subsequently transmuted into the movie *Cabaret*. Crime, murder and gangsterism were celebrated in popular culture and transformed into art by the paintings of Georg Grosz, the novel *Berlin Alexanderplatz* by Alfred Döblin and the songs of Kurt Weill and Bertolt Brecht in *The Threepenny Opera*. Café life and cabaret flourished as they had done in Munich's bohemian Schwabing district before the war. It was now in Berlin that the satirical magazines and pacifist periodicals flourished, with writers like Erich Kästner, Kurt Tucholsky and Carl von Ossietzky contributing to Berlin's *Die Weltbühne*, 'the world stage' magazine. Young women celebrated *Girlkultur* while nude reviews and prostitution, also favourite subjects for (male) artists, laid bare the degree to which sexual liberation could also mean sexual exploitation.

Viewed from Bavaria's 'centre of order' in post-revolutionary Munich, Berlin in the 1920s seemed the very negation of the kind of military, conservative, traditional Germany to which nationalists and authoritarians aspired. Little is said about this broader cultural history of the two cities in *Hitler's Berlin*, the last book by the late Thomas Friedrich, which focuses on Hitler's relationship with Berlin up to the Nazi seizure of power in 1933. Instead, the author focuses on Hitler's personal responses, which can only really be understood within this wider historical context.

As Friedrich notes, Hitler had been bowled over by the German capital's grandeur on his first visit, on furlough from the front in the First World War. In a letter to a fellow soldier in his unit, Ernst Schmidt, he called it 'a wonderful city. A real metropolis.' In 1920 Hitler still hoped it could be the starting point for the overthrow of Weimar democracy and the creation of a nationalist dictatorship. He had been in touch with the instigators of the Kapp putsch early in 1920 and flew to Berlin when it broke out. But on arrival he was met by striking workers occupying the airport. Disguised in a false, stick-on beard and passing himself off improbably as an accountant, Hitler managed to get through the checkpoint, but the obvious defeat of the putsch even before he arrived surely confirmed Hitler in his contempt for the German capital. Disillusioned, he denounced the fact that (as he saw it) 'the Berlin of Frederick the Great has been turned into a pigsty by the Jews'. Munich, by contrast, was pure, 'German', a city from which such unhealthy influences had been thoroughly expunged.

In 1923 Germany descended into chaos as monetary inflation spiralled out of control until the economy teetered on the verge of total collapse. The moment seemed right to the embittered nationalist opponents of the Weimar Republic to stage another putsch. This time, surely, it would succeed. But the failed attempt by Wolfgang Kapp three years before had suggested to Hitler that it was wrong to mount it in Berlin, where Communists and Social Democrats, the parties of the working class, dominated the scene. Friedrich suggests that Nazi hotheads were gathering in preparation for an attempt in Berlin, but the conditions were unfavourable, and the evidence for the claim that Hitler was thinking of a simultaneous *coup d'état* in both cities is skimpy, conjectural and unpersuasive.

For Hitler, by this time, Berlin was a sick, degenerate city that offered no hope for a nationalist revolution. Munich was to be the basis for Germany's regeneration. Once he had seized power there, he could use the 'centre of order' in Bavaria to overthrow the Weimar Republic. Mussolini's much-advertised 'march on Rome' the previous year, when the mere threat of moving his paramilitaries from the Fascist-controlled cities of the north down to take over the Italian capital by force, was one model for Hitler as he contemplated launching a putsch in Munich in 1923; another was the Turkish nationalist revolution of Mustafa Kemal, who had abandoned Constantinople and created a new, unsullied capital in faraway Ankara. 'In Turkey,' he declared at his trial for treason after the failure of the Beer Hall putsch, 'salvation could not come from the rotten centre, in Constantinople. Just as in our case, the city was contaminated by democratic-pacifist, internationalized people . . .' meaning, of course, the Jews.

Friedrich says far too little about this extremely negative period of Hitler's relationship with Berlin, preferring to skip quickly over the failed Munich putsch and move on to the period from 1924 to 1929, when Hitler began to reconstruct the Nazi movement. Berlin proved no more fruitful a recruiting ground for Hitler and his followers than before, and, as Friedrich remarks, 'within eighteen months of his party's re-emergence ... Hitler saw himself faced with the complete meltdown of the Berlin branch' of his party. His solution was to appoint Joseph Goebbels, at this time still a regional and rather left-ish Nazi leader in the Rhineland, to rebuild the party in the capital city. Like other Nazis, Goebbels found Berlin 'a den of iniquity!' and 'an asphalt wasteland'. But though Friedrich tries to deny it, it is clear that his attitude was fundamentally far more positive than Hitler's. 'Berlin,' wrote Goebbels, 'is the control centre. For us too. An international city.'

Soon Goebbels was revealing himself to be a gifted propagandist, organising marches and mass meetings, sending armed, brown-shirted stormtroopers to break up Communist Party events, and unfolding a campaign of violence that culminated in a pitched battle with Communist paramilitaries at the railway station in the suburb of Lichterfelde. In the affluent western thoroughfare of the Kurfürstendamm, Goebbels's thugs beat up Jewish passers-by. The respectable side of the Nazis was exhibited meanwhile by Hitler, who now considered it safe enough to come back to Berlin and deliver a cautiously worded speech there on May Day 1927. None of this fooled the Social Democratic police authorities in the city, who dissolved the party and its subsidiaries a few days later 'because the aims of these organisations run counter to criminal law'.

Typically for the Weimar Republic, this ban was first frustrated by the ultra-conservative nationalist judiciary's refusal to pass meaningful sentences on stormtroopers arrested for acts of violence, then the police's lifting of the ban on 31 March 1928 to allow the Nazis to campaign in the national elections. For all Goebbels's propagandistic genius, the Nazis did not do well in these elections, winning under

3 per cent of the vote nationwide. Their appeal, even in Berlin, was limited, as the Nazi Party's leading organiser Gregor Strasser conceded, mainly to members of the lower middle class. The election campaign in Berlin was further undermined by bitter rivalry between Goebbels and Strasser and constant rumblings of discontent from the stormtroopers. Yet the Nazis emerged from it strengthened, having relegated rival far-right groups to the sidelines. And Goebbels's weekly local paper *Der Angriff* ('Attack!'), founded the previous summer, was unfolding a skilful and demagogic publicity campaign that put the party firmly in the limelight.

Things improved still further with the campaign against the Young Plan, a rescheduling but not an abrogation of Germany's reparations payments to the former Western Allies from the First World War, in which Hitler and Goebbels were able to join forces with the far more prominent and more mainstream German Nationalist Party and use its newspapers to get themselves fresh publicity and make their pitch to the party's supporters (almost all of whom eventually deserted to the Nazi cause). What decisively changed the party's fortunes in Berlin as elsewhere, however, was the Great Depression, which arrived in Germany shortly after the Wall Street Crash of 1929. With business and bank failures and sharply rising unemployment fuelling massive discontent with the Weimar Republic and its institutions, people began to turn to the Nazi Party, largely because of its youth, its vitality and its promise of decisive solutions to the crisis.

On 17 November 1929 the party increased its share of the vote in the Berlin municipal elections more than three times over, winning support particularly in the city's better-off districts. Shortly afterwards, in mid-January 1930, the Communists handed Goebbels a propaganda gift when they shot a local stormtrooper leader, Horst Wessel, whose funeral after he had died of his injuries a few weeks later the Nazi propagandist turned into a massive celebration of young Germans' willingness to martyr themselves to save their country from Communism. Wessel's death became the subject of a new song that was turned into the official hymn of the Nazi movement. It is a pity that Friedrich does not devote more attention to this incident, perhaps the most famous of all involving the Nazi Party in the German capital before the seizure of power, and one of which every last detail has been turned over several times by historians. His failure to do so is indicative of his evident disdain for personal detail, anecdote and colour that make this, in the end, a book far duller than its topic deserves.

Wessel's murder kept Hitler out of Berlin for several months. The Nazi leader feared to tread in such a stronghold of his party's Communist rivals. Hitler, meanwhile, solved the internal squabbles of the party there by driving Gregor Strasser's brother Otto out for emphasising the 'socialist' in 'national socialist' over the 'national', while Gregor himself now toed the party line. During the national election campaign of 1930 Hitler scored a notable success with a major public speech at the Sportpalast, while the opening of the newly elected Reichstag, in which the Nazis had won more than a hundred seats, was accompanied by Nazi-orchestrated street demonstrations in which the windows of numerous Jewish-owned shops were smashed. Anxious not to alienate potential voters, the Nazis blamed all of this on Communist provocateurs, or, alternatively, declared roundly that they had not been involved in the violence at all.

Meanwhile, as the Nazi stormtroopers grew in number and in confidence, they began a local war of attrition against the Communists, attacking their meetings and using violence emanating from their self-styled Nazi 'storm centres' to force them out of their pubs and bars. It would have been interesting to have learned more about this process, but Friedrich moves swiftly on. Despite the electoral breakthrough, he notes, Hitler was still finding it difficult to make progress in the capital. Worried, Goebbels confided to his diary that the Nazi leader was 'giving too little time to Berlin' and opined that he 'must throw his personal weight' into the struggle there 'more than he has done until now'. Yet the propaganda chief was forced to admit that Hitler 'does not really want to do so: he hates Berlin and loves Munich. That's the crux of the matter. He refers to Potsdam, Washington and Ankara.

But why Munich?' As a Rhinelander, Goebbels did not understand the enthusiasm of his boss for the Bavarian city. But Hitler, it seems, was still thinking of transferring the capital to a smaller, purer, less degenerate centre than Berlin, to Munich, which he saw potentially as resembling the capital of the USA, Washington, or Turkey, Ankara, or Frederick the Great's residence, Potsdam.

Thus the Nazi Party headquarters stayed put in the 'Brown House' in Munich, where Hitler had an apartment, even though all the other national political parties had their quarters in Berlin; while in the national capital, he stayed at an hotel and grumbled about the conditions there, telling an Italian diplomat in 1931 that it was a city without traditions, half Americanised, half lacking in culture, and unable to provide him with the peace and quiet he needed to work. Already in *Mein Kampf* and in some of his early speeches he had ranted against the 'bestialised' mentality of the big city, its commercialism, in short, what he saw as its Jewishness; on 12 September 1931 this hostility was given brutal expression in a series of planned physical attacks mounted by around a thousand stormtroopers on worshippers as they emerged from a synagogue off one of western Berlin's main boulevards, the Kurfürstendamm. Some prosecutions resulted, but conservative judges handed down the most lenient of sentences to the perpetrators.

Meanwhile, the Nazi stormtrooper movement was gaining rapidly in strength, trebling its numbers in a few months in late 1931. Violence on the streets and at political meetings intensified, and the government of the conservative economic expert Heinrich Brüning banned the stormtroopers on 13 April 1932, raiding their premises and confiscating their equipment. Yet Hitler had been forewarned, and the stormtroopers carried on, disguised as sports clubs. Nazi sympathisers in the police ensured the ban was not strictly enforced. Meanwhile, Brüning was elbowed aside by another, more radical conservative, Franz von Papen, who became head of a government tasked by President Hindenburg with winning over the Nazis to provide mass support for the plans of his reactionary entourage to revise the Weimar constitution in an authoritarian direction and expand the armed forces in defiance of the restrictions imposed on them by the Treaty of Versailles.

Papen lifted the ban on the stormtroopers, and violence on the streets reached fever pitch once more, with hundreds killed in the course of 1931 and 1932. Nazi violence was directed not just at the Communists but also at the Social Democrats, who had provided the most solid support for the democratic institutions of the Weimar Republic from the very beginning. On 25 June 1932, for example, a gang of stormtroopers attacked the party's offices in the Kreuzberg district, leading to a gun battle in which three men were seriously injured. Every day, a respectable Berlin newspaper complained, 'shots are to be heard in the street'. The situation was becoming intolerable.

While he always used violence and the threat of violence to underpin his dealings with other parties, however, Hitler had decided after the failure of the Beer Hall putsch in 1923 to parallel this by also following the electoral road to power. There were plenty of opportunities in 1932, beginning with a Presidential election in which he came second to Hindenburg. Amidst a massive propaganda campaign the Nazis shot to national prominence. In July they won 37.4 per cent of the vote in nationwide Reichstag elections, making them the largest party in the country. As Friedrich points out, Berlin to some extent bucked this trend, with the Communist candidate Ernst Thälmann polling 23.6 per cent of the vote in the first round of the Presidential election, compared to only 13.2 per cent nationally, and 20.7 per cent in the second round compared to 10.2 per cent nationally. In the Reichstag elections in July, the Nazi vote in Berlin increased dramatically but still only reached 28.7 per cent. The combined support of the Communists and Social Democrats in the capital was almost double that of the Nazis. Thus Berlin underlined its reputation as a stronghold of the left. Again, Friedrich supplies far too little detail about the social geography of these elections, so that the forces supporting and opposing the Nazis at the polls in Berlin remain unclear.

As negotiations for the incorporation of the Nazis into a new government dragged on, frustrated by Hitler's insistence that this could only happen if he was appointed as the government's head, the Nazis began to run out of money and steam. In the November 1932 elections the party lost two million votes and in Berlin its support dropped to 721,000 votes while the Communists increased their support to 861,000, with the Social Democrats a strong third, at 647,000 votes. The circle around the President seized the opportunity of what they thought of as the Nazis' weakness and entered negotiations with them again. Under the threat of civil war posed by the rampaging stormtroopers, Hitler managed to get himself appointed head of a coalition government on 30 January 1933, with conservatives, including Papen, in the majority and hoping to keep him under control.

Less than a month later, on 28 February, the burning-down of the Reichstag building by a lone, deranged Dutch anarchist provided the excuse for the government to blame the Communists, suspend civil liberties and begin the mass arrest of their opponents. Elections held in March 1933 still failed to deliver an overall majority for the Nazis, who required the votes given to their conservative partners to get over the 50 per cent barrier. In Berlin the Communists managed to garner a quarter of the vote even in the face of mass terror unleashed by the Nazis. But now the Nazi assault on Berlin really began. Soon some two hundred makeshift, 'unofficial concentration camps' had been set up in the capital, many of them little more than cellars or warehouses, where hundreds of Communists and Social Democrats were tortured and murdered. Mass violence underpinned the Nazi seizure of power at every level, and by the summer of 1933 the other political parties had been dissolved, the conservatives pushed aside and all major institutions brought under Nazi control.

Hitler was now finally free to remould Berlin according to his own idea of how a great world capital city should look. Alongside an assault on 'degenerate art', satirical cabaret, jazz, and all the other things that had so disgusted him about the city in the 1920s, he now unfolded plans, as his secretary Rudolf Hess reported, for 'turning Berlin into the great metropolis of the new German Reich', beginning with the construction of a vast new sports complex ready for the 1936 Olympic Games, then planning new boulevards criss-crossing the city from north to south and east to west (one of which, renamed the Street of the 17th June after the popular uprising against Communist rule in East Germany in 1953, is still there). A vast triumphal arch was to be built, along with a huge Great Hall, and the grandiose new airport terminal at Tempelhof (also still there, though no longer in use). Massive demolition and clearance schemes began to make way for these projects; few were completed, and much of what was, such as the new Reich Chancellery building, perished in the bombing of the Second World War.

Hitler's continuing distaste for Berlin was demonstrated even in his megalomaniac scheme to make it into the new capital of the world: for the remodelled city was no longer to be called 'Berlin'; instead, it was to be renamed 'Germania'. All traces of what the Nazi leader had so despised about it in the 1920s were to be removed. Friedrich mentions these intentions, but fails to see their significance for Hitler's relationship with Berlin. Instead, the book advances the claim that 'Hitler identified with the city' (inside front flap) while all the evidence shows that he only identified with his own idea of what it should really be.

This lack of real historical insight, repeated elsewhere in its pages, is one of many disappointing features of this book. The story it tells is familiar, the details mostly well known, the writing colourless; time and again, the opportunity is lost to convey through anecdote and quotation the character of the city and its inhabitants. We are told very little about its social and political geography, and nothing at all about its municipal government; it is significant that *Hitler's Berlin* contains not a single map of the city. This is not so much a book about Hitler and Berlin as a narrative of the rise of Nazism in general terms, as it happened in the German capital, drawing not on local sources but on well-known documents like Goebbels's diaries and Hitler's speeches. Indeed, because of Goebbels's role as Nazi leader in Berlin, he features more prominently in the book than Hitler does.

Moreover, in the five years since the book was published in German, a great deal of research has appeared about Berlin during this period, so that the book was out of date even before it was translated. Friedrich was a museum curator in the city, not a professional historian, and while he was effective at presenting well-known facts to a wider audience, this book demonstrates, regrettably, that he did not really know how to do original or innovative historical research. This is, in sum, a disappointing book: the full story of the German capital during the Weimar Republic, and Hitler's relationship with it, remains to be told.

6. SOCIAL OUTSIDERS

I

There is now a substantial literature on social outsiders in the Third Reich. Much of it is the product of a realisation that Nazism had many categories of 'forgotten victims' whose fate had previously been little studied by historians. Although the Jews undoubtedly bore the main brunt of Nazism's policies of hatred and destruction of various forms of human life, other groups suffered, too. They included Gypsies (Roma and Sinti), homosexuals, the mentally and physically handicapped, 'habitual criminals', 'asocials', the 'work-shy', the homeless and itinerants, and Slavic and other subject peoples (both within Germany, as forcibly imported slave labourers, and beyond its borders). All these groups were subjected by the Nazis, in varying proportions and with varying degrees of severity, to arrest, imprisonment, brutal maltreatment in concentration camps, sterilisation, and murder.[1]

The impulses of discovery and documentation which have driven this research have inevitably meant that it has concentrated almost exclusively on the years 1933 to 1945. To be sure, many authors have traced back at least some of the roots of Nazi policies in this area to the social thought and practice of the Weimar Republic, or to racial and eugenic theories which came to the fore in the 1890s. But in sharp contrast to the immense literature on German antisemitism, which has given exhaustive coverage to the social, economic, ideological, cultural and political origins of the Nazi persecution of the Jews from the Middle Ages onwards, there is next to nothing on the long-term historical background to the Nazi persecution of other minorities in German *society*. German attitudes to the Slavs, and the history of foreign workers in nineteenth-century Germany, have been well documented.[2] Yet this is mainly because of the boost given to historical research on these topics by two major problems of West German politics in the 1970s and 1980s, namely the status and condition of millions of disfranchised *Gastarbeiter* in the country and the ever-present challenge of peaceful coexistence with the Soviet Union and the Warsaw Pact. By contrast, there has been very little debate on the long-term history of other social outsiders in modern Germany.

Yet it is on the face of it surprising that historians have not so far asked the same kind of questions in this area as they have in the history of German Jews and antisemitism. Did social outsiders play a particularly prominent role in German society from the Middle Ages onwards? Were the Germans particularly hostile to them? Did their situation improve or deteriorate over time? Do we have examples of their being made scapegoats in periods of trouble? Did they become more integrated or less into German society in the course of industrialisation? Did German liberals champion the cause of their emancipation during the political struggles of the nineteenth century? What difference did the coming of Weimar democracy make to their status and position? All these, and many other, similar, questions that spring to mind can be summed up by asking whether German society, as some historians of culture and ideas have supposed, was particularly conformist, regimented and hostile to outsiders. Did the Nazi persecution of social outsiders, in other words, meet with a ready response from the broader, conforming German population because the latter had always been hostile to social outsiders, to a degree perhaps unusual in other countries?

II

A start can be made by looking at the substantial literature which now exists on social outsiders in the early modern period, that is, from roughly the Reformation to the French Revolution and Napoleonic Wars. German society in this period was organised into status-based orders, or *Stände*, whose rights and duties were enforced by law and custom. All the elements of the social order were sustained by the notion that they possessed, in differing measure and in different ways, social honour (*Ehre*).

Outside this elaborate structure of honourable society, however, stood the heterogeneous group of the 'dishonourable' (*unehrliche Leute*), whose outsider status derived from five major sources: it could be inherited, it could be attached to an occupation, it could be the consequence of deviant conduct, especially (and above all for women) sexual, it could result from membership in a religious or ethnic minority, or it could follow from a criminal conviction. Distinctions between honourable and dishonourable groups were in part underwritten by the state, but it was above all the craft guilds that insisted on disqualifying a variety of social groups from membership by labelling them as infamous.[3]

Thus the dishonourable in early modern Germany included those who plied trades which brought them into contact with dirty or polluting substances: millers, shepherds, tanners, street cleaners, and, most dishonourable of all, skinners, knackers, mole-catchers and public executioners. A second larger and more amorphous group consisted of itinerants, people with no fixed abode: peddlers, Gypsies, travelling entertainers (bear-keepers, conjurers, and the like), mountebanks, knife grinders, and so on. Third, there were women who had lost their honour through sexual misconduct, above all, prostitutes and unmarried mothers. Fourth, infamy also attached to non-Christians, which in the German context meant above all the Jews, and subject linguistic-cultural groups such as the Wends. And finally, anyone, whatever his prior status, who had received a criminal conviction and suffered at the polluting hands of the public hangman at the pillory (called in German the *Schandpfahl*, or pillar of shame) was also considered dishonourable.[4]

Stigmatisation as dishonourable made it impossible to enter a guild, to acquire a citizen's rights, to buy most kinds of landholdings, and in general to carry on a decent existence above the poverty line. So concerned were guildsmen to distance themselves from the dishonourable that the merest accidental physical contact could provoke serious rioting, as in Berlin in 1800, when an executioner's assistant manhandled a journeyman spectator during a public execution, resulting in disturbances that only subsided when a senior and thus extremely honourable city official formally restored the journeyman's honourable status by shaking his hand (while at the same time calling out the troops just to make sure).[5] Executioners, indeed, were one of the few dishonourable trades where a decent living could be made and substitutes appointed to do the most dishonourable kinds of work. Even they had to drink in the local inn out of special mugs which nobody else was allowed to touch. Any guildsman who married an executioner's daughter was liable to find himself summarily expelled from his guild and deprived of his living.[6]

The guilds and other 'honourable' groups in urban and rural society excluded the 'dishonourable' in the teeth of growing opposition from the territorial state, which considered such restrictive practices harmful to the interests of the majority and productive of poverty and disorder among those whom it affected. It was not least its desire to reduce the power of the guilds that impelled the eighteenth-century absolutist state in repeated promulgations to attempt to reintegrate many of the dishonourable into society. The state's main concerns with social outsiders in the early modern period were to repress disorder and encourage industriousness. Thus it deployed a range of repressive strategies against those it regarded as disruptive or idle, such as bandits, beggars, confidence tricksters and some classes of itinerants such as travelling musicians, Gypsies, mountebanks, and bear-keepers, but it could not see why hardworking trades that contributed to the national wealth should be regarded as dishonourable.

In 1731 the Holy Roman Empire formally declared all trades apart from that of skinner/knacker/executioner (the three were usually combined) to be honourable, and in 1772 it extended this provision to the last-named group as well. In 1775 King Friedrich II of Prussia, followed in 1783 by Joseph II of Austria, reversed the previous policy of trying to drive out or exterminate the Gypsies and attempted instead to promote their integration into society. Numerous legal reforms drastically reduced the number of offences punishable by death, including sodomy (for which a young man had been burned at the stake in Prussia as late as 1730), and effectively decriminalised a wide variety of offences such as witchcraft and blasphemy. The replacement of Christian codes of conduct by Enlightenment rationalism led to the law codes of the late eighteenth and early nineteenth centuries which effectively abandoned sanctions against many consensual sexual acts including homosexuality.[7]

These laws, like so many of the proclamations of Enlightened monarchs, had a very limited effect on social attitudes and behaviour. Thus knackers and executioners continued to be excluded from respectable society and to form inbred dynasties of their own well into the nineteenth century.[8] Guilds continued to defy authority in enforcing a strict interpretation of the notion of honour. Moreover, the provisions of late eighteenth-century edicts ordering the integration of the Gypsies into German society in some ways merely amounted to novel forms of persecution. Gypsies were ordered to find a permanent residence, forbidden to marry each other, ordered to give all their children to German peasants to bring up, and banned from using their own language. These measures, too, proved impossible to enforce.[9]

The boundaries of honour and dishonour were often shifting and vague in the early modern period. Trades which were regarded as infamous in some areas were widely accepted as capable of forming guilds in others. Some kinds of conduct became less dishonourable as time went on, others more so. A particularly important example of the latter is prostitution, which suffered increasing discrimination and state regulation in the course of the sixteenth and seventeenth centuries. In almost all cases in early modern society, the ostracisation of the dishonourable was mitigated by the fact that they performed useful social functions of one kind or another. In an era when communications were poor, roads unmade or non-existent, resources limited and manufacturing often located many days' or even weeks' journey from the villages, small towns and farmsteads where the vast majority of people lived, itinerants such as knife-grinders, peddlers and the like were a necessary part of the rural economy. In a different way, knackers and skinners, millers, and shepherds also came into frequent contact with the population and were generally recognised as important to it. Travelling entertainers, mountebanks, quacks and tooth-pullers brought spectacle and diversion at fair time.

Moreover, mental or physical handicap was not, on the whole, a cause for dishonour. Life was neither long nor pleasant for village idiots or town fools, but on the whole they remained within the care of their family and were not social outsiders. Violent and disruptive mental disorder was likely to lead to confinement in a city prison, where the small number of criminal offenders who were imprisoned rather than whipped, branded or executed were also kept. Even here, however, honourable families would do their best to cope rather than resorting to such a drastic measure. Duke Wilhelm the Younger of Braunschweig-Lüneburg, for instance, was accustomed to run half naked around the streets of Celle giving people presents and gesticulating wildly, but it was not until he attacked his wife with a pair of tailor's shears that the ducal council agreed to confine him, and he continued to rule, subject to periodic bouts of madness, without being replaced by a regent, for another seven years, until his death in 1589.[10]

Just as madness led to total exclusion only when it became dangerous, so too itinerants only aroused the complete hostility of the population when poverty spilled over into destitution and they took to begging, thieving and banditry. Itinerant occupations provided an even more precarious existence than those of settled people. It was not surprising that the great robber bands which roamed many parts of Germany during the early modern period, above all in times of war and upheaval, were drawn mostly from the ranks of social outcasts, including not only itinerants, peddlers, beggars and Gypsies but also poor yet settled communities of outsiders such as Jews. When sweeping the countryside for suspicious characters, robbers and criminals, therefore, the early modern state paid special attention to the wandering trades. By stigmatising them in this way, the organs of the state thus reinforced their marginalisation.[11]

III

The eighteenth century saw not a general improvement in the position of social outsiders in Germany, but the beginnings of a restructuring of the notion of who was and was not an outsider, and the proclamation – though only to a limited extent the actual enforcement – of a new policy designed at integrating them into society. These processes were accelerated by the disintegration of the traditional social order in the course of population growth, economic change and the impact of British industrialisation on the Continent. The French and Napoleonic Wars lent new urgency to the reforming zeal of Enlightened monarchs and bureaucrats struggling to modernise their states and make them more effective in the face of the threat from France. A new bourgeois public sphere was emerging, whose educated members believed in equality before the law and the spread of civic freedoms and responsibilities in a free market and a liberal political order. Most important of all was the drastic reduction of the power of the guilds in the first decades of the nineteenth century, undermined by industrialisation on the one hand and attacked by the reforming state on the other. The transition from a 'society of orders' to a 'class society', from a *Ständegesellschaft* to a *Klassengesellschaft*, brought a new situation for social outsiders in the nineteenth century.

Many groups which had been excluded from society by custom and law were gradually, if in some cases imperfectly, integrated in the course of the liberal reforms which characterised the middle decades of the century. The Jews were the most obvious example, gaining civil equality by 1871 and abandoning their social isolation and religious identity in increasing numbers in the years up to the outbreak of the First World War. Of course they were still excluded from elite positions of power in the army, the civil service and politics. But while they continued to suffer discrimination, this did not make them social outsiders. Jews were integrated into German society before the First World War in a wide variety of ways. Even Kaiser Wilhelm II had a number of close personal friends who were Jewish, despite his occasional outbursts of antisemitic rhetoric. The same goes for other groups excluded from elite positions in the government and society of the Bismarckian and Wilhelmine Empire. The most numerous of these were women, who lacked even the vote, and only slowly gained a modicum of basic civil rights during this period. The feminists who tried to improve their lot were frequently subjected to petty acts of bullying by the police. More strikingly, the two largest political movements of the day, the Social Democrats and political Catholicism, were ostracised by the state political and administrative apparatus and subjected to wide-ranging legal discrimination and police harassment. In the end, however, these groups were a disadvantaged part of society, not excluded from it altogether; taken all together they formed the vast majority of people living in Germany at this time.

However, their predicament is not without relevance to the later history of state policy towards social outsiders. In particular, Bismarck's policy of labelling Social Democrats and Catholics as 'enemies of the Reich' and persecuting them in a variety of ways, from imprisonment on petty or trumped-up charges to wholesale proscription of many of their activities, set an ominous precedent for the future. At various points in the nineteenth century, conservative rhetoric had bracketed crime and revolution and argued for political radicals to be treated as common criminals. As heirs to this tradition, Bismarck and his successors used the criminal law to combat threats to the social and political order of the Reich in a manner which was still very much present in the minds of the many judges and penal administrators who survived the collapse of imperial Germany in 1918 and continued in their posts through the Weimar Republic.[12] In other countries, too, some political movements – most notably anarchism, responsible for a wave of political assassinations in late nineteenth-century Europe and America – was also subjected to police and legal repression, but in few countries west of tsarist Russia did such repression reach so wide or penetrate so deeply.

Political repression became enmeshed with criminal law and policing at a time when the state in Germany was rationalising its approach to social exclusion. As the power of the guilds dwindled, many trades, from milling to linen weaving, became more respectable. Others, such as shepherding, declined to marginal importance. Honour lost its significance as a means of sustaining the social order, and correspondingly dishonouring lost its significance as a means of punishment by the law and the state. On the other hand, steady work and a fixed abode, already prioritised by the Enlightened administrations of the eighteenth century, gained a more exclusive significance as criteria of social belonging in the nineteenth. Industrialisation and urbanisation brought rapid communication, mass production and distribution and the demise of the majority of itinerant trades. The remaining itinerants, like the remaining journeymen artisans, found it increasingly difficult to make a living and had to resort to a growing degree to begging. At the same time, by the late nineteenth century, economic growth meant a high demand for labour in the towns and cities. Many workers travelled the land looking for employment, and the instability and rapid fluctuations of industrial production often meant periods when they were unable to find it. Finally, the landed estates of the north and east were increasingly replacing settled with seasonal labour, which in turn attracted large groups of travelling agricultural labourers (often from Poland) looking for employment at various times of the year.

All this contributed to what contemporary social observers described as a growing problem of vagrancy in the late nineteenth century. Attempts to solve it ranged from the establishment of labour colonies to the beginnings of provision of cheap lodging houses for the homeless, funded by charitable foundations, often religious in their inspiration. All the while, however, the basic experience of the itinerant remained that of continual harassment by the police and the courts, who punished begging, failure to carry papers and tramping the land (*Landstreicherei*) with repeated short periods of incarceration in a workhouse or prison.[13] Poor relief in this period, under the influence of the so-called Elberfeld system, changed from a matter of indiscriminate charity to a project of closely supervising the destitute and forcing them to find employment either in a workhouse or in a poorly paid job, on pain of losing their entitlement. A similar policy was adopted toward the Roma and Sinti, who were constantly harassed by the police using legal instruments such as the requirement to carry identity papers, the tax law, the law against concubinage, and the requirement to register with the police on taking up residence in a district. In the context of virtually full employment and a growing elaboration of state and voluntary provision for the unemployed, vagrancy, begging, and tramping the countryside were seen not as responses to unemployment but as matters of personal choice by the 'work-shy' and the deviant. Such policies had their limitations, however. The absence of a national police force, and the responsibility of local officials for such matters, meant that the authorities were frequently satisfied by simply expelling Gypsies and vagrants from their district and abandoning responsibility for them to another. Often enough, indeed, local authorities would issue them with legitimation papers certifying that they were bona fide journeymen simply to get rid of them.[14]

The same kind of policy was applied to prostitution, which commentators tended to see, not as what it very often was, a temporary strategy for dealing with loss of income of employment by young women, or a means of dealing with the consequences of illegitimate motherhood and the consequent social stigmatisation, but as the expression of personal social and sexual deviance on the part of its practitioners. As a consequence prostitutes continued to be subject to police harassment if they resisted joining the small minority who were confined in state-regulated 'public houses' or bordellos. Most, however, were able to escape the attentions of the police.[15] At the same time the state was increasingly insistent upon the need to care for the mentally and physically handicapped in specially created institutions. The nineteenth century was the age of the great mental hospitals and lunatic asylums, when medicine and the law elaborated a series of medical definitions of deviant behaviour. With urbanisation and the relative decline of the proportion of the community living in rural communities, it became more difficult for the majority of families to support their mentally and physically handicapped members. The medical profession also increasingly intervened to enforce the committal of the mentally handicapped to institutions, even when the family of the person concerned resisted.[16]

It would be wrong to see such medical intervention in an entirely negative light. No doubt there were some kinds of mental disturbance which could be treated medically; and the situation of the mentally and physically handicapped in the poor quarters of Germany's great cities in the later nineteenth and early twentieth centuries was certainly not to be envied. Medical intervention and institutionalisation may well have prolonged the lives of some of them; in a few cases, indeed, they even saved a life by persuading the courts to avoid applying the death penalty on the grounds of a murderer's insanity.[17] However, the growth of the medical profession in the course of the nineteenth century undoubtedly led to a growing stigmatisation of certain kinds of mental and physical handicap as medically determined. The doctors were increasingly able to enlist the support of the state in compulsory certifications of insanity and mental incapacity.

What all this amounts to is the fact that social and sexual deviance in the nineteenth century was dealt with in the first place not by government policies and initiatives but in the everyday activities of what might be called low-level policing and administration. In some instances applying specific provisions of the criminal law, in others merely operating local regulations or police ordinances, the police harassed and harried itinerants, beggars, vagrants, Roma and Sinti, and prostitutes in much the same way as they harassed and harried recalcitrant Catholic priests during the *Kulturkampf* or Social Democratic activists under the *Sozialistengesetz* and, indeed, for long after. The illegality of male (though not female) same-sex relations according to Paragraph 175 of the Reich criminal code of 1871 was a further instrument in the hands of the police, who used it to harass homosexual men in big cities such as Berlin.[18]

The results were almost predictable. The lack of any coordinated national policy, coupled with inadequate police resources to deal with the numbers of people involved, meant that social outsiders such as these were stigmatised as deviants, identified and identifiable to the authorities through their numerous convictions, and subject to frequent and arbitrary interference with their way of life. There was no chance of police intervention actually reducing the numbers of the social outsiders or bringing about their integration into society. On the contrary, police harassment actually strengthened their identity as outsiders by arousing their resentment against society and forcing them to create and strengthen protective subcultures of their own. Thus a homosexual subculture grew up in Berlin just as a Catholic subculture grew up in the south and west; a subculture of vagrants, with its own jargon, its own meeting places and its own language of chalked signs on houses and street comers, paralleled the organisational subculture of German Social Democracy.[19] The culture of the Roma and Sinti, though little studied by serious historians, was similarly in all probability further cemented by such irregular but inescapable petty persecution.[20]

The same may be said of the criminal subculture in nineteenth-century Germany. As imprisonment replaced public physical punishment as the main penal sanction, so commentators began to note that the majority of prison inmates were persistent offenders who had been there many times before. Prison seemed to be a vehicle for the creation of criminals, not their reformation. Providing them with criminal records barred the way to regular employment had they wished to take it, while the company of other prisoners cemented their sense of criminal identity. Attempts to remedy this situation failed. Solitary confinement, the rule of silence, religious instruction and prison education, as advocated by reformers, were implemented too patchily to have any general effect. Voluntary associations for the care of released prisoners were too few to have more than a marginal influence, just as charitable 'Magdalen homes' for the reform of prostitutes, philanthropic labour colonies and charitable lodging houses for vagrants barely touched the fringes of the problem they were respectively trying to address.

The stigmatisation of these social outsiders indeed helped perpetuate the social threat which respectable society feared they posed. It reminded the bourgeoisie and the respectable working class alike of the fate that would await those who seriously deviated from social, sexual or legal norms. In a somewhat different category were Prussia's, and later imperial Germany's, ethnic minorities, principally Alsatians and Lorrainers, Danes and above all Poles. Here, too, the overwhelming drive was towards assimilation. Local German authorities attempted to suppress the use of Polish, French, Danish and Alsatian patois in official contexts, including state schools, encouraged German-speaking settlers and used the law in a variety of ways to the disadvantage of the local, non-German-speaking population. The result was as predictable as it was in other contexts, namely the growth of nationalist movements and the emergence of a strong regional or nationalist subculture which regarded the Germans as little better than an occupying power.[21] Finally, the physically and mentally handicapped were in a different category again. The extent to which they were able to fashion subcultures of their own within the institutions to which they were confined is difficult to assess; when they were isolated from their family and community and cut off to a large extent from the world beyond the asylum walls, they were the most vulnerable of all among nineteenth-century Germany's social outsiders.

IV

Despite the varied and changing kinds of discrimination outlined above, the history of social outsiders in eighteenth- and nineteenth-century Germany does not, on the whole, suggest that German society was particularly rigidly defined, or that it excluded larger numbers of people than other societies did, or that the German state persecuted deviants and outcasts more ruthlessly than other states did. In general, and with some qualifications, the processes which were taking place in the redefinition, investigation, isolation and stigmatisation of social outsiders in Germany were the same as those described by the French philosopher-historian Michel Foucault for England and France.[22] It was in the late nineteenth century that significant differences began to emerge. Eugenics, 'racial hygiene', and the theory and rhetoric of 'degeneration', though increasingly influential in many countries including Italy, France and the United States, seem to have struck a particular chord among German intellectuals from the 1890s on. By the eve of the First World War, increasing numbers of Germany's social outsiders were being regarded by growing numbers of those who wrote and thought about them in the light of theories of this kind.[23]

What this reflected was the growing influence of the medical profession in German society. At a time when it was gaining immense prestige through the triumphs of its research into the causes of tuberculosis, cholera, diphtheria and other major afflictions of the nineteenth century, German medicine was also gaining an all-pervasive social influence through the creation and rapid expansion of the medical and social insurance systems in which Germany was the undoubted pioneer. German doctors began to conceive the ambition of bringing other areas of society into their remit.[24] Among these were crime and social deviance. The German school of criminology, founded by men such as Franz von Liszt, and developed by specialists such as Gustav Aschaffenburg, gradually took the study of crime and deviance out of the hands of lawyers and moralists and placed it in the purview of psychiatrists and eugenicists. Adapting the ideas of the Italian criminologist Cesare Lombroso, himself also a medical man, they were arguing by the early 1900s that persistent, recidivist criminals were primarily the product of hereditary degeneracy, activated under particular social and economic circumstances. Other deviants, such as alcoholics, prostitutes, vagrants and tramps were placed in the same category of the hereditarily degenerate and eugenically substandard.[25]

Behind these arguments was a wider belief that with the decline in the German birth rate that set in around the turn of the century, and which was most marked among the upper and middle classes, 'less valuable' members of society were reproducing themselves faster than the 'fully valuable'. This language of *Minderwertigkeit* and *Vollwertigkeit* became almost universal among medical and other professionals involved in discussions of 'the social problem' by the eve of the First World War. However neutral and 'scientific' it may have seemed, it inevitably involved the moral and political judgement that some human beings were less than fully human; the very terminology broke down barriers to the abandonment of time-honoured liberal principles such as equality before the law and freedom of the individual. Eugenics could, of course, be applied in a positive sense, and was one of the factors behind efforts by the medical profession to improve standards of hygiene, nutrition, infant care and general public health; but the more the institutional network of health provision spread among the population, the more obvious it seemed to many of those involved in it that the minority who persisted in rejecting the benefits of a regular, sober, hard-working, law-abiding life must be doing so because of some innate hereditary defect such as the mentally and physically handicapped seemed to suffer from. Thus negative eugenics – the reduction or elimination of the 'less valuable' sectors of the population – followed as an almost inevitable consequence of the spread of positive eugenics – the improvement of the mental and physical state of the population as a whole.

By the eve of the First World War, the language of eugenics and racial hygiene was being widely used by criminal lawyers, state prose-cutors, penal administrators and social commentators in Germany as well as by those involved in Germany's rapidly growing profession of social welfare administrators. International organisations devoted to the application of medical ideas to criminal and penal policy were dominated by Austrians and Germans. Well before the outbreak of the First World War, penal reformers were arguing for the indefinite detention, castration or even execution of persistent offenders whose conduct over the years had in their view demonstrated their hereditary degeneracy and their unfitness to live in human society or pass on their character defects to the next generation.[26] In other countries such as the United States, eugenicists put forward similar views; but in Germany the movement was far more dominated by the medical and psychiatric professions, who applied the concept of degeneracy as a diagnostic tool to an increasing variety of social outsiders, including alcoholics, homosexuals and prostitutes.[27]

Even before the First World War, these new ideas were already having a discernible impact on attitudes towards serious and violent offenders, and in a popularised form were used in the legal profession, the press and political life as a means of justifying the death penalty. But it was only under the Weimar Republic that they became linked to two other sets of ideas in a new and fateful mixture. First, after Germany's defeat in the war, the idea of Nordic supremacy, along with its corollaries, belief in the inferiority of Jews, Slavs and other races, was adopted by increasing numbers of racial hygiene specialists, above all in the younger generation. Those eugenicists who opposed anti-semitism and racism became a minority. Second, the medical model began to be applied to political deviance. In the mid-nineteenth cen-tury, revolutionary activity and belief had been regarded by many commentators as a form of criminality. From the First World War, the idea began to gain hold that it was the product of a diseased or degen-erate mind. Already in 1916–18, indeed, Jehovah's Witnesses who refused military service on ethical grounds were being put into lunatic asylums after being diagnosed as suffering from 'religious mania'.

During the Weimar Republic they were widely regarded on the political right as deluded revolutionaries manipulated by Jews, with whom they were thought to share a number of religious beliefs.[28] The 1918 Revolution itself was seen by one leading criminologist as the product of psychic disturbance brought on by cosmic and climatic change which caused a reversion of the masses to an atavistic state of primitive bestiality not dissimilar to that diagnosed in criminals by the Italian theorist Lombroso.[29]

Racial hygiene became an established academic discipline under the Weimar Republic. The founding of the first chair in the subject, at Munich University in 1923, was followed in the next nine years by no fewer than forty courses on the subject at German universities in general. A variety of research institutes opened, criminological-biological collection stations were established to collect data on the personalities and families of offenders, and publications began to appear arguing for eugenically defective people to be killed because as 'ballast existences' they were imposing a financial burden on society at a time when economic crisis was making life difficult for those who did contribute to national production. Indeed, already during the First World War the deliberate withholding of supplies from lunatic asylums had led to a rise in the death rate among inmates so drastic that it is not much of an exaggeration to claim that tens of thousands of mentally ill patients met an untimely death at the hands of officials who knew well enough what they were doing and had few qualms about doing it.[30]

The elaboration of welfare services and the rise of the social work profession in the Weimar Republic accelerated this process rather than slowing it down. Whatever else they might have disagreed about, welfare workers were increasingly agreed on the need for legislation to replace outmoded policing measures and obsolete institutions such as the workhouse with modern homes in which tramps, vagrants, prostitutes and other 'asocials', as they were now widely known, could be interned without limit until they were judged fit to be integrated into society. All parties right of the Communists agreed on the introduction of a law decriminalising offences such as vagrancy and prostitution and introducing instead measures providing for the forcible and indefinite confinement of 'asocials' in secure homes of various kinds run by the welfare system.[31] A parallel debate took place in the case of habitual or 'incorrigible' offenders against the criminal law, who, many lawyers, criminologists and psychiatrists argued, should similarly be detained in 'security confinement' without limit of time, and for much the same reasons.[32] Thus they would be prevented from reproducing themselves and endangering the future health of the German race.

The spread of ideas drawn from eugenics and racial hygiene also affected other social outsiders in the Weimar Republic. Gypsies, for example, presented the welfare system with many of the same problems as 'asocials'. They were vagrants, they avoided laws about educating their children, they were thought to be involved in petty crime, and in addition they were clearly from a racial background altogether different from that of the Germans. As with persistent offenders and 'asocials', policy in the Weimar Republic was still largely a matter of policing, but the growth of the welfare system had an impact, too, in cementing their exclusion from society and prompting welfare agencies to argue more strongly than ever for their integration. 'Criminal biology' found it easy to describe them as 'primitive' and undeveloped human beings, racially inferior to the Germans. The idea of integrating them into society, therefore, came to be replaced in the minds of a significant number of policy-makers by the idea of cordoning them off from it altogether, in case they contaminated it through intermarriage, which, indeed, was occurring on an increasing scale in this period. A Bavarian law of 1926 sought to restrict their movements to designated sites, tried to prevent their forming 'bands' and threatened them with two years in a workhouse 'on grounds of public security' if they failed to prove regular employment. Officials began to compile a comprehensive register of Gypsies, with a view to keeping track of them in the criminal and welfare files as a separate racial group.[33]

The influence of medical and racial-biological thinking also made itself felt in discussions of homosexuality under the Weimar Republic. Already the sexologists of the turn of the century had classified homosexuality as a psychological disorder. As the birth rate declined, so worries among eugenicists about the contribution made to the decline by a possible spread of homosexuality began to grow. This was thought to be a disorder where, in the view of medical commentators, heredity, for obvious reasons, played only a subordinate role. Medical intervention could thus, in theory at least, effect a 'cure'. On the far right of the political spectrum, priority thus came to be given to the restriction and, if possible, elimination of the flourishing homosexual subculture of cities such as Berlin, in order to prevent young men who (it was thought) would otherwise have contributed to the reproduction of the race from being corrupted and seduced. In addition criminologists pointed to the criminal connections of the subculture (inevitable because of the illegality of male homosexuality under the criminal law). Finally, there were widespread worries on the right about the 'effeminacy' of male homosexuals and the effect this might have – in the eyes of some, was already having – on the masculinity of German men, their willingness to fight in a future war, and the manly vigour they should be transmitting to future generations. The sexologist Magnus Hirschfeld, a pioneering campaigner for equal rights for homosexuals, probably only fuelled such irrational anxieties by portraying homosexual men as neither masculine nor feminine but a 'third sex' somewhere between the two.[34]

Under the Weimar Republic the issue of social exclusion became heavily politicised. On the one hand, counter-revolutionaries and the political right increasingly lumped all kinds of social, political and religious deviants together in a single category of subversives thought to be undermining the German race. In this they were supported by at least some eugenicists and racial hygienists, although others resisted the political appropriation of the issue by the racist and antisemitic forces of extreme nationalism. More broadly, the burgeoning welfare apparatus of the Weimar period itself entered the political arena by demanding legislative action to take a variety of minorities, from the mentally ill to the persistent offender, from the vagrant and tramp to the alcoholic and the drug addict, out of the criminal justice and penal systems and into the realm of compulsory institutionalisation under medical supervision for an indefinite period of time.

Some groups of social outsiders became politicised, too. During the 1920s the Jehovah's Witnesses won massive new support in Germany; by 1926 there were more members of the sect in Dresden than there were in New York, and they became more thoroughly and uncompromisingly pacifist than they had been during the First World War, when a high proportion of them had agreed to serve in the German armed forces. Their forthright opposition to the growing menace of antisemitism enraged the far right and cemented the belief of ultra-nationalists that Jehovah's Witnesses were stooges of the Jews, hell-bent on preventing the resurgence of the German race after the catastrophe of 1918.[35] Homosexuals campaigned vigorously, and far more openly than under the Wilhelmine Empire, for the abolition of Paragraph 175 of the criminal code and the legalisation of homosexuality.[36] Anarchists such as Erich Mühsam and Gregor Gog attempted to politicise vagrants, although Gog's 'Vagabonds' Congress' in Stuttgart in 1929 had only a limited success, and the idea of organising tramps in a union was a predictable failure.[37]

Social outsiders also came to have a heavily symbolic political function under the Weimar Republic, when the forces of extreme nationalism were demanding that all right-thinking Germans should combat the Treaty of Versailles and fight subversive forces holding back national resurgence. Of no group was this more true than of the so-called 'Rhineland bastards'. During the 1920s, the left bank of the Rhine was under Allied military occupation, and in the French zone this meant colonial troops from Senegal, Madagascar and other parts of the French overseas empire. Virtually all German political parties including the Social Democrats protested against this policy of using what they openly declared to be racially inferior troops in the occupation, and particularly during the French invasion of the Ruhr in

1923, racist propaganda of this kind reached almost hysterical proportions, accusing the black troops of numerous rapes of German women. In *Mein Kampf,* indeed, Hitler ascribed this policy to a deliberate Jewish conspiracy to degrade and corrupt the German race. In fact, the colonial troops seem to have behaved with courtesy and consideration and the 'Rhineland bastards' were the offspring of entirely voluntary relationships with German women. Others so categorised were the children of older, entirely legitimate relationships between German colonists in America before the First World War and black American men or women, or white Germans and black colonial subjects. These distinctions, however, were ignored in the furore over the French occupation, and all mixed-race Germans were categorised as 'Rhineland bastards', a symbol of German humiliation so potent that officials in the Bavarian Ministry of the Interior were already asking the Reich government to sterilise them in 1927.[38]

V

Despite all these ominous developments it would be wrong to view the treatment of social outsiders in the Weimar Republic simply in terms of growing state discrimination and persecution. The 1920s also witnessed a widespread movement of social reform in the welfare, penal and policing apparatus of the state. Even those who believed in a strong hereditary element in social deviance of one kind or another generally considered that the majority of deviants were still capable of reintegration into society. Liberal and socialist ideas had some influence, and proposals to sterilise deviants or subject them to a policy of involuntary 'euthanasia' met with overwhelming rejection on all sides.

However, this situation did not last. The economic depression of 1929–33 exacerbated the problem of social outsiders in a number of ways. Mass unemployment on an unprecedented scale meant a huge increase in the numbers of homeless and vagrants. Benefits were cut and were removed altogether from the long-term unemployed, nearly a million and a quarter of whom were receiving no benefits of any kind by the beginning of 1933. The number of people sleeping rough and living on the streets in Germany was estimated at between 200,000 and 500,000 by the early 1930s. Cutbacks in state expenditure during the crisis fuelled the arguments of those who regarded the mentally and physically handicapped as 'social ballast'. Prostitution became once more a common means for young, mostly working-class women to earn a living when regular jobs were hard to obtain. And while crime rates did not increase as much as they had done during the hyperinflation of 1922–3, youth gangs or 'cliques' were particularly noticeable during the Depression and perceived as a serious threat to public order by many people in the middle classes.[39]

In this situation the boundaries between respectable society and its outcasts became vaguer and more fluid than ever. Even in normal times prostitution, for example, was generally a temporary expedient adopted by women who subsequently had little difficulty in reintegrating themselves into the working class. Vagrancy was less a permanent way of life than an unavoidable makeshift for the hundreds of thousands of mostly young men who were unable to afford a roof over their heads in the early 1930s; at other times it was little more than a phase for many who engaged in it. Theft, embezzlement and petty crime were a temptation to many in a period of mass unemployment and bankruptcy. In the longer run, too, an ethnic minority such as the 'Rhineland bastards' managed to find a role in society, above all in the circus and entertainment business. While some forms of mental and physical handicap were undeniably extreme and made it impossible for those who suffered from them to live a normal life integrated into society at large, others were ill defined and dependent on the whims of diagnostic procedures that were as vague as they were arbitrary.[40]

In normal times, as we have seen, policy and policing tactics could often harden these boundaries and turn what for many was a part-time or temporary role outside society into a more or less permanent condition. The medicalisation of penal policy and the rise of social

welfare had extended social exclusion in this way to increasing numbers of people who had previously escaped the net, while in no way
diminishing the impact of everyday policing on identifying and perpetuating the world of the 'asocial', the petty criminal and the repeat
offender. The collection of statistics on Gypsies, the creation of elaborate card indices by the 'criminal-biological collection stations' of
social outsiders thought to be hereditarily impaired and therefore to
pose a threat to coming generations, the information-gathering activities of the social welfare system, all this provided the basis long before
the coming of the Third Reich for the reassertion of boundaries
between society and its outcasts which the Depression in many ways
threatened to obscure.[41]

The Nazi regime sought to recreate these boundaries in an extreme
form. In doing so, it fused all the various elements which had previously been present in official, medical-psychiatric, administrative and
criminological thinking about social outsiders. Dividing their world
into 'racial comrades' and 'community aliens', *Volltsgenossen* and
Gemeinschaftsfremde, the 'ins' and the 'outs', the Nazis defined almost
any kind of refusal to contribute to their goals as deviant, sick, racially
motivated or degenerate. German society was probably, historically
speaking, no more hostile to outsiders than other European societies;
even in the traditional 'society of orders' (*Ständegesellschaft*), the
boundaries between the 'honourable' and the 'dishonourable' had
been changeable and fluid, and had largely been wiped away by the
middle of the nineteenth century. Industrial society had created new
categories of social outsider, notably among the physically and mentally
handicapped, while partly perpetuating, partly transforming others,
such as itinerants and vagrants. Social and to some extent official attitudes towards socially deviant acts such as sodomy and prostitution and
outsider groups such as the Gypsies became more lenient in the course
of the eighteenth and nineteenth centuries. Petty police harassment
was the lot of outsiders such as these until the turn of the nineteenth
century or thereabouts. It may have cemented their deviant identity
but it did not entirely sever their links with respectable society.

Three factors changed this situation in the period from about 1890 to about 1930. The first was the medicalisation of penal and welfare policy, coupled with a vast expansion of the state welfare system. Increasingly, and above all from the First World War onwards, a significant proportion of social outsiders were categorised by those who dealt with them as hereditarily tainted, degenerate, a threat to the future of the German race. The second, related factor was the rise of racial hygiene, the tendency to view German society and its relations with other societies in Europe and beyond in racial terms. This led to a gradual, if uneven, link between the discourse on social outsiders and the discourses of antisemitism and the fitness of the German race to survive in the struggle for supremacy with other races such as the Latins and the Slavs. The third factor was the increasing politicisation of the discourse on social outsiders, indeed the increasing politicisation of German society as a whole, above all under the Weimar Republic, when to many on the extreme right, drastic remedies seemed necessary to overcome the trauma of defeat in the First World War and regenerate the German nation as a virile, energetic, committed and united entity ready to re-establish on the world stage the world power it had failed to grasp in 1914–18.

These were the criteria which the Nazis applied to social outsiders in Germany from 1933 onwards. They often did so as much by riding roughshod over the careful distinctions drawn by the experts as by adopting their ideas and utilising the data they had so painstakingly collected under the Weimar Republic. As Nazism radicalised, above all during the war, so, too, did its policy towards the socially excluded. In this situation, distinctions between political, racial and social deviance almost completely vanished. By 1944 the definition of the 'community alien' had become a totally arbitrary instrument in the hands of the SS and police apparatus. According to the Nazi criminologist Edmund Mezger, a 'community alien' was 'anyone who, by his personality and way of life, and particularly through unusual deficiencies in understanding and character, shows himself unable to satisfy the minimal demands of the racial community by his own efforts'.[42] This encompassed far more than the categories of social out-sider which had borne the brunt of the Nazis' repression and extermination previously. It gave the enforcement agencies a practical carte blanche to arrest, incarcerate and kill almost anybody they wanted to. The biological term *Volksschädling* (racial parasite), com-monly used in Nazi legislation against wartime offences such as looting, testified to the permeation of Nazi thinking by the biological metaphor. Justice was explicitly proclaimed by leading Nazi jurists such as Roland Freisler and Otto-Georg Thierack to be an instrument of eugenic cleansing.

This was the end of a long road. It had begun, not with the survival of premodern forms of social exclusion inherited from the early modern *Ständegesellschaft*, but with the long-term autonomy and wide-ranging powers that the police in the majority of German states had inherited from the era of absolutism, powers which they used to harass and perpetuate the social exclusion of a variety of categories of deviant and outcast. The failure of penal reform in the nineteenth century, though far from unique to Germany, had played its part, too. But it was the eruption of racist, Social Darwinist and eugenic modes of thought into judicial, penal and social administration around the turn of the century, the medicalisation of these areas of thought and practice, and their politicisation during the Weimar Republic that set Germany on the fateful path towards the indefinite incarceration, sterilisation and eventually mass extermination of deviant groups. Of these, only the most radical step, that of mass murder, would probably not have been taken had the Nazis not come to power in 1933. For repressive poli-cies towards a variety of social outsiders were undertaken in other countries, too, from Sweden to the United States, in the interwar years, all the way up to forcible sterilisation, though on a much smaller scale than was involved in Germany. It was only in Germany that mass killing became state policy; and it began, not with the Jews, but with the men-tally and physically handicapped, in 1939.

Thus seen in a longer historical perspective, the confinement, ster-ilisation and extermination of social outsiders in Nazi Germany were the products of modernity, of political mobilisation and of scientific advance, or what was held to be such, in the half-century from around 1890 to 1940.[43] The process was not a regression into barbarism. To describe it as such is to use barbarism in a moral rather than in a historical sense, and hence to bar the way to an informed, historical understanding of the nature of Nazi exterminism. Instating barbarism as the central conceptual tool for understanding the Third Reich is to mistake moral condemnation for thought. Thinking of Nazi extermination instead as an aspect of the Janus-faced phenomenon of modernity involves recognising that there could be a dark side to modernisation, that – as Marx and Engels saw long ago – modernisation could have its victims as well as its beneficiaries. It does not mean rewriting the concept of modernisation until it is emptied of all positive connotations altogether.[44] It means recognising that science, in certain places and at certain times, and most notably of all perhaps in Germany between 1890 and 1940, could be a destructive as well as a constructive force, and that what some saw as social progress, others experienced as discrimination, oppression, suffering and death.

PART II

INSIDE NAZI GERMANY

7. COERCION AND CONSENT

In the decades that immediately followed the end of the Second World War there was a general consensus that Nazi Germany was a police state. Its all-encompassing apparatus of surveillance and control allowed the individual citizen little freedom of thought or action. The view that what principally characterised the Third Reich was the total destruction of civil freedoms and the rule of law in what the German political scientist Karl Dietrich Bracher called 'the German dictatorship' in his classic book of that title, went together with an emphasis on the top-down nature of decision-making in the Nazi regime, putting Hitler at its centre in what came to be known as the 'intentionalist' approach to the study of Nazi policy, in which things were seen to have happened because the Nazi leader wanted them to.[1] From the late 1960s onwards, however, this interpretation began to be pushed aside, as a new generation of historians began to explore the inner contradictions and instabilities of the Third Reich's system of rule. Local and regional histories uncovered a wide and changing variety of popular attitudes towards the Third Reich and its policies. This research emphasised by implication ordinary Germans' relative freedom of choice to resist or not to resist, and thus restored an element of voluntarism to their relationship with the Nazi regime.[2]

At the same time, the apparatus of the police state began to look a good deal less coercive than it had done in the 1950s. A variety of studies showed that the Gestapo, once portrayed as a universally intrusive institution of surveillance and control, was in fact a relatively small organisation, certainly when compared to the State Security Service of Communist East Germany, the Stasi.[3] And recently, a large-scale and methodologically sophisticated opinion survey of elderly Germans conducted in the 1990s by the American historian Eric Johnson and the German sociologist Karl-Heinz Reuband has claimed that a majority of those questioned admitted to being 'positive' or 'mainly positive' about Nazism at one time or another during the regime. Only a small minority ever feared being arrested by the Gestapo. 'Hitler and National Socialism', Johnson and Reuband have argued, 'were so immensely popular among most Germans that intimidation and terror were rarely needed to enforce loyalty.' The regime's popularity could also be clearly seen in the results of the elections and plebiscites it held at various intervals during the 1930s. The 99 per cent support the electorate gave to Hitler and his policies, according to the historian Robert Gellately, provided 'remarkable' evidence of 'popular backing' for the regime, a view endorsed by Hans-Ulrich Wehler, for long, until his death in 2014, Germany's leading historian, who claimed in his survey of the period that 'a systematic strategy of manipulation was not pursued' by the Nazis on these occasions.[4] The most sweeping claims in this respect have been made by the left-wing German historian Götz Aly, who has argued that 'the Third Reich was not a dictatorship maintained by force'. Instead, it was a popular regime, sustained by the enthusiasm of the vast majority for its achievement, early on, of material prosperity and social equality. Its decision-making structures were not 'top-down' but 'flat', giving maximum opportunity to participation in the formulation and implementation of policy.[5]

These arguments have been driven not least by a strong moral imperative, fuelled by the re-emergence of war crimes cases since the fall of Communism, and the launching of compensation and restitution actions on a variety of fronts, from looted art to slave labour. Anything that implies constraints on the free will of historical actors puts a potentially serious obstacle in the way of establishing their culpability. The language of the courtroom has been imported into history, as everyone who lived in Germany or Europe between 1933 and 1945 is categorised as a 'perpetrator', a 'bystander' or, less often, a 'victim'. Thus Hans-Ulrich Wehler argued that it would be 'mistaken to characterize the *Führer* state primarily as a terror regime in which a band of desperadoes under the leadership of an Austrian social outcast exercised a kind of alien rule over Germany to which the decent but defenceless majority had to bow'. Such a view, commonly found in West Germany in the immediate postwar period, provided an alibi for the majority, he argued, while it conveniently ignored the fact that there was a 'broad consensus' in support of the regime from the outset. This consensus, he claimed, was maintained above all by the charismatic appeal of Hitler and by a mixture of 'bread and circuses' for the masses. In consequence, there existed in Nazi Germany an 'unreserved agreement' between 'the rule of the *Führer* and the opinion of the people'.[6] For Wehler, admitting such a consensus underpinned the postulate of collective guilt that provided the primary integrating factor in Germany's post-unification national identity. This identity has never been uncontested, and there have been repeated attempts to provide an alternative, or to undermine its premises by portraying the Germans as victims of war and conquest as much as anybody else was. But it has achieved hegemonic status none the less. It rests on a shared sense of responsibility for Nazism's crimes that can now be observed almost everywhere in Germany, but above all in Berlin, where a monument and museum to Nazism's principal victims have been placed at the very heart of the nation's capital city.[7]

But the emphasis on a national consensus achieved by Nazism in the 1930s and early 1940s is not confined to those whose primary interest is in providing historical legitimation for a left-liberal concept of nationhood. It is now widespread among historians of Nazi Germany in whatever country they are based. 'In their successful cultivation of popular opinion,' Robert Gellately has written, 'the Nazis did not need to use widespread terror against the population to establish the regime.' 'The Nazi revolution,' he argues, 'did not begin with a sweeping onslaught on German society, but moved forward in tune with what the great majority of people wanted or would tolerate.' Terror, he says, was directed above all at small groups of social outcasts, and did not threaten the lives of the vast majority of ordinary Germans. Most Germans were indeed aware of the concentration camps and the terror apparatus, but their reaction was one not of fear but of approval. If terror did play a role in consolidating the regime, then it was the terror the Gestapo and the criminal police exercised against social outsiders, which helped convince the overwhelming majority of ordinary Germans that law and order were at last being restored after the chaos and disorder of the Weimar Republic. 'The silent and not-so-silent majority,' says Gellately, 'backed the regime.' This is not an isolated view. Indeed, a new consensus seems to have emerged according to which the Third Reich was thus, in a phrase used recently by a number of historians, both German and non-German, a 'dictatorship by consent', a *Zustimmungsdiktatur*, to quote the title of a chapter by Frank Bajohr in a recent collaborative history of Hamburg in the Nazi era.[8]

In what follows, I will take a critical look at three central propositions, or groups of propositions, on which this new consensus rests. These are:

(1) The Nazis did not seize power but won it legally and by consent. They only applied coercion to small minorities of social outsiders, and had the approval of the vast majority of the population in doing so.

(2) Nazi repression, exercised through the Gestapo and the concentration camps, was on a small scale and did not affect the majority of the population.

(3) The overwhelming popularity of the regime from the outset is demonstrated by the staggeringly successful results it achieved in national elections and plebiscites, by later opinion surveys of people's memories of the regime, by ordinary people's willingness to denounce to the authorities anybody who stepped out of line, and by the

widespread publicity given to the concentration camps, which thus appeared to be generally accepted as useful institutions by the German public.

I will return at the end to draw some general conclusions in the light of the points I have raised in these introductory remarks.

I

The first, and in many ways the most obvious, problem with the argument that Nazi Germany from the very outset was a 'dictatorship by consent' lies in the nature of the Nazi seizure of power. Of course, it has become conventional to criticise this concept, and to point out that Hitler did not seize power: rather, he was handed it on a plate by representatives of the conservative elites and the military establishment who secured his appointment as Reich Chancellor on 30 January 1933. Wehler, indeed, gives his description of Hitler's appointment the title 'The Handing-over of Power'.[9] What followed was, Robert Gellately maintains, a 'legal revolution', whose actions were legitimated by decrees and laws passed by elected legislative assemblies up to and including the Reichstag, thus reassuring the mass of the population that everything was in order.[10] But, of course, in reality, the Nazis were *not* 'handed power' on 30 January 1933. There was instead, as Bracher pointed out long ago, a power vacuum in Germany, in which no government and no political force, not even the army, was able to assert itself or gain popular legitimacy for its actions. Moreover, although Hitler did become head of the Reich government on 30 January, there were only two other Nazis in the cabinet, which was dominated by conservatives, headed by the Vice-Chancellor Franz von Papen, whose aim it was to outmanoeuvre Hitler and use his mass support to legitimise their own policies of establishing a counter-revolutionary authoritarian regime of their own. The Nazi seizure of power did not end on 30 January; in fact it only began at that point.

Nor was it legal, as Bracher, who actually coined the phrase 'legal revolution', pointed out. Hermann Göring's crucial actions as Minister-President of Prussia, for instance, lacked legal foundation because the status of his appointment was invalidated by the lawsuit brought by the Social Democratic government of Prussia that had been illegally deposed by Papen the previous June. The Enabling Act that provided much of the foundation for Hitler's legislative powers was passed illegally because Göring, as President of the Reichstag, broke the law in refusing to count the absent but legally elected Communist deputies in the total from which he reckoned the two-thirds majority needed for the Law's passage. The fact that it would have passed even without this illegal action did not make it legal. Göring's appointment of hundreds of thousands of Nazi storm-troopers as auxiliary Prussian police was of dubious legality given his own position's lack of legitimacy. And even if it had been legitimate, this would not in any way have legalised the numerous physical attacks, murders, lootings and other acts they went on to commit over the first half of 1933, as the many thousands of criminal prosecutions brought against them by state prosecutors' offices in the course of 1933 – all of them subsequently quashed on Hitler's orders – eloquently testified.[11]

Against whom was Nazi violence directed? Gellately in particular claims it was from the outset only visited upon small minorities. Both during 1933 and afterwards he argues, the concentration camps were overwhelmingly used as so-called re-education centres for social outsiders, including not only Communists but also habitual criminals, the work-shy, vagrants, homosexuals, alcoholics and the like. In fact, however, in 1933 the Communists were by some distance the largest category of people imprisoned in the camps. It was only later that social outsiders became a majority. And the Communists can only with difficulty be described as social outsiders, since they were strongly integrated into working-class communities all across the industrial regions of Germany; they were only social outsiders from the perspective of the middle classes, a perspective which Gellately too often unconsciously adopts. Nor were the Communists a tiny or marginal minority: in the Reichstag elections of November 1932 they gained 100 seats, more than half as many as the Nazis did.[12]

Much more important, however, is the fact that Nazi violence in 1933, and indeed well before that, was not directed exclusively against the Communists but also targeted the Social Democrats, whose representatives sat in town councils and regional parliaments across the land and who had led not only the Prussian but also the Reich government at various times before the Nazi seizure of power. Gellately dismisses Nazi violence against the Social Democrats as insignificant,[13] but even a cursory glance at the evidence reveals its shocking intensity and extent in the first six months of 1933 as the Nazis moved to crush what they called 'Marxism', by which they meant not Communism (which they termed 'Bolshevism'), but Social Democracy. Three thousand leading members of the party were arrested immediately after it was banned on 21 June 1933, beaten up, tortured and in many cases killed. An attempt at armed resistance in the Berlin suburb of Köpenick prompted the immediate arrest of 500 Social Democrats by Nazi stormtroopers, who in the course of the so-called 'Köpenick blood-week' tortured them so severely that ninety-one of them died. Senior political figures, far from being immune, were specifically targeted: the Social Democratic Minister-President of Mecklenburg, Johannes Stelling, was tortured to death and his body tied up in a sack and thrown into a river, from which it was fished out soon after along with the bodies of twelve other Social Democratic Party functionaries killed the same night. The Social Democratic mayor of Stassfurt was shot dead by Nazis as early as 5 February 1933. The ex-mayor of Breslau, the former editor of the town's daily paper, and the recently sacked chief administrator of the Breslau district, all of them Social Democrats, were arrested and imprisoned in a newly opened concentration camp by the stormtrooper leader Edmund Heines, who paraded one of them through the streets of the town dressed as a harlequin: Heines also kidnapped and arrested the former President of the Reichstag, Paul Löbe, another Social Democrat, and put him in the camp, too.[14]

A characteristic incident occurred in Braunschweig on 13 March 1933 when stormtroopers burst into a session of the town council, hauled off the Social Democratic mayor and forced him to resign; to underline the point, a gang of SS men then stripped him, beat him insensible and threw a bucket of water over him, after which they dressed him again and paraded him through the streets to the town prison. Social Democratic councillors and officials in the town were threatened with similar violence should they fail to resign their posts; one of them was beaten to death when he refused. The leading Social Democrat in Cologne, Wilhelm Sollmann, was tortured at Nazi Party headquarters and made to drink a mixture of castor oil and urine, while the director of the Social Democratic newspaper in Chemnitz was shot dead when he refused to tell a gang of stormtroopers where the party funds were. Incidents of this kind were repeated in different forms all across Germany in the spring of 1933 as the Nazis moved to take over town councils and city administrations. Five hundred municipal administrators and seventy mayors had been forcibly removed from office by the end of May 1933; not all of them were Social Democrats, of course, but many were.

These people were hardly members of a despised minority of social outcasts. Indeed, between them, the Social Democrats and the Communists had won 13.1 million votes in the Reichstag elections of November 1932, a good many more than the Nazis, who won only 11.7 million. In the Weimar Republic's system of proportional representation, these figures translated directly into parliamentary seats, which gave the combined working-class parties 221 to the Nazis' 196. The two working-class parties were, of course, bitterly divided against each other, and the many proposals of common action to stop the Nazis never stood a serious chance of success. These parties, particularly the Social Democrats, were closely affiliated to Germany's massive trade union movement, rendered largely ineffective by mass unemployment. Its premises were invaded across the land on 2 May 1933 by gangs of stormtroopers, their furniture and equipment looted, their assets seized and their functionaries arrested and thrown into concentration camps, where they were brutally mishandled; in the industrial town of Duisburg, four union officials were beaten to death in the cellars of the trade union headquarters.[15]

Overt coercion was applied in 1933 above all, then, not to despised minorities of social outcasts, but to the working class and its organisations. Many recent authors have failed to recognise this crucial fact and have differentiated simply between 'social outcasts' and the rest, describing the latter as a more or less uniform majority of 'the people', 'the masses', or 'the Germans', as Wehler, for example, frequently does. Both Gellately and Johnson and Reuband also fail to differentiate between social classes, and fail to recognise the fact that the major obstacle to the regime in generating support for its policies and actions both in 1933 and subsequently was posed by the mass allegiance of millions of workers to the ideals and principles of Social Democracy and Communism, an allegiance whose formal expression could only be broken by terror. Not surprisingly, as soon as the regime collapsed, in 1945, trade unions, Social Democratic and Communist Party organisations, strikes and other expressions of this allegiance reappeared almost instantly, and on a remarkably widespread basis, testifying to the inability of the Nazis to win the positive support of the great majority of working-class Germans.[16]

The middle classes and the peasantry were more amenable to the Nazi message, given their fear of Communism and their support in varying degrees for an authoritarian solution to Germany's political, social and economic crisis. Thus they required a much less concentrated application of violence and intimidation to force them to capitulate to the new regime and agree to their own dissolution. It was real enough all the same. The only other party with mass support besides the Nazis, the Social Democrats and the Communists was the Catholic Centre. Its Reichstag deputies were persuaded first to vote for the Enabling Law then to wind the party up, with some prodding from the Papacy, when the imminent prospect of a Concordat between the Vatican and the Third Reich was dangled before their eyes. Yet the party wanted a Concordat not least because of the massive intimidation to which it had been subjected since the end of February 1933. This included violent attacks on Centre Party meetings during campaigning for the elections of 5 March 1933, during one of which the Centre Party politician and former government minister Adam Stegerwald was severely beaten by Nazi stormtroopers (on 22 February). One after another in the spring and early summer of 1933, Catholic lay organisations were being forcibly closed down or merged with their Nazi counterparts, Catholic journalists and newspaper editors were arrested, especially if they had attacked the Nazi-led coalition government in print, and leading Catholics were brutally mistreated by the SA. The Württemberg State President Eugen Bolz, a leading Centre Party politician, was arrested and severely beaten on 19 June 1933, only the most prominent of many. In Bavaria, the new chief of the political police, Heinrich Himmler, ordered on 26 June 1933 the placing in 'protective custody' of all the Reichstag and Landtag deputies of the Bavarian People's Party, the autonomous Bavarian equivalent of the Catholic Centre in the rest of Germany: indeed, he went even further and ordered the arrest of everyone who had been 'particularly active in party politics', no matter what party they belonged to. The Catholic trade unions suffered the same fate as their socialist equivalents, and, crucially, Catholic civil servants were openly threatened with dismissal unless they resigned from the Centre Party. Not surprisingly, it was fear of the complete destruction of its lay organisations and the reversal of all the progress that Catholic laymen had made towards gaining equality of status with Protestants in the civil service and the professions over the previous decades that provided the major impetus behind the agreement of the Centre to dissolve itself in return for a Concordat in which the new regime would commit itself – with how little sincerity would soon become apparent – to preserving the integrity of the Catholic community and its institutions.[17]

Between them, the working-class parties and the Catholic Centre represented a majority of the electorate. Together they had won 291 seats to the Nazis' 196 in the last free Reichstag elections of the

Weimar Republic, in November 1932. The other parties had lost virtually all their electoral support since 1930 and were thus a less serious obstacle. Here too, however, violence and the threat of violence played a part. Like the Catholic Centre Party, the liberal State Party voted for the Enabling Law not least because of Hitler's blood-curdling announcement in the debate that their decision whether to support or oppose the Law was a decision 'as to whether it is to be peace or war', or, in other words, if the Law was rejected he would set two and a half million stormtroopers loose on everyone who had opposed it. All the same, many State Party politicians at every level from local councils upwards were subsequently arrested and the party forced to dissolve itself by the end of June 1933. The continuing dismissal of its members from the civil service seems to have been the main impulse behind the People's Party's decision to wind itself up, though its self-immolation did little to save their jobs in many cases. Hitler's Nationalist Party coalition partner, who like the Centre Party had no real commitment to the Weimar Republic or indeed to democracy by this time, was all in favour of the suppression of the labour movement and the parties of the left. What it did not expect, however, was that it would itself be suppressed. At the end of March 1933 the house of the party's parliamentary floor leader in the Reichstag, Ernst Oberfohren, was raided and his office searched, and a few weeks later he was found dead in suspicious circumstances. The warning was clear enough, and it was backed by explicit threats. Meeting with Hitler on 30 May 1933 to complain about the violence and intimidation to which their party representatives were being subjected, the Nationalist leaders were treated to what one of them called a 'hysterical outburst of rage' in which the Reich Chancellor announced that he would let the SA 'open fire' on the Nationalists and their paramilitary affiliates and 'arrange a bloodbath lasting three days long' if they refused to dissolve their party. To underline the point, he had one of their leading figures, Herbert von Bismarck, arrested. Within a few weeks, both the Nationalist Party and its paramilitary units no longer existed as autonomous entities.[18]

These events did not entirely subdue Hitler's conservative coalition partners, who became increasingly concerned about the violence of the SA, four and a half million-strong by 1934, by the increasingly openly declared ambition of its leader Ernst Röhm to replace the army, and by their own progressive political marginalisation. In the early summer of 1934, the imminent prospect of the death of Reich President Hindenburg prompted in the Vice-Chancellor, Papen, the ambition of regaining power by replacing him, hinted at in speeches denouncing the revolutionary rhetoric of the SA. Hitler quelled the restlessness of the SA at the end of June, arresting a number of its leading figures and having them shot by the SS. But it is important to remember that in the so-called Röhm Purge, or 'Night of the Long Knives', Hitler also struck a blow against the conservative right. Those killed included not only Röhm and his associates but also Papen's secretary Herbert von Bose, his speechwriter Edgar Jung, the leader of the Catholic Action organisation, Erich Klausener, former Chancellor Kurt von Schleicher, and others who were on a list compiled by Jung as possible members of a post-Hitler government. Papen was placed under house arrest and his predecessor as Chancellor, the Catholic politician Heinrich Brüning, escaped with his life only because he was outside Germany at the time. The warning to conservative and Catholic politicians to stay quiet was unmistakeable. Coercion over virtually the entire political spectrum was seldom more openly in evidence than in the 'Night of the Long Knives'.[19]

II

Nazi violence, real and threatened, was unevenly applied in the months of the seizure of power from February to June 1933. Physical coercion was directed with massive ferocity against Communists, Social Democrats and trade unionists, and with discriminating and symbolic or exemplary force against those such as liberals, Catholics, Nationalists and conservatives who were less diametrically opposed to the politics of the emerging Third Reich. Nevertheless, it operated across the board. As Richard Bessel has remarked, 'violence ... during the early months of 1933, was used deliberately and openly to intimidate opposition and potential opposition. It was used to create a public sphere permeated by violence and it provided a ready reminder of what might be in store for *anyone* who stepped out of line, who failed to show loyalty to the new order.'[20] How, then have some historians failed to recognise this fact and claimed instead that Nazi violence was directed only against small and socially marginal minorities? This brings me to the second proposition or group of propositions I want to discuss, namely that Nazi repression was exercised through the Gestapo and the concentration camps, it was on a small scale and it did not affect the majority of the population.

Wehler barely mentions the repressive apparatus of the Nazi state, except in passing, and when he does it is to allude to 'the instruments of terror: Gestapo, protective custody, revocation of citizenship, concentration camps'.[21] Gellately's most recent statement of his views does not mention other sanctions besides arrest by the Gestapo and imprisonment in a concentration camp.[22] Aly backs up his assertion that 'most Germans simply did not need to be subjected to surveillance or detention' by pointing out that 'the Gestapo in 1937 had just over 7,000 employees' who, 'with a far smaller force of security police ... sufficed to keep tabs on more than 60 million people'. By 1936, he adds, 'only 4761 people – some of whom were chronic alcoholics and career criminals – were incarcerated in the country's concentration camps'.[23] Similar assumptions are evident in Johnson and Reuband's statement, taking up a wider historiography, that:

> In the light of the large number of individuals arrested by the Gestapo and temporarily detained in concentration camps and the cruelty of the Gestapo's conduct – especially where the extortion of confessions was concerned – many authors have assumed that fear of falling into the hands of the Gestapo constantly plagued everyone in the Third Reich and concluded that fear and terror were the

decisive factors in shaping the German population's everyday behaviour. Our survey evidence, however, does not support this assumption and conclusion.[24]

There is a real circularity about these arguments, as the assumption that the Gestapo and the concentration camps were the only agents of control and repression in the Third Reich inevitably produces the answer, when this assumption is made the basis of interview questions, that they were not very significant, and so leads on to the sweeping conclusion that control and repression did not feature at all in the lives of the great majority of Germans.

Two points need to be made here. The first is that the principal instrument of terror in Nazi Germany was not the concentration camp but the law – not, to use Ernst Fraenkel's terminology, the prerogative state but the normative state, not in other words the coercive apparatus created by Hitler, such as the SS, but the already existing state apparatus dating back decades or even centuries.[25] This is not to belittle the camps' role in 1933, of course. During 1933 perhaps 100,000 Germans were detained without trial in so-called 'protective custody' across Germany, most but by no means all of them members of the Communist and Social Democratic parties. The number of deaths in custody during this period has been estimated at around 600 and was almost certainly higher. By 1935, however, the vast majority of these prisoners had been released on good behaviour and there were fewer than 5,000 of them left. Almost all the early camps had already been shut down by the end of 1933.[26] A major reason for this decline lay in the fact that the leading role in political repression was now being carried out by the regular courts and the state prisons and penitentiaries. A whole new set of laws and decrees passed in 1933 vastly expanded the scope of the treason laws and the death penalty. A law of 24 April 1933, for example, laid down that anyone found guilty of planning to alter the constitution or to detach any territory from the German Reich by force, or engaging in a conspiracy with these aims, would be beheaded: the concept of 'planning' included writing, printing and distributing leaflets, altering the constitution included advocating the return of democracy or urging the removal of Hitler as Leader, conspiring included anyone associated with the guilty parties. A law of 20 December 1934 went even further and applied the death penalty to aggravated cases of 'hateful' statements about leading figures in the Nazi Party or the state. Another law made 'malicious gossip' illegal, including spreading rumours about the regime or making derogatory remarks about its leaders. A whole system of regional Special Courts, crowned by the national People's Court, the *Volksgerichtshof*, was created to implement these and other, similar laws.[27]

It is important to remember the extreme extent to which civil liberties were destroyed in the course of the Nazi seizure of power. In the Third Reich it was illegal to belong to any political grouping apart from the Nazi Party or indeed any non-Nazi organisation of any kind apart from the Churches (and their ancillary lay organisations) and the army; it was illegal to tell jokes about Hitler; it was illegal to spread rumours about the government; it was illegal to discuss alternatives to the political status quo. The Reichstag Fire Decree of 28 February 1933 made it legal for the police to open letters and tap telephones, and to detain people indefinitely and without a court order in so-called 'protective custody'. The same decree also abrogated the clauses in the Weimar Constitution that guaranteed freedom of the press, freedom of assembly, freedom of association and freedom of expression. The Enabling Law allowed the Reich Chancellor and his cabinet to promulgate laws that violated the Weimar Constitution, without needing the approval of the legislature or the elected President. The right of judicial appeal was effectively abolished for offences dealt with by the Special Courts and the People's Court. All this meant that large numbers of offenders were sent to prison for political as well as ordinary criminal offences. In 1937 the courts passed no fewer than 5,255 convictions for high treason. These people, if they escaped the death penalty, were put into a state prison, often for a lengthy period of time. From 1932 to 1937 the prison population increased from 69,000 to 122,000. In 1935, 23,000 inmates of state prisons and penitentiaries were classified as political offenders. The crushing of the Communist and Social Democratic resistance ensured that these numbers had fallen by more than 50 per cent by the beginning of 1939; nevertheless, they were still far more significant than the numbers of political offenders in the camps after 1937, when the concentration camps expanded again; this time the camps really did function mainly as places of confinement for social rather than political deviants.[28]

The second point to be made is that legal condemnation for treason, malicious gossip and similar offences, and quasi-legal 'preventive detention' in concentration camps, were only the most severe of a vast range of sanctions that reached deep into German society in pursuit of the regime's efforts to crush opposition and dissent. Local studies give a good picture of the range of coercive measures open to the regime and its servants in these respects. In the small north German town of Northeim, for instance, the subject of William Sheridan Allen's classic study *The Nazi Seizure of Power*, first published in 1965, the Communists were arrested in the early months of 1933, along with some of the town's leading Social Democrats; the Social Democratic town councillors were forced to resign after attending a council meeting in which the walls were lined by brownshirts who spat on them as they walked past. Forty-five council employees were sacked, most of them Social Democrats working in institutions as varied as the town gas works, the local swimming pool and the municipal brewery. At a time of continuing mass unemployment they were unlikely to find other jobs. The local Nazis put pressure on landlords to evict Social Democrats from their apartments, and made sure the police subjected their homes to frequent searches in the hunt for subversive literature.[29]

At every level, too, the regime used coercion of a kind that did not involve arrest or incarceration when it sought to implement particular policies and secure the appearance of public support for them. Members of the Catholic, liberal and conservative political parties were coerced into joining the Nazis in the spring of 1933, and above all after the civil service law of 7 April, by the direct threat of losing their jobs in state employ, which in Germany included not only civil servants and local officials but also schoolteachers, university staff, prosecutors, policemen, social administrators, post office and public transport officials, and many others. When, some years later, it moved to abolish denominational schools and force parents to enrol their children in state-run secular educational institutions, in order to subject them more completely to Nazi indoctrination, the regime ran local plebiscites on the policy, and threatened parents who refused to vote in favour with the withdrawal of welfare benefits, including child support. A massive propaganda campaign was unleashed against monks and priests who staffed private schools run by the Catholic Church, accusing them of being paedophiles and bringing a large number of them before the courts in widely publicised trials. Parents, even schoolchildren, were then pressured to petition against being taught by alleged deviants such as these. Here, then, was a major proportion of the population, the Catholics, getting on for 40 per cent of all Germans, consisting of far more than mere social deviants or outcasts, that was subjected to persistent coercion and harassment when it stood in the way of a key policy of the regime.[30]

There were thus many kinds of coercion in Nazi Germany. It was particularly evident in the area of charity and welfare, where stormtroopers knocked on people's doors or accosted them in the street demanding contributions to Winter Aid. In all schools, pupils who failed to join the Hitler Youth were liable to be refused their school-leaving certificate when they graduated, destroying their prospects of an apprenticeship or a job. Because the Nazi regime acquired powers to direct workers to where it felt they were needed, it was able to use the threat of reassignment to dirty and difficult jobs as a sanction against troublemakers. Over a million German workers had been compulsorily reassigned to work in munitions and war-related industries by 1939, often being forced to live a long distance from their families, and sometimes transported to their destinations escorted by prison warders. Increasingly, as the rearmament programme began to create labour shortages and bottlenecks, skilled workers in key industries were punished by lesser sanctions such as these, rather than by measures, such as imprisonment, that would deprive the state of their labour. Being sent to work on the fortifications of the West Wall (the so-called 'Siegfried Line'), with its twelve-hour shifts of back-breaking manual labour, became a favourite instrument of coercion on the part of employers under pressure from the government's Four-Year Plan Office to produce more and keep costs down, and faced with workers demanding more wages or shorter hours, or overheard making derogatory remarks about their bosses, or about the regime, on the shop floor.[31]

The very wide range of coercive measures used by the regime at every level was enforced by an equally wide range of coercive agents. It is a mistake to focus exclusively on the Gestapo on the assumption that it was the sole, or even the principal, instrument of control in Nazi Germany. Detlef Schmiechen-Ackermann, for instance, has drawn attention to the 'Block Warden', or *Blockwart*, a popular name given to low-level officials of the Nazi Party, each of whom was responsible for a block of apartments or houses, where he had to ensure that people took proper air-raid precautions, hung out flags on Hitler's birthday and similar occasions, and refrained from engaging in illegal or subversive activities. The Block Wardens kept a close watch on former Communists and Social Democrats, listened out for expressions of dissatisfaction with the regime and could punish political or social deviance by a variety of means ranging from stopping the offender's welfare benefits to reporting their names to the district Party organisation for forwarding to the Gestapo.[32] In the workplace, Labour Front officials carried out a similar function, and were able to transfer recalcitrant workers to unpleasant jobs, increase their hours or deny them promotion. Surveillance, control and political discipline were exercised by Hitler Youth leaders, who were normally a good deal older than their charges. By 1939 membership was compulsory, and some 8.7 million out of a total of 8.9 million Germans aged ten to eighteen belonged to this organisation, so its effects were not limited to the deviant or the marginal.

Taken together, all these agencies of coercion added up to what one historian has recently called a polymorphous, uncoordinated but pervasive system of control, of which the Gestapo formed only one small though important part. Here, too, of course, their animus was directed most forcefully against former Communists and Social Democrats in working-class areas, but it was present as a looming threat in middle-class society as well.[33] It was not surprising, therefore, that most of Johnson and Reuband's respondents recalled that they had to be careful about what they said when speaking to strangers or to people they knew to be Nazis, 'such as the ubiquitous Nazi Party block leader'. One interviewee recalled: 'In the course of time, all people became cautious. They simply didn't speak with people anymore.' Ordinary Germans, as Johnson and Reuband rightly conclude, 'knew well that rash, politically unacceptable remarks and corresponding behavior could lead to serious punishment and possibly endanger their lives'.[34] In consequence, they withdrew more and more into the private sphere. Johnson and Reuband do not draw the obvious conclusion that people were living in a climate of fear, but even on the evidence they present it seems justifiable to conclude that they were. Ultimately, too, as their respondents suggest, the fear that formed the permanent backdrop to their daily lives was not a fear of the Gestapo, still less of ordinary citizens, friends or relatives, but a fear of active Nazis, low-level Party officials, and committed supporters of the regime: if you fell into conversation with a stranger, you might be able to tell whether he belonged to one of these categories by small signs such as, for example, whether he used the Hitler greeting, but you could never be entirely certain, so it was best to be circumspect, and if you knew the person you were talking to was an active Nazi, then you certainly had to be cautious.

III

Why was such a vast apparatus of coercion and control necessary if, as historians like Wehler, Gellately, Johnson and Reuband and others claim, the Nazi regime was viewed in such a popular light by the mass

of the German people? This brings me to the third proposition or
bundle of propositions I want to examine: that the overwhelming
popularity of the regime from the outset is demonstrated by the
extraordinarily successful results it achieved in national elections, by
later survey data on people's memories of the time, by ordinary
Germans' willingness to denounce to the authorities anybody who
stepped out of line and by the public support given to the concentration camps as indicated by the prominence given to them in the Nazi
press. Certainly, to begin with the plebiscites and elections that were
held at intervals under the Third Reich, the regime regularly won over
90 per cent of the vote when it put its policies to the people for
approval. But were these results really such striking indicators of the
regime's popularity as some have claimed? A wide range of contemporary reports strongly suggests that they were not. In the plebiscite
on Hitler's appointment as Head of State following the death of
Hindenburg in 1934, for instance, and in the plebiscite of April 1938
on union with Austria, and on other occasions, gangs of stormtroopers rounded voters up from their homes and marched them to the
polling stations. Here the electors were usually forced to vote in public,
since in many places the polling booths had been removed, or were
labelled 'only traitors enter here'; this was more than mere rhetoric,
since in 1938, when the plebiscite was coupled with a vote of confidence in Hitler, anyone voting 'no' was voting against Hitler and
would therefore – as Nazi officials and propaganda agents did not fail
to point out – be committing an offence under the treason laws.[35]

At all these elections, polling stations were surrounded by stormtroopers whose minatory attitude made clear what would happen to
anybody who failed to conform. Suspected opponents of the regime
were given specially marked ballot papers, and in many places rumours
were circulated beforehand that all the papers were secretly numbered,
so that people who voted 'no' or spoiled their ballot papers could be
identified and punished; and indeed people who took this course, or
refused to vote, were beaten up by the brownshirts, or dragged through
the streets with placards round their neck calling them traitors, or even

committed to mental hospitals. Just to ensure an overwhelming 'yes' vote, many former Communists, Social Democrats and other critics of the regime were arrested before the vote and only released when it was safely over, and ballot papers in many areas were already marked with a cross in the 'yes' box before electors arrived at the polling station; in some areas it was reported that so many 'no' votes and spoiled papers were replaced with one or more forged 'yes' ballots that the number of 'yes' votes actually exceeded the number of electors. None of this meant, of course, that in a plebiscite on an issue like unification with Austria, the government would have failed to obtain a majority for its actions; but it is surely safe to say that in a free vote, it would not have obtained the 99 per cent 'yes' vote it got by the tactics of manipulation and intimidation I have just outlined; in the plebiscite of 1934 it might even have failed to win a majority.[36]

Let us turn to evidence for the Nazi regime's supposedly overwhelming popularity from 1933 onwards provided by later opinion survey data. Johnson and Reuband claim that their interviews of elderly Germans during the 1990s show that 'Hitler and National Socialism were [so] immensely popular among most Germans'.[37] Yet their sample consisted overwhelmingly of people born between 1910 and 1928, people who therefore would have been between the ages of five and twenty-three at the beginning of the Third Reich and seventeen and thirty-five at the end. In the nature of things, more of them would have been born towards the end of the period chosen than towards the beginning. All we know about Nazi Germany, from the *Sopade* reports to the diaries of people like the Jewish professor Victor Klemperer, underlines the fact that Nazi propaganda was most effective in the younger generations of Germans, who after all had had few chances to form their own firm values and beliefs before the regime began, and who were subjected to massively intense and unremitting indoctrination from their schools, from the Hitler Youth and from the mass media orchestrated by Goebbels. It was overwhelmingly young people, for example, who joined in the antisemitic violence of the *Kristallnacht* and shouted insults at Victor Klemperer in the streets.[38]

And Johnson and Reuband themselves note that 'younger people . . . were disproportionately receptive to National Socialism'.[39] Their survey shows that 62 per cent of their respondents born in Berlin between 1923 and 1928 admitted to having been 'positive or mainly positive' about National Socialism, compared to only 35 per cent of those born between 1911 and 1916; in Dresden the comparable figures were 65 per cent and 39 per cent, in Cologne 45 per cent and 21 per cent. It would not be unreasonable to suppose that the figures for people born, say, before 1890 or 1880 would have been lower still. Their *overall* results, therefore, are skewed by the fact that most of their respondents were born in the 1920s.[40]

Moreover, as the authors themselves point out, when faced with their three questions – whether they believed in National Socialism, whether they admired Hitler and whether they shared Nazi ideals – only a minority (18 per cent) answered in the affirmative to all three, while 31 per cent answered yes to two. Thus, only 49 per cent of those who took part in the survey gave a clear yes to more than one of these three questions. Only when those whose answers appeared as ambivalent or neutral were added in did this become a majority. Johnson and Reuband's careful and exemplary detailed analysis of their survey data shows that the attitudes of most of the people they questioned were mixed: some viewed some aspects of Nazism positively but not others, while many people's attitudes changed quite markedly over time, a fact that emerges more clearly from some of the in-depth interviews than from the statistics provided by the opinion survey. All these variations and qualifications are spelled out in convincing detail in the text of Johnson and Reuband's book; it is a pity that they disappear entirely when it comes to summarising and presenting their conclusions.[41]

The third major strand of evidence presented by some historians in favour of the regime's popularity is the practice of denouncing law-breakers to the authorities. How much does the practice of denunciation actually reveal about people's attitudes to the regime? What it does not reveal, to begin with, is that Nazi Germany was a 'self-policing society', as Gellately has claimed, for people did not denounce offenders to each other, they denounced them to the authorities, including the Gestapo, and if the Gestapo and other agencies of state and Party control had not been there to act, either legally or extra-legally, against the objects of denunciation, then denunciation would have been meaningless. In practice, of course, denunciation was extremely rare: there were only between 3 and 51 denunciations a year in Lippe, where the population was 176,000, during the Third Reich, for instance; and a relatively high proportion of denouncers were members of the Nazi Party – 42 per cent in Augsburg, for example. In Düsseldorf, some 26 per cent of Gestapo investigations were triggered by denunciations from members of the general population; the other three-quarters were initiated by Gestapo officers or informers, Nazi Party organisations, the criminal police and the SS and state authorities of one kind and another. In addition, a study of recently declassified Gestapo files for the Koblenz and Trier region has revealed that the Gestapo made extensive use of paid informers and also kept a register of unpaid informers, whom they did not scruple to use repeatedly; around a third of these people were members of the Nazi Party or its affiliated organisations.[42]

In the case of contraventions of the Nuremberg racial laws, the proportion of cases that arose from denunciations was a good deal higher, but this was not least because such offences were largely committed in private, and few were likely to know about them apart from neighbours, acquaintances and family. In any case, as I have already noted, people were generally very cautious about what they said to strangers, so the relative prominence of family members, relatives and neighbours in denouncing people to the Gestapo might reflect among other things the fact that people often lowered their guard when talking to them. 'Malicious gossip' cases were more often than not begun by denunciations, above all, at least in the early years of the regime, from innkeepers and drinkers in bars, where alcohol loosened the tongue: significantly, however, as the consequences of loose talk gradually became clear, the proportion of malicious gossip cases in the Augsburg court, the focus of a particularly illuminating study, that derived from denunciations in pubs and bars fell from three-quarters in 1933 to one-tenth by the outbreak of the war. As Gellately has pointed out, moreover, many denunciations from ordinary citizens were made from personal motives, and say nothing about their overall attitude to the regime, its ideologies or its policies.[43]

In many cases, of course, denunciation would lead to prosecution, appearance before a Special Court, and imprisonment – not in a concentration camp but in a state-run jail. Nevertheless, above all in the first two years of their rule the Nazis made a point of publicising the concentration camps and their function, at a time when the repressive efforts of state and Party were directed mainly against political opposition and dissent. Did this, as Gellately claims, mean that everyone approved of the camps because they knew about them from newspaper reports and did not raise any objections to them? There is plenty of evidence to the contrary. To claim, as Gellately does, that camp prisoners in 1933–4 were 'social outsiders of one kind or another' is, as we have seen, simply incorrect. Not only were Communists not social outsiders, the camps were intended for Social Democrats, too; and the 'good citizens' of Germany in 1933, who Gellately portrays as rejoicing in the 'crackdown', included large numbers of Social Democratic mayors, councillors, deputies, officials, civil servants and others. Far from rejoicing, they were themselves now liable to be thrown into the camps.[44]

Articles and even pictures were printed prominently in local newspapers when the Dachau camp was opened in 1933, for instance, advertising the fact that not only Communists but also Social Democrats or 'Marxists' and political opponents of every hue were being 're-educated'. Once more, local evidence is telling on this point. In Northeim in 1933, for example, the local and regional papers ran stories on Dachau and the nearby camp at Moringen, and carried regular reports on the arrest of citizens for making derogatory remarks about the regime and its leaders. The guards at Moringen were drawn from the local population, and prisoners were released mostly after only a few weeks inside, so that knowledge of the camp must have been widespread in Northeim and the surrounding district.[45]

Of course, here as elsewhere there were multifarious contacts of other kinds with the local population, who were involved in constructing and supplying the camp and carrying out maintenance and repairs; but these did not necessarily indicate only support for its objectives: a plumber could repair leaky water pipes in the camp office building and still be afraid of what might happen if he stepped out of line or uttered an incautious remark. On occasion, the regime was explicit in its general use of the threat of the camps for people who made trouble: 'Concentration camp', declared the front page of Germany's newspapers in the immediate aftermath of the 'Night of the Long Knives', 'is threatened ... for rumour-mongering and offering slanderous insults to the movement itself and its Leader.' Mostly the threat was implicit.[46] Nevertheless, it was directed potentially at anybody, not just at social outsiders. It was only after the initial wave of repression in 1933–4 that the camps, having ceded their function of political 're-education' to the Special Courts and the state prisons, became repositories for social outsiders.

IV

Recent historiography has been rightly critical of older studies that reduce popular opinion in the Third Reich to no more than the product of coercion and propaganda. But to belittle the former and ignore the latter, in favour of a wholly voluntaristic approach, is not very useful as a means of explaining how the Third Reich operated. Propaganda was important, but it did not operate, of course, on a blank slate as far as most people's views were concerned. Nazi propaganda was at its most effective where it tapped into already existing beliefs, as Ian Kershaw demonstrated in his classic study of popular opinion in Bavaria under the Third Reich some years ago.[47] Where people, notably Social Democrats, Communists and Catholics, had formed their values and taken up their political stance well before the beginning of the Third Reich, it was less than wholly effective.

Propaganda also had an effect where it bore at least some relationship to reality: the Nazis won widespread if sometimes grudging approval, for instance, by the reduction of unemployment, the restoration of order on the streets and the successful re-establishment of Germany's international prestige and freedom of action. In the latter part of the war, by contrast, Goebbels's assurances of imminent victory were believed by few indeed.

Yet the more people clung to alternative values to those of Nazism, the more important terror was as a means of coercing them into submission. The Nazis themselves were the first to admit this. On 15 March 1933, referring to the semi-free elections that had taken place ten days previously, giving the Nazi Party and its Nationalist coalition partners a bare absolute majority of the vote, Goebbels declared that the government would 'not be satisfied for long with the knowledge that it has 52 per cent behind it while terrorising the other 48 per cent but will, by contrast, see its next task as winning over that other 48 per cent for itself'. Goebbels's speech was as remarkable for its frank admission of the role of terror in the establishment of the Third Reich as it was for its bold declaration of the importance of obtaining the ideological support of the whole of the German people. The story of the following years is in part the story of how the Nazis succeeded in key respects in doing this. Yet Goebbels's aim of winning over the majority of the people to wholehearted enthusiasm for Nazism was only partially fulfilled. The Nazi leadership knew by 1939 that most Germans paid its most loudly and insistently proclaimed ideals little more than lip service: they conformed outwardly while keeping their real beliefs for the most part to themselves. Nazism had succeeded in shifting the attitudes and beliefs of most Germans, particularly in the younger generation, some way in the direction it wanted, but it had not reached the ambitious goal it had set itself. This situation, attested above all in local studies such as Allen's *The Nazi Seizure of Power*, was in turn a reflection of the fact that, in the end, coercion was at least as important as propaganda in its impact on the behaviour of the vast majority of people who lived in Nazi Germany.[48]

Who operated the system of coercion, therefore? How many people were involved in its implementation? The fact that a great many agencies were involved implies that it was put into effect by a far larger range of people than those who belonged to the relatively small organisation of the Gestapo. The SA was nearly three million-strong by the beginning of 1934, four and a half million if incorporated paramilitary and veterans' associations like the *Stahlhelm* are included. There were around 200,000 Block Wardens by 1935, and no fewer than 2,000,000 of them, including their assistants and deputies, by the beginning of the war. Hundreds of thousands of Germans occupied official posts in Nazi Party organisations of one kind and another, such as the Hitler Youth, the Chambers of Culture, the Nazi teachers' and university students' leagues, the Labour Front, and so on. Particularly important in this context were the legal and judicial professions, including the regular police force and the Gestapo, most of whose officers were already serving policemen under the Weimar Republic. In Prussia only 300 out of around 45,000 judges, state prosecutors and officials were dismissed or transferred to other duties for political reasons by the Nazis in 1933; the rest stayed on and enforced the new laws enacted by the regime with only minimal and sporadic objections. If we count in all those many other Germans who held positions of responsibility in the state, the number of people who were willing to some degree or other to play a role in the coercive apparatus of the regime must have run into several millions. Even so, in a nation with a population of eighty million, they remained a minority. Just as important, too, they also knew, like everyone else, that they would fall foul of the regime if they stepped out of line: as many as 22 per cent of people tried for 'malicious gossip' in Augsburg in the mid-1930s were actually members of the Nazi Party. Nevertheless, exercising various kinds of coercion and violence, real or threatened, that would not be tolerated in a democratic society, had become a way of life for millions of Germans by the outbreak of the war.[49]

It is only by recognising that large numbers of Germans had become willing administrators of coercion and repression, and that millions of younger Germans had been heavily influenced by Nazi indoctrination, that we can explain the extraordinarily savage behaviour of the armed forces that invaded Poland in 1939. The invasion of Poland took place under favourable conditions, in good weather, against an enemy that was swept aside with contemptuous ease. The invading troops did not need to be convinced by political indoctrination that the enemy posed a huge threat to Germany's future; clearly the Poles did not. Primary group loyalties in the lower ranks of the army remained intact; they did not have to be replaced by a harsh and perverted system of discipline that elbowed traditional military values aside in favour of an extremist racial ideology.[50] Almost everything that was to happen in the invasion of the Soviet Union from June 1941 onwards had already happened in the invasion of Poland almost two years before. From the very beginning, SS units entered the country, rounding up the politically undesirable, professionals and the intelligentsia and shooting them or putting them in concentration camps, massacring Jews, arresting local men and sending them off to Germany as slave labourers, and engaging in a systematic policy of ethnic cleansing and brutally executed population transfers. From the very beginning, too, Nazi Party officials, stormtroopers, civilian officials and especially junior army officers and ordinary soldiers joined in, to be followed in due course by German settlers moved into Poland from outside. Arrests, beatings and murders of Poles and especially Jews became commonplace. Just as striking was the assumption of all the invading and incoming Germans that the possessions of the Poles and Jews were freely available as booty. The theft and looting of Jewish property in particular by German troops was almost universal.[51]

Toughness, hardness, brutality, the use of force, the virtues of violence, had been inculcated into a whole generation of young Germans from 1933 onwards. Among older troops and officials, propaganda also built on a deeper-rooted feeling that Slavs and Eastern Jews were subhumans. The violence meted out to Poles and especially Jews from the beginning of September 1939 continued and intensified actions and policies already established by the Third Reich. So, too, did the looting and expropriation to which they were subjected, in the same way as Communist, Social Democratic and trade union assets had been looted and expropriated in Germany in 1933 and Jewish assets at the same time and continuously thereafter. It was in direct imitation of the November 1938 pogrom in Germany that SS units burned down synagogues in some Polish towns in September and October 1939. And the regime's policy towards the Jews of Poland, which moved quickly towards ghettoisation, can only be understood in the light of its previous policy towards the Jews of Germany, who over the preceding six and a half years had been pushed out of their jobs, expropriated, deprived of their citizenship and their rights, and cut off by law from mixing in most ways with the rest of the population.

The substantial minority of Germans who implemented such policies of coercion, terror and mass murder had become accustomed to such things from the experience of the previous six years in Germany itself. Did the majority of the population give its consent to all this? Dick Geary has pointed out that to talk of 'consent' is meaningless unless it is freely given: 'consent,' he writes, 'can only be measured in situations in which individuals can choose between real alternatives.'[52] It is worth calling to mind, too, the fact that the legal definition of 'consent' (for example, in rape cases) lays down the principle that a person consents if he or she agrees by choice and has the freedom and capacity to make that choice. A threat of violence is held in law to rule out consent. Categories such as 'tacit consent' or 'passive consent' are in this context little more than vehicles of negative moral judgement based on an extreme and unrealistic model of active citizenship that assumes that if you do not openly protest against a government policy then you are giving your consent to it.

A more sophisticated approach to the question of consent in Nazi Germany has recently been offered by Peter Longerich, using the example of the regime's policies towards the Jews, but in a way that has implications for other areas as well. The more radical the regime's anti-semitic policies became, he argues, the less willing the mass of Germans became to go along with them. Before contacts between

Jewish and non-Jewish Germans became in many respects illegal, with the Nuremberg Laws of 1935, it had proved extremely difficult to persuade the mass of Germans to ostracise the Jewish minority. Both in the pogrom of November 1938 and later on, during the war, the majority of people, rather than being indifferent, disapproved of violence and murder towards the Jews. But they felt unable to do anything concrete because of fear of this violence being turned against themselves by the regime and its agents, because of fear of arrest and prosecution, or sanctions of other kinds. This fear reached an extreme in the last eighteen months of the war, as the regime, backed by the judicial and law enforcement system, ruthlessly suppressed so-called 'rumour-mongering' about its extermination of Europe's Jews. At the same time, the mass of the German population, who knew what had been happening in Auschwitz and Treblinka, began to repress their knowledge in the face of looming defeat, as the prospect of Allied revenge or retribution for the mass murder began to become more certain. What appeared as indifference was thus in fact something far more active, namely an increasingly desperate search for a way of denying responsibility for actions that almost everybody recognised as crimes. Here, too, therefore, fear played a key role in shaping people's behaviour, as indeed it had done throughout the Third Reich in other areas too.[53]

What implications, finally, does this conclusion have for the task, if we wish to pursue it, of reaching a moral judgement on these people's behaviour between 1933 and 1945? As Neil Gregor has recently pointed out in a critique of what he calls 'the voluntarist turn' in historical studies of the Third Reich, reaching a moral judgement does not require that all those who lived under the Third Reich 'were faced with completely free choices, the outcomes of which were determined only by their own personal convictions, moral codes, or desire for blood'.[54] 'Human agency', as Tim Mason pointed out, 'is defined or located not abolished or absolved by the effort to identify the unchosen conditions' under which it is exercised.[55] What we have to recognise in this context, hard though it may be, is the absolute centrality of violence, coercion and terror to the theory and practice of German National Socialism from the very outset. As Richard Bessel has remarked, 'Nazi ideology was, at its core, about violence ... The horrors unleashed by the Third Reich were a reflection of the fact that the Nazis made their ideology real.'[56] It is impossible to understand the terror vented by the Nazis upon people in the regions they conquered, especially in eastern and south-eastern Europe, and upon the Jews across the whole of the occupied areas of the Continent, unless we grasp the fact that they had already vented it upon large sectors of their own people before 1939: and not merely on despised and tiny minorities of social outcasts, but on millions of their fellow citizens, indeed at one level or another, to one degree or another, on the great majority of them.

8. THE 'PEOPLE'S COMMUNITY'

Why did the Germans keep on supporting Hitler and the Nazis until the end of the war? Why didn't they rise up against a regime that was committing mass murder and atrocity on an unimaginable scale? Why didn't the mass Allied bombing of German cities lead to a popular revolt against Hitler? Many historians have tried to answer these questions over the years since the Nazi regime collapsed in ruins in 1945. Older explanations looked to stereotypes of the German national character for an answer – militarism, love of violence, willingness to obey authority, desire for strong leadership, civil passivity and similar clichés of dubious validity. More recently, some historians have argued that propaganda played a central role in rallying the Germans to the Nazi flag; others have stressed the growing terror to which the Nazi Party subjected the German people, above all in the later stages of the war. A few years ago, the American political scientist Daniel Jonah Goldhagen suggested that the overwhelming majority of Germans were fanatical supporters of Nazi antisemitism from the very outset. Others have sought an explanation in the Germans' mindless enthusiasm for the charismatic leadership of Adolf Hitler.

None of these explanations by itself has proved very convincing. Simplistic notions of a German national character have foundered, like Goldhagen's sweeping generalisations, on the objection that a majority of Germans, in the Social Democratic and Communist parties, the

Catholic community and many other parts of society, refused to lend their support to the Nazis in any of the elections of the Weimar Republic, where the Nazis never got much more than a third of the vote. There is plenty of evidence that Nazi propaganda, though not wholly ineffective, was limited in its impact, especially among these previously resistant sectors of the population and above all in the second half of the war, when Germany was demonstrably heading towards defeat. Hitler certainly seemed immune from popular criticism, at least until 1943, but he was admired as much as for what he did as for the image he projected. And terror, though a very real, continuing, and in 1944–5 rapidly escalating force, was surely not enough in itself to keep a population of eighty million Germans in thrall.

In recent years, historians have turned to the Nazi idea of building a 'people's community' (*Volksgemeinschaft*) for an explanation. After bitter divisions of the Weimar years, the promise of uniting all Germans in cooperation and harmony, it is now frequently argued, exerted a considerable popular appeal. The following pages take a closer look at some of the evidence that has been put forward in support of the view that the 'people's community' was no mere propaganda ploy but had a real and widely supported content in terms of Germans' attitudes towards the Nazi regime.

I

Almost as soon as the Nazis came to power in Germany, they made the greeting '*Heil Hitler!*' a compulsory part of national life. Civil servants were legally obliged to sign documents with it, and anybody writing a letter to officialdom would have been well advised to do the same. Schoolteachers had to greet their classes with a '*Heil Hitler!*', raising their right arm stiffly in the 'German greeting' as they did so; train conductors had to use the greeting when they entered a compartment to collect tickets from passengers. In the street, Germans were supposed to use the Hitler greeting instead of 'Good morning!'. Postmen were meant to bark out a '*Heil Hitler!*' to customers before handing them their morning mail. Schoolchildren greeted their teachers every morning with '*Heil Hitler!*'.

Visiting his university in the summer of 1933, the Jewish literature professor and compulsive diarist Victor Klemperer began to see 'employees constantly raising their arms to one another' in the corridors as they passed. Giving the salute instead of simply saying 'good day' or 'hello' quickly became an outward, public sign of support for the regime, visible all over Germany as the Nazis were establishing the Third Reich. It was also an open, almost threatening gesture to those at whom it was addressed, implicitly admonishing them to conform by returning the salutation themselves. To a visitor from another country wandering the streets of German towns and cities in 1933, it looked as if everyone was fully behind the new regime.

Fans of Stanley Kubrick's movie *Dr Strangelove* will remember vividly the deranged Nazi scientist, played by Peter Sellers, struggling in vain to restrain his right arm at moments of excitement, as it involuntarily shoots upwards in the Hitler salute. As the arm straightens into an angle of 45 degrees, it reminds us in a single image not just that some military scientists in the postwar America had started their careers in Nazi Germany, but also that giving the Hitler salute had become second nature to the people who supported Hitler and its regime. By the middle of the 1930s, Germans of all classes, ranks and denominations seemed to have internalised the allegiance expressed in the Nazi salute.

But what exactly did it mean? '*Heil!*' didn't just mean 'Hail!'; the word also carried connotations of healing, health and good wishes. '*Heil Hitler!*' therefore involved implicitly wishing the Nazi Leader good health, and also invoking Hitler as a kind of Supreme Being who could grant good health to the greeting's recipient. In both cases, Hitler was introduced as an omnipresent third party whenever two Germans came across each other. People were aware of these added meanings, and some at least made fun of them. Treating '*Heil!*' as a command rather than a wish ('heal Hitler!'), you could reply to the greeting by saying 'heal him yourself', implying that the Nazi Leader was sick, or mentally ill; or you could feign innocence when somebody said '*Heil Hitler!*' to you by asking: 'What's he got to do with it?', thus implying that the salutation was unnecessary and out of place.

Moving your right arm up swiftly and stiffly to the required angle meant you had to step back from the object of your salute to avoid an accident (it was said that when the Nazi ambassador to London, Joachim von Ribbentrop, was presented at Court, he thoroughly alarmed the shy, stuttering King George VI by barking out '*Heil Hitler!*' to him and narrowly missing the monarch's nose as he swept his right arm upwards in a smart Nazi salute; no wonder the ambassador quickly became known as 'Von Brickendrop'). The distance this created replaced the intimacy of shaking hands and alienated people from one another, uniting them only in their allegiance to Hitler.

Since the Hitler salute was also routinely described as the 'German greeting', giving it was a signal of national identity. From 1937, indeed, Jews were banned from using it, so that the greeting became an emblem of supposed racial superiority and togetherness. In Catholic southern Germany, where people conventionally said hello to one another with the words '*Grüss Gott!*' – 'God's Greeting!' – it gave the Nazi Leader divine status by replacing 'God' with 'Hitler'. The salute thus replaced regional differences in greeting formulae – which varied from '*Servus*' in the south to '*Moin-Moin*' on the northern coastline – with a nationwide gesture, affirming people's collective identity above all as Germans, a single race united in a single Nazi cause.

As the sociologist Tilman Allert shows in *The Nazi Salute* (2008), the 'German greeting' brought the regime into every aspect of daily life. With everybody using it, those who were perhaps initially reluctant could feel hopelessly outnumbered. Eventually they, too, felt there was no alternative to it. The implications were far-reaching. When rendered in public, the 'German greeting' militarised human encounters; it stamped individuals as members of a society mobilising under Nazi leadership for war; it reduced people's sense of their own individuality; undermined their ability to take moral responsibility for their actions, placing the responsibility in the hands of Hitler instead.

In truth, however, people often rendered the gesture under duress. Particularly in the first months of Nazi power, when dissidents and opponents of the regime were liable to be beaten up by stormtroopers or hauled off to a concentration camp, many people conformed simply out of fear. The posters put up along Germany's streets proclaiming '*Germans* use the *German Greeting!*' implied that anyone who did not use it could not be counted as part of the 'national community' of Germans, was an outsider, an outcast, even an enemy. The journalist Charlotte Beradt was told by a former socialist acquaintance at this time that he had dreamed that Nazi Propaganda Minister Joseph Goebbels had visited him at his workplace, but that he had found it extremely difficult to raise his right arm to the Minister in the Nazi salute; he managed it eventually after half an hour of trying, only to be told by Goebbels, coldly: 'I don't want your salute.' Here in a single anecdote was all the fear, anxiety and doubt that characterised many non-Nazi Germans' attitude towards the salute at the outset of the Third Reich.

Even at this time, however, and increasingly as time went on, people often used a conventional greeting as before, following up the Hitler salute with a 'Good Day' and a handshake. People came to regard '*Heil Hitler!*' as a more or less irritating formality, to be got out of the way before you said your real hello, reconnecting yourself to your friend, relative, colleague or acquaintance and restoring the customary bonds of sociability that had briefly and annoyingly been violated by the formal gesture of the Nazi salute.

In any case, people very soon stopped using the Hitler salute, once the initial period of violence and intimidation was over. Visitors to Berlin were already noting in the mid-1930s that the salute had become less common than before. One narrow street in Munich is still known even today as 'Shirkers' Alley' because people dodged through it in order to avoid having to salute a nearby Nazi monument. In October 1940, when it was clear that Germany was not going to bomb the British into submission, CBS correspondent William L. Shirer observed that people in Munich had 'completely stopped saying *Heil Hitler!*'. After the German defeat in the Battle of Stalingrad, the SS security service reported that people were no longer using the 'German greeting', and, indeed, it had virtually disappeared, except among Nazi Party fanatics, well before the end of the war. In September 1941, Victor Klemperer noticed a decline in the use of the 'German greeting' and, with the pedantry that made him such a valuable diarist, he began to count. In one bakery where he went to shop, he noticed five customers saying 'Good afternoon' and two '*Heil Hitler*'; but in a grocery store he visited, all the customers said '*Heil Hitler*'. 'Whom do I see,' he asked himself, 'to whom do I listen?'

Even when they had to use it, Germans could sometimes turn it into a gesture of defiance against the regime. In 1934, travelling circus performers were put under police surveillance after reports that they had been training their monkeys to give the salute. And a photograph exists of miners in the Bavarian town of Penzberg, assembled for a ceremonial parade, waving their arms about in all kinds of ways, ignoring the Hitler Youth contingent standing behind them and showing them how it really should be done.

The fact that people saluted opportunistically, defensively, or even to express resistance, albeit veiled and modest, combined with the fact that Germans increasingly often refused or neglected to salute, or nullified the salute's effect by following it with a conventional greeting, gives the lie to Allert's claims that the salute 'brought about a breakdown in people's sense of self' as they 'tried to evade the responsibility of normal social intercourse, rejected the gift of contact with others, allowed social mores to decay, and refused to acknowledge the inherent openness and ambivalence of human relationships and social exchange'. Life isn't as simple as that, even if sociologists sometimes think it is.

II

Klemperer's question – 'whom do I believe?' – neatly encapsulates a debate that has continued among historians ever since the collapse of the Third Reich in May 1945. How far did ordinary Germans support

Hitler's regime? If they were not behind it, then why did they not rise up against it? Why did they carry on fighting until the bitter end? What was, in general, the relationship between 'Germans' and 'Nazis'? Were they one and the same by 1945? What difference did the persecution and extermination of the Jews make to their attitude to the regime? If they knew about it, how far did they approve? Did they carry on fighting to the end despite their knowledge of Nazism's crimes, or because of it?

Few historians would now accept the claim made by the overwhelming majority of Germans in the late 1940s and 1950s that they had remained unaware of the crimes committed in their name under the Nazi regime. The Security Service of the SS was already reporting in March 1942 that soldiers returning from Poland were talking openly about how the Jews were being killed there in large numbers. The Nazi Party Chancellery complained on 9 October 1942 that rumours about 'very harsh measures' against the Jews were 'being spread by men on leave from the various units of the armed forces deployed in the East, who have themselves had the opportunity to observe such measures'. With two-thirds or more of the thirteen million German men under arms engaged on the Eastern Front, reports spread rapidly, and before the end of the year most Germans knew full well what was going on there.

Debate still rages, however, around the extent to which ordinary Germans gave their approval to the genocide. Recent years have seen historians downgrade ideological factors in favour of practical ones. A whole range of studies has shown how citizens participated in the Nazi project for reasons that had little or nothing to do with ideology: because they wanted jobs and homes, because they wanted a better life, later on because they simply wanted to survive. Few people ever had cause to fear a visit from the Gestapo or imprisonment in a concentration camp, it has been pointed out, so for most of the time fear did not play much of a role. All of this had little to do with ideology. But the practical support Germans gave to the regime constituted, it has been argued, an implicit approval of what it did.

Arguments such as these represent what has been called the 'voluntarist turn' in the historical appraisal of National Socialism. The choices Germans made, it is generally assumed, were free and unfettered; otherwise how could they subsequently be held responsible for them? In *Life and Death in the Third Reich* (2008), the American historian Peter Fritzsche announces his intention, in the spirit of the 'voluntarist turn', of analysing 'the effort that Germans made to become Nazis' and 'the extent to which Germans made deliberate, self-conscious, and knowledgeable political choices in the Third Reich'. Fritzsche writes with his customary flair and verve, and packs an enormous amount into a relatively short volume. He is particularly good on the detailed analysis of small but revealing cultural phenomena, like, for example, the Hitler greeting, discussed above, or the 'Ancestral Certificate' that all Germans had to carry to demonstrate their racial purity. His immensely readable and intelligent book makes superb use of letters and diaries to communicate the experience of ordinary people under Nazism in a way that few other historians have been able to do.

Fritzsche is too knowledgeable and subtle an historian to follow the 'voluntarist turn' all the way. He convincingly explores the limitations of Nazification as well as its successes. He is surely right to argue that while Nazis and Germans were never identical, the relationship between the two was never static either. He shows with a wealth of detail how the 'conversion process' of Germans into Nazis changed over time in an 'ongoing process, riddled with doubt'. By 1942, Germans still loved the Third Reich, which had given them order, security and economic stability after the chaos of the Weimar years, but they had come to despise the Nazis, who were now destroying all of this by their refusal to admit defeat. 'In this way, the idea of Germany had been covertly Nazified as well as Aryanised. The majority of Germans preferred to win the war and keep the Nazis than to lose both the war and the Nazis. Very few hoped for Germany's defeat.' Two dates, Fritzsche correctly notes, dominated almost everything the Nazis did: 1914 and 1918 – the positive myth of national unity at the outbreak of the First World War, which they sought to recreate in the much-vaunted 'national community' of all Germans; and the negative myth of the 'stab-in-the-back', in which Jewish subversives at home had undermined then destroyed the cohesion and fighting spirit of the army at the front. There was to be no 'stab-in-the-back' in 1945.

Fritzsche is well aware that in many respects the Nazi project of creating a new national and racial consciousness among Germans failed to reach its objectives. The regime devoted massive efforts to instilling in Germans a belief in the virtue and desirability of war, yet the vast majority of Germans remained immune, demonstrating widespread anxiety as armed conflict loomed during the Munich crisis of 1938 and arrived for real in September 1939, and showing a corresponding degree of euphoria as the former was resolved without bloodshed and the latter ended, as they thought, within a few months in a series of cheap and rapid victories. There was a similar atmosphere of gloom and apprehension among ordinary people when the invasion of the Soviet Union began on 22 June 1941.

All the same, Fritzsche suggests, 'Germans worked to calibrate themselves to the new aims of National Socialism' after hearing of the invasion of the Soviet Union, just as they had in previous crises. Before long, there was a general feeling of pride in the war in the east and optimism about its outcome. Unfortunately, Fritzsche never actually supplies any concrete evidence to show that Germans were actively working to accommodate themselves to the purposes of the regime. Not even the diaries and letters he cites show such a process of self-propelled efforts by their authors to become Nazi. All he can offer is assertion. And this is backed up by a serious underestimation of the coercive and terroristic aspects of the Third Reich. Unlike some of the more extreme exponents of the 'voluntarist turn', Fritzsche is aware, of course, of the enormous extent of the violence and intimidation meted out by the Nazis to real and potential opponents during the 'seizure of power' in the first six months of 1933. But like them, he goes on to claim that there was little overt violence or coercion thereafter. Even on his own evidence, however, people were coerced into donating money to the Winter Aid programme, were intimidated by continuing antisemitic violence on the streets for most of the 1930s and were disciplined in a whole variety of residential camps, through which the great majority of the population had passed by 1939. But there were other aspects of compulsion, coercion and intimidation that he fails to mention, too.

Thus, for example, Fritzsche alludes, like many exponents of the 'voluntarist turn', to the fact that only 4,000 or so political prisoners remained in the concentration camps by the mid-1930s. But, like them, he fails to realise that a major reason for the low number was the fact that the task of repression had been taken over by the regular courts and judicial system, which had put more than 23,000 political prisoners behind bars in Germany's state prisons and penitentiaries by this time. His claim that the police left former Communists and Social Democrats alone after 1933 can be disproved by countless local examples: many were rounded up and incarcerated during the rigged plebiscites and elections that the Nazis organised from time to time, they were under constant surveillance and were liable to be hauled off to a concentration camp once the war broke out as potential 'subversives'. He does not note the huge expansion of coercive legislation during the war, which led to the prison population virtually doubling, and the number of executions reaching four to five thousand a year at home. And a major reason why the troops kept on fighting lay in the fact that coercion reached similar dimensions in the armed forces, where some 30,000 troops were put before firing squads in the course of the war (compared to a mere eighteen – eighteen! – during the First World War).

Most important of all, Fritzsche ignores the enormous range of lesser sanctions threatened and often used by the regime to enforce at least an outward show of conformity, from the deprivation of welfare benefits to the assignment of grumblers and dissenters to difficult and dangerous jobs far away from their family and home. Diaries and letters may not have mentioned fear of reprisal or punishment, as

Fritzsche points out, but then, their authors were habitually cautious about saying anything that might get them into trouble if their diaries should be discovered or their letters opened by the police or the military censors. Fear was all-pervasive in the Third Reich. One obvious example could be found in the precautions people took during the war against being found listening to a foreign radio station, an offence punishable by imprisonment or even by death. It did not matter in the end that there were relatively few prosecutions. The possibility of being discovered or denounced led people to hide themselves and their radio under a blanket when listening, or post a lookout at the apartment door, or lock themselves in the bathroom with their wireless set. The widely publicised cases of listeners being prosecuted and sentenced to a spell in a state penitentiary were not enough to deter people – the BBC reckoned that up to fifteen million Germans a day were listening to its broadcasts by 1944 – but they were enough to make them afraid.

Unless one realises the true dimensions of the terror exercised by the regime, which increased massively as the war went on and reached extraordinary heights towards its end, it is difficult if not impossible to understand the reaction of ordinary Germans to the deportation and murder of the Jews. In a fascinating chapter on this crucial topic, Fritzsche goes through the evidence carefully, and concludes that while Germans knew about the mass shootings of Jews carried out by the SS in the east almost as soon as they began, they did not know about the gas chambers of Auschwitz, Treblinka and the other death camps. But while the sources he uses – SS Security Service reports, private correspondence and so on – do indeed back up this claim, he ignores the fact that the gas chambers were mentioned frequently in BBC broadcasts to Germany from the latter part of 1942 onwards. Its fifteen million German listeners were left in no doubt as to what was going on. Here, as in other parts of the book, Fritzsche is too inclined to portray Germany under the Nazis as completely cut off from other parts of the world.

Not least for this reason, by 1942 ordinary Germans were disinclined to accept Propaganda Minister Joseph Goebbels's assurances that the war would be won. They fought on not because they believed in victory but because they saw no alternative. Although Fritzsche suggests that there was a positive response to Goebbels's exhortation to the German people to mobilise for 'total war' following the German army's catastrophic defeat at Stalingrad early in February 1943, the evidence even of SS Security Service reports on popular morale suggests otherwise. And the more it became clear that Germany was going to lose, the more ordinary Germans began to fear Allied retribution, fuelled – and here Goebbels's propaganda does seem to have borne some fruit – by a thirst for revenge by the Jews.

Fritzsche claims that 'most Germans thought of themselves as the innocent victims of Allied bombing attacks', but as he himself shows in some detail in another part of the book, the common reaction was a very different one: guilt at what they had allowed to be done to the Jews. 'Have we not murdered thousands of Jews?' – as the SS Security Service reported 'numerous people from all classes of the population' saying in Stuttgart in 1944 – 'Don't soldiers again and again report that Jews in Poland have had to dig their own graves? ... Jews are human beings too. By doing all this we have shown the enemy what they can do to us if they win.' Thus Germans began to keep silent about the Jews, preparing to deny all knowledge of what had happened to them when the Allies eventually came to exact their retribution. Fear of the enemy – and not just of the Red Army, though that was paramount and to a large extent, indeed, justified – was thus another factor in keeping Germans going to the end.

Fritzsche frequently fails to recognise the artifice and calculation behind many apparently spontaneous outbursts of popular acclamation for the regime, from the demonstrations that attended Hitler's appointment as Reich Chancellor on 30 January 1933 to the mass rallies held to celebrate Hitler's survival of Colonel von Stauffenberg's attempt to blow him up on 20 July 1944. Both were orchestrated by Goebbels, who was always concerned to generate images of popular enthusiasm for the Third Reich.

III

If propaganda wasn't entirely successful in bringing the German people round behind Hitler and his Nazi regime, then perhaps material inducements played a role. In a startling and absorbing book, *Hitler's Beneficiaries*, which caused a considerable storm in Germany on its publication in 2005, the left-wing historian Götz Aly advances another explanation. It was, he says, material factors that persuaded the great mass of Germans to support Hitler and the Nazis almost to the very end. The Nazi leadership, he claims, made the Germans into 'well-fed parasites. Vast numbers of Germans fell prey to the euphoria of a gold rush ... As the state was transformed into a gigantic apparatus for plundering others, average Germans became unscrupulous profiteers and passive recipients of bribes.' Already by the late 1930s, Aly argues, even former Social Democrats had become reconciled to the regime because it replaced the mass unemployment and economic misery of the Depression with full employment, prosperity and consumer satisfaction. During the war, he continues, 'the cascade of riches and personal advantage – all derived from crimes against humanity – ... led the majority of the populace to feel that the regime had their best interests at heart'.

Aly has offered this kind of materialist explanation before, in dealing with Nazi genocide, which he portrayed in his book *'Final Solution': Nazi Population Policy and the Murder of the European Jews*, published in English in 1999, as the outcome of rational, or perhaps one should say pseudo-rational, processes of state planning and ethnic reordering generated in the Nazi and SS bureaucracies rather than of ideological hatred and delusion. In *Architects of Annihilation*, published in English in 2002 (more than ten years after its first appearance in German), written in collaboration with Susanne Heim, Aly turned his attention to the planners, demographers, civil servants and academics who devised these plans, and argued that in the drive to adjust the ratio between productive and unproductive population groups in Europe, the planners 'advocated state-directed mass extermination as a necessary and logical component of social modernization', envisioning in the process 'not only one "final solution" but serial genocides, planned in detail to be carried out over several decades'.

This approach originates in a particular German far-left understanding of Nazism, which seeks at every juncture to link it to processes of modernisation culminating in the Federal Republic of the present day. In *Hitler's Beneficiaries*, for instance, Götz Aly loses no opportunity to mention prominent figures in postwar Germany who were enthusiastic about the Third Reich as young men. Not long ago, he raised a storm by indicting much-admired German university historians of the 1950s for what he saw as their role during the Third Reich in planning or justifying Nazi genocide. What makes Aly such an uncomfortable figure for Germans is the fact that his arguments are always buttressed by painstaking, meticulous and very extensive archival research. His voice may be that of an outsider, but it has to be listened to. On its first publication in Germany, *Hitler's Beneficiaries* caused an even greater upset than before by arguing that it was not only the elites whose support for the Nazi regime was based on rational, non-ideological grounds, but also that of the vast mass of the people. How do his new claims stand up to critical scrutiny?

Hitler's Beneficiaries, it has to be said, does not begin well. The opening pages on Germany in the years before the outbreak of the Second World War in 1939 contain many sweeping claims that have long since been exploded by serious research. Thus, contrary to what Aly says, the German middle classes were not impoverished by the hyperinflation of 1922–3 (it was advantageous for debtors, mortgage-holders and the like); relatively few Communists went over to Nazism in the early 1930s; the plebiscite that brought the Saar (an ethnically German region on the French border under the control of the League of Nations since 1919) back to Germany was not a free election; and the Nazi leadership did not make automobiles 'affordable to everyday Germans'. Nazism preached equality, but as with so many aspects of Nazi rhetoric, the reality was very different, and to speak repeatedly, as Aly does, of the Nazis' 'socialism' is to mislabel the Nazis' undoubted populism; real socialist regimes were very different in their basic political thrust, and few things in this book are more unconvincing than its attempt to show that the Third Reich was a genuinely redistributive regime that robbed the rich to pay the poor.

Desperate to demonstrate that the overwhelming mass of Germans enthusiastically supported Nazism from the start, Aly provides a highly selective list of examples of young people, some of them his own relatives, who waxed rhapsodic about the possibilities the regime offered them. Typically, he also quotes Hanns Martin Schleyer, who became president of the Employers' Association in postwar West Germany, enthusing in 1942 about the opportunities Nazism gave to the young: 'We learned at a young age during the movement's days of struggle to seek out challenges, instead of waiting for them to come to us – this and our constant efforts for the party, even after it took power, made us ready to take on responsibility much earlier than usual' (Aly neglects to mention that Schleyer was kidnapped and murdered in 1977 by ultra-left German terrorists from the 'Red Army Faction' founded by Andreas Baader and Ulrike Meinhof). He also cites two male relatives' entries in the Aly family guest book during the war, with slogans such as 'tomorrow belongs to us' and 'our country is heading towards a great and glorious future'. But one could of course cite just as many testimonies by Germans who were frightened and disturbed by what the Nazi regime was doing, even in the 1930s. Aly does not.

The leadership did not divert resources to fulfilling consumer desires 'to the detriment of rearmament' – rather, the opposite. True, the Nazis' charitable organisations such as the Winter Aid, designed to support the unemployed and their families at a time when jobs were few, or the Nazi People's Welfare, a larger, more formal institution aimed at doing more or less the same thing through the year, raised a lot of money for the less well-off. But a very high proportion of these funds were collected through contributions coerced from the population, including compulsory deductions from wages. The profits gained from the 'Aryanisation' of Jewish property were significant for those who availed themselves of them, but Jews made up less than

1 per cent of Germany's population, and not all of them by any means were rich or even well-off, so that the difference this made to the nation's living standard overall was minimal. Yet Aly claims that the Jews were dispossessed, and indeed eventually exterminated, not least in order for the German state to get its hands on their property and use it to raise the people's standard of living.

The *reductio ad absurdum* of all this is reached when Aly suggests that 'the Third Reich was not a dictatorship maintained by force', citing the small size of the Gestapo, and the fact that there were only some 4,000 inmates in concentration camps by 1936; but by this time the police, the state prosecution service, the courts and the state prisons were carrying out the bulk of the regime's coercive measures; the force used by the regime to maintain itself in power could be seen everywhere, in the intimidating presence of stormtroopers on the streets, in the daily newspaper reports of the trial and conviction of nonconformists, in whispered conversations behind closed doors about the sufferings of former Communists and Social Democrats at the hands of prison warders and policemen. Even more bizarrely, Aly describes the Third Reich as being run by a 'flat' decision-making process, dependent on individual initiative, rather than by a top-down hierarchy. The millions of people in Nazi Germany who were caught up in an undemocratic, totalitarian system governed by the all-pervasive 'leadership principle' where Hitler's most casual remarks were immediately translated into official policy, often with devastating consequences, would certainly have been surprised to have learned this. Aly makes such crude and sweeping generalisations because he appears to be unfamiliar with the English-language literature on Nazi Germany, which is too large, diverse and sophisticated to be ignored with impunity. One feels that here, as elsewhere, his grasp of what other historians have written is less than secure. His work rests overwhelmingly on documentary research. And here, once he gets beyond the simplistic account of Nazi Germany before the outbreak of the war, he has some interesting discoveries to present.

Long ago, the British historian Tim Mason pointed out that the

Nazis' monomaniacal drive to rearm in preparation for a general European war got the German economy into increasing difficulties by 1939, as growing shortages of materials and labour began to impose growing constraints on production. Workers were increasingly coerced into working longer hours; they responded with rocketing rates of absenteeism, and the regime reacted by drafting Gestapo agents into the factories to try and keep the workers' noses to the grindstone. In this situation, economic salvation lay in conquest and plunder. Aly shows that as well as appropriating huge quantities of raw materials from Eastern and Western Europe, and eventually forcing more than seven million workers from conquered and occupied countries to work for little or no pay in Germany itself, the regime also exploited the countries it occupied so as to prevent the mass of the German population at home from having to bear the real financial burden of the war. It did this, as Mason pointed out years ago, because Hitler and the leading Nazis were anxious to the point of paranoia about a possible recurrence of the 'stab-in-the-back' of 1918, when they believed – quite wrongly, of course – that a catastrophic deterioration of living conditions on the home front had led to a mass revolution, fomented by Jewish subversives, who had stabbed Germany's otherwise victorious army in the back and brought about Germany's defeat in the First World War. As the Nazis pursued this deadly fantasy, more than half of Germany's Jews were forced out of the country by 1939, and the rest were dispossessed and marginalised and from 1941 onwards were deported and murdered. However, from the Nazi leadership's point of view, this still left the problem of how to maintain a decent standard of living at home.

At this point in the argument, Aly's exposition becomes quite technical and very hard going for the reader, with a plethora of figures and calculations of tax burdens and exchange rates; but its broad outlines are clear enough. In every country they occupied, the Nazis either introduced a new currency or fixed exchange rates so that German soldiers, administrators and others could use a strong Reichsmark to buy up goods cheaply and send them back home to their families. Buying goods abroad also helped control inflation at home. Special credit arrangements were made to assist in this process, and German troops in other countries were specifically allowed to receive money from their families at home to spend on goods they could not get in Germany. Aly cites to dramatic effect the correspondence of a number of German soldiers who described with enthusiasm what they were buying up and sending back to their families, among them the young Heinrich Böll, who many years later was awarded the Nobel Prize for Literature for his novels and stories. 'I've got half a suckling pig for you,' he announced triumphantly to his family just before coming home from France on leave in 1940. After the regime lifted restrictions on how much could be sent home in this way, the number of packages sent from France to Germany by military post ran at more than three million a month. Soldiers' pay was increased towards the end of 1940 explicitly in order to help them purchase the foreign goods their families desperately needed.

At home, taxes on the general population were kept as low as possible in order to avoid discontent, while business was taxed more heavily, not least on the grounds that this would not incur the wrath of the population at large. Elaborate welfare arrangements and benefits were put in place to ensure that families did not suffer while their principal breadwinner was away on military service. More importantly, occupied Eastern Europe was subjected to a ruthless policy of exploitation and expropriation, in which foodstuffs were seized in vast quantities from the granaries of Ukraine to feed the population at home, while more than three and a half million Soviet prisoners of war were deliberately left to die of disease and starvation, and German war plans envisaged up to thirty, or in some versions fifty, million Slavic civilians perishing in the same way. A similar policy was put into effect as soon as the German army occupied Greece, with huge quantities of food being shipped off home while Athens succumbed to a famine of terrible dimensions. A key document laying down the main policy guidelines for the German occupation of the Soviet Union in 1941 urged the incorporation of 'Russia's food economy into the European framework', leading to 'the extinction' of 'large segments of the population', running into 'tens of millions.' Aly cites many similar documents. The German historian Christian Gerlach in particular has argued that the extermination of the region's Jews was hastened by the desire of German administrators to reduce the number of 'useless mouths' in a situation where the German armed forces had to live off the land, and food supplies at home constantly needed to be replenished from abroad. For Aly, indeed, a major reason for Hitler's decision to deport the remaining Jews in Berlin to the east in the summer of 1941 was the need to use their homes to rehouse Germans made homeless by Allied bombing raids.

Here, however, a fundamental weakness of Aly's approach becomes apparent. In all his work, including his earlier study 'Final Solution', he has applied a kind of economic reductionism that leaves other factors too much out of account – notably ideology and belief. His arguments are always stimulating and deserve the closest consideration, but they by no means tell the whole story, and they considerably exaggerate the impact of material factors on Nazi decision-making, which was fundamentally irrational at its core. In a series of complex calculations, Aly comes to the conclusion that no less than 70 per cent of the wartime revenues of the German Reich derived from occupied countries, from forced labour and from the murder of nearly six million of Europe's Jews (whose assets and possessions fell to the Reich once they were killed). One could, to be sure, make a case that Aly underestimates the amount of plunder extracted from the occupied countries, since he relies overwhelmingly on official documents and ignores the vast scale of the unofficial looting carried out by German soldiers as they marched into one country after another. Heinrich Böll described with disapproval how his fellow soldiers broke into deserted houses on their way into France, taking anything they wanted; and in Poland and the east, the troops stole food, jewellery, silver and gold, artworks of every description, and much else besides, from the country houses and monasteries they encountered on their victorious march towards Warsaw. The contribution all this made to the standard of living of the soldiers' families back home should not be underestimated, even if it is impossible to calculate.

But overall, Aly's figure is surely anything but an underestimate. Other calculations, notably by Adam Tooze in his history of the Nazi economy, *Wages of Destruction* (2006), put the figure more plausibly at around 25 per cent; still substantial but a long way from keeping almost the entire German people going by itself. Aly has relatively little in qualitative terms to say about the standard of living of Germans on the home front, and citing government social policy measures is no substitute. There can be little doubt that a deterioration in general living standards set in from 1941 onwards, as rations were steadily cut, people began to have recourse to the black market, where prices rapidly became inflated, and bombing raids began to have their effect. There is, moreover, a fundamental contradiction at the core of Aly's book. For if the overwhelming mass of Germans had been as positively committed to the Third Reich as he claims they were already before 1939, sustaining a 'totalitarian democracy' from below and participating fully in a 'flat' decision-making process, then why would the regime have felt it necessary to divert such enormous resources into trying to avoid discontent on the home front during the war? Ironically, too, the decision-making processes that Aly describes, from tax reform and welfare measures to the regulation of food parcels and the raising of soldiers' wages, originated with central figures and institutions in the regime, not least with Hitler and Göring themselves, and were implemented in a top-down fashion through the Finance Ministry. If the Nazi leaders had decided not to tolerate the plundering of occupied countries and stopped the troops from enriching themselves and their families, they could have done so, and things would surely have turned out differently.

A central feature of Nazi ideology and rhetoric, explored by many historians, but for obvious reasons completely ignored by Aly, was the cult of self-sacrifice, the appeal to self-surrender in the interests of nation and race. Much of this was coupled with promises that everything would get better once the war was over, but it also had a clear message for the present. Germany was everything, the individual nothing. The limits of such an appeal were clear; people had in the end to be fed, clothed and housed, and a vast welfare effort went into trying to ensure that this was done. At the same time, however, there is plenty of evidence that the deep-seated identification of a majority of Germans with the nation – their nationalism, in a word – was more important than anything else in maintaining their commitment to the war effort. In 1939, 1940 and the first seven months of 1941, this produced an almost hysterical euphoria, as with startling rapidity and ease German forces overran territories whose conquest had largely eluded them in 1914–18. From late 1941 to near the end of the war, coupled with growing and in many respects quite justified fear of the Red Army, it instilled a grim determination to preserve the nation in the face of its advancing enemies. At the same time, disillusion with the Nazi regime escalated, until by 1944 even Hitler was coming under increasing criticism from the populace, and the regular morale reports produced by the Security Service of the SS had to be stopped because they made too depressing reading.

When the Red Army finally overran Berlin, and Hitler committed suicide in his bunker, any remaining allegiance to his regime among the overwhelming majority of ordinary Germans collapsed. There can be little doubt that the material conditions of their life deteriorated sharply in 1945–7, now that the income and produce of occupied countries was no longer available to them, the country's huge arms and munitions industries had ceased to exist, the armed forces were demobilised and returned home to begin the difficult search for a job, millions of refugees and expellees flooded in from Eastern Europe, and the burgeoning black market fuelled inflation until it reached dangerous levels. Yet despite these appallingly difficult material conditions, there was no resistance to the Allied occupation and no serious attempt to revive National Socialism after its defeat. If material factors had been so central in creating Germans' loyalty to the Third Reich, one would have expected far more serious levels of discontent after it collapsed. As it was, the death of Hitler, the central, integrating figure of Nazism, had cut the bonds of people's allegiance to his movement. And a regime that had constantly insisted that might was right, and the spoils went to the strong, was now unambiguously

hoist by its own petard. It was not just the end of the good times, economically speaking, therefore, that tore people's allegiance away from
the principles and practices of National Socialism, important though
that was. Ideology, as always, was just as important, if not more so.
Götz Aly has once more done a service to our understanding of Nazi
Germany by drawing our attention to material factors, but as in much
of his previous work he has exaggerated their significance, and to concentrate on them alone is to show only half the picture.

IV

The same goes, in the end, for other, recent attempts to argue that the
much-vaunted 'people's community' was a social reality rather than a
propaganda myth. Already in the mid-1960s the sociological historian
David Schoenbaum, in his book *Hitler's Social Revolution* (1966),
argued that the Nazis succeeded in breaking down existing social barriers and creating a genuinely egalitarian society. Others, however,
rapidly undermined this position by showing that underneath the surface rhetoric of equality, old social hierarchies and class divisions
remained. Yet the more recent shift from social to cultural history,
combined with the 'linguistic turn' in historical studies, has focused
attention once more on the level of discourse, belief, collective psychology and other factors that cut across the class divide. Beginning
in the 1990s, too, the study of Hitler's Germany has concentrated
increasingly on the extermination of the Jews, and on the attitude of
the German people towards the antisemitic policies of the regime.
Race has pushed class to the margins as the central organising concept
of research into the Third Reich. The collapse of Communism and the
decline of Marxism as an intellectual force has further undermined the
role of social differences and antagonisms in the study of Nazi
Germany, as it has in other areas of historical interest.

The 'People's Community', it is often argued, had a real effect on the
life chances of the younger generation of German workers, who were

enabled in the Third Reich to improve their social position through organisations such as 'Strength through Joy'. Here it is widely argued that the socially levelling effects of the Third Reich laid the foundations for the 'levelled-out middle-class society' of West Germany in the 1950s and 1960s. Thus the 'People's Community', already foreshadowed in Kaiser Wilhelm II's declaration on the outbreak of the First World War that he recognised no parties any more, only Germans, became a reality in the 1930s that had a long-term effect on the structure of postwar German society. This view goes together with the recent, and highly persuasive tendency of historians to view Nazism as an essentially modernising force, rather than the atavistic, backward-looking movement portrayed by the historians of the 1950s and 1960s. However, it is far more plausible to argue that the real motor driving the breakdown of class barriers in postwar West Germany was the 'economic miracle', the long boom that delivered prosperity to people at every level of society, accompanied by the slow decline of the traditional working class with its roots in the fading iron, steel, coal and engineering industries of the classic era of high industrialisation in the late nineteenth century. Certainly, the political effects of Nazism in cutting off younger workers from the institutional bases of class consciousness – the trade unions, the Social Democratic Party, the organisations of working-class culture – cannot be denied. 'Strength through Joy' was popular, but this popularity did not stop workers from resenting the fact that its greatest benefits – such as cruises to Madeira – were reserved for the Nazi Party bosses, nor from noting that the money they paid in savings for the 'People's Car' never resulted in their being able to buy or drive one of their own.

For many groups in Nazi society, the idea of the 'People's Community' provided a justification for the realisation of their own deeply held aspirations. Medical researchers could break free of traditional ethical restraints and experiment on human beings rather than on animals; engineers could devote their efforts to new technology such as the atom bomb or the jet engine; economists and sociologists could draft plans for the complete racial restructuring of

Eastern Europe; planners could devise programmes for new towns and cities linked by broad-gauge railways; and everyone, including workers, could imagine themselves part of a newly dominant Aryan race, marginalising the inferior or the dangerous, and participating in the drive to make Germany the greatest nation on earth. If we accept the view propagated by Robert Gellately and others that Nazi Germany was a 'dictatorship by consent', then the success of the Nazi concept of the 'People's Community' can hardly surprise us. Yet, Ian Kershaw asks in a recent article, published in *Visions of Community in Nazi Germany* (ed. Martina Steber and Bernhard Gotto, 2014), 'how can we establish the reality of consent in a terroristic dictatorship? It is hard enough to do this in a pluralistic liberal democracy. Does it make sense to speak of consent when everyone who disagrees with the way things are going is locked up or compelled to remain silent?'

Certainly some aspects of Nazi policy were popular with some groups of people – for example, the revision of the Treaty of Versailles. But in many areas contemporary reports reveal widespread dissatisfaction, from the attack on the Catholic Church to the problems of the economy in the mid-thirties. The atomisation of society brought about by the throttling of any kind of independent political initiative drove people back on their own resources. Apart from a (very substantial) minority of politically committed Nazis, most Germans ended by paying lip service to the regime. During the war, and especially from 1943 onwards, as Allied bombing raids became more frequent and more destructive, people began to look to their own future rather than rally round the national community so insistently propagated by the Nazi Party. Already in January 1941 an official report from Upper Franconia, usually a stronghold of support for the Nazis, concluded: 'One cannot speak of a People's Community. Everyone is only thinking of his own advantage.' The disintegration of social cohesion became steadily more extreme as the war progressed, but in truth the 'people's community' had always been more propaganda myth than social reality.

9. WAS HITLER ILL?

After reports had begun to surface in the German media about the sudden flight of Hitler's deputy Rudolf Hess to England in May 1941 in pursuit of the delusion that he could persuade the British to make peace with Nazi Germany, a popular joke went the rounds in the pubs and bars of Berlin. 'So you're the madman', it had Churchill saying to Hess as he was brought before him for interview. 'No', Hess replies, 'only his deputy!' The idea that Hitler was insane was something many Germans came to believe in during the later stages of the war, and for some time afterwards, not least as a way of excusing themselves from responsibility for his actions. If they had known in 1932, when they voted for him in their millions, what they knew ten years later, they would surely have voted differently, they claimed; it wasn't their fault that six million Jews were murdered, countless Soviet and other soldiers and civilians killed, German cities devastated, and Germany as they had known it destroyed for all time; the fault was the Führer's and the Führer's alone.

The idea of Hitler's insanity was only one of an enormous range of speculations through which people tried, then and later, to explain the Nazi leader's actions. Hitler was antisemitic because he had Jewish ancestry, it was claimed, for example, ignoring all the genealogical evidence to the contrary; or because a Jewish doctor had deliberately helped Hitler's mother on her way when she was dying, and overcharged the family for his services (in fact, his treatments were conventional by the standards of the time and he hardly charged the family anything at all); or because he had caught syphilis from a Jewish prostitute in his youth (again, medical reports on his state of health oddly failed to reveal the symptoms of the disease). Hitler was a sado-masochist who projected his sexual perversions on to the world stage, in the view of the psychoanalyst Walter C. Langer, who reported to the American secret service during the war on 'the mind of Adolf Hitler'. According to one psychohistorian, Hitler's exterminatory mania derived from the fact that his mother breast-fed him as a baby instead of passing him over to a wet nurse, an act of 'breast-mouth incest' that made him 'unsuitable for any normal erotic relationship', though strangely enough it does not seem to have had this effect on the billions of other infants throughout history who have been through the same experience.

Hitler suffered from 'schizophrenic mania' according to a later German attempt to analyse his personality; or, in an even less plausi-ble scenario, he never woke up from the hypnosis to which he was allegedly subjected following the temporary, supposedly hysterical blindness he suffered after going through a gas attack on the Western Front at the end of the war. Neither of these two theories is supported by any evidence. The problem with many of such speculations is that the evidence they use is unprovable except on the basis of the kind of rumours that circulated round the bars of Europe and the USA during the war, and were retold and, no doubt, embellished, by barflies like Putzi Hanfstaengl, whose anecdotes provided much of the basis for Langer's psychoanalytical account.

And, of course, there was the little matter of Hitler's genitalia. Echoing the popular ditty 'Colonel Bogey', sung by British troops during the war, the notes of the Soviet forensic pathologist who exam-ined the Führer's remains after the war declared that 'the left testicle could not be found', though the same could be said of most of the rest of Hitler's body as well, since it had been thoroughly burned after his suicide in the Berlin bunker by his orderlies. In any case, when his doctors examined him during his lifetime, they found everything in perfect order, also giving the lie to the report, passed on through several intermediaries from a physician who had allegedly treated him during the First World War, and subsequently accepted by the dramatist Rolf Hochhuth, that Hitler's penis had been bitten off by a billy goat when he was a child. ('The goat must have had very good aim,' Henrik Eberle and Hans-Joachim Neumann comment in *Was Hitler Ill?* (2013), 'and Hitler no reflexes for his penis to have been bitten.') As for 'Colonel Bogey', the fact that it claimed that 'poor old Goe-balls had no-balls at all', when Goebbels actually managed to father no fewer than six children (all of whom he and his wife murdered before committing suicide themselves at the end of the war), suggests that it was not, to put it mildly, based on a sober assessment of all the available evidence.

Others, including the German historian Lothar Machtan, have suggested that Hitler was homosexual, thus purportedly explaining his murder in the 'Night of the Long Knives' in 1934 of known homosexuals like Ernst Röhm and, supposedly, anyone else who either knew about Hitler's sexual inclinations or indeed had actually had sex with him (Machtan's list of possible partners includes Hitler's chauffeurs Julius Schreck and Emil Maurice, his friend Putzi Hanfstaengl, and even Joseph Goebbels and Rudolf Hess, though strangely none of these people was targeted in the bloodbath of 30 June–1 July 1934). Precisely how homosexuality or the wish to deny it can explain the actions of a mass murderer Machtan did not care to say, and his prize witness, one of Hitler's comrades at the front during the First World War, was later convicted on several counts of forgery and sexual assaults on women, and changed his story about Hitler several times.

In fact, despite his concern to conceal his relationships with women from the public, in an effort to project an image of self-sacrifice and total, exclusive devotion to the German people, Hitler is known to have had sexual relationships with a number of women, and for the last years of his life was in a conventional heterosexual partnership with Eva Braun, a woman considerably younger than himself. Fit, athletic and energetic, she posed a challenge to his sexual prowess that he attempted to overcome with the help of his doctor, Theo Morell, who administered injections of testosterone and other hormonal preparations such as Prostakrin before he spent the night with her (nowadays, doubtless, it would be Viagra). The authors of *Was Hitler Ill?*, respectively a historian and a physician, list no fewer than eighty-two different drugs and other preparations, injected or taken orally, in a chapter entitled 'Hitler's Medicine Chest': they included sedatives, analgesics, stimulants, laxatives, painkillers, and much more besides, but not of course all at the same time, or for lengthy periods, or in large doses.

Hitler took such remedies for various, mostly commonplace ailments from which he suffered at various points of his life. More seriously, his service in the First World War saw him sustain a shrapnel injury in his left thigh, which gave him some trouble later on, and a temporary and partial bout of blindness on 14 October 1918 as the result of a mustard gas attack. And his constant speechifying, especially during election campaigns before he came to power, imposed a considerable strain on his vocal chords, causing hoarseness that was cured in April 1932 on medical advice by voice training from the celebrated tenor Paul Devrient; so, curiously, the heads of two major combatant heads of state in Western Europe during the Second World War, Hitler and George VI, had benefited from the attentions of a speech therapist, though for opposite reasons: the Führer spoke too much, the King found speaking too difficult to do it very often.

Hitler's hoarseness returned in 1935, leading him to fear that he had throat cancer and fuelling the anxieties about his own mortality that led him to speed up the pace of his foreign aggression over the next four years. Reports of this reached Stalin through Martha Dodd, who was not only daughter of the US ambassador to Germany and therefore privy to the gossip that did the rounds on the Berlin social circuit, but also a Soviet spy who regularly sent reports to Moscow. In fact, however, the cause was a polyp, which was surgically removed by a specialist and shown to be benign when put under the microscope; it came back in November 1944 – perhaps Hitler had been shouting too much at this late, desperate stage of the war – and was removed again, with no ill effects.

In August 1941 Hitler was ill with dysentery, nausea and vomiting, which knocked him out for a fortnight and robbed him of the power to make decisions, but this did not affect the course of the war, since he resumed command of the armed forces towards the end of the month and issued the fateful order to divert a significant portion of them from the attack on Moscow to the invasion of Ukraine. More generally, however, he was a long-term sufferer from irritable bowel syndrome. Some have blamed this on his strict adherence to a vegetarian diet from 1930 onwards: the authors reproduce the menu for Hitler's Christmas dinner on 25 December 1944, a miserable affair consisting of muesli, Vitamultin tea, noodle soup, breaded cauliflower, puff pastry and mashed potatoes; but, monotonous though his diet was, it is unlikely to have caused serious digestive problems; irritable bowel syndrome is normally caused by stress, and this is likely to have been the case with Hitler, especially during the war.

Eberle and Neumann discuss the possibility that Hitler suffered from high blood pressure and coronary sclerosis, and reproduce the results of a series of ECG tests; stress seems to have been a major factor here, too, and the authors conclude that a number of biographers have exaggerated the seriousness of his condition, which was not life-threatening. More serious was the tremor that people began noticing in Hitler's left hand and leg in 1941, along with a tendency to shuffle rather than walk; but while this fits the diagnosis of Parkinson's disease, it seems not to have affected Hitler very seriously until the very final stage of the war, since up to then neither his speech nor his thought processes became retarded. The most seriously wrong thing about Hitler's body was his teeth, which were badly decayed and had been poorly repaired when he acquired a new dentist in 1933; he must have had extremely bad breath. His dentist, Hugo Blaschke, was constantly treating them, extracting two as late as the autumn of 1944. By this time, Hitler's mouth was full of crowns and bridges, some of them quite possibly made with gold taken from the mouths of Jewish concentration camp victims – Blashke had a stash of fifty kilograms of it in his personal laboratory for use in his dental work, and, given the quantity, quite possibly for other purposes, too.

Hitler's health unquestionably suffered as the result of the bomb set off by Colonel von Stauffenberg in the tragically unsuccessful attempt to assassinate him on 20 July 1944. The blast shattered his eardrums, sent shrapnel pieces into his body, singed his hair and caused burns on his skin, but it did not stop him reacting quickly and with savage violence towards the plotters and their supporters and relatives immediately afterwards. Paradoxically, as he said afterwards, his trembling 'vanished almost completely as a result of the attack – not that I would recommend this kind of remedy'. Subsequently, however, it reappeared in his left hand, and his general state of health never completely recovered. By early 1945, as his Armaments Minister Albert Speer later reported, 'his limbs trembled, he walked stooped, with dragging footsteps. Even his voice became quavering and lost its old masterfulness. Its force had given way to a faltering, toneless manner of speaking.'

Was this because his physician Dr Theo Morell was pumping him full of unsuitable drugs? Certainly, Morell was known for his enthusiastic prescription of pills (Hitler was taking twenty-eight a day by the last months of the war), and injections (Hermann Göring dubbed Morell *Reichsspritzenmeister*, 'Reich Master of Injections'). Hugh Trevor-Roper, interviewing the surviving members of Hitler's entourage after the war, had no doubts about Morell's malign influence: 'He was a quack ... a charlatan ... totally indifferent to science or truth.' Morell's influence with Hitler, whom he had treated from 1936 onwards, derived not least from his reassuring bedside manner. His increasing power over the Führer aroused major jealousies in his entourage, particularly Hitler's other personal physician Karl Brandt; the opinions they purveyed to Trevor-Roper were full of personal animus and so were not to be trusted.

In fact, Morell was a qualified physician, and his remedies conformed to the accepted medical and pharmaceutical standards of the day. This included even his favourite remedy Vitamultin, a stimulant that may have included methamphetamine ('speed'); certainly reports of Hitler's behaviour during a summit with Mussolini in July 1943, when he was 'so euphoric and verbose that Mussolini was barely able to get a word in edgeways', strongly suggest that the pills Morell had given to the Führer shortly beforehand were based on this substance. Yet not all of the Vitamultin tablets, or the Vitamultin tea Hitler drank for breakfast, contained amphetamines; mostly they seem to have been caffeine-based, and there is no indication that Hitler ever became addicted to them. In the end, Morell was trying to deal with a gradual deterioration of Hitler's physical state during the war, and there is little convincing evidence to support Trevor-Roper's claim that he made it worse.

Hitler was never a particularly healthy man. He took little exercise, and when he did go for a walk in the Bavarian Alps, from his house on the Obersalzberg, he always walked downhill, making sure that there was a car ready to take him back up again when he reached the bottom. The contrast with the obsessive drive of his regime to breed and train a race of healthy Aryans through the daily gymnastics work- ers, teachers, soldiers, even schoolchildren were forced to undertake, was striking. The Nazi elite never cared much for conforming to the appearance or behaviour they demanded of other Germans – 'the true Aryan', a popular joke used to go, 'is as blond as Hitler, as nimble as Goebbels, and as slim as Göring'. Yet – unlike Göring, who undoubt- edly was addicted to drugs, or Goebbels, who suffered from a club foot – Hitler was no more unhealthy than many middle-aged Germans of the day; indeed, he neither drank alcohol nor smoked cig- arettes, making him a good deal healthier than many, despite his distaste for physical exercise.

Eberle and Neumann do a good job of clearing away all the redun- dant speculation of the decades about Hitler's state of health. Their answer to the question posed in the title – 'was Hitler ill?' – is a resounding 'no'; that is, he was no more ill than most other people are at some time or other during their lifetime. He certainly was not mentally ill, not at least in any sense known to medicine or psychiatry. Whether his actions and beliefs were rational is an entirely different matter: irrationality is not the same as madness, and as the authors go through various seemingly irrational decisions Hitler took during the war, they have no trouble in demonstrating that they were unaffected by any medical problems he might have had at the time. Hitler's beliefs and ambitions were shared by millions of Germans, and the picture so many of them painted after the war, of a nation of gullible dupes seduced by a raving madman, has never been a very convincing one.

Eberle and Neumann's retrospective diagnoses are compact, clear, authoritative and persuasive; but they are not particularly startling or original. For all this has been done before, by the late Fritz Redlich, an Austrian psychiatrist who emigrated to the USA in 1938 and subsequently became Dean of the School of Medicine at Yale University. In 1998, Redlich published *Hitler: Diagnosis of a Destructive Prophet*, in which he went over much of the same evidence, from Morell's notebooks to Hitler's electrocardiogram records taken at various times in the 1930s and early 1940s, and came to much the same conclusions. Redlich had the advice of the German historian Norbert Frei and other leading specialists in the history of the Third Reich, and it is to him that the credit for laying to rest so many myths about Hitler's illnesses must principally go. Eberle and Neumann ungenerously dismiss his work as based on unreliable sources but while they add detail and precision on some points, they do not seriously challenge his detailed medical arguments. Both books come to the inescapable conclusion that Hitler was not insane or deranged, or suffering from drug-induced delusions, or labouring under the effects of some chronic disease such as syphilis, or acting in an unresolved hypnotic trance: on the contrary, he was sane according to any reasonable definition of the term, and fully responsible for his actions.

10. ADOLF AND EVA

In the small hours of the morning of 29 April 1945, as the Red Army's guns and tanks could be heard bombarding the centre of Berlin, a curious event took place in Hitler's bunker deep under the garden of the old Reich Chancellery. Witnessed by Reich Propaganda Minister Joseph Goebbels and the head of the Nazi Party Chancellery Martin Bormann, a local Berlin official formally conducted a ceremony of civil marriage between the German dictator Adolf Hitler and a thirty-three-year-old Bavarian woman, Eva Braun, some twenty-three years his junior. After the ceremony was over, the party was joined in Hitler's living room by a small group of secretaries and leading Nazis for a glass of sparkling wine and, as one of those present later wrote, reminiscing 'happily about the old days'.

It was a marriage solemnised in the shadow of death. Shortly before, Hitler had dictated his 'political testament' to one of the secretaries in the bunker. In it he declared that since his life was now almost over, he had decided 'to take as my wife the woman who, after many long years of loyal friendship, came to the already besieged city ... It is my wish that she go with me into death as my wife.' On the afternoon of 30 April, the pair retired into Hitler's private quarters, where Eva Hitler, as she now was, sat down on a sofa. She bit a cyanide capsule and died instantly. Hitler, wanting to make doubly certain of his own death, did the same, while simultaneously firing a bullet through his right temple. Upon hearing the noise, some of the others present in the bunker entered the room and organised the removal of the bodies to the garden, where, acting on instructions, they poured petrol over them and burned them until they were unrecognisable. The still-functioning Nazi propaganda machine issued a statement claiming Hitler had died fighting to the end. No mention was made of his new wife. She died as she had lived, invisible to all but a handful of the Führer's intimates.

Who was Eva Braun? Why did she link her fate so inextricably to that of the German dictator? Why was her existence kept so secret for so long? Was she just a simple, apolitical, naive young woman capti- vated by Hitler's charisma? Was her relationship with the dictator merely platonic? In *Eva Braun: Life with Hitler* (2011), the first seri- ous, scholarly biography of the girl who after her death became one of the world's best-known women, the historian Heike Görtemaker sifts thoroughly and cautiously through the available documentation to try and find an answer to these perplexing human questions and pinpoint the exact nature of her relationship with the German dictator.

Historians have long been aware that Hitler relied on a small band of intimate friends and acquaintances to do things for him. Far from being professionally run, the Third Reich was governed by amateurs and outsiders. The role of his personal photographer, Heinrich Hoffmann, in this little coterie has, however, as Görtemaker shows, been insufficiently appreciated. Hoffmann was a Nazi almost from the very beginning, meeting Hitler before the Beer Hall putsch in 1923 and allaying the Nazi leader's anxieties about being photographed in unflattering situations by capturing his image in the most appealing possible way. Hoffmann's work ensured Hitler's picture was all over the media by the late 1920s. His photographs were always the best. He accompanied the Nazi leader virtually everywhere. Hoffmann's home provided Hitler with something like an ersatz family retreat. These services earned him Hitler's trust and later on brought him a large income and a good deal of power in the cultural world, includ- ing the selection of his paintings for the Great German Art Exhibition of 1937, the showcase for Nazi art. Relatively early in his career,

Hoffmann was able to expand his business and hire new staff. One of these new employees was the young Eva Braun.

Born on 6 February 1912, Eva was the second of three daughters of a lower-middle-class couple, Friedrich and Franziska Braun. Their marriage was neither happy nor stable. Indeed, in 1921 they had divorced, only to remarry just over eighteen months later, as rampant inflation was beginning to destroy the incomes of so many people like themselves: three children were cheaper to support in one household than in two. After the economy stabilised in the mid-1920s, the family, helped by an inheritance, recovered sufficiently to move into a large house, employ a servant and buy a car. But the situation at home remained tense, so much so that Eva spent most of her time living with the family of a friend, whose parents she ended up calling mother and father. After a period in boarding school, she answered an advertisement placed in a local newspaper by Heinrich Hoffmann and in September 1929 joined his rapidly growing staff.

By this time Hoffmann was advertising his studio as a Nazi enterprise. Friedrich Braun was an enthusiastic supporter of the Party and no doubt encouraged his daughter to apply for the job. The seventeen-year-old Eva served as a saleswoman and was trained in basic photographic techniques. Most of the studio's business was provided by the Nazi Party, so it is not surprising, especially in view of Hoffmann's close relationship with Hitler, that one of the first customers she came into contact with was the Party leader, for whom, one day, Eva was asked to fetch some food and drink from a nearby shop. As they all sat around eating, Hitler was clearly taken with his photographer's new assistant, even, according to a postwar book by a journalist who interviewed Braun's surviving relatives, offering to drive her home (she was back with her parents at this time). Soon Hitler was showering her with compliments on his frequent visits to the studio and giving her little presents. So taken with her was he that he secretly had her ancestry checked out to see if she was 'Aryan'. His investigators reported back: she was.

Unused to such attention, Eva Braun began to reciprocate. Soon there could be no doubt about the genuine nature of her feelings. Sensing that this would ingratiate himself still further with the Nazi leader, Hoffmann began to encourage the relationship (his later denials, as Görtemaker shows, are not credible). Within a relatively short time after their first meeting, the two had begun a sexual relationship, consummated most probably in an apartment rented by Hitler in the upmarket Munich district of Bogenhausen. Görtemaker eschews psychologising and speculation in this rigorously scholarly book, but it seems reasonable to suppose that Eva found in the much older Hitler a substitute for her unsatisfactory father. Beyond this, both of them came from similar social backgrounds, had comparable (somewhat rudimentary) levels of education and shared a common distance from the German social establishment of the day. Both of them, as those who knew them noted, were obsessed with personal cleanliness, maintained a tidy appearance and yet had spent much of their lives in unconventional surroundings, he in the bohemian world of prewar Munich and Vienna, she in the artistic milieu of the photographic atelier.

There can be little doubt that the relationship was a normal expression of heterosexuality on both sides. Görtemaker does not even bother to mention the wild speculations indulged in by American psychologists such as Walter C. Langer in his wartime analysis *The Mind of Adolf Hitler*, nor the bar-room gossip purveyed by the lounge lizard Ernst 'Putzi' Hanfstaengl, an intimate of Hitler in the 1920s, in the report he wrote for US president Franklin D. Roosevelt (who called it his 'bedtime reading' during the war), according to which Hitler engaged in sexual perversions of various kinds. Difficult though it may be to accept, it seems overwhelmingly probable that Hitler had a sex life that was conventional in every respect except that he kept it secret. Not everything about this most evil of men was necessarily twisted or perverted.

Hitler's liaison with Eva Braun soon began to pose problems for the Nazi leader; problems that only increased as their relationship deepened. Even before he came to power, Hitler started to avoid open displays of affection. There was more than one reason for this. For some time, he had been carrying on an affair with his half-sister Angela Raubal's daughter Geli, to whom he was subletting a room on Munich's grand Prince Regent Street. On 18 September 1931, Geli shot herself, perhaps from the guilt of her incestuous relationship with her half-uncle, perhaps because of jealousy, perhaps because she could not stand Hitler's controlling and restricting influence over her life. She did not leave a note behind, a fact that has caused some to doubt whether it was suicide at all. Others hinted, rather implausibly, that she had been murdered to avoid embarrassing revelations about the Nazi Party leader.

Whatever the truth about the affair, Hitler now decided that it was too dangerous to let his private life affect his public image, the more so since the Nazi Party was increasing rapidly in popularity and prominence. Even to intimates such as Goebbels he declared that he cared only for Germany and would never marry. Private happiness had to be sacrificed for the public good. From now on, as he said, 'I am married: to the German People and their fate!' As Hitler embarked on a period of feverish political campaigning, run from Berlin rather than from Munich, there was in any case little time in which to cultivate his new relationship with Eva Braun. Distraught, either in August or November 1932 (accounts differ) she took her father's pistol, loaded it, turned it toward her heart and pulled the trigger.

But Eva Braun's aim was poor. Whether by accident or design, the bullet missed all her vital organs and was easily removed in hospital, where Hitler, alarmed, visited her shortly thereafter. Hitler told Hoffmann that he 'must look after her' from now on; a second suicide scandal might ruin him. He now realised 'that the girl really loved him'. Hitler made no mention of his own feelings. But from that moment, his relationship with Eva became a fixed and significant part of his life. If her suicide attempt had been a cry for help, then it had succeeded. But she knew the rules by which the affair had to be conducted. It must remain under wraps. Not even on private occasions could any gestures of affection between the two be allowed if others were present. Marriage was out of the question. The public role of 'first lady of the Third Reich' was left to be fought for between the fanatical Nazi Magda Goebbels, wife of the Propaganda Minister, the actress Emmy Göring, second wife of the Reich's 'second man' Hermann Göring, and Ilse Hess, a committed Nazi of the first hour, married to Deputy Führer Rudolf Hess.

Braun's personal correspondence with Hitler was destroyed on his orders just before the end of the war, but a fragmentary – though clearly authentic – diary from 1935 survives, in which Eva wrote of her dismay when Hitler left suddenly for Berlin 'without saying goodbye' after spending 'two marvellously beautiful hours' with her up to midnight the previous day. During the following weeks, in which Hitler was preoccupied with major political issues, from the Saarland plebiscite to the introduction of conscription, 'love seems not to be on his agenda at the moment,' she wrote. At a reception in a Munich hotel, her expectation of a 'kind word' or 'greeting' from him was disappointed, and, as he parted, he merely gave her 'an envelope with some money inside as he had already done once before'. Worse still, Hitler was now seen at social events in Berlin in the company of a young and beautiful aristocratic woman, Sigrid von Laffert.

Faced with such seeming indifference to her, Eva resorted for a second time to a suicide attempt, on this occasion with an overdose of sleeping pills, that would really 'make "dead sure"', as she noted in the diary. In fact, she survived. But the tactic succeeded. She moved out of her parents' house into an apartment five minutes away from Hitler's own, in Munich, together with her sister and a domestic servant. The rent was paid by Hitler, using Hoffmann as an intermediary. A few weeks later, she was allowed to appear at the Nazi Party Rally in Nuremberg, and sat on the podium, much to the disgust of the leading ladies in the party hierarchy, who up to this point had been unaware of her existence. Shortly afterwards, Hitler's half-sister left his country retreat, the Berghof, in the Bavarian Alps, after seven years in charge of its daily management – that is, once she had made clear her dislike for her young rival, Eva Braun. It was obvious that Hitler would brook no criticism of the woman who had now become his permanent companion.

If Eva was seen with Hitler in public, at visits to the opera or on sporting or social occasions, then she had to be in the background. But she now travelled with Hitler often, even accompanying him on trips abroad, in the guise of a 'private secretary' or a member of Hoffmann's staff. Eventually she was provided with an apartment in the old Reich Chancellery in Berlin so that she could be with Hitler when he was in the capital. And behind the scenes, she slowly began to assert herself, above all at the Berghof, where she now lived for most of the time. Here Hitler came to relax and to resume the bohemian lifestyle he had enjoyed in the 1920s. While the establishment was run by Hitler's unobtrusively efficient factotum Martin Bormann, it was Eva Braun who established herself in the next few years as the hostess who orchestrated the retreat's social events and came to be recognised, willingly or otherwise, by Hitler's circle of intimates as the mistress of the household. Bormann was careful to maintain good relations with her, ensured she had whatever she needed, including money, and carefully made arrangements to conceal her existence from the general public.

Of course, since the fact that Hitler had a long-term partner was known to the senior figures in the regime, observant journalists could find out about it as well – if they so wished. For German reporters it was too dangerous. But Eva Braun's role did not escape the attention of some perceptive foreign reporters. Thus, for example, on 15 May 1939, in the true style of the gossip columns of the day, *Time* magazine ran a story under the headline 'Spring in the Axis', writing that a young, blonde woman called Eva Braun had been supplied with an apartment by her 'old friend in Berlin who always comes to see her when he is in town'. 'To her friends,' the article wrongly reported, 'Eva Braun confided that she expected her friend to marry her within a year.' The following December, indeed, America's *Saturday Evening Post* ran a piece: 'Is Hitler Married?' The German journalist Bella Fromm, who had fled her homeland for the United States in 1938, seems to have picked up gossip that led her to identify Braun as

Hitler's girlfriend as well; Fromm included it in her diary publication *Blood and Banquets* in London in 1942, noting that Hoffmann's former assistant 'Eva Helene Braun' seemed to have captured the Führer's heart. The Nazi censors, however, saw to it that such reports never reached the German-reading public.

While Hitler might have thought it necessary to keep the relationship quiet before he came to power in 1933, once he had established his dictatorship he could in effect do anything he wanted. Why, then, did the couple neither marry nor have children? In public, Hitler went out of his way to demonstrate his kindness to children, as to animals, and the offspring of intimates such as his architect and munitions supremo Albert Speer were always a welcome presence at the Berghof. Moreover, Nazi ideology emphasised the importance of 'Aryan' women such as Eva Braun marrying and having children for the Reich. Leading Nazis, such as Goebbels with his six children, or Bormann with an impressive ten, duly obliged. Eva Braun had photographs taken of her and Hitler sitting on a sofa together with the young children of her friend Herta Schneider and kept them in a special album, signifying her dream of having children with him after the war, in a parallel fantasy world to that conjured up by Hitler as he inspected models of the monstrous cityscapes he planned for Berlin or Linz once peace came. Hitler in turn allowed her to photograph him with children, not only because she sold the pictures to Hoffmann for propaganda use, but also because, Görtemaker suggests, he knew that these images allowed her to dream of the family life she was unable to have with him.

Hitler indeed deliberately avoided commitment to family life because he wished to project himself as an ostensibly lonely figure to whom all others had to defer, a man who stood above the social norms of the Third Reich. His model here was Karl Lueger, the popular, antisemitic mayor of Vienna, where Hitler had lived before the First World War, who had refused to marry his partner because, as he had said, he needed 'the women' in order to 'achieve anything' politically. 'Lots of women,' Hitler later declared, 'are attracted to me because I am unmarried.'

The Third Reich was what has been called a 'plebiscitary dictatorship'. Hitler repeatedly needed to demonstrate, not least to international opinion, the mass support his regime and its policies enjoyed; hence the lengths to which he went to manufacture majorities of 99 per cent in elections and referendums. Women voters – the majority, given the mass slaughter of German men in the First World War and their greater longevity – were an important source of electoral support for Hitler both before and after he came to power. And women, too, were vital in his view as supporters of the war effort, keeping their men committed to the cause and ensuring that soldiers had no reason to worry about their families on the home front. Marrying would, he said privately in 1942, create 'legal rights! So it's much more proper to have a lover. The burden drops away and everything remains a gift.' Aware of these views, Eva was careful not to use her position to try to influence Hitler in personal or political matters; while Hitler reacted allergically to any attempts by others to gain influence over him through her. When Hermann Göring lost power after the beginning of the war, he tried to regain it by encouraging his wife to become a personal friend of Eva's; Hitler brusquely put a stop to the manoeuvre.

Nazi ideology portrayed women as essentially passive, modest, simple and undemanding creatures, whose role was to adore their menfolk. Braun was no such woman. As her failed suicide attempts showed, she was prepared to go to some lengths to get what she wanted. Her position at the Berghof, in which she asserted her dominance over the much older would-be first ladies of the Reich, testified to her strength of personality. During the war, visitors noted how she became more self-confident, signalling to Hitler to shut up when he had launched into one of his interminable after-dinner monologues, or asking loudly what the time was when he showed no sign of retiring for the night. Still only in her twenties, she had become a figure to be reckoned with in Hitler's inner circle.

Eva failed to conform to the Nazi ideal of womanhood in other ways, too. A visitor to whom she was presented as the 'housekeeper' at the Berghof reported disapprovingly that Braun changed her dress several times a day. She did not, he noted severely, conform to the 'ideal of a German girl', who was supposed to be 'natural' in appearance. She bleached her hair and always wore make-up (Elizabeth Arden was her preferred brand). Moreover, as soon as Hitler left his Bavarian retreat, her mien changed – she smoked cigarettes (not only did Hitler himself not smoke, he also banned smoking around him), devised amusements for her friends, watched foreign movies, held parties, did gymnastics in a swimsuit, sunbathed in the nude and generally let her hair down.

Women were discouraged from pursuing professional work in Nazi Germany, but Hitler recognised Eva's claim to be a professional photographer – she not only took numerous, often very good photographs but also developed and printed them herself – by calling her the 'Rolleiflex girl'. One of the few gaps in this otherwise comprehensive study is Görtemaker's failure to discuss the extensive home movies Braun filmed at the Berghof; these are a significant source for our knowledge of the Third Reich leaders and their relations with one another. Braun's colour film of Hitler and his entourage is of rare immediacy, somehow, to the twenty-first-century eye, far more real than film shot in black and white. Some of it has been subjected to automated lip-reading technology, and in one particularly creepy moment, Hitler, while being filmed by Braun, begins to flirt with the woman behind the camera, giving those who view it the uncomfortable feeling that Hitler is flirting with them.

For all Eva's self-assertion, most of the men in Hitler's entourage who knew her portrayed her as an unassuming little thing, unaware of the big, wide world outside. Much of what is known about her comes from postwar reminiscences, notably those published by Albert Speer. Görtemaker shows once more how unreliable Speer's self-serving recollections were, like those of many others who knew Hitler's eventual wife. It was, after all, in their interest to suggest that she was naive and non-political, that life in the place where she spent most of her time, in Hitler's mountain retreat on the Bavarian Obersalzberg, was idyllically removed from the stresses and strains of political and military affairs, that neither she nor they discussed or knew about the persecution and mass murder of Europe's Jews, or the extermination of other groups, from Soviet prisoners of war to Germany's mentally handicapped.

Yet Hitler's inner circle, including Eva Braun, did not live exclusively at the Berghof, cut off from the events that took place in the great cities such as Munich and Berlin where they also spent much of their time. They witnessed the nationwide pogrom of 9–10 November 1938, when thousands of Jewish-owned shops were trashed by mobs of Nazi stormtroopers, hundreds of synagogues set ablaze and 30,000 Jewish men publicly rounded up, abused, maltreated and sent off to concentration camps. They saw the signs put up on the roads leading to villages around the Obersalzberg announcing that Jews were 'not wanted' in the locality. They read the newspapers, they saw the notices in town banning Jews from local amenities such as municipal libraries and swimming pools.

Though Eva left few concrete indications of her political views, some can be found in her photograph album, which included snaps of Hitler and his entourage during the tense period leading up to the outbreak of war, which she accompanied with typed captions such as: 'Poland still does not want to negotiate'; or: 'The Führer hears the report over the radio.' If Hitler listened to radio reports, then so, too, did she. There can be little doubt that Eva Braun closely followed the major events of the war, nor that she felt her fate was bound inextricably to that of her companion from the outset. 'If something happens to him,' she said, as she listened in the press gallery, weeping, to Hitler's declaration in the Reichstag on the outbreak of war that he would only take off the soldier's uniform he now wore 'after our victory, or not live through its end', 'I'll die too.'

The war changed the relationship. Hitler spent increasing amounts of time in Berlin or, after the invasion of the Soviet Union in June 1941, at his field headquarters behind the Eastern Front. It is reasonable to suppose he told her where he was going before he launched the invasion, and why he was going to spend so much time there. Certainly he told his young secretaries, giving the lie to the later claim that he never talked politics to women. Hitler's visits to the Berghof were now less frequent, though when the military situation allowed it, they could last for weeks or even months at a time. The atmosphere grew more depressed as the German armies suffered the disastrous defeat of Stalingrad at the beginning of 1943, and Allied bombers began to devastate German cities, including Munich, not long afterwards. As Hitler increasingly withdrew from public view, Eva's role grew more significant, and on 25 June 1943, Propaganda Minister Goebbels, whose voluminous diaries were by now intended primarily for postwar publication, began to mention her for the first time, and in sycophantically warm and admiring terms, in their pages.

Hitler's stay at the Berghof from February to July 1944 was his last. He left only when rumours of an impending assassination attempt drew him back to Berlin. Before leaving, he made arrangements with Eva for the eventuality of his death; her response, he told Goebbels, was once more to tell him that if he died she would kill herself. Given the fact that she had already tried to do this twice so was no stranger to the idea, and knowing that her enemies, who by now included the increasingly power-hungry Bormann, would drive her out if Hitler were no longer around, this was perhaps not so surprising. But it also clearly reflected genuine emotional identification. When the assassination attempt came on 20 July 1944, with Colonel von Stauffenberg's bomb in Hitler's field headquarters, Eva repeatedly tried to reach Hitler by phone in the ensuing hours of uncertainty, telling him when she eventually did get through: 'I love you, may God protect you!'

In October 1944 Eva made her last will and testament, alarmed by reports of Hitler's increasingly frail health. Leaving everything to her family and friends, the will once more made it implicitly clear that if Hitler died, from whatever cause, she would perish, too. In November, as Hitler moved back to Berlin, Eva joined him in the apartment in the old Reich Chancellery, later, when constant bombardment from enemy planes and guns made life above ground too dangerous, relocating to the underground bunker where they were to end their lives. Here she gave her full support to Hitler's fanatical determination to fight to the end, hoping for victory in the face of overwhelming evidence that total defeat was only weeks away. When Hitler had his doctor, Karl Brandt, arrested and condemned to death for daring to send him a report detailing the catastrophic situation of medical services in the Reich, Eva stood by him, despite her previous friendship with Brandt, describing the physician's conduct as mad and disgraceful. (Brandt managed to evade his fate in the chaos of the final weeks, only to be executed by the Allies after the war for medical crimes.)

After a brief farewell visit to her family in Munich, she returned to the bunker on 7 March 1945, a few weeks later writing to a friend that she was 'happy to be near *him*'. She rejected all attempts to get her to persuade Hitler to leave Berlin. She not only kept up appearances herself but also insisted Hitler do so, too, encouraging him to believe that the situation could still be turned around, or at least to behave as if it could. By projecting this image of an undiminished will to fight on, Eva Braun undoubtedly contributed to hundreds of thousands of deaths in the last weeks of the war.

Even if she sometimes became impatient with them, Eva Braun listened to many of Hitler's political monologues, large numbers of which Bormann had noted down for posterity, and, as his fervent admirer, with the barely formed views of a teenager, she no doubt accepted without question his racism, his antisemitism, his murderous hatred of his opponents, his megalomaniac belief in Germany's mission to rule the world. Many of Hitler's friends and associates whose education and maturity were well above her level accepted these things, too. Heike Görtemaker's meticulously researched biography disposes of once and for all Hitler's associates' later, and often self-serving, claims that his private life, including his relationship with his companion, was entirely shut off from the larger world of Nazi politics and ideology. Thus it makes a major contribution to our understanding of the intimate world of the dictator and his entourage, and, beyond this, to our judgement, both in general and in innumerable matters of detail, of the many postwar reminiscences in which they sought to justify themselves.

If Hitler emerges from this story as a man with normal human desires for domestic bliss and sexual fulfilment, does this make him seem less evil? Do we somehow need to believe that people who commit evil deeds are evil in every respect of their lives? Is it somehow more comforting for us to think that a man who deliberately causes millions of innocent people to die, often in the most horrible circumstances, is in some way not really human?

One of the familiar clichés of writing about Nazism is the concentration camp commandant who plays Bach on the violin when he gets home from a day's murder and listens to Mozart on the gramophone for relaxation. Such dichotomies were present in Hitler's life, too. Most biographers of Hitler have written him off as a man without a real human character, a kind of black hole at the centre of Nazism, cut off from normal human emotion by his violent and alienating upbringing, incapable in adulthood of any true feelings except hatred and ambition. *Eva Braun: Life with Hitler* shows that this is too simple a view to take; and for that reason it is deeply troubling to read. For if a man like Hitler was capable of ordinary human love for another person, then what power does love possess?

PART III

THE NAZI ECONOMY

11. ECONOMIC RECOVERY

In the decades since the end of the Cold War, living in a unipolar world dominated by the US has changed the way scholars view the history of twentieth-century Europe. For someone in his mid-thirties, like the British historian Adam Tooze, author of *The Wages of Destruction: The Making and Breaking of the Nazi Economy* (2006), the rise of America to the superpower status it has enjoyed for most of his adult life is the fundamental fact of the last century as well as the present one. Already in the decade from 1924 to 1935, the national income of the US averaged three times more than that of Great Britain, four times more than that of Germany, and five times more than that of France or the Soviet Union. Over the same period, British per capita Gross Domestic Product was running at 89 per cent of the comparable US figure, French at 72 per cent, German at 63 per cent and Soviet at 25 per cent.

European contemporaries were very much aware of these facts; and none more so than Adolf Hitler. Already in his unpublished *Second Book*, written in 1928, he was declaring that 'the European, even without being fully conscious of it, applies the conditions of American life as the yardstick of his life'. For Hitler, who read the Wild West novels of Karl May during his childhood and adolescence, it seemed obvious that America had achieved its industrial advantage and high standard of living through its conquest of the west and its extermination of the Native American population. If Germany, as Europe's leading power, did not do something similar, the 'threatened global hegemony of the North American continent' would degrade all the European powers to the level of 'Switzerland and Holland'. Far from being the revival of some medieval dream of conquest sparked by the example of the Teutonic Knights, Hitler's drive to conquer Eastern Europe was based on a very modern model, a model of colonisation, enslavement and extermination that had its parallels in the creation of European empires in Africa and Australia, or the nineteenth-century Russian conquest of Central Asia and Siberia.

Here, for Hitler, lay the key to Germany's achievement of European dominance: 'In future,' he wrote, 'the only state that will be able to stand up to North America will be the one that has understood how ... to raise the value of its people in racial terms and to bring them into the state form most appropriate for this purpose.' That state form, of course, was the dictatorship of the Third Reich, and as soon as Hitler came to power, he threw off the shackles of the peace settlement concluded at the end of the First World War, which had restricted Germany's army to a maximum of 100,000 men and banned the construction of tanks, aeroplanes, battleships and other essential instruments of modern warfare.

Adam Tooze, whose work so far has focused on the emergence of economic statistics in early twentieth-century Germany, gathers extensive economic data to demonstrate conclusively that rearmament was the motor that drove German economic recovery from the outset of the Third Reich. The Depression had thrown more than a third of the workforce into unemployment, and the Nazis made great play with so-called job creation schemes like the construction of the new freeways, the *Autobahnen*, but in reality even these were meant to serve military purposes (ferrying troops and equipment rapidly around the country); and the number of jobs they actually provided was very small. Unemployment remained at high levels until the introduction of mass conscription soaked up entire generations of young men from 1935 onwards.

Tooze is saying nothing very new here; and his claim to be

overturning an entrenched orthodoxy that puts civilian job creation at the centre of the Nazi economic recovery has to be taken with a pinch of scepticism. Similarly, although he suggests that the evidence he presents for the recovery beginning in the late summer of 1932, six months before Hitler came to power, 'contradicts all subsequent portrayals of the German economy under National Socialism', the fact is that economic historians have long known that the Nazis were lucky in their timing, taking over the German economy just as it was beginning to come out of the Depression. What his book does offer is a mass of evidence that finally puts these arguments beyond dispute. Hitler's drive to rearm was so obsessive, so megalomaniacal, that he was prepared to sacrifice almost anything to it. In particular, consumers suffered as resources and foreign exchange were diverted into arms expenditures. Cotton imports, for example, were hard hit, and people started to complain about the poor quality of the synthetic-fibre clothing that they were forced to wear. Tooze here completely explodes the German historian Götz Aly's claim that the Nazi regime deliberately cushioned the civilian population for fear of alienating it. Contrary to what Aly suggests, Tooze points out that Germany's population was the most heavily taxed in Europe.

In the competition between guns and butter, it was always the former that won out, at least in the short term. Indeed, butter was among the foodstuffs that had to be rationed from the mid-1930s on, as the arms industry began to draw workers away from the farms into Germany's large cities; and the backward peasant-farming sector failed to cope with the demands imposed on it of making the country self-sufficient in food supplies. Hitler was only too aware of the fact that 600,000 German civilians had died of malnutrition and related diseases under the impact of the Allied blockade during the First World War, and he did not want the same thing to happen again, most of all because he thought that the demoralisation this had caused had been one of the factors in Germany's defeat (through the mythical 'stab in the back' supposedly meted out to the German armies by revolutionaries at home).

Lacking the overseas colonies and transatlantic connections of Britain and France, and the resources provided by the vast Eurasian empire of the Soviet Union, Germany was forced, Hitler believed, to fall back as far as possible on its own resources until it could harness the oilfields of the Caucasus and the granaries of Ukraine to its own use. That would be the moment when the sacrifices of the German people would be rewarded with an affluence far beyond anything they had experienced. To achieve this, as he said on numerous occasions from the early 1930s onwards, the conquest of the east, preceded by sharp and decisive blows against Germany's enemies in the west (which meant in the first place France), would be necessary. Hence the need for a huge army, backed by an air force that would be bigger than any other in Europe.

So extensive was Hitler's drive to rearm that it was absorbing over a fifth of German state expenditure by the eve of the war. So much raw material had to be imported to feed the Moloch of the arms industry that serious foreign exchange crises hit the country in 1934 and again in 1939, forcing severe cutbacks in arms expenditures. Among Tooze's most original contributions is his demonstration that these well-known problems had their root in Hitler's refusal to devalue the Reichsmark despite the urgings of numerous economics experts, although he does not really explain why Hitler was unwilling to take this step. So severe was the shortage of hard currency that the regime even undermined its own policy of forcing Germany's Jews to emigrate by banning them from taking their assets and savings with them; this caused a drop in emigration until the violence of the November 1938 pogrom and the forcible dispossession and expropriation of Germany's remaining Jews pushed the figure up again.

Shortages of steel – particularly because of a lack of imports of suitable iron ore – made a mockery of Hitler's irrationally ambitious aim of deploying an air force of 21,000 planes at the beginning of the coming European war, and the army and navy were similarly unable to find the raw materials to equip themselves properly. Gangs of stormtroopers roamed the country tearing down iron railings around parks, cemeteries and even private gardens to be melted down for arms and ammunition, and the chemists of IG Farben worked around the clock to devise synthetic substitutes for rubber and gasoline; but it was all to no avail. Very much aware of these problems, and conscious by the middle of 1939 that Britain and France were rearming apace, Hitler decided to get in the decisive blow while Germany's armaments were still superior to those of its potential enemies. The crisis in armaments was not, as the historian Tim Mason argued, a general crisis of the whole economy, leading to rising worker unrest, but it was severe enough all the same to make Hitler, as he told Mussolini in March 1940, 'begin immediately ... even at the risk of thereby precipitating the war' with 'the Western powers two or three years earlier' than he had always envisioned.

Tooze makes effective use of the work of military historians over the past few years in showing that the famous *Blitzkrieg* strategy of short, decisive blows by rapidly moving armoured columns against an enemy pulverised by heavy air strikes was the result of improvisation, not of careful planning designed to minimise the burden of war on Germany's civilian population. German plans for the invasion of France originally envisioned a direct and probably lengthy confrontation of the main armies. It was only the chance discovery of the plans by the Allies that forced their abandonment and the substitution of the celebrated though extremely risky push through the densely forested Ardennes and the subsequent 'sickle-cut' that disposed of the Allied armies in France and Belgium in the space of a few weeks in 1940. When it came to the invasion of the Soviet Union the following year, the *Blitzkrieg* strategy had an even shakier foundation. It depended for its success on the racist assumption that a country populated by supposedly subhuman Slavs under the leadership of a political elite the Nazis regarded as 'Jewish-Bolshevik' exploiters would collapse after the first defeat, leaving the Third Reich to pick up the pieces. When this did not happen, the Nazis found themselves embroiled in a war they could not hope to win.

Looked at from an economic perspective, indeed, the cards were stacked against the Germans from the outset. Tooze perhaps over-stresses the point when he describes Germany, as he frequently does, as a 'medium-sized European power'; even according to his own fig-ures it far outclassed all other European states with the exception of Britain and the Soviet Union. The point was, however, that by the end of 1941 it had arrayed against it the combined might not only of these two countries, together with the British Empire, still at this time the largest the world had ever seen, but also of the United States. To try to counter this, Hitler more or less abandoned the construction of costly and generally ineffective battleships and poured resources into the U-boat campaign with which he hoped to cut off British supplies from across the Atlantic and force a separate peace. Yet there were too few submarines to make an impact, especially against an enemy that organised an effective convoy system and had the advantage, thanks to the Ultra decodes, of being able to decipher German signals in advance of the operations they unleashed. Once more, the raw materials needed to build and fuel a submarine fleet large enough to overcome these obstacles were simply lacking.

Tooze points to a similar problem with the projected invasion of Britain in the summer and fall of 1940. Irrespective of whether Hitler was really set on this course, he simply lacked the resources to estab-lish the air superiority that was the *sine qua non* of a successful crossing of the English Channel. A third of the initial strength of the German air force, the Luftwaffe, had been lost in the western campaign in the spring. The Germans lacked the trained pilots, the effective fighter planes and the heavy bombers that would have been needed. Moreover, before long the German attempt to gain control over the oil-rich Middle East and also threaten British control over the vital artery of the Suez Canal had suffered a fatal blow when Britain defeated a German-sponsored uprising in Iraq and seized Syria from the Vichy French.

Germany, of course, had at its disposal the resources of conquered countries in Europe, from France in the west to Belarus in the east. The Nazis had no compunction in ruthlessly exploiting the defeated nations to their own advantage. Tooze notes that by 1944 the Germans had taken nearly four million shells, over five thousand artillery pieces and more than two thousand tanks from the French. Nearly half of all German artillery guns in March 1944 were non-German. Enough tin and nickel was seized after the victories in the west to cover German needs for a year, enough copper for eight months. France was drained of almost all its gasoline supplies. Yet such exploitation contributed to a collapse of the French economy in 1940, and the confiscated resources did not last for very long. This was another reason for Hitler's avoiding any further delay in pushing on with the invasion of the Soviet Union.

When German armies marched into the Soviet-controlled part of Poland and then Ukraine in June 1941, they soon scored a series of stunning victories, surrounding and killing or capturing millions of Red Army troops. Here, too, shortages of fuel and ammunition quickly affected the German armies as their rapid advance stretched their supply lines to the breaking point. More serious still was the food situation. It was no use commandeering the Ukrainian collective farms if there was no gasoline to run the tractors and combine harvesters. Millions of German troops had to be fed, and more resources still were needed to sustain the civilian population back home, not to mention the foreign workers who were being forced into the country by the million to boost the labour supply.

The Nazis and the German military decided to deal with this problem through the planned starvation of the native population of the occupied areas of Eastern Europe. At least three and a third million Soviet prisoners of war were deliberately killed in German captivity, allowed to die of starvation, disease and neglect, or simply shot. Nearly three-quarters of a million people perished during the German siege of Leningrad as a deliberate result of the blockade. German plans for the region envisaged the deaths of up to thirty million of its civilian inhabitants over the following years as German settlers were moved in to populate its towns, cities and manor houses. This was mass murder on a historically unprecedented scale.

Nazi antisemitism was being fuelled by 1941 by Hitler's growing obsession with Franklin D. Roosevelt, who was steering American supplies to Britain and, soon, the Soviet Union in ever-increasing quantities. In December 1941, assuming that America would be preoccupied with the Japanese following the attack on Pearl Harbor, Hitler declared war on the US. Convinced of the existence of a Jewish axis uniting Stalin, Churchill and Roosevelt (or, rather, of dark Jewish forces he imagined were manipulating them), he had already embarked on a campaign of mass murder against Europe's Jews. Here, too, however, there were contradictions.

Killing millions of able-bodied Jews hardly seemed rational at a time of increasingly desperate manpower shortages in the German economy. Tooze argues that the idea of 'annihilation through labour' was a compromise between the SS, who wanted to kill all the Jews, and economic and political leaders who wanted to make use of those judged fit for work. In practice, of course, the latter were a very small proportion of the whole. Tooze suggests that at the Wannsee Conference early in 1942, arranged to coordinate the logistics of the 'Final Solution of the Jewish Question in Europe', as the Nazis euphemistically put it, Himmler's deputy Reinhard Heydrich, in the chair, 'referred neither to gassing nor shooting as a means of disposing of the Jewish populations of Poland or Western Europe. Instead, he proposed that they should be evacuated eastward in giant construction columns', and used on the building of roads. But in fact the minutes of the meeting identified two and a half million Jews who lived in the 'General Government' part of occupied Poland as unfit for work. Nobody present at the conference was left in any doubt that they were to be killed. Goebbels recorded in his diary that around 40 per cent of the Jews were to be used on construction schemes. From the outset, however, they were kept on inadequate rations, beaten, housed in desperately unsanitary conditions and generally regarded as expendable, as, to an only slightly lesser degree, were the foreign workers who were now brought into the German economy in growing numbers.

Unlike some German historians who have recently written about this topic, Tooze is alive to the importance of ideology and the role of Hitler in directing the extermination programme. Yet there is a danger here of making it all seem too instrumental. If, for example, food shortages in April and May 1942 were the key factor in prompting the Nazi leadership to kill the remaining Jews of Poland and occupied Eastern Europe, how does one explain the fact that Western European Jews were already being shipped off to the extermination camps by this time? The war was still going relatively well for Hitler in the spring of 1942. Yet the resilience of the Soviet Union was as unsettling as it was unexpected. Largely independently of US aid, Stalin's industries, safely located well behind the battlefront, were outperforming their German counterparts and producing considerably greater quantities of arms, ammunition and equipment. By 1942, the Soviet Union managed to build four tanks for every German tank, three guns for every German gun and two combat aeroplanes for every German one. The Soviet effort was successfully concentrated on turning out a small range of armaments in huge factories. German war production was already using up virtually all the available resources. But according to Albert Speer, Hitler's personal architect, who took over as Armaments Minister in early February 1942, it was chaotic and poorly organised, and frittered away resources on far too many different products. After the war, Speer claimed to have taken the process by the scruff of the neck and boosted German war production simply by getting it properly organised. Portraying himself as an unpolitical technocrat, he took a perverse pride in his achievements, underlining them by claiming further to have had no knowledge of, or participation in, the genocidal policies being pursued by his master, Hitler.

Tooze comprehensively demolishes the myth so carefully crafted by Albert Speer, a myth that deceived generations of historians and journalists, from Joachim Fest to Gitta Sereny. Of course, he is not the first to try to puncture its dubious claims, but once again, he provides so much information so convincingly that he leaves no more room for doubt. Speer, he shows, not only fixed the statistics to make it look as if he was achieving more than he actually did; he also managed to take the credit for improvements in production that were already in the pipeline when he took over. Other economic managers, notably the air force's Erhard Milch and the Economics Ministry's Hans Kehrl, played an important part here, a part Speer successfully managed to obscure in his postwar testimony. He was never the complete armaments supremo he later claimed to have been. Armaments production did increase in 1943 and 1944. Much of this was owing to the dispatch of forced labour, including Jews and concentration camp inmates, to the arms factories, where appalling living conditions ensured high mortality rates, and draconian rules and regulations prescribed shooting or beheading for the most trivial offences. Moreover, quality was sacrificed to quantity, with resources being diverted into mass-producing inferior tanks and aircraft that were no match for those being built by the British, the Americans and the Soviets.

Of course, there was a range of new, technically very sophisticated weaponry under development, including jet fighters, rockets, U-boats that could stay underwater for prolonged periods of time, and, notably, the atomic bomb. But research and development on such 'wonder-weapons' inevitably took years, and Germany did not have years. Development was mostly rushed and botched, and these weapons never made much difference to the war; even the V-2 rockets that rained down on London in the final phase of the war were not able to carry the warheads they needed to have a really serious effect on the outcome of the conflict. In any case, what was really needed at this time was some means of defending Germany against Allied air raids from the west and the onward march of the Red Army from the east. The former caused real devastation to arms factories and military facilities in heavy industrial areas like the Ruhr, and progressively damaged German civilian morale until people even began to lose confidence in Hitler, who responded by ratcheting up terror and repression against his own people in the final months of the war. Conditions deteriorated rapidly in Germany's towns and cities, with inflation spawning an ever-expanding black market and living standards plummeting.

Tooze does not give much credence to the German historian Götz Aly's argument that, until this point, the regime had done its best to cushion the civilian population against the effects of the war. But even on his own admission, it held off raising taxes on private incomes, preferring to place the burden on businesses instead. Its failure to mobilise women for work in the hard-pressed armaments factories has been the focus of a great deal of attention from feminist historians. Tooze bypasses this by pointing out that female participation in the labour force was already very high in Germany, so that the room for increasing it was extremely limited. There is surely more to say about it than this. Nazi ideology did not allow any campaigns for the recruitment of the German equivalent of Rosie the Riveter, the brawny young woman featured on American recruiting posters. Hitler was keen to avoid discontent on the home front by providing allowances to the wives of soldiers that were generous enough to dissuade them from seeking jobs. Nevertheless, however much it tried, the regime could not protect people from bombing, food rationing and increasing economic misery; Aly is certainly wrong in his claim that, even during the war, the German people had 'never had it so good'. Ideology, as Tooze demonstrates, was the real force behind what Speer was trying to do. More realistic economic managers had already concluded in 1942 that the war could not be won. For Speer, however, anything was possible through the 'triumph of the will'. Of all the leading fanatics in the regime who were most adamant that the war should be fought to the bitter end, Speer was one of the most vocal and persistent.

The Wages of Destruction will doubtless excite discussion and debate for years to come. In his relentless focus on the economics of armaments, Tooze perhaps neglects other aspects of the Nazi economy, such as the role of big business, the 'Aryanisation' of Jewish enterprises and the living standards of the military and civilian population. All of these, of course, are mentioned, but one wishes he had more to say about them. For the moment, however, Tooze's book takes its place immediately as the leading account of the economic history of Nazi Germany in any language, including German. Parts of it are inevitably somewhat technical, or clogged with statistical detail, and the use of some specialised economic jargon was doubtless unavoidable. Nevertheless, Tooze has a gift for narrative and an ability to coin a striking phrase, and few have come closer to making economic history genuinely readable. If his approach makes the outcome of the war seem all too predetermined, that, at least, is a valuable corrective to those many accounts that have little or nothing to say about the 'sinews of war' without which no battle could have been fought, and no victory won.

12. THE PEOPLE'S CAR

When I first went to Germany in the early 1970s, the roads were swarming with the squat, misshapen little beasts, bustling about the city streets or rattling along the autobahns with their noisy, air-cooled engines, their curved roofs tapering to a point at the back, and, in the older models, their tiny oval back windows, so small that I wondered how the driver could see anything at all in his rear-view mirror. The ugliness of their exterior appearance, however, was nothing in comparison to the horror of actually being taken for a ride inside one of them: sitting in the back seat, as I often had to when I was being driven around with a group of friends, I was oppressed by the sense of claustrophobia imposed by the low roof, while the loud rattling and whirring of the engine behind me quickly gave me a headache, made worse by the repulsive smell of the heating system when it was turned on during the winter months. Turning corners at speed – or such speed as the vehicle could muster – was a nightmare, as the car rocked and rolled and churned up my stomach.

I much preferred my father's pale blue Morris Minor, with its upright design, roomy interior and quiet, front-mounted engine. With the British car there was the additional charm of the quaint semaphore-style left and right indicators, which emerged from the bodywork to stick out horizontally like tiny, glowing amber arms (which, however, always threatened to break off when you opened the front door). Faced with this practical and yet somehow elegant vehicle, who would want to buy a Volkswagen Beetle? Yet the Beetle was the most successful car of its time, selling more than any other, as Bernhard Rieger notes in *The People's Car* (2013), his entertaining, illuminating and elegantly written new study of the vehicle's history. While a total of more than 1.3 million Morris Minors were sold over the decades, Beetle sales were exceeding one million *each year* in the late 1960s and early 1970s, when one car in every three on West German roads was a Volkswagen. In 1972 its total sales even passed those of what had been up to that point the most popular passenger car of the century, Henry Ford's Model T.

Like other popular small cars, the Morris Minor was, of course, exported and manufactured under licence abroad, but it was so emphatically English in style and conception that its popularity was mostly confined to countries of the British Empire and Commonwealth like New Zealand, where the last models rolled off the production line in 1974 and plenty of them were still on the roads when I first visited the country in the mid-1980s (nowadays all the cars there seem to be Japanese). The Beetle, by contrast, was a truly global vehicle, achieving large sales in the United States and still being manufactured in Mexico after the turn of the century.

What was the secret of its extraordinary popularity? Its origins were hardly auspicious. Though most people chose to ignore the fact after the war, the Volkswagen Beetle began life in the 1930s. When he came to power, Hitler was determined to bring Germany up to what he thought of as the level of modernity common in other advanced economies like Britain and America (Rieger's account is another nail in the coffin of the old interpretation of Nazism as a backward-looking, atavistic sociopolitical force). Relatively few people owned a radio, for example; so Hitler's Propaganda Minister, Joseph Goebbels, introduced the People's Receiver (*Volksempgänger*), a cheap and cheerful little wireless, set to short-wave so that listeners couldn't tune into foreign broadcasters. Fridges were even rarer, so the Nazi government introduced the People's Refrigerator (*Volkskühlschrank*). Soon there were many other products with similar names and similar intentions. The People's Car (*Volkswagen*) belonged to this milieu; in fact, though it was widely referred to by this name, its official title was the 'Strength through Joy Car' (*KdF-Wagen*), signifying its association with the Labour Front's leisure programme (though to anyone who's ever been in a Beetle, neither strength nor joy seems an appropriate term to describe the experience).

From the outset, Hitler was determined to modernise Germany's roads. In the early 1930s, Germany was one of Western Europe's least motorised societies. This was partly because its public transport even then was second to none – smoothly efficient, quick, omnipresent and all-encompassing. Germans mostly felt they didn't really need cars. And in any case even had they wanted cars, they couldn't have afforded them. The economic disasters of the Weimar Republic had depressed domestic demand. So empty were German roads, indeed, that Berlin, the Weimar Republic's lively metropolis, did not find it necessary to install any traffic lights until 1925.

Three-quarters of Germany's population were labourers, artisans, farmworkers and peasants, unable to purchase the expensive products of Daimler-Benz or any of the country's twenty-seven separate car manufacturers, whose inefficient production methods and small outputs led to models that only the intermittently affluent bourgeoisie could buy. To reach current American levels of car ownership, Hitler told the automobile show in Berlin in 1934, Germany had to increase the number of cars on its roads from half a million to twelve million. Even the British had six times more cars relative to their population than the Germans did. To the further dismay of German nationalists, the country's most successful mass vehicle manufacturers were both foreign – Ford, who opened a factory in Cologne in 1931, and General Motors, who operated the Opel car factory at Rüsselsheim. By the early 1930s, Opel cars were dominating the German passenger vehicle market, with 40 per cent of annual sales.

Hitler pursued his motorisation project on several levels. Building the famous motorways, the *Autobahnen*, was one, though the loudly trumpeted benefits it brought to employment were grossly exaggerated by Goebbels's propaganda machine. Another was the promotion of motor-racing, where hefty government subsidies brought the German speedsters built by Daimler-Benz and Auto-Union victory in nineteen of the twenty-three Grand Prix races held from 1934 to 1937. Ideology played an important role here. Pursuing its stated goal of national unity, the government replaced local regulations with a Reich-wide Highway Code in 1934. Far from imposing a straitjacket of regulation on drivers, as one might have expected, the Code placed its trust in the Aryan individual's consciously willed subordination to the interests of the racial community. Owners of expensive cars had to put 'discipline' and 'chivalry' first and thus bridge outmoded class antagonisms on the roads. The Jews, of course, couldn't be trusted to do this, so they were banned from driving or owning cars from 1938 onwards.

The automobile, Hitler declared, responded to the individual will, unlike the railway, which had brought 'individual liberty in transport to an end'. So the new Highway Code abolished all speed restrictions on German roads. The results were catastrophic. In the first six years of the Third Reich the annual figure of deaths on the roads rose to nearly 8,000, with up to 40,000 seriously injured each year, the worst accident rates in Europe (worse even than those of Great Britain, where speed limits had been abolished in 1933 in the belief that Britons would behave on the road like gentlemen – they did not, of course, and speed limits were introduced again in 1934, just as the Germans were abolishing theirs). By May 1939 the Nazi regime had to admit defeat and reimposed speed restrictions on all roads except the motorways, which continue to be without them even today, making them the most terrifying roads to drive on in the whole of Europe.

Cars, Hitler proclaimed, had to lose their 'class-based, and, as a sad consequence, class-dividing character'. They had to be available to everyone. What was needed was a home-built vehicle that bridged the social divide.

He commissioned the Austrian engineer Ferdinand Porsche to design an affordable car for ordinary people (in a typically Nazi addendum, officials required him to ensure that a machine gun could be mounted on the bonnet if necessary). Ambitious and politically skilled, Porsche secured Hitler's backing for a huge new factory built on the most modern lines to reduce costs by streamlining production. The Labour Front put its vast funds at Porsche's disposal and sent him on an inspection tour of car factories in the United States, where he hired a number of engineers of German extraction to take back with him to work on the new car. Hitler opened the Volkswagen factory near Fallersleben, in what is now Lower Saxony, in 1938. A new town was begun to accommodate the workers, and all seemed set to go.

The Labour Front unfolded a vigorous propaganda campaign designed to get people to join a savings scheme for the new car. Rieger shows an illustration of the official savings book, in which people stuck red stamps worth five Reichsmarks each until they reached the total of 990 Reichsmarks required to buy their first Volkswagen. Over a quarter of a million people enrolled in less than eighteen months. Impressive though this total seemed, however, it fell far short of the millions envisaged by the regime. With this level of enrolment, the scheme would never even remotely have covered the costs of production. Most of the savers were middle-class, and a third of them had a car of their own already; the masses simply couldn't afford the level of savings required. Moreover, as Rieger points out, the mass abstentions from the scheme reflected a widespread anxiety about the future generated by the Nazis' increasingly bellicose foreign policy. Rather than invest their hard-earned Reichsmarks in what was still, for them, a relatively expensive car, the working classes preferred the much cheaper motorbike instead, whose sales soared from 894,000 in 1934 to 1,582,872 in 1939. This was the true 'people's vehicle', even though its popularity was still dwarfed by that of the humble pushbike, of which there were some twenty million in Germany on the eve of the war, underlining yet again that most Germans cycled to work and thought of the motor car as a leisure vehicle if they thought of it at all.

Ordinary Germans were right to be sceptical about the savings scheme. Not one of the people who signed up ever got a Volkswagen of their own, at least not from the funds they invested in the Nazi era. The money all went into arms production. So, too, did the factory. Only 630 production models of the Beetle were made before the war, most of them snapped up by leading officials in the regime. In 1939, as the workers in the Volkswagen factory were whisked off to labour on the western fortification lines of the Reich, the regime was only able to keep production going by obtaining 6,000 labourers from Mussolini's Italy. They were housed in wooden barracks, since only 10 per cent of the planned accommodation in the new city had been completed by September 1939. The product they worked on was a military version of the Beetle, with the chassis used as the base for a German version of the jeep, the 'bucket vehicle' (*Kübelwagen*), which saw service wherever the German armed forces operated, from North Africa to the Eastern Front.

The Volkswagen factory was not at the top of Bomber Command's list of military facilities to be destroyed. At the end of the war, Ivan Hirst, a major in the Engineers, arrived from Britain to inspect it. He found that 70 per cent of its buildings and 90 per cent of its machinery were still intact. The British Zone of Occupation had to cater for the transportation needs of some twenty-two million inhabitants with a mere 61,000 motor cars, nearly two-thirds of which were described as 'worn out'. Railway track and rolling stock, which had been on Bomber Command's list, were in ruins. Needing rapid improvements in communications, the British military government ordered Hirst to start up production of the Beetle again. Applying the ideas and methods of 'trusteeship' derived from British colonial experience in Africa, Hirst set to work, using the existing staff at the factory. When more than 200 senior managers and technical experts were dismissed by denazification tribunals, Hirst found substitutes or had the verdicts overturned, in a triumph of necessity over legality and morality typical of the late 1940s in occupied Germany. He also managed to recruit 6,000 workers by the end of 1946. But Volkswagen's resurrection had been too hasty. The cars were dogged by mechanical and other problems. British auto engineers who visited the factory concluded that the noisy, smelly and underpowered Beetle had no future. The idea of relocating the vast factory to Britain was deemed impracticable. So it was handed over to the Germans.

The situation was rescued by Heinrich Nordhoff, an Opel engineer who enjoyed close contacts with the company's owners in America, General Motors. Although he was not a member of the Nazi Party, Nordhoff had contributed to the war economy by running the Opel truck factory, the largest in Europe, and was banned from employment in the American sector because of his extensive use of forced foreign labour. The British did not mind. Nordhoff threw himself into his new job with manic intensity, working fourteen hours a day to streamline the production process, eliminate the car's technical deficiencies, expand the dealership network and establish an effective, hierarchical management structure at the plant. The car was offered for sale in bright colours, or, as Nordhoff put it, given a 'paint job absolutely characteristic of peacetime'. Production figures began to climb, and sales started to improve.

But it was not so easy to shake off the Volkswagen's Nazi past. The factory town was now named Wolfsburg after a nearby castle (though some may have recalled that 'Wolf' was Hitler's nickname among his cronies, so the name could be translated as 'Hitler's Fortress'). As housing construction got under way, Wolfsburg was crowded with refugees and expellees from the east – some of the eleven million ethnic Germans thrown out of Poland, Czechoslovakia and other Eastern European countries at the end of the war. Burning with resentment, they proved easy prey for ultra-nationalist agitators, and by 1948, unusually for postwar West Germany, the neo-Nazi German Justice Party was garnering nearly two-thirds of the local vote, while factory walls were repeatedly daubed with swastikas and many ballot papers were marked with the words 'we want Adolf Hitler'. As a new town, Wolfsburg lacked politicians with the experience to counter this kind of extremist nostalgia. Only gradually did the established political parties manage to push the neo-Nazis back into the shadows.

They were aided in this task by Heinrich Nordhoff, who insisted that Germans' travails in the late 1940s were the result of 'a war that we started and that we lost'. This unusual frankness had its limits: he did not mention the mass murder of the Jews or any of the Nazis' other crimes. He even, no doubt unconsciously, echoed Nazi language in urging workers to overcome the difficulties that faced them and focus on 'achievement' (*Leistung*), just as Hitler in 1942 had urged 'a battle of achievement for German enterprises' in war production. Whatever the resonances of the rhetoric, the workers certainly did 'achieve'. While the Opel and Ford factories, badly affected by war damage, were struggling to get production under way again, the Volkswagen plant was already turning out Beetles in large numbers. Its efficiency improved steadily during the 1950s as Nordhoff introduced full automation on lines pioneered in Detroit. In August 1955 the millionth Beetle rolled off the production line, gold-painted, with its bumper encrusted with rhinestones, before an audience of 100,000. Twelve marching bands played tunes by Johann Strauss, a troupe from the Moulin Rouge danced the cancan, a black South African choir sang spirituals and thirty-two female Scottish dancers performed the Highland Fling to the sound of an ensemble of bagpipes. Reporters were wooed with lavish entertainment, while the event, and the achievement of the Volkswagen factory, were brought to the wider public in a seventy-five-minute movie.

The Volkswagen Beetle, as Rieger plausibly argues, achieved iconic status in West Germany during the 1950s by taking its place as a typical product of the 'economic miracle': not flashy or glamorous, but solid, functional, dependable, inexpensive to acquire, cheap to run and easy to maintain: everything the Third Reich was not. It was so lacking in frills that it wasn't even fitted with a fuel gauge: drivers had to keep a record of their mileage or risk running out of fuel. Through the 1950s and 1960s modifications were introduced, including hydraulic brakes, a fully synchronised gearbox and a larger and more powerful engine, but its basic appeal remained. While Nordhoff continued obsessively to root out and solve minor technical problems, he also established a dense network of dealerships and service stations where the cars could be quickly fixed if anything went wrong. As West Germany became a 'levelled-out middle-class society', the Beetle became the levelled-out middle class's car of choice.

Lacking obvious symbols of national identification, Germany to the west of the fortified border that divided it from the Communist east fixed on the Beetle as a national icon. Car ownership suited the retreat of German society into private and family life in reaction to the over-heated and overpoliticised public sphere of the Nazi era. The liberty to drive anywhere, where and when you chose, was celebrated by politicians as a key aspect of Western freedom in the era of the Cold War. The Beetle's Nazi associations were forgotten in a 'historical car-wash' that ascribed its origins to the individual genius of Ferdinand Porsche. War veterans liked it because they fondly remembered driv-ing its relative, the jeep-like 'bucket vehicle', on campaign. Younger Germans liked it for its utilitarian sobriety. It represented for Germans the 'new landscape of desire' of the sober, conservative 1950s.

Before long, however, car-owners were personalising their Beetles by purchasing accessories, sticking on chromium strips, respraying the exterior in garish colours, or adding so many decorations that the car looked like 'a rolling Christmas tree', as one critic put it. Small vases installed in the interior to carry flowers picked on outings were par-ticularly popular. Journalists noted with amusement the owner's ritual of washing the car, devoting to it 'a degree of love and care that could lead detached observers to believe he was flirting with a new lover'. Rieger is particularly good on the gendered nature of Beetle-owner-ship. At a time when less than 20 per cent of car licences in West Germany were held by women, the Beetle became a vehicle for 'auto-motive misogyny' as men did all they could to keep women away from the steering wheel. Advertising campaigns underscored the male-dominated nature of car-ownership by portraying the left half of a man's face merged with the right half of the front of a Beetle under the slogan: 'His Better Half'. Only gradually, during the 1960s, did women begin to assert themselves, but it's arguable the Beetle always remained largely an object of a specifically masculine desire.

Desire of another sort found expression in the car's interior as young couples used it as a 'zone of privacy', away from overcrowded apartments and disapproving adults. A car manual solemnly pointed out that sex in a Beetle did not qualify as indecency in the eyes of the law so long as the car was not parked in a prominent location. Thirty years after having sex with his girlfriend in the back of a Beetle, a journalist from Bremen confessed that he was still overcome by a 'strangely fascinating weakness in the groin' whenever he saw one of the cars in the street. It was left to the Mexicans, however, to discover the full erotic potential of the Volkswagen Beetle (known there as a *vochito*). 'It is not just that many *vochitos* were made in Mexico', one owner said later: 'many Mexicans were also made in *vochitos*.' It's hard to imagine: they must all have been contortionists.

The car started to be manufactured under licence in Mexico in 1967, with the millionth vehicle coming off the production line in 1980. Like its German counterpart, the expanding Mexican lower middle class found the Beetle an attractive alternative to imported American gas-guzzlers including the misnamed 'compacts'. When economic crisis hit the country in the 1980s, the manufacturers cut the price of the car by 20 per cent, opening it up to new purchasers. It became the vehicle of choice for taxi-drivers. The *vochito* appealed not only to petty-bourgeois ideals of reliability and sobriety but even to Mexican national pride: manufactured in Mexico by Mexicans, it needed very little to keep it going and survived in rough conditions, just like the Mexicans themselves. As one fan explained, the *vochito* was like a 'small tank'. This was meant as praise rather than criticism.

The Beetle also came to be manufactured in Brazil, and it is a pity that Rieger does not say anything about its image and its popularity in South America's largest country. He is very good, however, on its appeal in the United States, where it became the second car of choice for many homeowners in the expanding suburbs of the 1950s and 1960s, as American manufacturers were unable to keep pace with the rapidly rising demand for vehicles. By 1968 the Volkswagen company was shipping more than half a million Beetles across the Atlantic every year, accounting for 40 per cent of its total production. Altogether it was sold to no fewer than five million Americans. In sharp contrast to the situation in Germany, the Beetle was overwhelmingly driven in America by women, and used for practical purposes such as driving to shopping malls. By the 1970s it had even become an icon of the counterculture, with John Muir's *How to Keep Your Volkswagen Alive* selling more than two million copies. Muir encouraged readers to 'feel with your car'; its 'Karma,' he wrote, 'depends on your desire to make it and keep it – ALIVE'. The startling culmination of this process of anthropomorphisation came with the 1969 Disney movie *The Love Bug*, where a Beetle with a personality rewarded his owner, an unsuccessful competitive driver, with success and, in the end, love. The vehicle's improbable association with sex had even found its way on to the big screen.

All of this illustrated the sturdy and reliable Beetle's outstanding global capacity to adapt to whatever environment it happened to find itself in. Foreign sales kept the company going even as the era of the Beetle came to an end in Germany itself, when the oil crisis of 1973–4, along with changing fashions, tough new safety regulations and a failure to keep up the pace of automation, caused domestic sales to slump. With the end of the 'economic miracle' came the end of the Beetle, its prime symbol. West Germans began to demand cars that were faster, roomier, more comfortable, more elegant in design. The new Volkswagen Golf fitted the bill, along with its smaller, cheaper version, the Polo. In 1978 Wolfsburg stopped manufacturing the Beetle altogether. In due course, Volkswagen introduced a 'New Beetle', appealing to the American fashion for retro-chic but also making it clear that this was a vehicle that fully met the demands of twenty-first-century motorists ('Less Flower – More Power' as one advertisement put it). It was made in Mexico, and models for sale in Germany were now exported across the Atlantic. 'It was as if a movie was running backwards,' remarked one journalist on seeing the cars being unloaded at the quayside from which so many Beetles had been exported in the past. The new Beetle was a symbol not only of postmodern irony but also of transnationalism and globalisation. Its curving silhouette was deliberately designed to echo that of the original model.

Yet owners of the old Beetle know it's not the same. They now gather at locations around the world for rallies where they can indulge in nostalgic admiration of historic models and imaginative customisations. One such meeting has been held every year since the 1980s at the old site of the Nazi Party's own Nuremberg Rallies, in front of the grandstand from which Hitler used to deliver his speeches. Nobody seems to notice. The wheel of history hasn't really come full circle, however; the Beetle has long since become a globalised product, for most if not all people entirely detached from its Nazi origins. In 1998, when the *New York Times* columnist Gerald Posner told his mother-in-law, whom he described as a 'conservative Jew', that he had bought a New Beetle, she replied: 'Congratulations, darling. Maybe the war is finally over.'

13. THE ARMS OF KRUPP

'Of all the names which have become associated with the Nuremberg Trials,' declared the prosecutor at the proceedings intended to bring the surviving Nazi leaders to justice at the end of the Second World War, 'I suppose that none has been a household word for so many decades – indeed for nearly a century – as that of Krupp.' Its history, the indictment continued, had made the firm 'the focus, the symbol, and the beneficiary, of the most sinister forces engaged in menacing the peace of Europe'. Krupp was very much a family enterprise: 'Four generations of the Krupp family,' the indictment noted, 'have owned and operated the great armament and munitions plants which have been the chief source of Germany's war supplies.' The tradition of the Krupp firm, and the 'social-political' attitude for which it stood, was exactly suited to the moral climate of the Third Reich. There was no crime such a state could commit – whether war, plunder or slavery – in which these men would not participate. Long before the Nazis came to power, Krupp was a 'National Socialist model plant'.

At the Nuremberg trial, and at the subsequent trial of leading industrialists held in 1947–8, 'Krupp' came to stand not so much for Nazism as for the economic impulse behind the deeper forces of militarism which the Allies were equally determined to drive out of German politics, culture and society. Given the sinister international reputation of the firm, as the arms manufacturer behind Germany's military aggression from Bismarck's wars of unification through two world wars, it's not surprising that it has attracted the attention of many different historians writing from different points of view. The most widely read was *The Arms of Krupp,* a thousand-page epic published in 1968 by William Manchester, better known for his account of the assassination of his wartime friend John F. Kennedy, *Death of a President.* Written in a racy, sometimes sensational style, the book was full of sweeping generalisations about Germany and the Germans, whom Manchester, not least as a result of his war experiences, clearly did not like. The Krupps were demonised from start to finish, and there was more than a whiff of muckraking about Manchester's whole approach. The book received a mixed reception even in the popular press, with reviewers unhappy about its sarcastic style and what *Time* magazine called the 'swarms of errors' that littered its pages. Nevertheless, with his customary thoroughness, Manchester had worked hard in the Krupp company and other archives, in the Nuremberg trial documents, and in many other sources, and he had interviewed a substantial number of people. He unearthed a huge mass of material, much of it previously unknown, and on particular issues, such as the question of Krupp's attitude to Hitler in 1932–3, before the Nazi seizure of power, he clearly stuck to the documentary record and did not make claims that went beyond it.

Manchester was not an economic historian, and he was more interested in the personalities of the Krupps than in their business. Before he published there had been hardly any historical studies of major German companies and their role in the Third Reich, and his book was not only pioneering in this respect but held the field for many years, until other studies began to appear from the 1990s onwards (one of the reasons for the delay was that German companies, including Krupp, were so incensed by Manchester's book that they made it very difficult for some time after its publication for historians to gain access to their archives). In the last few years, however, serious accounts of the firm's history have begun to appear, and now they have been joined by a chronological overview from Harold James, a British economic historian who teaches at Princeton. The sober style of *Krupp: A History of the Legendary German Firm* (2012) could not be more different from Manchester's, and its focus on the technological and economic history of the business is a world away from Manchester's relentless exposure of the personal foibles and misdemeanours of the company's successive owners.

Like Manchester, James begins at the beginning, though his coverage is roughly even across time, where *The Arms of Krupp* focused heavily on the Nazi years. As James notes, the company's beginnings could hardly have been more inauspicious. Its founder, Friedrich Krupp, was a risk-taker of no mean proportions, and most of his industrial gambles ended in abject failure. His grandmother, Helene Amalie Krupp, the first of a series of powerful women who would play a pivotal role in the dynasty's history, left him a fortune based on her canny investments in retailing, trade and property. Her business interests included a small but unprofitable ironworks, in which Friedrich had gained some of his earliest experience, and though it had been sold off, Friedrich was left with a strong desire to produce steel and steel products 'in the English manner', combining toughness and malleability.

Friedrich squandered his grandmother's inheritance in pursuit of this obsession. He experimented with different raw materials, different locations and different techniques. Debts piled up, he was crossed off the official list of local businessmen in 1824, and in 1826 he died, exhausted, at the age of thirty-nine. His widow Therese, however, continued to have faith in his vision, and carried on the business, assisted by their fourteen-year-old son Alfried, who Anglicised his name to Alfred in homage to England's domination of industry and technology at the time. In 1838, indeed, he travelled to England (incognito, as 'Herr Schropp'), returning in 1843 and continuing to send agents there to learn the latest factory designs and industrial techniques, to win new customers and to spread his reputation in what was then the world's richest country.

Alfred was a workaholic, who later reminded people that in those early days 'I was the chief executive, clerk, treasurer, smith, smelter, coke beater, nightwatchman at the cement oven, as well as much else, and one run-down horse served our transportation needs.' His father's one indisputable success had been in developing a process for casting steel for the manufacture of steel stamps used in the production of coins. Soon Alfred was supplying coining rolls to the Austrian mint, and branching out into the production of rolls for the manufacture of spoons, which he marketed in France, Russia, England and even Brazil. His real breakthrough came with the railway boom of the 1840s, when he began supplying axles and crankshafts to the Prussian state railways. Continuing technical innovations enabled him to produce cast steel rings for use on railway wheels – three intertwined rings became what is still the company logo – then rails, as well as steel plates and propellers and shafts for steamships. All this allowed Krupp to buy up other firms and acquire iron ore mines, while the introduction of the Bessemer and Siemens-Martin processes allowed him to make more and bigger steel products, employing 12,000 workers on a 35-hectare site in Essen by 1874, three times the size it had been a decade earlier.

Alfred Krupp was well aware that skilled and reliable workers in the conditions of rapid industrial growth that characterised the Ruhr in his time were often hard to come by. They frequently changed jobs in order to get better wages or conditions. They needed discipline and organisation to operate the dangerous process of casting steel with the precision it required. Yet Krupp wanted 'loyal workers ... who are grateful in heart and deed for the fact that we offer them bread'. In order to induce them to work for him and to stay once they had arrived, he set up a health and pension fund for his employees, built housing blocks in which more than 25,000 people were living by the end of the century, opened fifty-five company stores and canteens, set up schools and eventually provided a hospital, a convalescent home and a library.

There was a flipside to this paternalism, however. Alfred declared that 'nobody shall dare to rise up against a benevolent rule; I'd rather it was all blown up.' To enforce discipline, he declared in 1871: 'I wish to introduce for ever the practice of photographing workers, and a much stricter control of the workforce, of their past, their impulses, their life. We must have a private police that is better informed than the municipal service.' Photography was indeed used to deal with what James calls 'troublemakers'. Krupp told his staff that 'the best and most skilled worker or master is removed as soon as possible if he even appears to incite opposition or to belong to an association': by which he meant a trade union.

The workers were *Kruppianer*, and Alfred even wanted to oversee their morals. 'Morality,' declared the Krupp General Regulation of 1872, 'allied to order and loyalty, had a beneficial effect – without it there will be deceit, disorder, depravity, disloyalty with ruin in its train.' In 1877, before a national election, as Manchester noted, Krupp posted notices in all his shops telling his workers to leave politics to their betters: 'Issues of high policy require more time and knowledge than the workman has at his command.' After the elections he summarily dismissed thirty employees for allegedly spreading socialist propaganda. He required his workers to swear an oath of loyalty and was dissuaded from issuing them with uniforms with gold braid for good service only by the argument that the foul factory air would quickly ruin them. His private police force was larger than the municipal one in Essen, and was used to levy fines for lateness for work, insolence towards superiors and much else besides. The policemen were instructed to ransack the rubbish bins outside Krupp shops and housing blocks for socialist literature and 'used toilet paper' with seditious text printed on it. He even told his employees to marry and have lots of children 'to provide the state with plenty of loyal subjects and to develop a special breed of workers for the factory'. This neo-feudal management style did indeed foreshadow the later development of the 'Nazi model plant', with its 'leaders' and their 'retinue', and its combination of welfare provisions with authoritarianism.

James says far too little about this aspect of the Krupp enterprise, which is covered in detail by Manchester; indeed, the workers barely get a mention, and where they do it's only to emphasise the company's paternalism, not its almost totalitarian regimentation of its employees. This is emphatically a top-down history of the company. James is at pains to stress, too, that armaments made up only a part of its production, except in time of war. Yet even if Krupp did not begin as an arms manufacturer, there was, as James notes, 'a synergy between military and nonmilitary production' that now underpinned the company's rapid expansion through all the economic vagaries of the coming decades. As the railway boom began to fade, growing international tension caused European countries to arm, and Krupp was well placed to take advantage of this new development.

Unlike his father, Alfred was a skilled promoter of his own products, a showman who believed publicity could win him customers. He used multiple crucibles simultaneously to case a 4300-pound steel block which he showed at the Great Exhibition in 1851, winning a medal for it. But he also exhibited a shiny steel cannon, undermining the claim advanced in the exhibition catalogue that 'the Palace of Industry was a Temple of Peace'. 'The English will have their eyes opened,' he claimed exultantly. (Subsequently, the firm produced the Paris Gun, which bombarded Paris with 94-kilogram shells fired through a barrel 34 metres long at a distance of 120 kilometres in the final months of the First World War, and an 80cm cannon called 'Dora', mounted on a huge railway chassis, in the Second. These gigantic weapons made little impact, but they served their purpose in keeping the firm in the public eye.)

In the 1870s, Alfred began building a grandiose villa on a hill eight miles from the factory, overlooking the Ruhr valley: the Villa Hügel, built to his own designs and using large amounts of Krupp iron in its construction. It was not so much a home as a place for customers and visiting dignitaries to stay, keeping them away from the technical secrets of the factory. 'The commercial manufacturer,' Alfred declared, 'must be a waster of money in the eyes of the world.' To underscore the point he even employed the composer Engelbert Humperdinck to play the piano for the amusement of his visitors. At the Chicago World's Fair of 1893, Krupp spent $1.5 million on creating a replica of the Villa Hügel with his name on the façade; inside, visitors could inspect a cannon capable of firing a shell at a target thirteen miles away.

Visitors came to Essen from all over the world, including China and Japan. Krupp sold arms to the Russians, incorporating innovations suggested by their military technicians, as well as railway equipment to Brazil. He invited representatives of eighteen states to a gunnery demonstration in 1879 and circulated advertisements for his products to British MPs. His vision encompassed the supply of railway equipment to the whole world, with railway lines, as he said in 1875, 'linking and crossing the great continents of Africa, America and Asia so that they will come to the status of civilised countries and with connecting and branch lines will keep industry busy until the end of the world – as long as some windbag does not destroy this expectation by developing air transport'.

Yet for all the global scope of his enterprise, repeatedly underscored by James, Krupp ultimately hitched his fortunes to those of the Prussian state, first to the booming railways, then to the army, the institution that played a central role in Bismarck's wars of unification in 1864, 1866 and 1870. Krupp lobbied hard to get orders for his weaponry, and built four new production halls for cannon between 1861 and 1870 to meet the rapidly growing demand. James describes Krupp himself as an 'un-political German', but he cultivated close relations with Kaiser Wilhelm I and told his son Friedrich Alfred: 'You must be to the future Kaiser what I am to the present one, then no swindler can damage the factory.' In 1871, Alfred declared: 'My achievement will stand and fall with Prussia's greatness and military supremacy.'

Friedrich Alfred, who took over the business on his father's death in 1887, was an enthusiastic moderniser under whose influence nickel steel armour plating, electrical detonators and much more besides came into production. He conducted mergers and acquisitions at a frenetic pace and oversaw a major increase in the size of the factory, whose employees grew in number from 13,000 in 1887 to 25,000 in 1899. Friedrich Alfred had no qualms about using the new mass press and popular political mobilisation to further his business interests. A major opportunity came at the end of the century, with Kaiser Wilhelm II's decision to build a large new navy. Krupp not only acquired a major shipyard, trebling its workforce in a few years, but also hired a journalist, Victor Schweinburg, to publish articles favourable to his business. Schweinburg founded the popular Navy League to whip up popular pressure for the construction of a battle fleet. Within a year it had nearly a quarter of a million members. Krupp's links with Schweinburg, as well as his own presence on the League's executive board, did not go unnoticed, and both were forced to resign from the Navy League under heavy political pressure. It was discovered that the firm was making a profit of 60 per cent as the only supplier of armoured plating for the new fleet. Never very healthy (he suffered badly from asthma as a child), Friedrich Alfred spent increasing amounts of time away from these political storms on the island of Capri, where he dabbled in marine zoology and distributed his largesse to the local inhabitants.

Scandal ensued as rumours of wild homosexual orgies with underage Italian boys began to reach Berlin. Accusations and counter-accusations flew about in the press and the Reichstag. The storm of publicity reflected a widespread horror at homosexuality, which was illegal according to the German Criminal Code; it was portrayed by the straitlaced Social Democrats in particular as evidence of the deep moral turpitude of the ruling capitalist elite. Friedrich Alfred's marriage broke down under the strain. He had his wife confined to a mental hospital and shortly afterwards, on 22 November 1902, he died, killed by a stroke according to his doctors, by his own hand according to rumour.

James dismisses the allegations of Friedrich Alfred's pederasty as the product of political opposition to him on Capri and 'a sustained and vicious attack that used all the instruments of the new politics of scandal and sensation' in Germany itself, but Manchester provides a great deal of circumstantial evidence, including Krupp's habit of inviting young Italian boys to stay with him at the Hotel Bristol in Berlin when he was there. Manchester has no doubt that Krupp committed suicide, noting that there was no official autopsy and that the doctors placed the corpse immediately in a sealed casket that not even relatives were allowed to open. Whatever the truth, James puts the most favourable gloss on events and glides smoothly over the controversy, attaching any opprobrium to Krupp's socialist critics.

With the death of the last male Krupp, the family firm was turned into a joint-stock company, though one in which all but four of the 160,000 shares were owned by Friedrich Alfred's sixteen-year-old daughter Bertha. Managers moved in to take over the firm, which continued to innovate and expand, achieving a particular triumph with the patenting of a new kind of non-rusting steel (4500 plates of which covered the top of New York's Chrysler building from 1929 onwards). In 1906, the situation changed again when Bertha married the diplomat Gustav von Bohlen und Halbach. Delighted, the Kaiser issued a royal patent allowing him to take the name Krupp. By 1909, Gustav Krupp von Bohlen und Halbach, as he was now called, had become chairman of the supervisory board. In the same year, the Pan-German businessman and media mogul Alfred Hugenberg, who was to become Hitler's main coalition partner in 1933, became chairman of the executive board. This was the team that led the firm into the First World War.

Krupp soon adjusted to the new situation in 1914. The company's shipyard went over to making U-boats and, assisted by large subsidies under the Hindenburg Programme of 1916, undertook a dramatic expansion of arms production. 'The company,' James remarks, 'had become in practice part of the German state.' The workforce grew rapidly, reaching almost 170,000 by the middle of 1918. By this time, worker discontent was also growing. As the Allied blockade throttled the country's food supplies, prices began to rocket and a vast black market in food emerged. Workers began to agitate for wage increases in order to feed their families, and Gustav began to worry about 'the sliding of our monarchical and state authority down the slippery road to democracy'. Anxious to stop the rot, the Kaiser visited the factory and delivered a characteristically bombastic speech to the workers. But it was too late.

In November 1918, the Kaiser was overthrown and Germany became a republic. The newly powerful trade unions negotiated agreements with the firm that established a works council. A slimmed-down workforce went back to producing for the state railways. Meanwhile, in an attempt to enforce the demilitarisation policies of the Treaty of Versailles, a posse of British and French officers descended on the Essen factory and ordered the destruction of 10,000 machines used for producing military hardware. Not only did Krupp manage to evade these controls but the firm also began making weapons in secret with the encouragement of the German army, the Reichswehr, in collaboration with the Swedish arms company Bofors. From 1926 it began building tanks ('tractors') and had them tested in the Soviet Union by the Red Army.

Meanwhile, Krupp was profiting from the hyperinflation that overtook Germany in the early 1920s. In the summer of 1922, for instance, it borrowed a billion marks from the banks, worth 1,140,000 marks in gold; when the firm repaid the sum in October 1923, its value had sunk to a mere 53,000 gold marks. When the French occupied the Ruhr after Germany fell behind in reparations payments, production ground to a halt; Gustav was arrested for organising resistance to the occupation and jailed for seven months. In the final stages of the inflationary period the economy all but collapsed and Krupp made major losses. It had to negotiate a large American credit and obtain further help from the German government.

Recovery had barely begun when the Wall Street crash of 1929 plunged the German economy into the Depression. Krupp had not solved the problem of overcapacity that had plagued it during the 1920s. Wages and salaries were repeatedly cut, hours of work were reduced, and between 1928 and 1932 the workforce was cut in half. In 1928, Krupp had joined his fellow steelmakers in an unprovoked lockout of workers in the Ruhr in an attempt to cut wages still further; characteristically, James devotes most of his coverage of this event to stressing Gustav's reservations about it, though the fact is that he participated in it fully and a quarter of a million men had to suffer the loss of their jobs at a time when they could ill afford it.

Despite his new role as chairman of the Reich Association of German Industry, Gustav, as James points out, played little part in the complex behind-the-scenes negotiations that led to Hitler's appointment as Reich Chancellor on 30 January 1933. He even declined to meet Hitler when invited, and did not put money into his election coffers when asked to. While Manchester agrees with this finding, he points out that Gustav thought the political parties incapable of solving Germany's problems and that he wanted Hindenburg to appoint a government to do the job. Krupp joined a group of industrialists in signing a petition submitted to Hindenburg by the Nazi banker Kurt von Schröder in November 1932 urging him to appoint Hitler. And he welcomed the suppression of the unions and the onslaught on Communism that followed Hitler's appointment.

Krupp gave in easily enough to Nazi pressure to dismiss Jewish employees, and his firm benefited almost immediately from the new regime's drive to rearm. 'The next five years,' Hitler told his cabinet on 8 February 1933, 'must be dedicated to the rearmament of the German people.' The orders began to flow in. By 1934–5 the company was making heavy artillery again. Its shipyard, which had been struggling for a long time, launched its first new submarine in 1935. The outbreak of the Second World War in September 1939 increased the pressure on arms manufacturers. James argues strongly that, far from driving the Third Reich to war, Krupp was pulled along by the regime, which was certainly making the running. Nevertheless, the Nazi state afforded excellent opportunities for Krupp to expand, and the firm made substantial profits from rearmament.

The Krupp tradition of a family firm run by a single person rather than a board of directors fitted in well with the Nazi ideas of leadership (Führerschaft) and heredity. On 12 November 1943, Hitler decreed that 'the owner of the Krupp family wealth is empowered to create a family enterprise with a particular regulation of succession'.

Bertha transferred ownership from the ailing Gustav to her eldest son, Alfried, who had taken up a management role a few years before. Alfried had joined the SS in 1931 as a 'patron' – an early indication of his political sympathies – and the Nazi Party in 1938. He eased out the managing director, Ewald Löser (an old-style nationalist who had been deputy mayor of Leipzig under Carl Goerdeler, a central figure in the conservative resistance to Hitler), and devoted himself to serving the regime. Characteristically, James underscores his relative lack of dynamism and commitment, and the growing government interference in production, especially after Albert Speer became Armaments Minister. But the fact remains that Alfried Krupp was chairman of the executive board and so bore the major responsibility for the firm's actions.

The most controversial of these in retrospect was the company's increasing use of forced foreign labour. The Krupp concern no more remained a passive agent of government policy in this field than it did in any other. From the autumn of 1941 onwards, as German workers were drafted in growing numbers to the front, the firm lobbied energetically for an allocation of labourers from the prison camps of the Reich and its satellites; indeed, the firm was criticised by the regime for what were regarded as excessive demands. James says that it had no alternative but to use forced labour, but Krupp's demands went far beyond what was necessary. 'Krupp placed orders for workers speculatively, without always being sure they were actually needed', Ulrich Herbert noted in *Hitler's Foreign Workers* (1997), while its demands met with a positive response mainly because the firm 'traditionally enjoyed excellent relations with the Berlin central authorities'.

Companies were supposed to guarantee food and accommodation before any allocation was agreed, but the numbers demanded by Krupp far outran the firm's capacity to cater for them. The company's agents picked suitable workers from camps in Holland and made sure French workers were well cared for, but the many Soviet labourers were kept behind barbed wire and fed rations so meagre that their health rapidly deteriorated. Local managers sometimes tried to improve things to get a better performance out of the men, but in one instance Krupp's head office declared that 'Russian prisoners of war must not be permitted to become accustomed to West European food', and a complaint about inadequate ration allocations made by the board of directors to the prisoner-of-war section of the armed forces supreme command met with the counter-complaint that the prisoners 'are being beaten' and were 'not receiving the food and free time they are entitled to'.

James admits that the firm did 'remarkably little' to improve the dire conditions for forced labourers but the evidence shows its sins were not merely ones of omission. Eventually, he says, rations were increased and the barbed wire removed from the perimeter of the camps in which Soviet workers were housed. Yet according to Herbert, 'the old barbed wire often remained in place', and bombing raids nullified the small attempts at improvement made by Krupp officials anxious not to lose the right to procure more foreign workers. Some of the camps in Essen became, Herbert says, 'breeding grounds for corruption and petty crime', including the misappropriation of food rations supposed to go to the inmates and the sexual exploitation of female workers.

The company security force, 2,000 men armed with leather truncheons, administered savage beatings in a cellar of the main administration building to foreign workers who caused trouble. One Soviet prisoner caught trying to steal a loaf of bread was shot dead by a company guard, who received no punishment. Many were 'beaten up simply because they were Eastern workers, and plant security had been given power over them'. Manchester provides page after page of evidence taken from Nuremberg trial papers documenting a regime of horrifying brutality exercised by Krupp's security force. At the end of the war, Gustav Krupp von Bohlen und Halbach was arraigned at Nuremberg, but by this time he had become senile following a series of strokes, and proceedings against him were abandoned. Instead, Alfried and almost all the Krupp directors were charged in the industrialists' trial in 1947–8. They were convicted of employing slave labour and plundering occupied Europe and sentenced to varying terms of imprisonment. Krupp's fortune was confiscated. Some might think this was only just, but James waxes indignant about the industrialists' trial. 'There appears [*sic*] to have been many and in some instances multiple violations of standard judicial practice,' he says. All he will concede is that the firm was 'a participant in a massive web of ideologically driven immorality' for which the regime of course bore the responsibility.

Other German industrialists, themselves just as deeply implicated in the crimes of Nazism, were predictably outraged by the trial. In January 1951, as the Cold War gathered pace, the Allied high commissioner, US General John McCloy, amnestied Alfried Krupp – who, he claimed, had 'exerted very little if any influence in the management of the company' – and revoked the confiscation of his property. He amnestied the other directors too, though they had, it seems reasonable to suppose, exercised a more considerable influence on the management of the company. This was part of a wider American policy of forgive and forget, given the perceived need to bolster West German morale in the face of the Communist threat from the east – the rapid recovery of the economy trumped the fading desire to settle accounts with war criminals.

Like many other German businesses, Krupp adapted seamlessly to the new world of the postwar economic miracle. As a symbol of German militarism, the firm was initially supposed to be broken up, but although a few parts were split off, the company basically remained intact. The young banker Berthold Beitz, appointed managing director not least because, during the war, he had saved several hundred Jewish workers as manager of an oil extraction company near Łódź, managed to secure delay after delay in the process of selling off the firm's steel and coal holdings, while it expanded production in these areas and invested in new technology.

Now out of prison and back at the helm, Alfried began to think of the future. His son, Arndt, had no interest in taking the firm over, preferring, as James says, 'to cultivate an ostentatious and hedonistic life as a homosexual playboy'. In 1966, Alfried found a solution to the problem by converting the firm into a public company controlled by a charitable foundation. Arndt was bought out of his inheritance with an annual income of two million marks. This had the effect of keeping the firm intact and protecting it from corporate raids and takeovers. It also, of course, protected the family fortune. But this had little meaning any more, since the name Krupp, added by the Kaiser's proclamation of 1906 to the surnames solely of Gustav and his heir, Alfried, lapsed with the latter's death in 1967. Beitz duly announced: 'There is no Krupp family name any more.' In due course, it merged with other companies, notably the Thyssen concern, though it has subsequently always remained conscious of its unique tradition.

It was to celebrate that tradition that the foundation commissioned Harold James to write this book, which first appeared in German in a much larger format, with lavish full-colour illustrations, to celebrate the firm's 200th anniversary in 2011. Doubtless copies of the German edition now adorn coffee tables in the Villa Hügel and are given away to valued customers and prominent visitors. Although James thanks the foundation for its financial support, he does not reveal this background or the existence of the German commemorative version in his preface. He should have done. The book's true nature as a celebratory official history is betrayed by the imprint page, which reveals that the copyright is held not by the author or publisher but by the Alfried Krupp von Bohlen und Halbach Foundation. James insists that all the views and interpretations in the book are his own, but at every juncture the book denies or passes briefly over the dark side of the firm's history. One is left with the impression that the author has taken much too seriously his brief of providing an official history that will not cause any upset at the Villa Hügel.

14. THE FELLOW TRAVELLER

I

When I was just starting as a graduate student at Oxford, in 1970, I was approached by a history don at the university who asked me if I would like to apply for a new scholarship that had been set up by the F.V.S. Foundation in Hamburg. I already had a grant from the then Social Science Research Council and didn't need the money, but I didn't want to offend him, so I applied and was duly awarded it – there were two of them on offer, and there wasn't much competition.

They were called the Hanseatic Scholarships and they provided a year in Hamburg and a second year in Germany wherever one needed to go (I went to Berlin). The founder was a man called Alfred Toepfer, a wealthy businessman who, as his secretary explained to me at the welcoming dinner in his guesthouse in Hamburg a few months later, had been inspired by the example of Cecil Rhodes to convert his fortune into a Foundation under the Weimar Republic. Toepfer's youthful experiences in the celebrated *Wandervogel* youth movement before the First World War had led him, she said, to devote his life to fostering understanding between the youth of different nations.

In the early days of Appeasement between the wars, the Rhodes Trust had reinstated the two Rhodes Scholarships offered to Germans (who had been expelled from the Anglo-Saxon club in 1914) and now, after the Queen's state visit to Germany in 1965 had sealed the renewal of friendship between the two nations, they had been revived again after going into abeyance for a second time in 1939. On both occasions – the first after an interval of a few years – Toepfer's Foundation had established two Hanseatic Scholarships as a kind of quid pro quo, Rhodes Scholarships in reverse. Even the amount of money paid to the Hanseatic Scholars was the same, converted into German marks, as was paid to a Rhodes Scholar. So far, so admirable.

But as the dinner progressed, I soon began to realise that what Toepfer meant by international friendship wasn't quite the same as was generally understood by others in the 1970s. This was the period when Edward Heath's Tory government was securing Britain's entry into the European Community (later European Union), and in welcoming myself and my fellow scholar to Germany, Toepfer declared that this was another step in the furthering of cooperation between the different nations of the Anglo-Saxon race (and he really did speak in these terms, unthinkable in Germany today).

In particular, Toepfer lamented the fact that such cooperation had been so sadly lacking in the past. If only England, as he called it, had joined the European Community in the fifties, along with the Scandinavian nations! The preponderance of the Latin race in the European Community, he said, had caused many difficulties and had been a great hindrance to its development. This visibly embarrassed the British Consul-General Mr Purves, who by this stage was holding his head in his hands, and indeed it embarrassed almost everyone else present. I thought it best not to mention that, being Welsh, I was not an Anglo-Saxon myself.

Later, I found myself engaged in a lively debate with Harald Mandt, the chairman of the Hanseatic Scholarships committee and himself a former German Rhodes Scholar, about apartheid in South Africa, which he wholeheartedly supported. Then I talked to Toepfer's deputy Herr Riecke, who said he had been interned by the British occupation authorities after the war. I asked him what he felt about it now. He had paid his dues, he said, with a shrug of his shoulders. Later, when everyone had gone, I looked round the bookshelves in the Foundation's guest house, where I was staying the night. With a slightly queasy feeling, I noted several works of what we would now call Holocaust denial on them.

There was worse. As I signed the guest book in the morning, the housekeeper gushed to me about another visitor who had recently stayed over: Albert Speer, Hitler's friend and Armaments Minister during the war, who had been released not long before from the twenty-year prison sentence imposed on him at the Nuremberg War Crimes Trials. Such a gentleman, she said, such perfect manners.

Did this mean Toepfer was a neo-Nazi? It wasn't easy to find out in 1970. West German historians hadn't undertaken any research on ex-Nazis in their own society – that didn't come for decades. All one had to go on was the *Brown Book* published by the Communist regime in East Germany, listing hundreds of Nazi war criminals in the West German political, judicial and economic elites. Toepfer's name wasn't in it. Moreover, his staff assured us that he had remained uninvolved with the Nazi regime, indeed had actually been imprisoned by it for a while because he opposed it. And the company he kept was nothing unusual in West Germany at the time, as the *Brown Book* indicated; the entire postwar economy was crawling with serious Nazi war criminals, including retailers like Josef Neckermann who had profited from the 'Aryanisation' of Jewish businesses in the Nazi years, businessmen like Krupp and Flick who had been found guilty in the Nuremberg industrialists' trial of using slave labour, senior managers in the IG Farben conglomerate like Fritz ter Meer, who had set up a factory at Auschwitz from which underperforming workers were periodically 'selected' for the gas chambers, senior officials in the Degussa company, suppliers of Zyklon-B to the gas chambers, and many more. Toepfer didn't seem to belong in this company. Indeed, his staff pointed out that he had been completely exonerated by a denazification process after the war, unlike many other businessmen.

True, he almost seemed to make a point of employing former Nazis in his Foundation. But this didn't mean he was a Nazi himself. Even the most respectable West Germans didn't seem to mind keeping company with ex-Nazis. For many years, Chancellor Adenauer himself had employed as the head of his own office Hans Globke, the civil servant who had written the standard commentary on the Nuremberg race laws in the 1930s. One of Adenauer's concerns, indeed, was to get old Nazis to commit themselves to democracy by integrating them into the West German establishment, no questions asked, so they wouldn't harbour resentments or gravitate towards neo-Nazism. And there was no sign that Toepfer was peddling any kind of neo-Nazi ideology. His racist views, I realised as I learned more about the intellectual and political world of Germany before 1914, were common among German elites long before Nazism even existed. And most probably the Holocaust denial books in Toepfer's library were unread. Toepfer did not strike me as a well-read or well-educated man; indeed, in most matters apart from business he seemed, as his speech at the inaugural Hanseatic dinner suggested, rather naive.

Nor did Toepfer and the Foundation try to influence us in any way in our own political or historical views. The Foundation seemed to have little idea of what to do with us Hanseatic Scholars and certainly gave no indication of any political intent in its administration of the scholarships. We were expected to study at Hamburg University but we never bothered, since, as doctoral students, we were more concerned with researching and writing our theses than with going to lectures; without telling the Foundation, we spent a lot of time in archives away from the city; and the Foundation only ever showed an interest in us when it required our presence at a dinner of one kind or another, which was not very often.

My doctoral project assessed the complicity of the liberal German bourgeoisie, or at least its female half, in the rise of Nazism. I was inspired to do so by the work of Martin Broszat on the support given to Hitler by German elites. My fellow Hanseatic Scholar was investigating the sexual habits of Bavarian peasants in the early nineteenth century. Subsequent Hanseatic Scholars also worked unhindered on other critical investigations of the darker side of modern German history. The idea that the Foundation would try to interfere in our research or our extra-curricular life was simply absurd. On my return to Oxford, I lost contact with the Foundation, and felt more obliged to it for introducing me to some of the dubious realities of the West German establishment in the 1970s than for anything else.

Meanwhile, the Foundation continued its educational and cultural work unabated. Over the subsequent decades, more than eighty graduate students or postdoctoral fellows from Oxford and, more recently, Cambridge as well, benefited from the Hanseatic Scholarships. The Foundation established many more exchange scholarships with other countries, particularly in Eastern Europe. It awarded prizes for cultural achievements of various kinds, some of them from the 1930s, others founded since the war. The recipients read like a galaxy of twentieth-century political and cultural stars. The Shakespeare Prize for cultural achievement was awarded, for example, to Ralph Vaughan Williams, Benjamin Britten, Ian McEwan and A. S. Byatt, among others.

II

Some years after that memorable welcoming dinner in Hamburg, the Foundation's prizes began to run into trouble. A particular problem was posed by the Upper Rhenish Cultural Prize, set up in 1966 and awarded in turn to figures from France, Germany and Switzerland. The idea was to support the idea of a common culture across artificial state boundaries in this area. Allegations surfaced that portrayed the F.V.S. Foundation's support for cross-border cultural ties as part of a prewar German imperialist tradition aimed ultimately at the annexation of eastern France and northern Switzerland to Germany.

The charges were levelled by a French schoolteacher, Lionel Boissou, who alleged that the Upper Rhenish Cultural Prize was awarded by a 'bare-faced agitator' for German aggrandisement in Switzerland and Alsace – namely, Alfred Toepfer, a man with, as he said, 'a dubious past'. This led not only to the prize being withdrawn, in 1996, but also to the Basel Burckhard Prize being withdrawn by the Foundation itself the previous year. In 1999 Boissou persuaded the French Senate to prevent the use of its premises for the ceremony awarding the Foundation's Robert Schuman Prize to a former Polish Foreign Minister.

Boissou was in fact a vehement French nationalist who campaigned for the compulsory use of French as the medium of instruction in all French schools, and regarded the minority language campaigns in Brittany and the French Basque country as part of a German plot to dismember France, reminiscent of similar plots in the interwar years. In 1997, Boissou stated that post-1990 Europe was in danger of being 'wholly subjected to German domination'. The Maastricht Treaty's insistence on minority language rights in a 'Europe of the regions' simply fuelled this paranoia. His campaign, therefore, despite achieving results, was very much that of a loner on the fringes of politics.

However, Boissou received support from the German historical geographer Michael Fahlbusch, who had published a study of the German People's Research Association in the Nazi period. This organisation sponsored ethnic maps of Europe that were later used by the Nazis in ethnic cleansing and mass murder operations in Eastern Europe. The German People's Research Association had close personal and financial ties with Toepfer and his Foundations. But Fahlbusch's thesis that these maps were drawn up specifically in order to facilitate mass murder was not borne out by the evidence. The Nazis' genocidal intentions and plans had an entirely independent genesis. So, in the end, it was scarcely legitimate to allege from all this that Toepfer funded 'academic support of the Holocaust', as Fahlbusch claimed.

Another campaign unfolded against Toepfer in Austria. When, in 1990, the Foundation set up the Grillparzer Prize, for cultural achievements in Austria, linked to two travel scholarships for young Austrians, the drama student Christian Michaelides launched a campaign against what he called a 'neo-German form of power-politics' and a 'shameless act of cultural colonisation'. Michaelides was heavily criticised by the Austrian journalist Ulrich Weinzierl, who called his campaign 'a broth of half-truths, exaggerations and insinuations', and 'a symptom of the latent discomfort in Austria in the face of the new enlarged Germany' following reunification in 1990. Nevertheless, when the Austrian novelist Hans Lebert was awarded the prize in 1992, he sent an actor to the ceremony to repeat a litany of similar allegations of German cultural imperialism ('First missionaries come and change our world picture, then come the businessmen and corrupt the chiefs of the tribe with more or less valuable gifts, and lastly come the occupying forces and hoist up an alien flag').

Austria is a German-speaking country, whose inhabitants overwhelmingly welcomed the German annexation of 1938 and since the Second World War has struggled to find a convincing national identity. No wonder Austrians were worried in 1992. The prize was in fact awarded on the recommendation of the Austrian Academy of Sciences (the reason for the mockery poured over it by one of its recipients, the writer Thomas Bernhard, hilariously recounted in his novella *Wittgenstein's Nephew*). But the paranoid campaign against Toepfer and his Foundation continued and culminated in the mailing of forged letters to numerous Austrian authors telling them they had won the Grillparzer Prize. Not surprisingly, the Foundation by this time had had enough and discontinued it.

Clearly, therefore, the Foundation was being put on the defensive in the 1990s. After Toepfer's death in 1993 it commissioned a thorough investigation of what his businesses and his Foundation had done during the Nazi period, no doubt expecting the historians it engaged, led by the leading German specialist on the Third Reich, Hans Mommsen, and including French and Swiss as well as German contributors, to exonerate them. But they did not. On the contrary, the results of their investigations, when they appeared in 2000, were devastating. They revealed that Toepfer's involvement with the Nazi regime had been far greater than he had admitted. Even his staff were shocked. It took some time for them to come to terms with the revelations, which were not published in book form until 2006. Two years later one of the contributors, Jan Zimmermann, published a biography of Toepfer containing fresh discoveries and adding more material about the Foundation's history after 1945.

These findings were initially ignored by Oxford and Cambridge. But in the April 2010 issue of *Standpoint*, the lively conservative intellectual monthly edited by Daniel Johnson, they were presented to an English-speaking readership in a lengthy article by Michael Pinto-Duschinsky, a writer on elections and party funding, with a few extra discoveries of his own. Under the headlines: 'The prize lies of a Nazi tycoon' and 'A Nazi shadow over Oxford', Pinto-Duschinsky described Toepfer as a 'sponsoring member' of the SS who was enormously helpful to Hitler. In the 1930s, he said, Toepfer channelled money via his Foundations to influence public opinion in Britain and elsewhere in Europe in favour of the Third Reich and played an important role in Nazi subversion in Austria, the Czech Sudetenland, Alsace-Lorraine and elsewhere.

Moreover, he charged, 'his closest henchmen were unrepentant Nazis who had been key figures in murdering hundreds of thousands of Jews and in starving to death countless numbers of Russian prisoners of war'. Since his death in 1993, he alleged, the Foundation had been assiduously 'greywashing' the Holocaust and its founder's role in it. 'The current leadership of the foundation used this unfortunate colour metaphor to avoid the reality that, if ever there were crimes that were irredeemably and completely evil, they were those of Nazi Germany.' Toepfer's money was 'severely tainted'. 'Greywash becomes whitewash.' The inevitable conclusion was that Oxford and Cambridge should sever their links with the Foundation and that the 'tainted scholarships' funded by the Foundation should be discontinued.

III

Who was Alfred Toepfer? Both the historical commission report and the biography by Zimmermann presented a mass of material on the man and his views that enabled the careful reader to reach an informed judgement. Born in 1894 to humble parents (a sailor and a farmer's daughter), Toepfer left school early to go into trade, served in the army during the First World War, won the Iron Cross, First Class, and was wounded on three occasions, on none of them seriously. Before the war, as indeed his secretary had told me, he had been inspired by his membership of the rebellious youth movement, the *Wandervogel*, which took adolescent boys into the hills and woods to commune with nature and sing patriotic songs round the campfire. If this gave Toepfer's nationalism one kind of flavour, then his youthful reading of a book he referred to throughout his life as having exerted a huge influence on his outlook lent it another: this was Julius Langbehn's *Rembrandt as Educator*, a vastly popular work that treated the Dutch painter Rembrandt as racially German, saw community with nature as the essence of the German soul and condemned Jews and Slavs as uncreative and worthy only of being destroyed.

With such beliefs it was not surprising that Toepfer volunteered after the war for the Maercker *Freikorps*, a band of armed irregulars that 'restored order' in a number of central German towns following the German Revolution of 1918–19. After things had calmed down, he went into business, and quickly made a fortune in grain trading and the supply of raw materials for construction work. He got lucky with exchange rates in the German inflation of the early 1920s. Like other German-nationalist conservatives he welcomed the Hitler coalition cabinet of 30 January 1933, in which, after all, German-nationalist conservatives were in a majority. But like most of them, too, he did not object when Hitler established a Nazi dictatorship. Toepfer regarded its restoration of the German economy with satisfaction, and its organisation and disciplining of young people in the Hitler Youth with approval. The order he saw emerging – ignoring the massive violence with which it was established – seemed to him an indispensable basis for the expansion of business. Like other businessmen, he set about forging useful contacts with the regime and its servants.

Was Toepfer antisemitic? Pinto-Duschinsky did not allege that he was, and indeed there is not a single instance of his uttering even an implicitly antisemitic remark in the whole course of his very long life. In this he was not untypical of Hamburg's business elite, which under the Weimar Republic included many Jews. Only gradually during the Nazi period did businessmen in the city move to take commercial advantage of 'Aryanisation', for example. Early in 1933, it is relevant to note, Toepfer openly advocated the election of Jews to the board of the grain merchants' division of the Hamburg Stock Exchange, to the horror of hard-line Nazis. There is no evidence to support Pinto-Duschinsky's supposition that the award of prizes to Jews such as Martin Buber after the war was intended as a cynical fig leaf to make it easier to award prizes to old Nazis as well. Toepfer simply wasn't that sophisticated. And of all the messages conveyed by *Rembrandt as Educator*, antisemitism seems to have had the least effect on him.

What was unusual about Toepfer, indeed very unusual, was his decision to convert his fortune into a Foundation and use it to award cultural prizes and scholarships. As the Swiss historian Georg Kreis had noted, 'Toepfer was a somewhat naïve idealist, a completely self-taught man who combined, again in a rather strange way, a reverence for the acknowledged giants of the contemporary worlds of art and science with a kind of proprietorial attitude to them.' Through the work of the Foundation he sought to gain the respect his humble background had initially denied him. He dreamed, in fact, of gaining the status and respect of a Cecil Rhodes.

Yet under the Third Reich, this ambition was almost bound to get him into trouble. After the rapid *Gleichschaltung*, or 'coordination', of almost every organisation in Germany apart from the armed forces and the Churches, the F.V.S. Foundation was by the mid-1930s unique, the only such body in Germany. The Nazis began to put Toepfer under pressure to make it over to them, spreading rumours about him and gathering what they could use to incriminate him. On 14 June 1937, basing themselves on knowledge of his complex international financial dealings, including transfers of funds between the F.V.S. and its sister Foundation, the J.W.G., in Switzerland, the Gestapo arrested Toepfer for alleged currency offences. Pinto-Duschinsky accepted their claim that he was involved in 'tax evasion' and infringements of currency controls and that Toepfer's Foundation and its sister Foundation in Switzerland were no more than tax-avoidance devices. He claimed that 'the weight of evidence does not support' the argument that this was a pretext or that the real reason for his arrest was political.

But he provided not a shred of evidence to back up this assertion. It was in fact a typical Nazi tactic to trump up charges of tax evasion and currency fraud against people the regime did not like, but these did not stick either. On 23 May 1938 Toepfer was released without the charges ever having been proved, despite a minutely detailed prosecution audit of the books of his Foundations and his company. Nor was there any evidence to back Pinto-Duschinsky's assertion that by moving currency between banks in different countries – surely a normal activity for an international businessman – Toepfer was aiding the Nazi regime. The circumstances of his arrest in fact reflected Nazi hostility to his Foundation.

And how did Toepfer secure his release? Here Pinto-Duschinsky was on firmer ground, for Toepfer acted in the same way as many other businessmen in the Third Reich: he worked to win powerful patrons within the Nazi regime, securing, for example, the good offices of Hermann Göring, and appointing top SS men to senior positions in his Foundation. Contributing money to Heinrich Himmler's benefit fund can't have done him any harm either (this is what made him, like many businessmen, a 'sponsoring member' of the SS, which did not mean, however, that he was actually an SS officer or anything like it). In May 1938, he ceded his 'founder's rights' in the Foundation to Werner Lorenz, a senior SS officer who ran the Association for Germans Abroad, an organisation with which Toepfer had close connections. This was enough to bring about his release from custody. It looked as if the SS had now taken over. But in fact Lorenz had agreed not to exercise these rights in any way; and in 1942 Toepfer acquired them again. The whole business had been a manoeuvre that said much about Toepfer's determination to do anything to keep the Foundation going, but little about his own ideological convictions.

Pinto-Duschinsky was undoubtedly right in detailing the manner in which Toepfer made his country estates at Gut Siggen and Kalkhorst available to Austrian and Sudeten Nazis, who spent their time plotting the incorporation of their homelands into the Third Reich. Many of those who stayed there later distinguished themselves as mass murderers and a number were condemned after the war. Some, like Konrad Henlein, the leader of the Sudeten Germans in Czechoslovakia, or leading figures in the clandestine Nazi Party in Austria, were already involved in violence and terrorism at the time when Toepfer gave them practical support. Toepfer was involved, through members of the Foundation's board, in Nazi subversion in Switzerland and Alsace-Lorraine as well, funding local Nazis through the J.W.G. Foundation run by his brother Ernst.

In doing all this, Toepfer seems to have been acting on his own initiative rather than at the behest of the Nazi authorities. To say, as Pinto-Duschinsky did, that he was 'enormously helpful to Hitler', implies a personal relationship between the two men; there was none. Rather, Toepfer was pursuing his own German-nationalist belief, which neatly dovetailed with early Nazi foreign policy, that German-speakers in Austria, Czechoslovakia, Alsace-Lorraine and Switzerland should be 'brought back to the Reich' – a belief shared not only by the vast majority of Germans of all political hues at the time, but also to some extent at least by politicians and statesmen outside Germany, such as British Prime Minister Neville Chamberlain, who accepted the *Anschluss* of Austria and brokered the incorporation of the Sudeten-land into Germany at the Munich Agreement in 1938.

On reacquiring his Foundation in 1942, Toepfer used personal connections to get an appointment to the counter-espionage division of the German armed forces (*Abwehr*) in Paris, where he was in a division responsible for securing armaments for Germany and for dealing with sabotage and subversion in enemy states. Whether he actually did anything active remains obscure. The *Abwehr* was a strange organisation, full of opponents of Hitler who were to play a role in the plotting that led to the attempt to blow him up on 20 July 1944. Toepfer was certainly not one of these, but he may well have shared the view of its Paris office that shooting hostages was counter-productive. In any case, he left the *Abwehr* in the middle of 1942 at the point when the SS took over the combatting of resistance, in view of what it regarded as the *Abwehr*'s softness.

From the start of 1943 Toepfer was commissioned by the Reich Economics Ministry to acquire hard currency for the Reich by secretly selling to foreign countries goods that were not needed in Germany. His first enterprise was the sale in Spain of half a million bottles of champagne that had been confiscated from the French by the German armed forces. There followed transactions with confiscated motor vehicles, cigarette papers, radio aerials, turbines and much more besides. Not a penny of this went into Toepfer's own pocket, though he did make a contribution in this way to the Nazis' exploitation of the French economy – a rather pathetic one, given the vast scale of the exploitation they carried out in other parts of the economy.

Is there any evidence that Toepfer profited from the mass murder of Jews? Pinto-Duschinsky claimed that a subsidiary of the Toepfer business supplied slaked lime to the German ghetto administration in Lódź, and noted that slaked lime was 'used among other things to cover cadavers'. However, there is no evidence that Toepfer himself was aware of any sale, and no reason why he should have been involved in the day-to-day management of this business, though he certainly did visit its branches in Posen and Kraków, was kept regularly informed about their business activities and ensured that he retained a controlling financial interest in them. The subsidiary in question was a construction company, and slaked lime is used as an ingredient in whitewash, mortar and plaster, as well as being an element in sewage treatment. There is no evidence that it was used to cover dead bodies of murdered Jews, indeed this is not even a reasonable supposition.

Pinto-Duschinsky did not mention that slaked lime was not the only thing the Toepfer subsidiary delivered to the ghetto administration in Lódź: it also supplied cement, suggesting its involvement in construction here as elsewhere in Eastern Europe, and food materials such as flour and peas. In journalistic accounts of Pinto-Duschinsky's article, for example in *Cherwell*, the Oxford student magazine, a hypothetical possibility became a fact, in 'the supplying of slaked lime to cover bodies in the Polish Ghetto city of Lódź'. Moreover, it is interesting to note that when the Gestapo arrested all the Poles employed at the yard shared by Toepfer's firm and various other construction companies in Posen after the Polish resistance had burned it down, it was Toepfer's company that interceded for them and helped eventually to secure their release.

In fact, Toepfer's businesses were involved in political activities in another way, for by supplying building materials for German settlements in occupied Poland, or organising the delivery of foodstuffs to Germany from Turkey, in helping with the construction of military emplacements in the Polish General Government or carrying out 'cultural work' in the region, they were both underpinning the Germanisation of conquered Poland and contributing to the German war effort in a more general way. Business and ideology went hand-in-hand with Toepfer as it did with other German businesses at the time. But for men like him it was German nationalism rather than Nazism that supplied the ideology; closely related and overlapping though they may have been, they were not identical.

IV

After the war, Toepfer underwent a period of two years' internment by the British occupation authorities, who eventually decided to classify him, reasonably enough, as a 'fellow traveller' of the Nazis before handing him over to a German-run denazification tribunal. Like many in the same situation, he had obtained testimonials from a variety of respected figures, and made claims to have been involved in resisting the Nazi regime that were exaggerated, to say the least. So he got a clean bill of health to serve as an alibi later on. In the 1950s and 1960s Toepfer rebuilt his businesses and amassed a large fortune, which he poured into the reconstruction and expansion of the Foundation and the establishment of new prizes and scholarships. He fitted seamlessly into the new world of the West German 'economic miracle' and quickly made friends with the Christian Democratic establishment of Konrad Adenauer and Ludwig Erhard; an establishment, as I have noted, that was full of former Nazis with records far worse than his.

Pinto-Duschinsky implied that Toepfer continued to be a closet Nazi while leading a 'double life' through feigned conversion to European unity on the surface, and using the award of his prizes to 'a smattering of Jews' to provide a fig leaf for his award of prizes to a variety of 'Nazi associates and a series of antisemitic, *völkisch* (racist) writers and scholars'. But there is no meaningful evidence to support the claim of a 'double life': Toepfer's European enthusiasm was genuine, even if it still had significant continuities with the beliefs he had held before 1945.

Toepfer seems to have thought at that time that the 'new order' in Europe established with the Nazi victories of 1940 would pave the way for a new era of European cooperation under German leadership. That it involved the extermination of millions of Jews and Slavs, which he must have known about, since the overwhelming majority of Germans knew about it, does not seem to have troubled him. Pinto-Duschinsky quoted a publication of 1940 in which Toepfer praised Nazism for achieving 'social justice' in Germany, abolishing unemployment and educating the young of all classes in body as well as in mind. Nazism had, he said, achieved *völkisch* unity, by which he seems to have meant the absorption of supposedly Germanic elements in other European countries into the Reich. He did not seem to care that it did so at the cost of many lives and enormous suffering to others.

By 1943 the dream of German-led European cooperation had been rudely shattered by ruthless Nazi exploitation of the conquered countries. Like many other supporters of the 'new order', Toepfer seems to have turned to the postwar order that, after the Battle of Stalingrad had clearly announced the inevitability of German defeat, would resurrect European cooperation in a new form. Thinking along these lines was tolerated by the regime, which in the latter part of the war presented itself as fighting for Europe against the threat of American and Soviet domination. Such ideas flowed easily into the lightly modified form of Toepfer's Euro-enthusiasm after the war.

How deep were Toepfer's sympathies with Nazism after 1945? One of Pinto-Duschinsky's undoubted discoveries was that Toepfer's daughter Gerda visited Oxford in 1951 to hand over the 1938 Shakespeare Prize to John Masefield, the Poet Laureate. While in Oxford, she talked to C. A. Macartney, a Fellow of All Souls and leading historian of modern Hungary, who wanted to interview three men who had been senior German officials in Hungary during the brief period when the German occupation brought the fascist and antisemitic Arrow Cross movement to power, leading directly to the murder of more than 400,000 Hungarian Jews in Auschwitz. Pinto-Duschinsky claimed that subsequent correspondence implied that Gerda Toepfer wanted Macartney to use his good contacts in the British government to press for the early release of Edmund Veesenmayer, one of these officials, from prison in return for being granted access to him.

Pinto-Duschinsky did not have direct evidence to support this claim. He was right to say that, after his release, Veesenmayer joined the staff of Toepfer's Foundation, but in fact this was only as a representative for the branch of his business that existed in Tehran; and Toepfer fired him after two years anyway. This was hardly being 'closely associated' with him, as claimed in *Cherwell* magazine. However, Veesenmayer's personal secretary from 1940 to 1945, Barbara Hacke, became Toepfer's private secretary. Pinto-Duschinsky quoted a letter of 1952 in which, he said, Hacke 'effectively justified the Holocaust', and indeed it implicitly defended the German-Hungarian extermination of the Jews as part of a Pan-European rather than a nationalistic enterprise. Moreover, Veesenmayer's deputy Kurt Haller also joined Toepfer's staff, becoming his legal counsel in 1947.

As for Herr Riecke, whom I met at that dinner in 1971, Pinto-Duschinsky noted that he was an SS major-general who had been

State Secretary in the Food Ministry and a senior member of the Ministry for the Occupied Eastern Territories; in these capacities he had been responsible for plans to starve the local population. In addition, Toepfer wrote a letter of recommendation for an old acquaintance, SS Major-General Hermann Lauterbacher, for use if he succeeded in escaping from hiding to join other wanted Nazis in Argentina. In addition, Toepfer helped fund the defence of the senior SS man Werner Lorenz, who had helped rescue his Foundation when he was arrested in 1937, before a US tribunal in Nuremberg. He had ties with the leading SS man Werner Best and the Nazi Rector of Hamburg University, Adolf Rein (who had been responsible for firing Jews from his staff), and helped the former Nazi mayor of Hamburg, Carl Vincent Krogmann, when he got into financial difficulties.

Why did Toepfer support these criminals? In his memoirs, Riecke noted that after 1945 Toepfer gave jobs to four (not necessarily mutually exclusive) categories of people: trained accountants and businessmen; former comrades-in-arms from his days in the army during the First World War and the Free Corps immediately afterwards; men who had behaved 'decently' during their postwar imprisonment; and men of the Third Reich who had fallen on hard times because of being unjustly treated by the Allies. Riecke and Veesenmayer were undoubtedly experienced and highly qualified in business matters, otherwise Toepfer would not have employed them; but they also fell into the last two of the four categories Riecke mentioned, so that it was clear, as the historian Christian Gerlach noted, that Toepfer employed them for political as well as business reasons. This was not, however, because they were Nazis. Like most conservatives in the 1950s and 1960s, Toepfer distinguished between Nazis and Germans, and excused the latter from the crimes of the former – crimes which he recognised as such, but treated as if they had been carried out by a tiny occupying force of bandits that had nothing to do with the real Germany of men like himself and those he employed. Like the vast majority of Germans, he resented the war crimes trials and denazification procedures of the Allies, and thought of men like

Best and Riecke as victims of victors' justice. Unlike most Germans, however, he was in a position to help them. So he did.

V

What, then, of the Hanseatic Scholarships? As his remarks over dinner suggested, Toepfer regarded the revival of the Hanseatic Scholarships in 1970 as a gesture of reconciliation between England and Germany, and although the racist background to his initiative was clear to those who knew him, still, it was basically no different from that of the original Rhodes Scholarships when they were founded before the First World War, with their primary aim of enabling men from the white 'Anglo-Saxon' world, from countries such as the USA, Canada, Australia, New Zealand, South Africa and Germany, to study at Oxford. But such views had long since lost any relevance to Oxford or Cambridge by the 1970s, by which time Rhodes Scholars included female and non-white students, and they had no relevance to the Hanseatic Scholars themselves either.

Of course, the Hanseatic Scholarships set up in the mid-1930s were a different matter. This was the world of Appeasement, in which the symbolic political pay-off to be derived from their establishment was clear to Joachim von Ribbentrop, Hitler's ambassador-at-large before his appointment to the London embassy in August 1936. Pinto-Duschinsky was undoubtedly right in pointing to Ribbentrop's encouragement of the Scholarships, which he clearly saw, along with many other initiatives (such as his founding of the Anglo-German Society in 1935), as a means of improving the image of Nazi Germany in the UK. But there is no evidence that the Scholarships had much effect in this regard; on the contrary, after a series of humiliations as ambassador, Ribbentrop began to hate the British and started working for a war against them. And Nazism was long gone by the time the Scholarships were revived in 1970. Although the money for the Hanseatic Scholarships is provided exclusively by the Foundation, the selection committee that meets every year is entirely independent; the Foundation is not directly represented and has no right of veto over the candidates selected. Toepfer's racial vision of a community of 'Anglo-Saxon' youth is no longer relevant; the current statutes of the Scholarships declare that 'they should serve to develop and strengthen relationships between Germans and Britons, while inspiring and promoting European solidarity'.

One of Pinto-Duschinsky's major points in urging Oxford University to terminate the Hanseatic Scholarships scheme was that 'the way in which the Holocaust is taught – or, more accurately, is relatively little taught – at Oxford [is] affected by the university's sources of funding'. He alleged that the 'dangers' of 'funding ... modern German history and politics' were 'particularly pronounced' because 'the source of funding affects the opinions and the results of the research' in this, as in other areas. In an article published under the heading 'Holocaust Denial' in the *Jewish Chronicle* on 10 June 2010, he called the Toepfer Foundation's historical commission's history 'apologetic' and among the most 'prime examples of the distortions that mar so much recent Holocaust history'. 'At Oxford,' he added, '... academic studies of modern European history and politics are heavily dependent on money from German companies and foundations with strong motives in laundering their pasts.' Laundering, he implied, was the job of the Foundation's 'sponsored historians', who provided 'a selective version of a tainted history'. In so doing, he charged, they were peddling a respectable form of Holocaust denial.

But where was the evidence to back these claims? My own experience neither of the early 1970s nor of later, British and German government-funded research grants, supports this bizarre innuendo. In fact, though a whole variety of funding bodies, from German government agencies like the DAAD or the *Deutsche Forschungsgemeinschaft* to private foundations like the Volkswagen Foundation, have long funded research into German history, they have not tried to influence the way this research has been carried out or the conclusions it has reached. Nothing has been able to stop historians uncovering Nazism's crimes and the complicity of many German institutions and individuals in them from the outset. From the days of Alan Bullock, A. J. P. Taylor, Hugh Trevor-Roper and later Tim Mason, Jane Caplan and Nicholas Stargardt, Oxford has always been a major centre for research into Nazi Germany, as, indeed, has Cambridge over the same period, where historians from Jonathan Steinberg to myself have not only written extensively about the Nazi extermination of the Jews and supervised numerous Ph.D. theses on Nazi Germany but have also served on restitution and reparations commissions of various kinds.

Jane Caplan and Nicholas Stargardt, who teach a course on 'Nazi Germany: A Racial Order' at Oxford, angrily rebutted Pinto-Duschinsky's accusations. They pointed out that antisemitism and the Holocaust featured in every one of its eight weeks of teaching, three of which were devoted solely to the topic. Two thousand pages of set documents (in English translation) confronted students with the most harrowing details of the subject. As an advanced university course, it obviously avoided works such as Sir Martin Gilbert's popular documentary collection *The Holocaust* (1986) that were intended for the general reader. These would merely replicate what the students had already learned – some of it in the modern European history outline courses that they took in their first or second year of study. Caplan and Stargardt found it 'truly disturbing that a fellow academic feels entitled to smear Oxford's historians and their teaching with outrageous insinuations and unfounded claims of guilt by association in this way' and declared themselves 'personally and professionally affronted at the imputation that our teaching has even the faintest association with Holocaust denial'.

Over a number of years, I have had direct experience of Holocaust denial in a variety of forms. At the turn of the century I was involved as an expert witness in the libel action brought by the writer David Irving against Deborah Lipstadt and her publisher, Penguin Books, over her allegation that he was a Holocaust denier who manipulated and distorted the evidence for the Nazi extermination of European Jews. Researching the subject for the trial, which ended in Irving's comprehensive defeat, brought me into contact with many varieties of Holocaust denial, many of them nauseating, all of them upsetting. Neither the work of the Alfred Toepfer Foundation's independent historical commission, nor that of Jan Zimmermann, nor the website and publications of the Foundation itself, nor teaching and research in German history at Oxford and Cambridge has anything to do with Holocaust denial.

Pinto-Duschinsky misunderstood the process that forced often reluctant German companies and foundations in the 1990s to commission independent histories of their role in the Third Reich. As the Holocaust came to public prominence, especially in the USA, it became increasingly damaging to their international business interests to be seen as covering up their role in it. Moreover, in almost every case, from the Dresdner Bank to Mercedes-Benz, from the publisher Bertelsmann to the constituent companies of IG Farben, many of them household names today, this role was far, far more prominent and far, far more murderous than that of Toepfer and his Foundation, which played no direct part in mass murder or financing it.

As far as the historical commission was concerned, Pinto-Duschinsky's complaints were directed mainly against the introduction to its report, the only part to have been translated into English; he complained, for example, that Toepfer's postwar employment of Veesenmayer was mentioned 'only in a footnote'. In fact it is discussed on page 378; similarly he claimed that the slaked lime was not mentioned in the introduction, but did not say that it was discussed in the text. His claim that significant facts were buried 'in obscure parts of a turgid tome' is meaningless: they are there for anyone who reads German to see, and the turgidity of the style in which they are written, characteristic of so much German academic writing, is neither here nor there.

Was the independent historical commission's report a piece of 'grey-washing'? Was it in fact independent? One of its authors, Christian Gerlach, complained subsequently that there were 'massive efforts to influence me' and 'to render my text harmless (in particular by cutting it)'. Furthermore, the Foundation showed 'a thoroughly defensive

attitude' towards interpretations of Toepfer's role in the Third Reich.
And indeed, this was undoubtedly the case in the year 2000. But the
pressure on Gerlach, and possibly on others, was exerted not institu-
tionally, by the Foundation but personally, by its archivist, a long-term
friend of Toepfer's, who clearly tried to withhold documents from the
researchers and angrily demanded that Gerlach's contribution should
be axed altogether. He was backed by one of the senior historians on
the commission, Arnold Sywottek. The commission's independence
was also compromised by the presence of members of the Toepfer
family at its meetings.

However, Gerlach published his chapter as written, after threatening to publish it in full elsewhere. There is no evidence to support
the view that the commission's findings were bowdlerised by the
Foundation. On the contrary, they were upsetting both to the
Foundation's staff and to Toepfer's family. No wonder it took them
time to adjust. But, in the end, the Foundation has adjusted. It has put
the commission's principal findings on its website in English, German
and French and distributed it free of charge to libraries and interested
parties, including Hanseatic Scholars. The Foundation points to the
fact that it has changed its programmes in the light of the historical
commission's findings. It has developed active support for initiatives
of remembrance and tolerance in the Hamburg region, including the
placing of small round brass plaques known as *Stolpersteine* on the
pavement outside formerly Jewish-owned houses, with the names of
their murdered owners or tenants on them. It has funded publications
on the persecution and murder of Hamburg's Jews under the Nazis. It
has supported Jewish organisations and awarded scholarships, including Hanseatic Scholarships, to students researching into the history of
Germany and other countries in the Nazi era. 'Pinto-Duschinsky's
claim raised in his letter to the editors of the *Frankfurter Allgemeine
Zeitung* that this Foundation gives token grants to Jewish organisations for purely cosmetic reasons is therefore,' it says, 'as insulting and
inappropriate as his even more absurd insinuation that this organisation sets out to trivialize the Holocaust.'

Why, then, in view of all this, does the Foundation continue to include Toepfer's name in its title and documents? Could it not simply revert to the 'F.V.S. Foundation', the title it held before its founder's death in 1993? To do so, however, would surely invite the accusation that it was trying to cover up the fact that he had established it in the first place. Yet to use the name invites the accusation that it is continuing to honour someone who should not be honoured. The colloquial expression 'heads I win, tails you lose' comes to mind here. The Foundation has decided to keep Toepfer's name 'rather as an act of transparency than as an attempt to honour Toepfer'. Far from glorifying him, as Pinto-Duschinsky alleges, it now uses this association to signal its responsibility deriving from its past. Its website contains a large amount of information helping prospective prize-winners and Scholars to make up their own minds, including the *Standpoint* article by Pinto-Duschinsky itself, and it informs prize-winners about the history of the Foundation before they decide whether to accept a prize from it.

All of this seems admirable. The funding the Foundation provides for young British scholars and graduate students to study in Germany is not 'tainted money'; it did not come from the 'Aryanisation' of Jewish businesses or the supply of poison gas to Auschwitz or the employment of slave labour or the plunder of occupied countries or anything similar. The Foundation has openly acknowledged the complicity of its founder, Alfred Toepfer, with the Nazi regime, and is absolutely transparent in its provision of information with which people can make up their own minds about how far it went. Its openness is a model that others could follow.

NOTE
This article sparked a prolonged controversy with Michael Pinto-Duschinsky, which can be followed in the lively right-wing magazine *Standpoint*, edited by Daniel Johnson: for the original article, see Michael Pinto-Duschinsky, 'The Prize Lies of a Nazi Tycoon', Issue 21 (April, 2010), pp. 39–43; idem, 'The Holocaust: excusing the

inexcusable', Issue 34 (July/August, 2011), pp. 34–9; and 'An exchange: Toepfer and the Holocaust', Issue 35 (September, 2011), pp. 16–18, with articles by Pinto-Duschinsky and myself. At this juncture, wisely perhaps, the editor brought the debate to a close. However, this left a number of the points at issue unresolved. In his final contribution to the discussion, Pinto-Duschinsky accused me of being 'unwilling to face up to the defiance and excuses of the Toepfer Foundation'. Yet the Foundation has shown contrition for what he rightly calls the 'dubious past' of its founder and confronted it with admirable honesty, even if it has only got around to doing this in the past few years. Nobody familiar with its website could possibly think it is making excuses or showing defiance to Toepfer's critics. There is no possible reason why I would not be willing to criticise it if this was not the case.

Similarly Pinto-Duschinsky thinks I have 'too complacent a view about German historiography of the Holocaust'. He has no basis for this assertion. If he really does think German historiography has not confronted the Holocaust openly and critically then he needs to cite the literature that would justify this claim. In fact he cannot, because of course the mainstream of professional historians of the Holocaust in Germany have been in the forefront of uncovering its horrors for many years. He claims I have revised my judgement of the report of the independent historical commission set up by the Toepfer Foundation to investigate their relationship with Nazism because while I earlier described its findings as 'devastating', I now say it 'pulled its punches'. I have not changed my mind. There is no contradiction between these two statements. As I noted in *Standpoint*, the editorial gloss on the commission's findings did indeed conclude (wrongly in my view) that Toepfer was not a fellow traveller of the Nazis. It did so, no doubt, because that was the verdict of the German denazification court after the war. But I go on to say that the error of this claim is made clear by the commission's individual chapters. It is these chapters that contain the devastating findings. And they were devastating because up to that point Toepfer's claim not only to have been distant from but actually to have opposed the Nazis had been accepted by the Foundation and even by his own family.

Pinto-Duschinsky persists in calling the report an 'official history' and its authors 'sponsored historians'. This is rhetorical sleight of hand; the report was independently researched and compiled by an independent group of professional historians. Of course they were provided with research facilities and access to the documents by the Foundation. But so, too, was Pinto-Duschinsky, whose work also appears on the Foundation's website. Does this make him a 'sponsored historian'? He brings the commission's report into association with a report commissioned previously by the Foundation from a PR agency, but he should know that the PR agency's recommendations were not acted upon and did not affect the commission's work.

Pinto-Duschinsky makes great play with the fact that I declined to carry out a full check on the documents, sources, emails and correspondence generated in the course of Oxford University's investigation of his charges against the Toepfer Foundation when he asked me to do so. I declined, however, not only because I was unwilling to spend the very considerable amount of time it would have involved doing this, but also because he himself has all this material in his own possession. Perhaps he could say why he was unwilling or unable to do the checking himself?

Pinto-Duschinsky asserts that I have 'relied on summaries prepared by the Toepfer Foundation and its sponsored academics as well as documents on the Foundation's website'. The implication here is that I have used this material uncritically. I can assure him I have not, and indeed he presents no evidence to suggest this is the case. The material in question includes, of course, the chapter in the commission report by the 'sponsored historian' Christian Gerlach which Pinto-Duschinsky himself repeatedly relies on (it is the only one in the book he consistently uses). The documents on the Foundation's website include Pinto-Duschinsky's own articles, which, of course, I have used as well. He presents no evidence to back up his assertion that the materials on the Foundation's website are 'misleading and selective', nor that the commission's report was in any significant respect 'bowdlerised'.

To give one example: Pinto-Duschinsky claims that Gerda Toepfer, Alfred's daughter, visited the Hungarian history specialist C. A. Macartney in Oxford to persuade him to use his good offices to secure the release of the war criminal Edmund Veesenmayer. The Foundation has dug up and made available her correspondence with Macartney, in which there is no mention of this alleged intent at all; the correspondence makes it clear, on the contrary, that Macartney was only interested in interviewing Veesenmayer for his research. Thus Pinto-Duschinsky's claims are shown to be entirely without foundation. If he wants to substantiate them, he will have to produce a properly incriminating letter. So far he has not done so. Thus my conclusion is that the Foundation is right on this score. I fail to see how this amounts to an uncritical swallowing of the Foundation's point of view. Just because the Foundation says something doesn't mean it is necessarily wrong.

It is unfortunate that Pinto-Duschinsky relied for some of his arguments on the French ultra-nationalist Lionel Boissou. It is a pity that a serious historian like Pierre Ayçoberry came to endorse Boissou's exaggerated criticisms of the Toepfer Foundation, which Boissou portrayed as engaged in a plot to detach Alsace-Lorraine from France (in the 1990s!!). The University of Strasbourg should not have given in to the pressure exerted by Boissou. Pinto-Duschinsky also alleges that the commission deliberately ignored a critical article published in 1999 by the left-wing activist, doctor of medicine and historical researcher Karl-Heinz Roth on the Toepfer Foundation. In fact it is mentioned in the commission's report, including in the introduction (notes 21 and 24, p. 27).

Zimmermann's careful and balanced analysis of Pinto-Duschinsky's allegations notes that his discoveries, which are very few in number, add little of importance to what the commission and (in his later biography) Zimmermann had already uncovered about Toepfer; the commission had not suppressed, but simply (and, in retrospect, ill-advisedly) neglected to investigate the Foundation's postwar employment of ex-Nazis (reflecting its conception of its mission as investigating the activities of Toepfer and the Foundation *during* the Nazi period). Zimmermann provides detailed support for his allegation in his correspondence with Pinto-Duschinsky and in his analysis of the first *Standpoint* article.

The extent of Toepfer's postwar association with ex-Nazis, war criminals and Holocaust perpetrators was no greater than that of many leading conservative businessmen, politicians and civil servants in Adenauer's Germany. The fact that Toepfer and his Foundation behaved in a way typical of the West German establishment after the war does not make their behaviour any less reprehensible, of course, but it does make Pinto-Duschinsky's attempt to claim that Toepfer's practices in this respect were somehow exceptional, unusual or extreme in their nature and extent entirely untenable.

Pinto-Duschinsky's claim that the Toepfer archive was weeded to remove incriminating material was changed in his final *Standpoint* contribution to a reference to a statement by Toepfer's son that part of Toepfer's own *private* papers (specifically, papers that revealed his *private* views on Nazism) were destroyed after 1945. This is not the same thing. We do not know how or why they were destroyed. And destruction is not the same as weeding. There is no evidence of any subsequent 'redaction' of the archives of the *companies* and the *Foundation*, both of which were freely used by the commission's researchers. As Zimmermann notes, the material in them, especially relating to the postwar period, is incriminating enough to make it clear no weeding was carried out.

Toepfer's companies did not manufacture munitions, tanks or poison gas; they did not build concentration camps or gas chambers or crematoria; indeed, they did not produce anything specifically designed for use in the war or the Holocaust at all. They did not employ slave labour or concentration camp prisoners, though hundreds of other German firms like the Krupps were doing so at the time. Unlike many German companies, Toepfer's did not profit from the 'Aryanisation' of Jewish property. He did not commit any war crimes, nor did he profit from them. Toepfer ran construction companies but they were not engaged in military construction let alone work for the SS. The most that can be said is that they operated in a part of Poland that had been re-incorporated into the Reich after the invasion of Poland, doubtless to the satisfaction of nationalists like Toepfer since it had been part of Prussia before 1918. By operating there, of course, the companies endorsed Germany's war aims and implicitly backed the occupation. But this does not make the money they generated indelibly 'tainted'. Moreover, this money constituted only a minute fraction of Toefper's fortune, most of which was made after the war and came from the grain trade.

And, to reiterate a detailed but crucial point: slaked lime is different from quicklime. Gerlach is wrong to claim that the former was used for covering and dissolving cadavers. Nor did he claim that the slaked lime that Toepfer supplied to the SS administration of the Lódź ghetto was used for covering corpses; his claim only had a general application to the chemical in general, and here, as I have noted, it was in any case wrong.

As for Edmund Veesenmayer, who, for a brief time after the war, was a business employee of Toepfer in Tehran, I did not describe him in a 'euphemistic way'. I described him as a 'former Nazi' and a 'senior German official in Hungary' (at a time when, as everyone knows, the German administration was sending more than 400,000 Hungarian Jews to Auschwitz) and I pointed out that his ex-secretary wrote implicitly justifying the Holocaust after the war. And although Pinto-Duschinsky claims he did not describe Edmund Veesenmayer as a close associate of Toepfer, on page 327 of the German edition of his first *Standpoint* article, he says the following: 'Thus *three* [his italics] of the closest associates [*Mitarbeiter*, lit. 'co-workers'] of Toepfer had assisted in deeds of murder: *Edmund Veesenmayer* [my italics], Kurt Haller and Hans Joachim Riecke, as well as Barbara Hacke as his private secretary.' In fact, Veesenmayer's association with Toepfer was so tenuous that Toepfer is not even mentioned in the standard critical biography of Veesenmayer by Igor-Philip Matic published in 2002.

One of Pinto-Duschinsky's favourite tactics is to establish guilt by association. He refers to my recollection that Toepfer's guest house in Hamburg in 1971 contained Holocaust denial literature, that I met ex-SS Major-General Hans-Joachim Riecke in the house, and that Albert Speer had been a recent guest of the Foundation, but while these were indeed disturbing to me as a young British student making my acquaintance with Germany for the first time, I did not even then fall into the error of supposing this made Toepfer either a Holocaust denier, or an ex-SS man, or a pro-Nazi. I did indeed try to find out more about him, but was assured by the Foundation that Toepfer had resisted the Nazis, and that Riecke was no longer in its employ. Speer, whose memoirs had recently been published, was at that time widely seen in Germany as 'the acceptable face of Nazism', as it were, and his claim not to have known about the Holocaust was generally believed. Even experienced anti-Nazi journalists like Gitta Sereny were unable to penetrate the mask. Only gradually, and much later, did it become clear how many lies, evasions and half-truths he had been telling the world about his role in the Third Reich and its knowledge of its crimes. Moreover, as I delved into the background of the West German establishment with the aid of the (East German) *Brown Book* listings of prominent ex-Nazis in its ranks, it became clear that pretty well every institution in West Germany was swarming with ex-Nazis. Despite this, Toepfer's name was not on the list.

This does, of course, raise a more general question about historical research and its funding. Should I, for example, have accepted, as I did in the mid-1980s, an exchange grant from the East German government to work in the old Reich archive in Potsdam and local and regional archives in Leipzig and Dresden, even though the regime was responsible for the deaths of many unfortunate citizens who had tried to escape to freedom across the Berlin Wall? The answer must surely be yes. It was impossible to work on German history without making such compromises, and, crucially, they had no influence on what I wrote about the regime on the basis of my researches. Marxists in the 1960s used to talk of 'useful idiots', capitalists and their fellow travellers who could supply money and resources to those who were willing to take advantage of them and use them to undermine capitalism, and this is very much how, *mutatis mutandis*, young historians like myself regarded institutions like the East German regime or, indeed, the Toepfer Foundation and its like. Our agenda at the time, following the lead of German historian Martin Broszat in his brilliant book *The Hitler State*, was to uncover the true breadth and depth of complicity of German social, economic and political elites in the rise, triumph and rule of the Nazis. Part of the excitement lay in the knowledge that these elites were still very much in charge of West Germany, even though 1968 and the generational change associated with it were beginning to loosen their grip. Toepfer and his Foundation belonged squarely within this frame of reference.

It is difficult to see why Pinto-Duschinsky has pursued the Toepfer Foundation so obsessively. He initially claimed that Toepfer and his Foundation had provided 'enormous help to Hitler' and played a 'key role in the Third Reich'. In fact, neither the Foundation, nor its founder, nor its activities, nor the Toepfer businesses were particularly significant or important during the Nazi era. They were fellow travellers whose contribution to the Third Reich and its crimes was at most minor and marginal. The Foundation does not even provide funds to Oxford University – the Hanseatic Scholarship money is given directly to the recipients, and the selection committee is entirely independent of the Foundation and the University. In pursuing the remaining unresolved legacies of the Nazi past in present-day Germany it is important to choose the right targets. In the end, for all their toleration of Nazism, its servants and its crimes, Toepfer and his Foundation are the wrong ones.

PART IV

FOREIGN POLICY

15. HITLER'S ALLY

Shortly after he was forced out of office in November 2011, Italy's longest-serving postwar Prime Minister, Silvio Berlusconi, told the press that he was spending his time reading the last letters written by the Fascist dictator Benito Mussolini, who had ruled the country from 1922 to 1943, to his mistress Clara Petacci. 'I have to say,' he confessed, 'that I see myself in many aspects of those letters.' In the dictator's view, Italy was ungovernable. 'The Duce wondered: "What sort of democracy is this?"' When one of the journalists suggested to Berlusconi that it might not be entirely accurate to describe Mussolini's Italy as a democracy, the former Prime Minister replied: 'Well, it was a democracy in a minor way.'

The right-wing parties that have dominated Italian politics since the end of the Cold War have consistently rejected the legacy of resistance to Fascism represented by the Christian Democrats and the Communists, the two parties that dominated Italian politics from the late 1940s to the early 1990s. Exploiting Italians' deep frustration at the chaotic instability and corruption of the postwar political system, the New Right has based its appeal not least on its claim to represent law and order, Italy for the Italians, respect for the Catholic Church and its values, and, not least, financial rectitude and political stability. Neo-fascist and self-styled post-fascist political groupings have played a full part in the political manoeuvrings and mergers that have characterised Italian politics over the past two decades, moderating their policies and their rhetoric where necessary in order to obtain a share in power.

In this situation, serious public criticism of Mussolini in Italy has become increasingly rare. His rule is widely portrayed as relatively benign. 'Mussolini,' Berlusconi told the *Spectator* in September 2003, 'never killed anyone.' If he did send his opponents into internal exile it was to holiday resorts. Politicians like Gianfranco Fini who began their careers in the neo-fascist Italian Social Movement, the MSI, had no problems in attaining high political office under Berlusconi (Fini was Foreign Minister for several years in the first decade of this century). In 1992 Fini declared that Fascism had been 'part of the history of Italy and the expression of permanent values'. Alessandra Mussolini, the dictator's granddaughter, has been a member of the Italian legislature as part of Berlusconi's right-wing alliance after playing a prominent but repeatedly disruptive role in post-fascist politics. In 2008 Gianni Alemanno, the former secretary of the youth wing of the MSI, was elected mayor of Rome on the promise of expelling illegal immigrants from the city. His victory speech was greeted with arms raised in the Fascist salute and chants of '*Duce! Duce!*' from the cheering crowd.

In Mussolini's home town of Predappio, souvenir shops until recently lined the main street, selling black shirts, Fascist banners, statues of the Duce, books and DVDs celebrating his life, and, more disturbingly still, *manganelli*, or clubs, inscribed with words such as *molti nemici, molto onore* ('many enemies, much honour'). Every year, on the anniversaries of Mussolini's birth and death and his March on Rome in 1922, thousands of sympathisers, many of them dressed in black shirts and wearing Fascist badges, have marched from the town centre to the mausoleum where his body is interred, chanting Fascist songs and slogans. Dozens, sometimes hundreds, of people come to the mausoleum daily and leave their comments in the visitors' book placed before the tomb. What they have to say is overwhelmingly positive; almost always, their words are addressed directly to the Duce himself: 'You alone believed in a strong and free Italy and you loved your people unto death' (2007). 'Only under your wise guidance did Italy become a "nation", a nation that was feared, respected, fruitful, and envied' (2008). 'If you were here, we would not be in this mess' (2011). Many of these messages have an intimate, personal quality, and religious phrases and sentiments are common: 'If you could see how low our poor Italy has sunk,' wrote one visitor in 2007, 'return, reincarnated in one of us! Now and for ever.'

It would be impossible to imagine similar sentiments being expressed by Germans about Hitler, former Nazis and neo-Nazis joining a present-day German government, German politicians claiming Hitler never killed anyone, Hitler's granddaughter (if he had had one) being elected to parliament, a former German head of government seeing himself in Hitler's letters to Eva Braun, German crowds chanting Nazi slogans, or German souvenir shops openly selling Nazi memorabilia. While Italians are widely dissatisfied with their political system and even more with the state of their economy, there has seldom been a political system that has enjoyed such widespread support as that created in 1949 by the Basic Law of the German Federal Republic: it has delivered stability and prosperity, and nurtured in the Germans a palpable smugness that is sometimes hard to bear, however justified it may be. The destruction of Germany at the end of the war was almost total; in Italy, despite widespread damage inflicted by the military conflicts of the final phase of the war, after the country had come under German occupation and been invaded by the Allies, the destruction was nowhere near as widespread or severe. Germany was occupied for years by massive Allied forces, while the postwar occupation of Italy was only very brief. Italy remained territorially pretty much intact, while Germany lost huge swathes of its traditional lands and was divided into two mutually hostile states for more than forty years after the war; for the overwhelming majority of Germans, their country's fate was inescapably the consequence of Hitler's megalomaniac military and political ambitions.

In the absence of a consistent policy of prosecuting Italians for war crimes, symbolised by a general amnesty for political and military prisoners issued in June 1946, Fascist bureaucrats and administrators stayed in office, with sixty out of the country's sixty-four regional prefects in 1960 and all 135 police chiefs in the same year having begun their careers under Mussolini. The judge appointed in 1957 as president of the Constitutional Court had been president of the tribunal set up in 1938 to judge issues stemming from the Fascist racial laws. Surviving senior figures in the regime went unpunished. There was no general reckoning with Fascism's crimes either at home or abroad. All this was in sharp contrast to the situation in Germany, where only a handful of former Nazis escaped the net of denazification, and war crimes trials continued for several years, giving shocking publicity to the misdeeds of the Third Reich and its servants.

Above all, perhaps, the reorientation of German public memory since the end of the Cold War, reflecting a far more widespread trend, especially in the USA, towards placing what at that point came to be called the Holocaust at the centre of any retrospective assessment of the Third Reich, as a defining aspect of Hitler's rule, has created a gulf between past and present that no German can conceive of bridging. Such has been its power, indeed, that even Italian neo-Fascists have felt obliged to distance themselves from Mussolini's introduction of racial and antisemitic laws in the late 1930s. Yet the fact that for most of his time in office Mussolini did not persecute Italy's Jews, who were sent to Auschwitz only after the Germans occupied Italy following the Duce's fall in 1943, has preserved the memory of his regime from the fate that has overtaken its German counterpart, whose primary responsibility for the Holocaust is undeniable.

While a considerable body of research now exists documenting the nature and extent of ordinary Germans' support for Hitler during the Third Reich, there is nothing comparable on Fascist Italy. In *Fascist Voices* (2012), Christopher Duggan fills the gap by examining a wide range of diaries and the numerous letters sent to Mussolini by private citizens during the two decades of his rule. Among the most striking material is the correspondence between Petacci and Mussolini, fleshed out by extracts from Claretta's diaries. This material often expressed the same unforced intimate feelings towards the Duce and his regime as the messages left in more recent times on his grave. It enables Duggan to deliver not merely a detailed account of popular attitudes towards the regime, but, far more, a general history of Fascism that for the first time treats it not as a tyranny that gave ordinary Italians no possibility of expressing themselves freely, nor as the brutal dictatorship of a capitalist class that reduced the great majority of the country's citizens to the status of victims, but as a regime rooted strongly in popular aspirations and desires.

Yet this material, by its nature, quite possibly exaggerates the degree of popular success enjoyed by Mussolini. In *The Fascist Party and Popular Opinion in Mussolini's Italy* (2012), Paul Corner paints a very different picture, arguing that corruption and mismanagement had made the Fascist Party deeply unpopular by 1939. And other sources used by Duggan himself reveal a more complex picture than the diaries and letters he quotes from suggest.

True, Mussolini was careful not to antagonise the faithful, and his Concordat with the Papacy in 1929, ending the mutual hostility of Church and State that had begun with the unification of Italy in the nineteenth century, and putting in place arrangements that have endured to the present day, marked the symbiosis between the two that made Catholicism one of the regime's most important props. This extended even to Mussolini's antisemitic racial laws, which were backed by leading Catholic periodicals and praised by the rector of the Catholic University of Milan, Father Agostino Gemelli, as the passing of the 'terrible sentence that the Deicide people has brought upon itself' as 'the consequences of that horrendous crime pursue it everywhere and at all times'. Nor would conversion release Jews from this sentence: their race meant they would never be assimilated to what Gemelli called Italy's new Fascist unity 'of descent, of religion, of tongue, of customs, of hopes, of ideals'. Mussolini himself was repeatedly the object of ecstatic mass adulation when he spoke, as he often did, in public, in what he described to Claretta as 'fanatical scenes, delirious, mad: they were weeping, kneeling, shrieking, arms stretched out . . . ' The enthusiasm expressed in the letters ordinary people sent to him made it clear that this was far more than stage-managed.

Yet Duggan also makes clear the extraordinary degree of surveillance and repression imposed by the regime on real or potential dissenters. Known critics of Fascism were targeted, with the house of the liberal philosopher Benedetto Croce being broken into by armed blackshirts in November 1926 and its contents trashed before the eyes of his terrified family. The police guard thereafter permanently stationed outside his house was posted there less for his own safety than in order to note down the names of his visitors, who now rapidly dwindled in number. Soon his friends were obliged to meet him 'in deserted streets and in solitary corridors'. Even greater isolation was the lot of those exiled to the remoter rural parts of southern Italy – 13,000 of them in all, including not only political opponents and critics but troublemakers of all kinds, as well as homosexuals and petty criminals. Far from being 'holiday resorts', the villages where they were sent, far from their families and their jobs, were godforsaken places, as even their inhabitants admitted (*Christ Stopped at Eboli*, the classic account of exile by Carlo Levi, takes its title from a saying of the inhabitants of the area south of the town of that name). Absorbed in the daily struggle for existence in a harsh and unforgiving rural environment, the peasants there had little time for intellectuals, politicians or even the Italian state, whatever its political complexion; for them, Rome, as Levi noted, 'is the capital of the *Signori* [gentlemen], the centre of a foreign and malicious state'.

The Political Police, or *PolPol*, formed in 1926, was given a huge budget, fifty million lire, fully half that assigned to the country's entire police force, and liaised with local police through what Duggan calls 'another vast tentacular organisaton', OVRA (short for *piovra*, 'octopus') opening and copying the correspondence of political dissidents. A Special Confidential Service tapped the phones not only of dissidents but also of leading figures in the Fascist movement, if Mussolini should need to use their tawdry secrets in order to blackmail them. By 1938 the Service was employing 462 stenographers just to transcribe the conversations it overheard. OVRA – according to Mussolini, 'the strongest organisation in the world' – employed a large number of spies, recruited from many walks of life, often under the threat of exposing their own personal vices. Some of them were former socialists or Communists persuaded to work for the regime by payments that rescued them from the financial ruin into which so many of them had fallen.

The result of all this was a pervasive atmosphere of suspicion and distrust, in which even the schoolchildren whose diaries Duggan quotes became wary about expressing any criticism of the regime. A law of November 1926 banned statements that were 'seditious or damaging to the prestige of the authorities', and the displaying of 'symbols of social subversion', though (unlike in Germany) the political jokes that proliferate under every dictatorship seem mostly to have gone unpunished. But arrest and imprisonment were far from being the only sanctions against dissent; in the economic depression of the late 1920s and 1930s, dismissal from a job, however low-paid, could spell ruin, and was frequently used. As in Germany, too, many people sent in denunciations to the police when they witnessed imprudent remarks or behaviour, though Duggan says rather charitably that this was mainly because they were worried that if they did not report them to the authorities they might themselves risk an accusation of complicity in such deviant acts.

Yet such repression did not extend into the moral sphere, despite the regime's strong links with the Catholic Church. Indeed, sexual libertinism seems to have been as prominent a feature of Italian political life then as it has been more recently. When Silvio Berlusconi declared that he could see himself in the letters exchanged between Mussolini and his mistress Claretta Petacci, he could also have been referring to their often highly sexual content. The Duce's ill-concealed sexual voracity, like Berlusconi's, projected an image of virility that many Italians, in both cases, found deeply impressive. Just as Berlusconi was repeatedly reported, in his seventies, to have held orgies with bevies of young, sometimes very young, female dancers and good-time girls,

Mussolini spent huge amounts of time on his sex life, his official image as a loving and faithful family man paralleling an unofficial one as a man of uncontrollable priapic urges.

Women, he liked to boast, threw themselves at him, and he did not even pretend to try and fend them off. Some of the letters Duggan quotes must have left him in no doubt as to what was being offered, if they managed to make their way to him through the 1,500 pieces of correspondence from private citizens that reached his office every day: 'So many kisses and caresses I would give my dear Benito,' wrote one of them: 'I would embrace him so he could not escape!' Most of these women, he told Claretta, he only made love to once, and never saw again. He simply used them, he told her, 'for my carnal satisfaction', and to reassure her, he phoned or wrote to her a dozen or more times a day after their relationship began in 1936.

The libidinous nature of the regime's satraps was also a matter of public knowledge. During the disastrous military campaign in Greece in the winter of 1940–1, Mussolini's son-in-law Galeazzo Ciano installed himself and his entourage in a large hotel in Bari, where twenty or more girls were brought by government officials every week for orgies in which the participants divided into teams and squirted water from soda siphons at each other's genitals while hacking at clothes with scissors. Just to make sure everyone knew what was going on, the windows were left wide open. All of this was a world away from the priggishness of Hitler, who concealed his own, single, and utterly conventional sexual relationship, with Eva Braun, from the public until they finally married on the eve of their mutual suicide at the end of the war. When he found out that the Nazi Propaganda Minister Joseph Goebbels was conducting a passionate affair with the Czech actress Lida Baarova, Hitler gave him a furious dressing-down and forced him to break it off.

No harm was done to Mussolini's standing with the Italian public by all this. People might grumble about one thing or another, but, as in Nazi Germany, the Leader became a successfully integrative figure, bridging social, cultural, generational and regional differences to help bind the nation together. 'If only the *Führer* knew' was an exclamation frequently uttered by citizens of the Third Reich outraged at yet another peccadillo of a corrupt Gauleiter or party boss, and it was paralleled exactly in Fascist Italy: 'If only the *Duce* knew'. Mussolini seemed sacrosanct however much his subordinates were reviled.

He reached the height of his popularity with the invasion of Ethiopia in October 1935, as the regime pursued wild fantasies of imperial wealth and expressed its determination to exact revenge for liberal Italy's defeat at the hands of the Ethiopian Emperor Menelik II forty years before. Determined to avoid a repeat of the disastrous ground campaign of 1896, Mussolini ordered poison gas to be dropped on the enemy forces from the air and sprayed indiscriminately from aircraft on to military and civilian targets alike. This, too, was widely supported. Any means were justified to punish the 'inhuman, vile . . . bestial Abyssinian people', a group of students told him: 'Chemical weapons are expensive, it is true, but the Italian people are ready to make the financial sacrifices required to save their sons.' Critics in Geneva and elsewhere were told the chemicals only knocked people out for a short time, while those who pointed to press photographs of mustard-gas victims were informed that they had died of leprosy.

Duggan quotes a couple of diarists who expressed doubts about the conduct of the Italian troops during the war, during which, for example, the party secretary, Achille Starace, used Ethiopian prisoners as target practice, shooting them first in the testicles and then in the chest. But the overwhelming majority of responses were ecstatic. As numerous testimonies quoted by Duggan demonstrate, Mussolini reached the absolute pinnacle of his popularity at this point, the embodiment of Italian national pride and national achievement. 'It is right that we look for a place in the sun,' wrote one diarist: 'Today Italy is a nation, a people, conscious of its worth, that knows what it wants and how to get it. The Italy of 15 years ago is finished, dead.'

War in Ethiopia kindled in the regime a new optimism about remoulding Italians into aggressive, well-disciplined and fanatical members of a new master race. Among other things, this meant reforming Italian manners, getting rid of 'bourgeois' customs such as the handshake (declared to be 'soft' and 'Anglo-Saxon' and replaced with the Fascist salute), and the formal mode of address, *Lei* (branded a 'foreign import' with connotations of 'servility'). Coffee-drinking was condemned as decadent (even more of a lost cause than the other behavioural reforms). Mussolini announced his intention of making Italians 'less nice' and more 'odious, tough and implacable: in other words, masters'. In April 1937 the Duce made it illegal for white Italians to have sexual relations with blacks, a measure prompted by the mass sexual exploitation of Ethiopian women by Italian troops following the invasion. As the twenty-six-year-old Fascist journalist Indro Montanelli, who had enrolled as a volunteer for the campaign in 1935, wrote: 'We will never be dominators without a strong sense of our pre-destined superiority. There is no fraternising with negroes ... No indulgences, no love affairs ... The white must command.' This did not stop him purchasing from her Ethiopian father a twelve-year-old wife for himself for 500 lire, though he was prudent enough to leave her behind when he returned home.

However, all this was bought at a heavy cost. Together with Mussolini's large-scale intervention in the Spanish Civil War, the conquest of Ethiopia imposed unsustainable financial burdens on the Italian state, making it impossible to invest seriously in military equipment or the expansion of the armed forces. Mussolini thought he was militarily invincible, and no one dared tell him otherwise. In his conversations with Claretta he poured scorn on the other peoples of Europe: the English were 'a disgusting people ... They think only with their arses.' They were cowards who were afraid of getting their clothes wet when it rained: 'People who carry an umbrella can never ... understand the moral significance of war.' The Spanish were 'lazy, lethargic' and the French a 'hotchpotch of races and scum, a haven for cowards ... spineless and gutless people' corrupted by 'alcohol and syphilis'. Only the Italians and the Germans were able to 'love that supreme, inexorable violence which is the chief motor force of world history'.

In 1939 it finally dawned on him that the Italian armed forces were woefully unprepared for a European war, with obsolete equipment, poorly trained troops and severe shortages of arms and ammunition. He had no alternative but to adopt a stance of 'non-belligerence' when war broke out in September 1939, to the relief of most Italians. As German victories multiplied, however, Mussolini grew increasingly irritated at his countrymen's evident distaste for a European war: 'I have to say they nauseate me. They are cowards and weaklings ... It's disappointing and soul-destroying to see that I've failed to change these people into a people with steel and courage!' Popular reaction to Italy's declaration of war on France and Britain on 10 June 1940 was mixed; some were enthusiastic, others were apprehensive. The doubters were right to be concerned.

If the Italian attack on France was a fiasco, the Italian invasion of Greece was a catastrophe. Instead of the anticipated lightning victory, the poorly prepared Italian forces were humiliated by superior Greek troops in the Balkans, while the British quickly routed the Italians in Libya and Ethiopia. Hitler had to step in to rescue the situation, and the ease with which the Germans drove the British out of Greece, combined with the stunning victories of Rommel in North Africa, only rubbed salt into the wounds of Fascist pride. The letters and diaries quoted by Duggan now mingled patriotic and Fascist commitment with increasing doubt and scepticism. When Mussolini visited wounded soldiers in hospital he was greeted with cries of 'assassin!' (a second visit gave better publicity, since the injured had been replaced in the beds by policemen). People refused to buy the 50 cent stamp with the picture of Hitler and Mussolini on the front, complaining that 'they're even forcing us to lick his backside'.

When Mussolini was overthrown by the Fascist Grand Council following the Allied invasion in 1943, there were, Duggan reports, 'explosions of collective joy' everywhere. The Fascist movement disappeared without trace. As Corner shows, the everyday experience of Fascist rule had alienated most people long before the regime melted away in 1943. Fascism had never succeeded in breaking free from its roots in local and regional politics, and had become the vehicle of the personal and financial ambitions of local power-brokers. Just as nineteenth-century nationalism had tried to 'make Italians', so twentieth-century dictatorship had tried to 'make Fascists'; both, in the end, failed. Italians greeted the surrender to the Allies in September 1943 with huge relief, only to be rudely disabused when the Germans occupied Italy and arrested most of the Italian troops, sending them back home for forced labour in the factories and fields of the Fatherland. Just as it had begun in civil violence, so the regime ended: as Mussolini was rescued from captivity by the Germans and installed in the puppet regime of Salò in the north, a partisan resistance movement emerged, meeting with brutal reprisals from Mussolini's remaining loyal followers, backed by the Germans. More than 50,000 people were killed on both sides, including Mussolini and Claretta, shot by partisans while trying to flee northwards. Their bodies were strung upside-down from the gantry of a petrol station in the suburbs of Milan after being reviled, spat on and urinated on by rejoicing crowds, a large part of whom had most probably been cheering the Duce to the rafters only a few years before.

16. TOWARDS WAR

'It is with Hitler and Hitler's intentions,' remarks Zara Steiner at the beginning of her magisterial contribution to the Oxford History of Modern Europe series, *The Triumph of the Dark: European International History 1933–1939* (2011), 'that any student of European international history must start.' From the moment he became Chancellor, Hitler acted and other statesmen reacted.

His intentions were fixed long before he came to power. They were breathtaking in their ambition. Hitler was not a conventional European statesman. Governed by a Social Darwinist belief in international affairs as a perpetual struggle between races for survival and supremacy, Hitler repeatedly told his leading military and naval officers that Germany would conquer Eastern Europe, aggrandising its vast agricultural resources for itself and pushing aside those who lived there to make way for the expansion of the German race's 'living space'. France, Germany's traditional enemy in the west, would be subjugated to allow Germany to become Europe's dominant nation. This was not a normal German foreign policy in any sense; nor was it determined by the structural factors inherent in the international system of Europe since the nineteenth century, as some have argued.

Of course, Steiner concedes, Nazi Germany was not controlled by a monolithic policy-making structure, and different groups and individuals in the higher echelons of the regime often pursued their own agendas. This was particularly the case with Joachim von

Ribbentrop, who graduated from being head of the Nazi Party's foreign affairs bureau to being the ambassador in England and then Foreign Minister. 'Vain, aggressive, and self-important', in Steiner's words, Ribbentrop developed a rabid Anglophobia and did his best to dissuade Hitler from pursuing the idea of an Anglo-German alliance. Britain, he said, was 'our most dangerous enemy'. Fuelled by perceived slights during his time in London, where his tactlessness earned him repeated and increasingly outspoken criticism in the press, the Foreign Minister eventually succeeded in weaning Hitler away from the alliance project. The Nazi leader continued to hope for British neutrality in the coming conflict, however.

Others, such as Hermann Göring, also on occasion ploughed their own furrow, or influenced Hitler in one direction or another. Yet in the end, it was Hitler – rather than an ill-defined 'polycracy' – who determined Germany's foreign policy. 'Whether Germany was led by Bismarck, Wilhelm II, or Hitler made a vital difference to its policies', Steiner observes. Germany, Hitler declared in *Mein Kampf*, would 'either be a world power, or cease to be.' Once hegemony had been achieved in Europe, so Hitler adumbrated in his *Second Book*, Germany would enter into a power struggle with America for world domination. In order to achieve this, Germans, equated by Hitler with the 'Aryan' race, would have to deal with their arch-enemies the Jews, whom Hitler's paranoid political fantasies portrayed as engaged in a global conspiracy to subvert German civilisation.

Increasingly, Hitler came to identify America as the epicentre of this supposed conspiracy, with Jewish capital working through US President Franklin D. Roosevelt. All of this would involve war – not a limited war for limited and arguably rational objectives, but war on an unimaginable scale, waged at least in part for its own sake. 'We can be saved only by fighting,' Hitler told leaders of the armed forces in February of 1933. Normal rules of diplomacy saw as their ultimate aim the avoidance of conflict and the settlement of international disputes by negotiation. Hitler did not play by these rules, though he repeatedly tried to reassure people publicly that he intended to do so. It took other European statesmen a very long time to realise this. Their mis-judgements form the heart of this important book.

Neville Chamberlain, the British Prime Minister from 1937 to 1940, has had several defenders, but Steiner is not one of them. Her thorough command of the German and French literature and source material enables her to reach a properly contextualised judgement of his policy of appeasement, of giving Hitler what he demanded in the hope that it would satisfy him. Chamberlain, she argues persuasively, was a man of limited insight and imagination, repeatedly prone to wishful thinking. During the Munich crisis he mistakenly thought that all Hitler wanted was to absorb the German-speaking part of Czechoslovakia, when what he really wanted was the total destruction of the country, which he achieved in violation of the Munich settlement a mere six months later.

Chamberlain also put too great a burden on his own abilities. As Steiner writes, his 'hubristic ambitions and self-confidence were extraordinary'. He stubbornly refused to recognise reality. Right to the end he viewed Mussolini as a calming and restraining influence on Hitler – 'a judgment', Steiner comments, 'which was entirely wrong'. He had no idea of Mussolini's ambitions in the Mediterranean. It is true that Chamberlain pursued a policy of rapid rearmament from 1936, but he did so in order to deter Hitler, not in order to prepare for a war. As late as 23 July 1939, he told his sister that 'Hitler has concluded that we mean business and that the time is not ripe for the major war. Therein,' he concluded with ineffable smugness, 'he is fulfilling my expectations . . . the longer the war is put off the less likely it is to come at all.' Just over two months later Britain was at war.

Anthony Eden, the British Foreign Secretary who later portrayed himself as a resolute opponent of the Nazis and of the policy of appeasement, does not fare much better in Steiner's account. In developing policy towards the Germans, Eden was 'wobbly and unclear in his own mind', and 'gave no consistent lead', so that it was scarcely surprising that Chamberlain 'was thoroughly annoyed by his Foreign Secretary, who needed constant prodding to take any positive action'.

Vacillating and indecisive, he did not join the anti-appeasers around Winston Churchill even after he (Eden) had left office in 1938. Lord Halifax, Eden's successor, was easier for Chamberlain to manage, especially once the Prime Minister had restructured the policy-making machinery to give himself control over foreign affairs. Halifax dutifully pursued Chamberlain's chimerical vision of a general European settlement involving non-aggression pacts, collective security and disarmament (in 1938!), a policy that led Hitler to remark to Halifax's face that the British government was living in 'a make-believe land of strange, if respectable, illusions'. Steiner notes that Halifax, 'though patronizing about Hitler and his advisers, was clearly out of his depth in dealing with them'.

Chamberlain's and Halifax's defenders have sometimes argued that the peace they achieved by sacrificing the integrity of Czechoslovakia bought Britain and France time to rearm. It is one of the many strengths of this book that it includes detailed assessments of the state of military readiness and arms production of the major European powers at various stages in the run-up to the war. The figures show that it was in fact Germany that benefited from the year's peace that followed the Munich agreement. The Wehrmacht was so poorly prepared for a general war in September 1938 that leading generals were even considering arresting Hitler and staging a climb-down if a general European war became a serious prospect. It is often forgotten how close Europe came to armed conflict at that time. British children were evacuated to the country and Londoners were issued gas masks for the eventuality of German bombing raids.

Steiner speculates that if Chamberlain had joined forces with the French and threatened war instead of opening negotiations, Hitler might have been forced to back down. Popular opinion, strongly opposed to war, might have swung round behind the British and French governments. A military conflict would most likely have brought a stalemate, especially if the modern and efficient Czech army had held its well-prepared defensive positions against a German attack. But 'like so many counterfactual scenarios', Steiner concedes, this is in the end implausible, and 'the arguments for war in 1938 seem much stronger in retrospect than they did at the time'. The British and the French had not held the staff talks needed to coordinate military action, and both overestimated German military strength. Chamberlain still believed in the possibility of a general European peace settlement. And he was committed to avoiding war at almost any cost.

The leading French statesman of the day, Edouard Daladier, did not share such illusions. He was clear in his mind that Hitler intended to destroy Czechoslovakia, and that his word could not be relied on. 'Within six months,' he predicted correctly after the Munich agreement, 'France and England would be face to face with new German demands.' Throughout the crisis he tried to persuade Chamberlain to stand firm. A senior official in the British Foreign Office called his argument 'awful rubbish'. By failing to build a viable system of alliances with the smaller East European states, the French had made themselves reliant on the British. After the Munich agreement, Daladier told his colleagues: 'I am not proud.' He knew it was an abject capitulation, and he was right.

Daladier's relative clear-sightedness was not shared by the leadership of the other major European power confronted by Hitler's relentless expansionism in the second half of the 1930s. The Soviet Union. Joseph Stalin sought as far as possible to keep his country out of any coming war. He had been building up arms at breakneck speed since the mid-1930s but still he felt unprepared, in part because of the damage he himself had inflicted on the higher levels of the military leadership in the purges and terror of 1937–8. He regarded the capitalist powers in Central and Western Europe as bound by common interests and was persuaded by Chamberlain's weakness in the face of Hitler's demands that Britain and Germany would eventually make a deal with each other. The British government's attempt to bring the Soviet Union into an anti-Hitler coalition foundered not least on the anti-Communist prejudices of Chamberlain and Halifax, but the understandable nervousness of the smaller Eastern European states also played a part.

'Common sense suggests that it would have been an act of desperation [for Hitler] to have attacked Poland in the face of an Anglo-French-Soviet alliance,' Steiner concludes. But common sense was not one of Hitler's characteristics. He described himself as a gambler who always went for broke. The alliance in any case did not come to pass. Stalin concluded that time was best bought by concluding a deal with Hitler and letting the capitalist powers fight it out among themselves. Pragmatic, defensive interests predominated in Stalin's mind. This was not a prelude to world revolution. It was important, he told the head of the Communist International, not to fall into the over-optimistic frame of mind shown by the Bolsheviks in the 'First Imperialist War': 'We all rushed ahead and made mistakes! ... Today we must not repeat the position held by the Bolsheviks.' If he did not provoke Hitler, Stalin thought, the pact would hold. These were all illusions that, as Steiner notes, 'would cost his country dear in 1941', when the Germans invaded without any warning, and proceeded to conquer vast swathes of territory, inflicting huge losses on the Soviet people, military and civilian, before they were eventually stopped.

By the time of the Hitler-Stalin pact, the system of international relations had changed beyond all recognition from two decades before. After the First World War, the victors had hoped to create a new way of doing business, with the end of secret negotiations and bilateral pacts and the creation of the League of Nations to monitor international disputes and settle diplomatic crises. Disarmament talks would make the world a safer place and contribute to the avoidance of another destructive general war. Hitler's accession to power put paid to disarmament talks: after he walked out of them in 1933, there was no point in carrying on, and the World Disarmament Conference was indefinitely adjourned in June 1934. Italy's invasion of Ethiopia in 1935 'irreparably damaged the League of Nations', notes Steiner. Before 1914 the invasion would have been written off as a minor colonial adventure, but the new rules of international behaviour ensured that it took on a far greater significance. While statesmen issued ritual expressions of moral outrage, the British and the French, on whose cooperation the League ultimately depended, approved the imposition of only the mildest of sanctions against the Italians, while behind the scenes they agreed to propose the partition of Ethiopia, with a large chunk of the country going to Italy.

When that agreement – the Hoare-Laval Pact – was leaked to the French press, the international storm of protest almost brought down the British government. Had they been serious about stopping Italy, the British and the French could have cut off Italian supplies by closing the Suez Canal. The fiasco of the Hoare-Laval Pact made it clear that the League was no longer an effective international forum for resolving disputes or enforcing peace. Recognising the realities of the situation, it voted for the end of sanctions. Italy, after using poison gas bombs to destroy the Ethiopian army from the air, occupied the whole country with impunity. This convinced Hitler that he need fear nothing from the British and the French at this stage, and he brought forward his plans for the unilateral remilitarisation of the Rhineland, another nail in the coffin of the Peace Settlement of 1919. For his part, Mussolini became convinced that his ambition to create a new Roman Empire in the Mediterranean was now feasible. This, too, was an illusion: Italy's resources simply did not allow it, as was to become clear later on when Italian troops failed ignominiously to conquer Greece, Yugoslavia and North Africa.

From then on, international relations were conducted through old-style secret bilateral negotiations of the kind the Peace Settlement had sought to abolish in 1919. The scale of the virtually unchecked intervention by Germany, Italy and the Soviet Union in the Spanish Civil War served to underline the impotence of the League. It still continued its human rights, health and welfare programmes. But even here it met with failure when confronted with the greatest challenge of the late 1930s: the rapidly swelling flood of refugees. It is important, Steiner notes, not to be anachronistic in our judgement of this issue: 'Few statesmen believed that the abuse of human rights was the concern of the international community.' The urgent issues of war and peace relegated the question of refugees to the bottom of the international agenda.

Yet something had to be done. The prospect of large numbers of Jewish refugees coming not only from Germany and particularly Austria following the *Anschluss* of March 1938, but also from Hungary and Romania, prompted the calling of an international conference at Evian in July 1938. It was called not on the initiative of the League but at the invitation of Roosevelt. The results were meagre. One country after another declared itself saturated with immigrants and unable to do anything. 'Openly antisemitic speeches provided the Nazi press with a field day,' Steiner writes. The League centralised its policy under a high commissioner for refugees towards the end of 1938, but his office was underfunded and lacked the means to negotiate with the Germans. Other institutions with a potential role in humanitarian aid, such as the Papacy, did not think that Jews were their concern.

Attitudes only began to change with the nationwide pogroms carried out by the Nazis on the night of 9–10 November 1938, when synagogues across Germany were razed to the ground, thousands of Jewish-owned shops trashed and 30,000 Jewish men seized and carried off to concentration camps, from which they were released only after promising to emigrate. These events shocked international opinion. Chamberlain described them as 'barbarities', but no concerted action followed, least of all any action undertaken by the League of Nations. Britain eased visa restrictions and over the following months individuals and non-governmental organisations in the United Kingdom and other European countries launched a variety of schemes to bring German Jews to safety, particularly children. Many were saved. But these actions were still on an extremely modest scale. For Hitler, the war, from the very beginning, was, as Steiner rightly says, a 'racially motivated war' against what Nazi propaganda already in September 1939 was calling 'international and plutocratic Jewry' across the world. International opinion never really recognised this fact.

If the First World War arguably began in August 1914 as a result of misunderstandings and errors of communication, the same was not true of the Second World War. Yet although Hitler wanted a war, Steiner writes, the war that ensued 'was not the war he had wanted, nor the one for which Germany was prepared'. Hitler was determined that there should be no repeat of the Munich agreement; nothing would stop him from invading and conquering Poland, as he had been stopped, for a while at least, from invading Czechoslovakia. Already jolted into a less sanguine view of Nazi Germany and its intentions by the savagery of the 1938 pogrom, the British and the French government had come to the realisation when the German armies stormed into the rest of Czechoslovakia in March 1939, for the first time conquering territory where the majority of the inhabitants were not German speakers, that Hitler really did intend to do more than simply revise the provisions of the 1919 Peace Settlement in Germany's favour. Daladier was proved right.

Anglo-French guarantees to Poland and other East European countries in the event of a German invasion now followed. Both governments realised Munich had been in vain. Serious military plans were laid. The British arrived at a more realistic, and therefore less exaggerated estimation of German military strength. Yet the British and the French decided not to launch an independent attack on Germany if Poland was invaded, though they left the Poles under the impression that they would come to their aid. The French promised to send over some obsolete aircraft as military aid. Polish officials unwittingly encouraged this relaxed approach by boasting to the British of their own military strength, a policy Steiner describes as foolhardy. In reality, once the Hitler-Stalin pact was sealed, Poland's fate was sealed along with it.

In the final weeks before the outbreak of war, public opinion in Britain and France, though apprehensive, recognised that Hitler had to be stopped. Yet Chamberlain and Daladier still hesitated. Mussolini was clearly reluctant to come in on Hitler's side – the Italians in fact waited several months until they did so – so perhaps he could be used as honest broker in bringing about a settlement that would avert war. Once again, Steiner comments acidly, both Chamberlain and Halifax misunderstood the nature of Hitler's intentions. Surely the differences between Germany and Poland could be resolved without bloodshed? They simply did not see that Hitler actually wanted bloodshed. As Steiner notes, 'rational to a fault, Chamberlain could not imagine that anyone in his right mind ... would actually want war. To the very end, this stiff, controlled, and stubborn man sought to convince himself that some way existed to avoid the looming catastrophe.'

Chamberlain seriously misread the changing mood of the British House of Commons in 1939. When he appeared there immediately following the German invasion of Poland, it was to announce in vague terms that he was seeking mediation through the good offices of Mussolini. He was virtually shouted down. The cabinet met hurriedly without him and forced him to issue an ultimatum to the Germans to withdraw. The appointed hour passed without any withdrawal; consequently, Chamberlain told the British people in a radio broadcast whose sepulchral tones betrayed his deep disappointment that mediation this time had not been possible, that Britain was now at war with Germany. 'Everything I have worked for, everything that I have hoped for, everything that I have believed in during my public life,' he told the House of Commons, 'has crashed into ruins.'

Hitler did not want this particular war either. Right to the end, he hoped for Anglo-French neutrality, or at least inaction. Chamberlain's and Daladier's actions had only strengthened him in this view. As the situation neared the brink, he became apprehensive and postponed the invasion at the last minute. But in the end, he took the risk. Britain and the British Empire, together with France and the French Empire, and with the tacit support of the United States, just beginning to come out of isolation in the realisation that Hitler's long-term ambitions would seriously affect its own long-term interests, would, Hitler's advisers warned, be the inevitable winners in a war of attrition. Germany's resources simply could not match up to theirs in the long run. The best chance of success was now, before Germany's enemies were fully prepared. And so began the greatest war in history, a war that was to last until 1945, a war in which more than fifty million people would lose their lives, a war that would end in the destruction of Germany and the collapse of the European overseas empires, including the British and the French. Few could have seen these outcomes at the time; but few thought in the end that war could be avoided.

Zara Steiner's *The Triumph of the Dark* is a masterly sequel to *The Lights that Failed* (2005), her equally commanding study of international relations from the end of the First World War up to the Nazi seizure of power. Her two-volume account will stand the test of time. It is as impressive in its breadth as it is in its depth, covering economic developments and relations, arms production, diplomatic negotiations, politics and war with equal authority. Steiner's command of the scholarly literature and documentation in several languages is little short of awe-inspiring. Her book is brilliantly written, full of pungent judgements, arresting phrases and sarcastic asides, and conveys often complicated sequences of events with limpid clarity. It is a magnificent work of scholarship, narrative and authoritative historical judgement and will remain the standard account of these terrible years for a long time to come.

17. NAZIS AND DIPLOMATS

I

When the career diplomat Curt Prüfer, born in 1881, sat down at the end of the Second World War to think about his career and what he had done during the Third Reich, he could look back on nearly four decades of moving steadily up through the ranks of the German Foreign Office. An Arabist who had worked as an intelligence officer in the Middle East during the First World War, Prüfer had served as deputy director of the Anglo-American and Oriental Division of the Foreign Office in Berlin from 1930 to 1936, when he was put in charge of the Personnel Division, before becoming ambassador to Brazil in 1939. In 1942, following Brazil's entry into the Allied camp, Prüfer returned to Berlin, but ill health, age and the fear that Germany would soon be defeated led him to obtain leave to go and live with his family in Switzerland, where he received confirmation of his official retirement just before the end of the war.[1]

Prüfer did not look back over his life with either nostalgia or satisfaction. Despite his relatively humble origins, he had quickly become, through his command of Arabic and his knowledge of the Arab world, part of the conservative elite whose values and beliefs dominated the Foreign Office during the 1920s. But, he said, during the Hitler years this elite had been pushed aside by younger newcomers shoehorned into the Foreign Office by the Nazis. They were particularly prominent

in the Germany Division (*Abteilung Deutschland*), which was responsible among other things for liaison with the Nazi Party and the SS.
Prüfer thought it created unnecessary paperwork and got in the way of
the proper functioning of the diplomatic service. The Nazis brought
into the Foreign Office by Joachim von Ribbentrop, the Party man who
had replaced the conservative Konstantin von Neurath as Foreign
Minister in February 1938, were, he thought, mere dilettantes
appointed for their ideological commitment rather than their expertise. Men like Under-Secretary of State Martin Luther knew nothing of
foreign affairs, and key parts of the Office, including the Information
and Oriental Divisions, were being ruined by the newcomers. The old
diplomatic elite, Prüfer insisted, had remained professional and correct,
hostile to Hitler and distrustful of his adventurism. The German people
was not to be blamed for the outbreak of the war, but had instead been
prepared systematically for it by a clique of Nazi warmongers. Left to
get on with the job, he implied, the diplomats of the Foreign Office
would have managed to solve Europe's crisis peacefully.[2]

In recollecting his past, Prüfer had the huge advantage of being able
to refer to the diaries that he had kept all his life. Prüfer was almost
unique among senior diplomats in keeping a private journal, so it is
particularly valuable as a source. In many of the entries quoted in the
book he prepared for publication at the end of the war, Prüfer's disillusion with the Nazi regime and its leader shines through. Reporting
on 19 July 1943 on the dramatic decline in Germany's military fortunes, above all in Italy, his diary noted:

> Perhaps the ultimate reason for this dreadful reversal is that the twi-
> light of the gods is now upon the mass of the people who followed
> Hitler with such blind faith. It has become clear that the wrong
> road was chosen; that everybody was duped; and that all the
> unimaginable sacrifices were offered to a false idol, sacrifices which
> will earn us no reward, only punishment. These realizations have
> drained our courage, throttled our enthusiasm, and raised doubts
> as to the justice of our cause.[3]

Prüfer was also highly critical of Nazi policies towards the Jews, about which he said in his entry for 16 October 1942, the stories he heard were 'so dreadful that we held them to be "atrocity stories", or at the very least exaggerated'.⁴ On 21 November 1942 he reported that stories of the extermination of the Jews would cause Germany 'unspeakable harm' 'if these stories really correspond to the facts'. As far as the Jews were concerned, 'everyone speaks of them with the greatest sympathy'.⁵ On another occasion, he noted, 'The persecution of these innocent people, who are being annihilated solely because their existence does not conform to the ideal projection of the National Socialist "Weltanschauung", has burdened the conscience of every individual who knew about it.' Regrettably, coercion and 'the oath of allegiance' had kept people (including, of course, himself and his fellow diplomats) in line. Most Germans, he wrote on 19 July 1943, wanted Hitler to be removed, 'but as long as the enemy insists on unconditional surrender [...] the nation will keep resisting'.⁶ Thus the absence of resistance was mainly the fault of the Allies.

Unfortunately, Prüfer never actually wrote these words in his original diaries. He inserted them for the benefit of his later readers, in 1946. In the original version of the entry for 19 July 1943, quoted above, he merely wrote: 'The Führer is a great, a very great man, who made our nation – at that time facing ruin – into the most powerful country on earth.' Germany's decline was 'terrible to see,' he wrote, 'because I was sincerely converted to some of the beautiful ideas of National Socialism'.⁷ The entry for 16 October 1942 in which he reported his scepticism about the extermination of the Jews never existed in the original; he wrote it in 1946. Nor did the original entry for 21 November 1942 contain even a single word about the Jews.

Prüfer doctored his diaries not least to conceal the fact that he was himself deeply antisemitic. His belief in a Jewish conspiracy to subvert Germany had already manifested itself during the General Strike that overthrew the Kapp putsch in 1920. Walking through Berlin during the strike, he found groups of people 'standing around debating everywhere. The speakers are nearly exclusively Jews, behaving as if they were friends of the people. It is repulsive to see how the stupid Germans allow themselves to be ensnared by international Jewry.' For Prüfer, the strike was 'the Jewish affair'.[8] His antisemitism had a practical side, too. During the Nazi era, Prüfer rushed to cover up the fact that one of his wife's ancestors was a baptised Jew by bribing an official to expunge the fact from the records, while later on he had no qualms about purchasing 'Aryanised' property in Baden-Baden.[9]

On 14 April 1943, he wrote of 'the abysmal hatred of the Jews against all European Gentiles' and asked: 'How can there ever be peace if Jews are the advisers of our enemies?'[10] His report on 22 November 1942 that he had heard of the mass murder of the Jews in the east ('today every child knows this in the smallest detail') was without comment on its morality, and was replaced in the revised version by the expression of doubt ('if these stories really correspond to the facts') and the invented story of people's sympathy for the victims.[11] One of Prüfer's principal jobs during the war, after his return from Brazil, was, as an expert on Arab affairs, to deal with the Grand Mufti of Jerusalem, Haji Amin al-Husseini, whom he defended against the intrigues of his rival Rashid Ali al-Gailani, the Iraqi nationalist who had fled to Germany after a failed uprising against the British in 1941. The Mufti, Prüfer wrote in his original diary on 17 July 1943, 'kept insisting on "getting rid of the Jewish settlements in Palestine"', by which was meant, as the Mufti told Hitler on another occasion, exterminating the Jews there. However, this entry was simply cut from the revised diaries.[12]

Prüfer did not publish his diaries; after he had revised them, he realised that they would incriminate his old boss Joachim von Ribbentrop, who was standing trial in Nuremberg for war crimes. But he kept them and after his death in 1959 passed them on to his son, who eventually made them available for scholarship. They are interesting not least because they show how consciously Prüfer doctored the historical record to make himself, and the professional diplomatic elite to which he belonged, seem as if they had been politically neutral during the Third Reich, had despised Hitler and the leading Nazis, had known little or nothing for sure about the extermination of the Jews, and on the basis of what they did know had condemned the Nazis for their antisemitism, which, like the mass of the German people, they had not shared themselves. Prüfer's biography, and the story of his doctored diaries, can be taken as a dramatic example of how history can be manipulated and legends manufactured. Prüfer was not only unable to learn from the past, he actively engaged in covering it up.

II

How typical was Curt Prüfer? How far did the old-style career diplomats who served in the German Foreign Office during the Nazi period cover up their own involvement in Nazism's crimes? How deep was their involvement in any case? For decades after the war, the Foreign Office showed little or no inclination to confront these questions. Reconstituted in West Germany in 1951, it described in a pamphlet published in 1979 its history in the years 1933–4 in three sentences:

> The Foreign Office mounted tough, persistent resistance to the plans of the Nazi regime, however without being able to prevent the worst. The Office long remained an 'unpolitical' institution and was regarded by the National Socialists as a hotbed of opposition. In the entrance hall of the new Office there is a memorial plaque which commemorates those officials of the Foreign Office who gave their lives in the fight against the Hitler Regime.[13]

This account became more or less dogma in the Foreign Office and remained so up to the end of the twentieth century and even beyond. On a number of occasions it was challenged, but attempts to pillory the Foreign Office as a tool of Nazism seemingly had no influence on its collective memory.

In 2003, as was its custom, the German Foreign Office published in its in-house magazine a respectful obituary of a recently deceased career diplomat, in this case the former Consul-General in Barcelona, Franz Nüsslein. On reading the obituary, Marga Henseler, a retired Foreign Office translator, protested to the Foreign Minister, the Green Party politician and former student activist Joschka Fischer, and to the Social Democratic leader of the coalition government, Gerhard Schröder, pointing out that it neglected to mention the fact that Nüsslein had served during the war as a state prosecutor in German-occupied Prague, where he had among other things been responsible for considering appeals for clemency by Czechs condemned to death for their involvement in the resistance; he had, she alleged, turned down more than a hundred such appeals. In 1948 Nüsslein had been condemned to twenty years' imprisonment by a Czech court, before being returned to Germany in 1955 as a non-amnestied war criminal. Nüsslein claimed merely to have been 'interned' and indeed successfully sued for compensation as a late-released prisoner of war. Thanks to his personal connections he had almost immediately obtained a post in the Foreign Office, where he served in various capacities, including dealing with claims for compensation for wrongful dismissal.[14] Despite widespread publicity given to his Nazi past in the late 1950s and early 1960s – orchestrated by East German propaganda but backed by a West German former diplomat, who had been refused compensation by Nüsslein for his dismissal by the Nazis – the diplomat stayed in post until his retirement in 1974.

Foreign Minister Fischer, shocked that a man with such a past could receive a respectful obituary, one which, to boot, made no mention of his past crimes, banned the writing of any more obituaries for former members of the Nazi Party in the Foreign Office. The following year, another retired diplomat, Franz Krapf, former German ambassador to Japan and head of the German delegation at NATO headquarters, died, and since he had been a member not only of the Nazi Party but also of the SS, Fischer's ban meant that there could be no obituary published by the Foreign Office's in-house magazine. The reaction among retired diplomats was furious. It was dishonourable conduct on the Minster's part, complained one. Members of the Resistance to Hitler within the Foreign Office, such as Adam von Trott zu Solz, had themselves been members of the Nazi Party. Would they, too, have been denied an obituary had they survived? Krapf himself, they said, had been a close friend of another official, Erich Kordt, who had opposed Hitler throughout his life and had testified after the war to Krapf's sympathies with the resistance to Nazism. Outraged by the ban, 128 retired officials signed a lengthy obituary notice in the conservative newspaper *Frankfurter Allgemeine Zeitung*, honouring Krapf's memory in respectful terms.[15]

This was an open act of rebellion that the Foreign Minister could not afford to ignore. Fischer's reaction was to commission an independent group of professional historians to investigate the 'history of the Foreign Office in the National Socialist period, the way it dealt with this past after the re-founding of the Foreign office in 1951, and the question of personal continuities or discontinuities after 1945'.[16] The members of the commission originally included two conservative elder statesmen of the profession, Henry Ashby Turner and Klaus Hildebrand, but ill health forced them both to resign, leaving the Germans Eckart Conze and Norbert Frei, the American Peter Hayes and the Israeli Moshe Zimmermann to organise the research and writing. All had experience of working variously on the Nazi period and the postwar years. All, however, were extremely busy men, so in turn they commissioned twelve junior colleagues to do the work, and a thirteenth to carry out the task of editing. The role of the four senior historians in the project is unclear, but it seems to have been in practice fairly minimal, and indeed with commendable honesty they list at the very end the actual authors and the passages for which they are responsible. At the same time, however, the chance removal of the two most senior and most conservative historians on the original commission (Turner and Hildebrand) placed the direction of the project in the hands of a younger generation of historians with a rather different set of attitudes, while the research and writing were carried out by men and women predominantly of a younger generation still. This was to have profound consequences for the interpretations advanced in the book, entitled *Das Amt und die Vergangenheit* (The Office and the Past, 2010).

By this time, the Social Democratic-Green Party coalition had long since given way to a more conservative government, and Fischer had left office, but at the book's launch he declared triumphantly that this was the obituary that the diplomats had really earned. In an interview with the news magazine *Der Spiegel*, Eckart Conze summed up its findings. The Foreign Office, he said, 'participated as an institution in Nazi crimes of violence up to and including the murder of the Jews. To this extent one can say: the Foreign Office was a criminal organization.' This put it on the same footing as the SS, condemned at the Nuremberg War Crimes Trials as a 'criminal organisation'. Conze went on to claim that most diplomats and officials 'already felt that the Nazi assumption of power in 1933 was a kind of redemption'.[17] Far from being 'unpolitical', they were opponents of democracy and were sufficiently antisemitic to make them sympathetic to the anti-Jewish measures taken by the Nazis. The replacement of Neurath by Ribbentrop made no difference. The old guard of professional diplomats were as bad as the new Nazi officials; and only a tiny proportion of them were involved in any kind of resistance.

The book's publication caused an enormous storm in the media. The huge publicity given to the book's launch, especially with the presence of Fischer and other senior politicians, helped – along with the book's undeniably clear and readable style – make *Das Amt* into a bestseller. Initial reactions in the press were overwhelmingly positive.[18] But soon, critics were denouncing its conclusions as too sweeping, its research filled with innumerable errors of detail, its arguments consistently biased and unsupported by the evidence. *Der Spiegel's* writers Jan Friedmann and Klaus Wiegrefe complained that the book repeatedly referred to 'the' diplomats as if they were all involved in Nazism to the same degree; or that the book equated knowledge of mass murder with approval or even responsibility.[19]

The commission's work, complained the historian and journalist Rainer Blasius, 'violates scholarly standards and nurtures prejudices'.

It virtually ignored the role of individual diplomats in the resistance to Hitler, and consistently put the worst possible interpretation on their conduct. It repeated old propaganda stories concocted by the German Democratic Republic in an effort to discredit the Federal Republic.[20] Other critics pointed to the fact that, although the commission presented its research as if it broke a whole series of taboos for the first time, there had in fact been a number of serious academic studies of the Foreign Office's involvement in the Holocaust, notably by Christopher Browning[21] and Hans-Jürgen Döscher, who had also published major studies of the Foreign Office in the Nazi and postwar years.[22] Critics found considerable fault with the book's lack of reference to other relevant secondary work.[23] Hans Mommsen and Johannes Hürter both criticised the commission's narrow focus on the Holocaust, to the neglect of other issues, and complained once more of the book's tendency to sweeping and undifferentiated judgements.[24] Mommsen added that none of the four editors was an expert on the history of the Holocaust – a plainly unfair remark,[25] since Peter Hayes has published major research work on the involvement of companies such as IG Farben and Degussa, and Norbert Frei is one of the few remaining senior historians in Germany who has written extensively on the Third Reich, while the major part of the book, on the postwar period, surely required the expertise of a historian like Eckart Conze, author of a recent history of Germany since 1945.[26] Still, his point could none the less be fairly applied to a number of the researchers who actually wrote the book, who included young scholars who had not even finished their Ph.D.

The fact that the four responsible historians did not actually write the book has not prevented them from leaping to its defence. Moshe Zimmermann accused Hürter in particular of speaking for the conservative Institute for Contemporary History in Munich, which, he alleged, was constantly trying these days to exculpate the old German elite. It was abstruse to accuse the authors of focusing too much on the Holocaust, said Zimmermann. The critics were running a political campaign to rehabilitate the Foreign Office of the 1950s and to discredit the editors of *Das Amt* because they were outsiders.[27]

While there might well have been some plausibility in these charges as far as some of the critics were concerned, however,[28] it is not plausible to accuse Hürter of speaking on behalf of the Institute for Contemporary History in Munich or of trying to exculpate the old elites – he is author of a major critical study of the army officer corps in the Third Reich that is anything but exculpatory – and in any case other critics, particularly Mommsen, have no connection with the Institute and no conservative axe to grind. Ascribing political motives to the book's critics is not an answer to their criticisms. The points they raise are serious ones and have to be confronted head-on. Any discussion of the book needs to ask, therefore: are the critics right? And if they are, do their criticisms add up to a vindication of the traditional Foreign Office position on the ministry's role in the Third Reich and its treatment of that role in subsequent decades?

III

The opening section, by Lars Lüdicke, at the time of writing a doctoral student at Potsdam University and author of a short study of German foreign policy from 1933 to 1945, published in 2009,[29] that, obviously, is closely linked to his lengthy contribution to *Das Amt,* deals with the period up to the outbreak of war. Devoting a good deal of attention to the internal personnel structures and policies of the Foreign Office, Lüdicke argues convincingly that the attempts made in the Weimar Republic to modernise the service were a failure. In 1933 its upper echelons in particular were still dominated by diplomats who had learned their trade under the Kaiser. Many of them were aristocrats and shared the aristocracy's prejudices against democracy, egalitarianism, reform – and Jews. Very few officials in the Foreign Office chose to resign when the Nazis came to power – Friedrich von Prittwitz und Gaffron, ambassador in Washington and a convinced democrat, was a solitary exception in the top ranks of the diplomatic service, for although some of his colleagues also considered resignation, he was the only one who actually put his principles into action. As dyed-in-the-wool imperialists and expansionists, the vast majority welcomed the advent of the Nazis, whom they did not view as 'party-political' in the sense that, say, the Social Democrats were. The Foreign Office collaborated willingly with the Nazis in identifying Jewish officials and applying the law of 7 April 1933 that forced most of them to leave the service, obliged the regime by issuing rebuttals of foreign press accounts of antisemitic outrages in Germany, and took a full part not only in revoking the citizenship of anti-Nazis like Albert Einstein but also in keeping a close watch on their activities in exile.

Yet all of these activities could be defended at the time as part of the normal business of a foreign ministry. What was not normal was not the activities, but the nature of the regime they served. As with other key institutions, such as the officer corps, the university professoriate or the judiciary, it seems legitimate enough, for all the terror and coercion in operation in Germany in the first half of 1933, to use the term *Selbstgleichschaltung* ('self-coordination') to describe this process of more or less voluntary adaptation.[30] Soon, too, officials were using the 'German greeting' and swearing a personal oath of allegiance to Hitler. None of this should be particularly surprising. The comparison between the legal profession, where 4,000 lawyers lost their jobs in 1933, or the medical profession, where 2,000 were sacked, shows merely how few Jews and how few left-wing or liberal political activists had made it into the Foreign Office, in comparison to medicine or the law.[31]

Yet this conformity was not enough for the Nazis, least of all for Joachim von Ribbentrop, the self-proclaimed foreign policy expert in the Party. From 1933 onwards the Foreign Office grew rapidly in size, reaching a strength of 2,665 in 1938 and 6,458 four years later.[32] The number of men in the higher service rose from 436 in 1933 to 596 in 1939.[33] In the course of this expansion, many young, committed Nazis came into the service. Most of them were in relatively junior positions, though, as Jan-Erik Schulte, an expert on the SS who has written an excellent monograph on its economic empire,[34] shows in the final section on the peacetime years, Ribbentrop's closest links were with the new men rather than the old.[35] No fewer than twenty-eight members of Ribbentrop's Party Office (the *Dienststelle Ribbentrop*) joined the service in peacetime. Men in the upper reaches of the service increasingly joined the Nazi Party, though this did not necessarily signal adherence to its central beliefs. Heinrich Himmler and the SS tried to gain influence by appointing leading officials to positions in the SS, which obliged them, of course, to give at least lip service to SS ideas and principles.[36] Lüdicke concludes his contribution by arguing that, despite these changes, the old elite remained dominant at the higher levels of the service, above all in the embassies and consulates. It was only during the war that the number of people brought into senior positions for ideological reasons underwent a serious expansion. At the same time, the old elite did not remain immune from the influence of Nazism, and many of them – one could cite the example of Curt Prüfer – either applauded or approved of the antisemitic policies of the regime or remained silent about them while continuing to justify them abroad.

These findings are persuasive and illuminating, though far from surprising. Nevertheless, Lüdicke's section has a number of serious weaknesses. First, on occasion the author exaggerates the importance of the Foreign Office in key areas of Nazi policy. After describing the reports on anti-Nazi press reports and actions in the USA in the early months of 1933, for instance, Lüdicke concludes that these provided the decisive excuse for the anti-Jewish boycott launched on 1 April 1933 at the behest of Hitler and Goebbels, indeed the indirect trigger for the boycott.[37] But in fact neither Goebbels nor Hitler needed to read Foreign Office reports to know what was going on in America: they could read the daily papers. Lüdicke provides no direct evidence to back up his point. The idea of a boycott had been around for two years at least; and by the time the dispatches cited by Lüdicke as decisive had been sent, from 26 to 29 March 1933, preparations for the boycott had already been under way for a fortnight, the cabinet had discussed it on 24 March, and the final decision had been taken two days later.[38]

Similarly, Lüdicke ascribes to the Foreign Office a large part of the responsibility for the introduction of the antisemitic Nuremberg Laws in September 1935, noting State Secretary Bülow's statement in a meeting on 20 August 1935 that spontaneous antisemitic actions were damaging Germany's image abroad.[39] Yet there is no direct evidence for this link. In the voluminous scholarly literature dealing with the genesis of the Nuremberg Laws, the Foreign Office plays only the most minor of roles, if any at all. If there was a driving force within the civil administration, it was Reich Economics Minister Schacht, but the key role was played by Hitler himself, who already cracked down on individual violence against Jews on 8 August 1935 and saw the Laws as a way of neutralising the remaining 'radicals' within the Party.[40]

Lüdicke's treatment of these two cases points to a major weakness in his contribution, as in many (though not all) of the other chapters in *Das Amt*: the failure to consult the relevant secondary literature. The archival documentation used as the basis for the research should have been backed up by a systematic evaluation of the scholarly work carried out by others on the subjects discussed. Particularly weak is the coverage of the English-language literature. Research on National Socialist Germany has long been international – and in no area more obviously so than in its foreign policy. Yet even standard works are not cited where they should have been, and more specialised work is frequently missing altogether. A case in point is provided by the diary and biography of Curt Prüfer with which this essay began. Despite their obvious relevance and importance, they appear nowhere in the notes to *Das Amt* and are apparently completely unknown to its authors. Perhaps this is a reflection of the tight deadlines to which the researchers had to work; perhaps it is a result of their conception of how to go about their task, namely just by ploughing through the Foreign Office archives; either way, it means that the book does fall short in a crucial respect of the scholarly standards one should expect from a commission report of this importance.

Another, equally problematical aspect of Lüdicke's contribution, is its failure to deal with foreign policy and diplomacy. This is a particular deficit in the treatment of the peacetime years because it was so central to the prosecution case in the war crimes trials from 1945 onwards. As Astrid Eckert notes in her account of the trial of the major war criminals in Nuremberg, including the two Nazi Foreign Ministers Neurath and Ribbentrop: 'At the heart of the prosecution lay the concept of a criminal conspiracy that prepared the German war of aggression and was intended to lead to the German domination of Europe and in the end, the world.' The diplomatic manoeuvres carried out by the Foreign Office under their direction were not necessarily criminal in themselves, but took on a criminal character by virtue of their embedding in this conspiracy. Two years later, in the 'Wilhelmstrasse' trial, leading diplomats were confronted with the same accusation. By this time, the emerging Cold War was having its influence, and the accused men – former State Secretary Ernst von Weizsäcker at their head, followed by many other members of the old diplomatic elite – managed to rally round numerous supporters to testify to their innocence to ensure that only three of them were found guilty of launching a war of aggression, and two of these verdicts were quashed later on. The court abandoned the charge of conspiracy. The forty-eight charges facing eight accused led to a mere fifteen guilty verdicts, mostly for crimes against humanity.[41]

Nevertheless, given the fact that Eckert quite rightly criticises the 'Wilhelmstrasse' trial for its extreme leniency, and thus, presumably, considers that the accused, along with many other senior officials in the Ministry, were in actual fact guilty of conspiring to launch a war of aggression, in violation of the 1928 Kellogg–Briand Pact, to which Germany had been a signatory, it is astonishing to find in the earlier sections of the book no mention of the Foreign Office engaging in these activities either before September 1939 or afterwards. Even if one concedes that the book's authors had to stick to their brief of researching the crimes committed by the Foreign Office and its members rather than writing a general history of the institution, it is still surprising that they failed to deal with the preparation of an illegal and criminal war of aggression, in comparison to which the issues on which Lüdicke spends so much time – the surveillance of émigrés, and even the sacking of officials regarded by the regime as Jewish – pale into relative insignificance. The reason for this surprising omission, as Johannes Hürter has pointed out, is all the more extraordinary since the classical realm of diplomacy that lay at the heart of this criminal activity was still dominated by the old elites.[42]

IV

The book's narrow focus on the involvement of the Foreign Office in the persecution and, ultimately, the mass murder of Germany's, then Europe's, Jews, becomes even more relentless in the sections dealing with the war. In his introduction to this part of the commission's report, Jochen Böhler, author of an important if controversial book on the German invasion and occupation of Poland,[43] notes that the Foreign Office was involved in the requisitioning of slave labour, the theft of cultural objects and artworks and the extermination of the Jews[44]; but in the coverage of the war the first two points are barely mentioned. As Böhler notes, the *Sonderkommando Künsberg*, which plundered occupied territories across Eastern and South-Eastern Europe on a massive scale in 1941–2, focusing particularly on library books and cases of champagne, was directly subordinate to the Foreign Office, and carried out numerous tasks for Ribbentrop.[45] But the cultural depredations of the occupying German forces in many other countries, notably France and Italy, were also vast in scale, and far too little space is given in the rest of the book to elucidating the role of the Foreign Office in what was probably the greatest act of wartime looting in history.

In Poland, as Jochen Böhler and Irith Dublon-Knebel, editor of *German Foreign Office Documents on the Holocaust in Greece, 1937–44* (2007), note, the Foreign Office and its representatives urged mod-

eration, concerned that the brutal and murderous policy of the occupying forces was alienating the local population.[46] Similarly, in France,
Ambassador Otto Abetz – not a member of the traditional elite –
tried to soften the harsh repressive policy taken by the SS against the
resistance and to go slow on the requisitioning of forced labour, for
much the same reason. We learn little, however, of the wider activities
of the ambassadors in France, Holland, Belgium, Denmark or Norway,
and almost nothing at all about the involvement of Foreign Office
envoys in the occupation of Tunisia and other parts of North Africa,
or their role, often carried out in conjunction with army units such as
the *Panzerarmee Afrika*, in propaganda and political warfare. The
focus is overwhelmingly on the involvement of the Foreign Office in
the deportation of the Jews. In a number of instances this did indeed
spill over into the active advocacy of mass murder.

Thus, in Serbia, for instance, the Foreign Office plenipotentiary
Felix Benzler, prompted by mounting army concerns about the growing military resistance to German occupation, concerns that were
expressed in large-scale shootings of Jews as the supposed originators
of this resistance, repeatedly pressed Berlin for the deportation of
Serbian Jews. When this was ruled out as impracticable, Ribbentrop
sent Franz Rademacher, head of the Foreign Office's Jewish Department, to arrange, as Rademacher put on his application for travel
permission, the 'Liquidation of Jews in Belgrade'. Once in Serbia,
Rademacher pressed hard for the complete extermination of all the
Jews on the spot. Even if the primary driving force here was the army,
aided and abetted by the SS, there is no doubt that, as the authors put
it: 'The boundary between the treatment of foreign-policy aspects of
the Jewish Question and an active participation in murder is thereby
washed away – and it was crossed'. By contrast, the Reich
Plenipotentiary in Athens, the diplomat Günther Altenburg, distanced himself from the actions taken against Greek Jews and took
steps, partly successful for a while, to reduce the severity of SS actions
against the local population.[47] There were, therefore, choices that
could be made.

Yet Foreign Minister Ribbentrop himself was temperamentally and ideologically inclined always to take the harshest measures against the Jews. How significant was this fact? On page 185 of *Das Amt* we find an extraordinary claim:

> The top echelons of the Foreign Office participated directly in the decision for the 'Final Solution'. The Jews' fate was sealed on 17 September 1941: on this day Hitler held a meeting with Ribbentrop. Immediately before the meeting Hitler issued his order to deport the Jews, who had just been forced to wear the 'Jewish star', to the East. What had already become clear in connection with the Madagascar Plan now continued following the German invasion of the Soviet Union: The Foreign Office took the initiative in the 'Solution of the Jewish Question' on a European level.

It should hardly be necessary to point out that there is an enormous and almost unmanageable scholarly literature on the question of when, how and by whom the decision to exterminate Europe's Jews was taken. This literature is neither referenced nor discussed in the book: indeed, the bold claim quoted above is not even footnoted. The standard research literature on the arrest and deportation of the Jews from Holland, Belgium, France and other occupied countries is not mentioned. In all of this literature, and in the most important syntheses on the extermination of the Jews, the Foreign Office is often mentioned as involved, but it is never portrayed as the driving force.

As this voluminous literature shows, Ribbentrop's meeting with Hitler on 17 September 1941 was only one of a whole series of meetings over several days, involving Hitler, SS chief Heinrich Himmler and his deputy Reinhard Heydrich, and other SS officials, along with Ambassador Abetz. According to Christopher Browning's authoritative account of these meetings, the actual impetus to deport German and French and potentially all European Jews to the east came from Eastern Minister Rosenberg (who wanted retaliation for Stalin's deportation of the Volga Germans), Otto Abetz (who in conjunction with military and SS officials wanted reprisals for acts of resistance in France, which they blamed on the Jews), and the Gauleiters of Hamburg and Cologne (who wanted to evict Jews to rehouse non-Jews made homeless in bombing raids). All accounts are agreed, however, that the decisive intervention came from Himmler. Ribbentrop was not even informed of the decision to deport the German Jews once it had been taken, even though, as Browning notes, he had 'played a small role in the decision-making process'.[48] Peter Longerich's account of the same series of meetings suggests that Hitler had already in essence decided to start the deportations even if he was confirmed in his intention by the interventions of Himmler, Ribbentrop and others.[49] Thus their neglect of the secondary literature feeds the authors' tendency to overinterpret the sources. If they had taken the trouble to put them into their historiographical context they would have been in a position to deliver a more nuanced and more accurate account of the Foreign Office's role. This would not have prevented them from echoing Döscher's conclusion, reached already in the mid-1980s, that 'the collaboration of the Foreign Office with the Reich Security Head Office in the "Final Solution of the Jewish Question" functioned without any noticeable friction from the beginning onwards', and, crucially: 'Most of the responsible officials of the Foreign Office who took part were not old Nazis but career diplomats who had mostly only joined the NSDAP or one of its organizations after 1933.'[50]

It was, as Irith Dublon-Knebel and Lars Lüdicke note, in the Foreign Office that plans to deport the Jews to Madagascar were – obviously – worked out, but these came to nothing in view of the British domination of the seas.[51] The actual implementation of the extermination was a very different matter from the concoction of such impracticable plans. And here the role of the Foreign Office, as the detailed accounts in the book show, was very much smaller. To begin with, in Denmark and Norway, the Foreign Office had little influence compared to the SS and the Nazi Party, and, like Rosenberg's Eastern Ministry, it was outflanked by these institutions and by the armed forces in Poland and in the occupied areas of the Soviet Union after its invasion in June 1941. The influence of the Foreign Office was greater, as the authors show, in Hungary, especially as Hitler and Ribbentrop ratcheted up the pressure on the Hungarian leader Admiral Horthy in 1943–4, and in Croatia and Slovakia. In France, Ambassador Abetz played a significant role in the deportations. In some of these areas, such as Greece or Hungary, the representatives of the Foreign Office argued against harsh reprisals against acts of resistance so as not to alienate the local population. But as the authors rightly note, this policy of mildness never extended to the Jews, unless they were foreign nationals from non-combatant countries, in which case they were to be protected in the interests of good bilateral relations.[52]

None of this suggests that the Foreign Office was a hotbed of resistance to the regime and its policies. In a notably brief treatment of the resistance the authors (Jan-Erik Schulte, Irith Dublon-Knebel and Andrea Wiegeshoff – another Ph.D. student) note that the few men within the Foreign Office who had contacts with the military leaders of the resistance in its various phases were mostly young officials in the information department, which had expanded rapidly and recruited people from unconventional backgrounds in comparison to those of the mainstream career diplomats. A few had connections to the Kreisau Circle, in which private discussions were held about the contours of a post-Nazi Germany. A small number, including the young Adam von Trott zu Solz, the retired diplomat Ulrich von Hassell, and the head of the Russian department, Friedrich Werner von der Schulenburg, were involved in the plot to kill Hitler that failed to achieve its aim on 20 July 1944.[53]

The authors give equal status to other individuals such as Fritz Kolbe, another outsider who advised Ribbentrop on the war economy and regularly supplied secret information to the American Secret Service, or Gerhart Feine, a more conventional diplomat who nevertheless worked tirelessly from his office in Budapest against the extermination of the Jews in Hungary and did his best to save as many as he was able. This breadth of coverage is surely right. It has the effect of downgrading the uniqueness of the July bomb plot and therefore further undermining the account of its past constructed within the Foreign Office after the end of the war. Even before 20 July 1944 Hitler and Ribbentrop had begun to purge the Foreign Office of men with 'international connections' and what the regime regarded as dubious links, for example to the families of the higher nobility. A good number were dismissed. Yet this was not evidence of any major role played by the Foreign Office in the resistance. On the contrary, a tiny minority of largely isolated figures, or *groupuscules*, had undertaken a variety of steps to distance themselves from, oppose, or in very rare cases try to overthrow the regime or circumvent its policies. These all deserve commemoration, perhaps at greater length than they receive here, but their behaviour and attitudes should in no way be taken as typical of those of the Foreign Office as a whole.

V

The later chapters of the book are devoted to the second part of Foreign Minister Fischer's brief, namely how the Foreign Office dealt after 1945 with its role in the Nazi period and how much continuity there was from that era to the years from 1951 onwards, when it was refounded in the Federal Republic, in personnel terms. As Katrin Paehler, a German scholar who has worked on the siege of Leningrad and its role in memory, and now teaches in the USA, shows, the Foreign Office was quickly dissolved as an institution in 1945, its officials scattered everywhere, some in Soviet prisons (especially if they were Nazi stormtroopers), some in interrogation centres, some arrested and tried for war crimes; a few took part in the massive wave of suicides that rolled over the official world in Germany in the first half of the year.[54] Many found new careers in industry, academia, the law, the civil service, local government and even the Church. Their high social background, education and abilities stood them in good stead. The process of denazification, as Thomas Maulucci, an American professor who works

on American policy in the Cold War, shows, resulted in 108 higher officials in the Foreign Office being excused (*entlastet*), 70 untouched (*nicht
betroffen*), 15 being classified as fellow travellers (*Mitläufer*), 5 amnestied
and 39 unaffected by the entire process. Nevertheless, in their correspondence with one another, former diplomats continued to complain
about what they saw as the unreasonable prejudice of the Occupying
Powers against former German diplomats.[55]

The 'Wilhelmstrasse' trial of alleged Nazi war criminals in the
Foreign Office (1947–9), is analysed by Astrid Eckert, yet another
German historian teaching in an American university, author of a
useful study of the return of captured German files to the Federal
Republic. Eckert covers the proceedings in detail. She shows clearly
how the trial focused on the top layer of officials, notably the State
Secretaries and Under-Secretaries, who were regarded by the
American prosecutors as responsible for the Foreign Office's crimes,
so that many middle-ranking officials who had been directly involved
in crimes such as the murder of Europe's Jews (Rademacher, for example) were not dragged into the net. The only one who had been
directly involved in the murders and stood in the dock was Edmund
Veesenmayer, who had been Ribbentrop's roving emissary in
Yugoslavia and Slovakia and Reich Plenipotentiary in Hungary in the
crucial period of 1944 and sent large numbers of Jews to their death,
even suggesting methods for improving their transportation to the gas
chambers. Veesenmayer was responsible among other things for subversion in countries about to be invaded by the Nazi regime, and had
been closely involved in setting up the genocidal puppet governments
in Croatia and Slovakia. Despite pressure from those who wanted
these particular crimes to be highlighted, the emphasis was very much
on the issue of conspiracy to launch a war of aggression.[56] This, as
Annette Weinke, author of several studies of the prosecution of
German war criminals, shows in her excellent discussion of the creation of the myth of the Foreign Office as a centre of resistance,
allowed former officials, taking up their informal social and professional ties once more, to organise a coordinated defence particularly

centred on the key figure of former State Secretary Ernst von Weizsäcker, whose family played a significant part in all this.[57]

The picture these men put together was much as Curt Prüfer had painted it for himself in his doctored diaries immediately after the war. They portrayed the marginal figures who had taken part in the active resistance to Hitler as if they had been mainstream figures in the Foreign Office. They presented the isolated and diffuse resisters as having worked together in a coordinated group centred on Weizsäcker. And they distinguished them from the 'traitors' who had leaked information to the Americans or the Soviets. Assisted by influential journalists such as Marion Dönhoff and Margaret Boveri, they convinced the Nuremberg Court and the public that the overwhelming majority of diplomats had stayed on rather than resigning purely in order to moderate the extreme policies of the Nazis. It was the new ideological men brought in after Neurath had given way to Ribbentrop who overrode the continuing scruples of the old hands, forcing them to sign incriminating documents in order to protect themselves from harm. They claimed that the Foreign Ministry had the highest rate of executions of officials of all Ministries after the July 1944 bomb plot. They obtained innumerable testimonies of good character – known popularly as *Persilscheine* or 'Persil Certificates' because, like the eponymous detergent, they washed 'whiter than white' – from former Jewish officials and members of the military-aristocratic resistance to testify to their opposition to the regime. They did their best, often in the most unscrupulous manner, to smear the prosecutor Robert Kempner, an experienced Jewish-German lawyer who had been arrested and forced into exile by the Nazis. Finally, they put the whole prosecution, like those of the industrialists and the army officers, down to an attempt by egalitarian Americans to discredit Germany's traditional aristocratic elites.

To his credit, Weizsäcker's son Richard, a key member of the defence team and later President of the Federal Republic (1985–95), regarded such smear tactics as counterproductive and tried to moderate them. But the Cold War was now under way, and American sentiment had veered towards leniency so as not to upset West Germans with the appearance of vindictiveness. Ernst von Weizsäcker was duly released, only to die of a stroke shortly afterwards. As the American historian William Gray, author of *Germany's Cold War* (2007), notes, even the lenient sentences passed down in the 'Wilhelmstrasse' trial soon came to be considered too harsh, and a commission of inquiry recommended a reduction. Even the odious Veesenmayer's prison term was halved, for instance, on the grounds that he had been 'only a roving ambassador' and had merely reported to Berlin and conveyed the German government's views to the Hungarians, as any ambassador would. His only crime had been membership in a banned organisation – the SS. Veesenmayer's real activities were now conveniently forgotten.[58]

The Federal Republic was duly permitted by the Allied Occupying Powers to establish first a consular service, then, in 1951, a full-blown Foreign Office. As with other areas of professional life, West Germany found that it needed men with professional expertise whatever their role had been before 1945. To represent the emerging state of the Federal Republic abroad, people with technical and linguistic expertise were needed, along with experience of diplomacy and its often arcane rules and conventions. As Weinke shows, Federal Chancellor Konrad Adenauer was keen to avoid any resurrection of the old Wilhelmstrasse, but in practice he lacked the detailed information on personnel to prevent it. A key figure here was the head of the Foreign Office's Political Division, Herbert Blankenhorn, who had managed somehow to convince his American interrogators at the end of the war that he had been a member of the resistance. Gaining Adenauer's confidence to the extent that he became his personal assistant before his move in 1951 to the Foreign Office, Blankenhorn provided the means whereby substantial numbers of old Foreign Office hands from the Nazi years found their way back into the diplomatic and consular service and its administration in Bonn. One after another, they were presented as having been distant from Nazism or even involved in the July 1944 bomb plot.[59]

Remarkably, as Weinke shows, this aroused the criticism above all

of a group of former *Sicherheitsdienst* (SD) men who had been deliberately recruited to *Der Spiegel* by its editor, Rudolf Augstein. A
sixteen-part series on the new Foreign Office by Horst Mahnke, who
had worked in the Reich Security Head Office's section for research
into ideological opponents of Nazism and considered the men of July
1944 to be traitors, poured scorn on the claims of the diplomats to
have been involved in the resistance. But there were other criticisms,
too, from left-leaning newspapers like the *Frankfurter Rundschau* to
the propaganda apparatus of the German Democratic Republic,
which never tired of exposing old Nazis in high places in the West, culminating in its publication of Albert Norden's *Brown Book: War and
Nazi Criminals in West Germany, State, Economy, Administration,
Army, Justice, Science* in 1965. After failing to suppress it, the West
German authorities dismissed it as a tissue of lies and fabrications. It
turned out in the end to be largely correct.

Nevertheless, the Foreign Office was able to shrug off all these
attacks. In 1953, for instance, it re-employed Otto Bräutigam, a career
diplomat who had worked during the war on the sequestration of
Polish property – 'one of the most extreme acts of plunder in the history of the world, and a mockery of international law' – as he
characterised it with remarkable honesty in his memoirs.[60] Attached to
Rosenberg's Eastern Ministry, Bräutigam had become an energetic
spokesman for its view that it would be more useful for Germany in the
long term not to maltreat the Slav population of the occupied areas, a
view that had little influence on the actual course of events. It was a different matter with the Jews. During the war Bräutigam had pressed for
the deportation of the Jews as retaliation for Stalin's maltreatment of
the Volga Germans, taken part in a meeting on the use of gas vans for
mass murder and chaired a discussion held in the wake of the Wannsee
Conference to deal with the definition and treatment of Jews and half-
Jews in the east at which Rosenberg's Ministry had declared the latter
were 'racially just as undesirable as full Jews'.[61] In 1950 a district court
in Nuremberg had none the less cleared Bräutigam of the charge that
he had participated in the extermination. But evidence of his role

began to be publicised, notably through the pioneering work on the Holocaust by Gerald Reitlinger.[62] In the Foreign Office strenuous efforts were made to expunge Bräutigam's name from the German edition of Reitlinger's book, along with other damaging evidence, but the press furore led to the cabinet forcing the abandonment of Bräutigam's appointment as envoy to Brazil in 1955 and his suspension from office the following year. Although the East Germans made the maximum political capital out of the affair, and questions were raised about his past in the British House of Commons, Bräutigam was reinstated in 1957 on the grounds that he had tried to avoid the worst excesses of Nazism's genocidal policies, and he ended his career as Consul-General in Hong Kong.[63]

In fact, in the new Foreign Office, as Andrea Wiegeshoff shows, the higher up the ranks one went, the more likely one was to encounter diplomats and officials from the old Wilhelmstrasse. Between a quarter and a third of ambassadors and consuls belonged to this category; and with the rapid expansion of the Foreign Office during these years (1,000 personnel in 1951, over 4,500 in 1955), there were soon actually more Nazi Party members in the new Foreign Office than there had been in the old one before 1945. Some of them even taught courses to young officials on the countries where they had been stationed during the Third Reich: thus, for example, Werner von Bargen, who had spent the war years in Belgium, gave lectures on the Benelux states, while Werner von Grundherr, who had run the Scandinavian department of the Foreign Office during the war, and been involved in the financing of the puppet Norwegian Quisling regime and the abortive attempt to deport the Jews of Denmark, taught a course on Scandinavia. Herbert Müller-Roschach, responsible for 'Jewish Questions' in the Germany Division during the Nazi period, found himself teaching about European integration. In the end, therefore, there is no doubt that many committed former Nazis who had been seriously involved in the persecution and extermination of the Jews or in other crimes of the Nazi era were re-employed in responsible positions in the Foreign Office after 1951.[64]

This is not always easy to find out in detail from the pages of this book. One of the most serious problems in these accounts for the reader, and a symptom of the slack editorial control that can be detected throughout the book, lies in the fact that many of the individuals mentioned in the postwar sections do not appear at all, or at most only fleetingly, in the prewar chapters. Thus there is little or no continuity, and it is difficult to get a clear idea of how important these people were in the 1930s and early 1940s. Werner Blankenhorn's name, for instance, does not appear at all until we get to the postwar years; similarly with Müller-Roschach and many others. This makes it all the more difficult to get a clear picture. It would have been simple enough to ensure that figures who play a major role in the post-1945 sections of the book were given adequate treatment in the pre-1945 sections. But the editors failed to do this.

VI

With time, the proportion and influence of the old guard within the Foreign Office declined. At the same time, however, they succeeded in some respects in stamping their views on their successors. Thus, long after this generation's departure from office, the Foreign Office's way of dealing with the past remained deeply problematical. Annette Weinke demonstrates that the old Wilhelmstrasse hands now conveniently re-edited their memories, just as Curt Prüfer had done, devoting considerable efforts to researching the history of the resistance and those few of their colleagues who had actually taken part in it, quietly ignoring the history of the officials who had been dismissed or persecuted for their political beliefs or their race, and treating those who had collaborated with the enemy, like Fritz Kolbe, as traitors.[65] Astrid Eckert has some distressing tales to tell about former officials in this category or their widows being denied recognition or compensation for their dismissal or execution by the Nazis, particularly if these men had had connections with the so-called Red Orchestra, now regarded as a Soviet spy ring rather than the loosely organised network of resisters of varying ideological convictions that it actually was.[66]

Did the presence of a network of former Nazis in the Foreign Office have any effect on the actual conduct of foreign policy? It was certainly relevant to issues such as relations with Israel or the Foreign Office's legal obligation to offer assistance to German citizens standing trial in foreign courts (such as, for example, Adolf Eichmann in Israel). It played a role in the Foreign Office's withdrawal of a grant subsidising an American lecture tour of the historian Fritz Fischer, whose book on Germany's aims in the First World War was described by the conservative historian Theodor Schieder in a phone call to the Office as a 'national catastrophe'.[67] Eckert's account of the internal debates in the Foreign Office on the invitation gives a fascinating picture of the institution in a moment of transition. While the conservatives won out in the end, the much-publicised protest of senior American and German-American historians like Gordon Craig, Fritz Stern, Klaus Epstein and Hans Rosenberg, who ensured that the money was raised to enable the lecture tour to go ahead, provided precisely the kind of bad publicity that the old hands in the Foreign Office had hoped to avoid.

How much did all of this really matter? The ex-Nazis in the Foreign Office did not revive Nazi ideas or policies. The Cold War enabled them to translate their Nazi anti-Communism smoothly into an advocacy of the Western orientation of the new Federal Republic. They did not conspire against democracy or try to revise the peace settlement. If one of Adenauer's purposes was to reintegrate former Nazis into the West German establishment and convert them to new ways of thinking more in tune with the postwar world, then the evidence of the Foreign Office suggests he succeeded. Yet, at the same time, the presence of many former officials and diplomats from the Nazi years in the Foreign Office, and the relative success they had achieved in covering up their past and that of the institution to which they belonged, had serious implications for the conduct of West German foreign policy. The memory of National Socialism and its many crimes remained very much alive outside Germany, however much it might be obscured or manipulated within the country, and continued, as indeed it still continues today, to frame the world's attitudes towards the Federal Republic. Germany's reputation in the world depended, and depends, not least on its ability to convince the world that it has come to terms openly and honestly with the Nazi past. The continued presence in the Foreign Office of men implicated in the crimes of Nazism and the persistence of a culture of exculpation in its attitudes to the past made this aim more difficult to achieve.

Has it been achieved by this book? This is not, as it claims to be, 'a systematic and integrating total representation' of the history of the German Foreign Office from 1933 to the end of the twentieth century, 'based on working through the sources and the secondary literature'.[68] Both the immediate background to Foreign Minister Fischer's establishment of the commission and the terms in which he framed its task prioritised the question of how far the Foreign Office and its civil servants were involved in or responsible for the crimes of Nazism, how far those who were responsible reappeared to serve in the Foreign Office in the 1950s and subsequently, and what the attitude of the Foreign Office was to its involvement in the Nazi past. Thus the approach of the researchers and authors is not merely necessarily highly partial and selective, it is also cast in moral terms dictated by the questions raised in the present, rather than in purely historical terms suggested by a more strictly academic approach. The moral charge carried by Fischer's original commission could not fail to find its way into the research and the writing of the book. In terms of its *political* effects, which have been considerable, this may be in the end no bad thing.

Yet there is no doubt that this book is deeply flawed as a work of scholarship. The research is not properly embedded in the context of the secondary literature, and neglect of the current state of knowledge in a number of the topics studied leads to errors and misinterpretations. There is a persistent tendency to exaggerate the active participation of the Foreign Office in a number of the criminal activities of the Nazis. At the same time, the field of vision is too narrow, so that warmongering, a key aspect of the Nuremberg indictments, is almost entirely left out of the frame, although it is surely of direct relevance in the present day; other crimes, such as wartime looting and spoliation, also fade into the background. The almost exclusive concentration on the Holocaust may reflect the way in which the Nazi regime is viewed by the younger generation of historians, and by the public, in the early twenty-first century, but this does not help a broader understanding of Nazism, what it did and how it worked.

There is no doubt that this book was needed. Previous work by Browning, Döscher, McKale and others touched on the problems it covers and explored some aspects of them with exemplary thoroughness, but these books were mainly addressed to a scholarly readership and had little wider resonance. This deficit has now been remedied by *Das Amt und die Vergangenheit*. Despite its unevennesses and inadequacies, this book has unquestionably succeeded in proving beyond reasonable doubt that the Foreign Office was an essential part of the machinery of government in the Third Reich; that it subscribed to and carried out Nazism's ideologically driven policies, including the persecution and extermination of the Jews, insofar as they lay within its area of competence, which at particular moments and in particular places they did; that its old-established diplomats and officials in their overwhelming majority believed in and happily implemented these policies; and that after the war these same diplomats and officials did their best to cover up what they and the Foreign Office had done during the Nazi years. The myth of the Foreign Office's resistance has been publicly exploded by this book.

All the more pity, therefore, that the book's deficits and exaggerations make it easier for those who still believe in this myth to try and discredit it. The importance of the topics it covers deserved better. The blame for this lies squarely with the editors. If you are going to employ Ph.D. students as researchers, then it is your duty as a senior historian to go carefully through their work to make sure it properly references the secondary literature, avoids overinterpretation, and strikes a proper balance in its coverage. The editors have failed in this duty. Other departmental histories have more recently been commissioned, notably of the Finance Ministry and the Intelligence Service. Let us hope that more care is taken over their research and presentation, and that they avoid some of the weaknesses and failings of the present work.

For in undertaking research of this kind, historians need to be fair, and they need to be precise. There is a whiff of the witch-hunt about this book, as if the authors saw it as their job to hunt down the complicity of diplomats and officials in the Holocaust and slap on the most serious charges they could find. Even given the brief they had to carry out, however, they should have remembered that the historian is not a prosecutor and history is not a court. And even if it were a court, the fact still remains that it's important to differentiate, to be exact, and to avoid sweeping generalisations. As one of the greatest historians of Nazism, Tim Mason, once wrote:

> The precision of the identification matters [...] While systems of domination and exploitation cannot be represented as individual moral actors can, it can be demonstrated that they generate barbarism. The demonstration of exactly how they have done so is often complex, but complex historical arguments are not indifferent to moral issues just because they are complex. If historians do have a public responsibility, if hating is part of their method and warning part of their task, it is necessary that they should hate precisely.[69]

NOTE

Two of the editors of *Das Amt und die Vergangenheit*, Peter Hayes and Norbert Frei, published a spirited rejoinder to these and other reviews in the *Bulletin of the German Historical Institute, Washington*, Vol. 49 (Fall, 2011), p. 55, along with contributions by Johannes Hürter, Christopher R. Browning, Holger Nehring and Volker Ullrich ('Forum: The German Foreign Office and the Nazi Past', pp. 53–112). Frei and Hayes followed established academic bad practice in trying to discredit the book's critics by noting minor errors and slips, though in the case of the above article they could only find one (the mis-naming of Herbert Blankenhorn as Werner). However, they do make perhaps three points in the book's defence that are worth comment-ing on.

They begin by asserting that Curt Prüfer was not a significant figure and therefore did not deserve coverage in their volume. But, of course, the point is not that he was irrelevant, nor, more seriously, that he did not play a part in postwar myth-making about the Foreign Office: the point is that his attitude to the past was typical of that of the entire diplomatic profession in Germany after the war, and the demonstra-ble and concrete falsifications he engaged in provide an example of this attitude that is second to none in its clarity, presenting direct evidence of the doctoring of the Nazi past by a former diplomat that is too valu-able to overlook. The fact that Prüfer did not serve in the West German Foreign Office after 1951 is irrelevant to this fundamental point. *Das Amt* does indeed mention McKale's two books on Prüfer in the bibliography, but nowhere does it cite them in the notes, let alone use them in the text; a mere listing is no evidence that the books were actually read. So my charge is not 'spurious', as the editors claim, but entirely justified.

In their interesting *Nachwort und Dank* ('Afterword and Acknow-ledgements') the editors describe among other things the process through which the volume came together. They point out that each of them took responsibility for a particular segment of the book, and that some of the oral history interviews were carried out by them, or with their participation. They refer in very general terms to the fact that 'at all times the members of the Commission and their assistants worked constructively together', and then list the pages which each of the latter wrote. There is no mention here at all of the later claim of Professors Frei and Hayes that 'each chapter emerged through a process of repeated give and take among the drafters named there and the member of the Commission primarily responsible for the relevant time period or topic and then at successive sessions of the Commission'. No reader of the book could possibly have guessed this from the way its composition is presented there. In later interviews Professor Conze in particular claimed that the editors and their assistants wrote the book together (http://www.zeitgeschichte-online.de/thema/die-debatte-um-das-amt-und-die-vergangenheit, which gives an excellent account of the controversy and deals with all the criticisms as well as the editors' replies to them). It remains extremely hard to believe that the very weak sections on the National Socialist period, especially on the war, were seriously discussed in sessions of the Commission, or that the responsible editors, senior historians with a good knowledge of the period, gave the drafts composed by their assistants the careful and critical readings that they should have done, let alone took part in the drafting themselves.

Professors Frei and Hayes complain further that it is unjust to accuse the volume and its authors of failing to deal with the preparation of an illegal and criminal war of aggression, in their obsession with the role of the German Foreign Office in the 'Final Solution of the Jewish Question in Europe'. They take refuge in the fact that only Ribbentrop and Neurath, the two Nazi Foreign Ministers, were convicted of this charge after the war. Surely they are not claiming that this exonerates the civil servants who worked for them? Or perhaps they were 'only obeying orders'? Such an argument is an unworthy defence of a book that in other areas goes into great detail of the crimes committed by the Foreign Office's diplomats and administrators, even though here they were still under the command of the Minister. The fact remains that *Das Amt und die Vergangenheit* focuses far too narrowly on the Office's role in antisemitic policy-making and its implementation. A great deal of work remains to be done on its broader role in other areas.

PART V

VICTORY AND DEFEAT

18. FATEFUL CHOICES

The war that began in September 1939 was not the one Hitler envisaged. Britain came in; Italy stayed out. In the west there was a period of inactivity, known as 'the phoney war'. By the early summer of 1940, however, things were going his way, following a series of stunning military victories. Yet peace with Britain did not follow. A year later Germany was at war with the Soviet Union as well; and by the end of 1941 the United States had entered the conflict too. Within another year Germany was clearly losing the conflict. How much were these stark reversals of fortune the result of 'fateful choices' made by Hitler and the other war leaders such as Stalin, Churchill and Roosevelt? Or were they simply borne along on the tide of events?

This is the question Ian Kershaw sets out to answer in *Fateful Choices: Ten Decisions that Changed the World, 1940–1941* (2007). Kershaw's earlier work focused on the reactions and attitudes of ordinary German people to Nazism, showing a huge variety of popular responses to Adolf Hitler and the Nazi regime, ranging from resistance and opposition through dissent and indifference to enthusiasm and praise. His book *Popular Opinion and Political Dissent in the Third Reich* (1983) attacked the cliché of universal obedience to Hitler. In this vision, relatively few Germans were committed Nazis; most were lulled into acquiescence by Nazi propaganda and Nazi achievements in one or another area, objecting – sometimes with success – only when the regime interfered directly with the innermost values of their daily lives, most notably in matters of religious practice. All of this, of course, raised the question of how the regime managed to put its policies into effect. In *The 'Hitler Myth'* (1987) Kershaw showed how the propaganda image of the Führer provided until near the end of the war a repository for people's hopes and aspirations that deflected many of their discontents on to his subordinates or held out the prospect that he would eventually find a remedy. People were reluctant to believe that in reality Hitler was a man driven by a fanatical hatred of the Jews, a boundless desire for conquest and, at bottom, a deep contempt for the mass of ordinary Germans.

Kershaw's pioneering study of Hitler's propaganda image thus seemed to point naturally to the next step, a biography of the man himself. After a decade of research, the resulting two volumes – *Hitler 1889–1936: Hubris* (1998) and *Hitler 1936–1945: Nemesis* (2000), totalling nearly 2,000 pages – established themselves immediately as the standard biography on the German dictator. Among their many virtues were their scrupulous scholarship, their meticulous sorting out of fact from myth and, not least perhaps, Kershaw's new, more relaxed style of writing, displaying a hitherto unsuspected talent for taut narrative, gripping description and the atmospheric recreation of past events and situations.

Kershaw came to the biography, as he confessed at the time, from the 'wrong direction': not from the history of high politics and decision-making but from the history of everyday life and opinion in Nazi Germany. What resulted was a book that for the first time related Hitler convincingly to his historical context, that showed him as created by his times as much as acting independently upon them. The biography, indeed, rushes impatiently through Hitler's obscure early life, dismisses psychological speculation about his motives (his alleged fears of Jewish ancestry, supposed homosexuality, early failure as a painter, etc.) and devotes only minimal and evidently somewhat irritated attention to the few episodes we know about in his personal life later on.

In Kershaw's account Hitler appeared, in many ways, as a kind of blank space on which Germans, or, rather, key groups of them, projected their ambitions and aspirations. As time went on and he came to believe in his own myth, largely fashioned for him by others, Hitler assumed a more decisive – and ultimately disastrous – role in the formulation of policy, especially with regard to the war. This structuralist approach to the dictator's role in the Third Reich has led to the charge, levelled most recently by Christopher Browning in *The Origins of the Final Solution* (2004), that 'Kershaw portrays Hitler's role in actual decision making on Jewish policy', as in other areas, as 'passive, simply assenting to pressures and proposals from others'.

Perhaps, then, it is not surprising that in his latest book, Kershaw returns to the theme of decision-making, this time on a much broader scale. Here he offers a narrative and analysis of ten decisions, each influencing the ones that followed, starting with Britain's decision to fight on in the spring of 1940 and Hitler's decision to invade the Soviet Union, and moving through Japan's decisions to ally with Germany and Italy and then to strike at Pearl Harbor, the Italian Fascist leader Benito Mussolini's somewhat belated decision to join the war, US President Franklin Delano Roosevelt's decisions to aid the British and then to escalate this into undeclared war against Germany, and Hitler's decisions to declare war on the United States and to attempt the extermination of Europe's Jews. As one might expect from Kershaw's previous record, he does not delve too deeply into the psychology of the world leaders whose actions in 1940 and 1941 shaped the course of the Second World War, and thus the parameters of the postwar order. Like Hitler in his two-volume biography, they remain remarkably bland and elusive. Indeed, at times they virtually disappear as individual actors altogether. Thus, for example, Kershaw concludes that 'the colossal risks which both Germany and Japan were prepared to undertake were ultimately rooted in the understanding among the power-elites in both countries of the imperative of expansion to acquire empire and overcome their status as perceived "have-not" nations': power-elites, not leaders.

Insofar as he is interested in the leaders as individuals, Kershaw is most fascinated by the constraints under which they operated and the broader factors by which their freedom of action was limited. Thus when Hitler rejected the advice of his military leaders to give priority to North Africa and the Mediterranean after the stunning victories they had achieved over France and the other Western European countries in 1940, he was, to be sure, driven by the ideological emphasis he had always laid on the conquest of the Soviet Union. Yet at the same time, Kershaw argues cogently, 'the decision to attack and destroy the Soviet Union ... was strategically forced upon him. He had to gain victory in the east before Stalin could build up his defences and before the Americans entered the war.'

Such decisions, Kershaw underscores, depended not least on previous decisions taken by people in various positions of authority, and some of these were less governed by force of circumstance than others. The decision with which he opens the book is a case in point. In late May 1940, as it became clear that France had been defeated and it looked as if the British forces sent to aid the French would be killed or captured before they could be evacuated from the Continent, powerful voices within the British Cabinet, led by the Foreign Secretary, Lord Halifax, began to be raised in favour of seeking mediation through the Italians, first via Roosevelt, then, when that failed, in a direct Anglo-French approach to Mussolini. Newly appointed British Prime Minister Winston Churchill had to use all the rhetorical force at his command to quash the idea:

> Signor Mussolini, if he came in as mediator, would take his whack out of us. It was impossible to imagine that Herr Hitler would be so foolish as to let us continue our rearmament. In effect, his terms would put us completely at his mercy. We should get no worse terms if we went on fighting, even if we were beaten, than were open to us now.

If Britain sued for peace, he said, it would be forced to disarm and become a slave state, under a puppet government run by British Fascist leader Sir Oswald Mosley. In the event, the French decided to go it alone; their peace feelers were rudely rebuffed by Mussolini, who did indeed want to 'take his whack'. Nearly 225,000 British troops were evacuated from the Continent at Dunkirk, an event that Churchill's stirring rhetoric remarkably turned from a calamitous defeat into some sort of victory. And Britain fought on.

What would have happened if Halifax and his allies had carried the day in the Cabinet? Here, following Churchill's lead, Kershaw engages in some fascinating counterfactual speculation. Certainly, he argues, in the event of a peace between Britain and Germany in May or June 1940, Hitler would have demanded the sacking of the Churchill administration. But more likely as a successor than the unpopular and discredited Mosley would have been a widely admired politician such as David Lloyd George, Britain's Prime Minister in the First World War and a self-professed admirer of Hitler. Lloyd George indeed envisaged a role of this sort, possibly under a restored King Edward VIII, whose sympathies with Nazi Germany and belief in the need for a separate peace with Hitler were also on record. This would have been something like the regime installed in France in 1940 under the hero of France's army in the First World War, Marshal Philippe Pétain, though initially at least without its Fascist leanings. A rival government, possibly under Churchill, might have been set up in Canada. But with Britain effectively on Germany's side, the swelling tide of American aid would have been stopped and Hitler would have been free to marshal all his forces, whenever he wanted to, for the long-desired invasion of the Soviet Union. And whatever he might say, Hitler would not have waited long before embarking on the dismemberment of the British Empire, contrary to the view expressed by some later historians such as Maurice Cowling, Alan Clark and John Charmley, who argued that a separate peace with Germany in 1940 would have been the best way to have preserved it.

How legitimate is this kind of speculation? Kershaw is careful not to take it too far; indeed, he does not go much beyond the scenarios painted by Churchill himself on this occasion. Rather than draw imaginative pictures of what might have happened, Kershaw seeks to assess the alternatives open to the decision-makers. He does no more than hint that a peace with Britain in 1940 might have increased the chances of Hitler's defeating the Soviet Union. But in fact, those chances were never very great. Though Germany might have had 'all the Continent's material resources at its disposal' in such an event, the Nazi exploitation of the defeated French and other economies was so ruthless that these counted for relatively little in the long run. The Soviet Union was the decisive force in the defeat of Germany.

Hitler's decision to invade Russia was made in the summer and autumn of 1940, prompted, Kershaw argues, not least by the German dictator's knowledge that with Britain still in the war, the vast resources of the US economy would soon be pouring into the British war effort in ever-increasing quantities. It is possible to imagine, as Kershaw does, that if the counsels of the German generals had prevailed and the German war effort been directed toward the conquest of North Africa and the Middle East, gaining vast oil reserves desperately needed by the Nazi economy and cutting off the main British supply route to the East through the Suez Canal, the fatal confrontation with the Soviet Union might have been postponed, perhaps indefinitely. Possible, but unlikely.

As it was, Hitler got the worst of both worlds. Turning to Mussolini's decision to join the war on the German side after the crushing defeat of France, Kershaw portrays the Italian elites as avid for a share of the spoils. Remaining neutral would have enabled Italy to have husbanded its weak resources in the traditional manner by playing one side off against the other. Mussolini should, perhaps, have remembered the sarcastic remark of a Russian negotiator at a peace conference in the late nineteenth century, that since the Italians were demanding an increase in their territory, he supposed they must have lost another battle. Disappointed with Hitler's refusal to accede to his demands in the west, Mussolini made the fatal decision to invade Greece. Soon, Italian military failures there and in North Africa had sucked the Germans into a theatre of war in which they did not really want to fight.

Hitler would later complain that this diversion of German resources cost him the war by forcing him to postpone the invasion of Russia, officially known as Operation Barbarossa. If the invasion had taken place earlier, he claimed, the Germans could have defeated the Red Army before the rains bogged down the German advance in the autumn. But as Kershaw points out, bad weather in May and early June would have postponed the invasion anyway. What is more, in the first weeks of the Russian campaign, Hitler anticipated victory well before the autumn. Hundreds of thousands of Soviet troops were surrounded and killed or captured in vast encircling movements driven forward by fast-moving German armour backed up by complete German domination of the skies. The collapse of the Soviet regime seemed imminent.

Responsibility for the Russians' near defeat, Kershaw argues, must lie principally with Soviet dictator Joseph Stalin, whose decision to ignore the warnings pouring in from intelligence agents about an impending German invasion in June 1941 forms the subject of another chapter. What alternatives were open to Stalin? One that was put to him by leading generals the previous month was to launch a pre-emptive strike. The documentary traces of this have provided fuel for those who have tried to argue that Hitler invaded in order to stop the Red Army from marching westward. But Kershaw persuasively rejects this 'far-fetched interpretation'. Operation Barbarossa had been in preparation for many months before the idea of a pre-emptive strike by the Red Army was first mooted. Therefore the strike was always intended to have been a defensive move.

After the war, one of its principal authors, General Georgy Zhukov, admitted it would probably have been a dismal failure anyway. The Red Army and its leadership had been crippled by Stalin's purges in the late 1930s. The frantic arms programme launched in 1939 had not got very far; Stalin did not think the Soviet military would be in a position to fight the Germans successfully until 1942. He rejected the idea out of hand. 'Have you gone mad?' he exploded: 'Do you want to provoke the Germans?' Stalin knew how poorly prepared his forces were, and he was playing desperately for time, even continuing deliveries of goods and raw materials under the Nazi–Soviet Pact signed in 1939 up to six days before the invasion.

Ideologically blinkered, the Soviet dictator would not tolerate any dissent from his own complacent assessment of the situation. Kershaw does not say what Stalin's ideological preconceptions were, but as a good Marxist-Leninist, Stalin was convinced that Hitler's regime was the tool of German monopoly capitalism, so that if he made available everything German business wanted, there would be no immediate reason to invade. Moreover, he thought it inconceivable that Hitler would launch an invasion while the war with Britain was still in progress. Surely the German dictator was aware of the folly of waging a war on two fronts? But Hitler held the Soviet Union in boundless contempt. One push, he thought, and the whole edifice of Communism would come crashing down.

It did not. By the end of 1941 the German armies had been fought to a standstill before Moscow, and though they made further, major advances in 1942, the factor most feared by Hitler, the growth of US aid for Britain and to a lesser extent also the Soviet Union, now came increasingly into play. Kershaw devotes two chapters to decisions made by Roosevelt. On 30 October 1940, the President promised American mothers and fathers: 'Your boys are not going to be sent into any foreign war.' By this time, however, he had already long been convinced that German expansionism posed a fundamental threat to the United States. He was right.

As Kershaw remarks, Hitler had always envisaged in the longer term 'a war of the continents' in which a German-dominated Europe would launch a final struggle for world supremacy with the United States. But Roosevelt knew that he would never get Congress to support a declaration of war on Germany. So he proceeded cautiously, step by step, to shore up first the British and then the Soviet war effort. 'I do not think we need worry about any possibility of Russian domination,' he declared shortly after the launching of Operation Barbarossa. Lend-lease, which made available vast quantities of war materiel to Britain and later Russia, was followed by the Atlantic Charter, implicitly allying the United States with Britain by stating the common democratic principles they sought to uphold, while a clash between a German U-boat and an American destroyer provided the pretext for persuading Congress to approve American warships' protection of Allied merchant ships and convoys in the American half of the Atlantic in the interests of the 'freedom of the seas'.

Roosevelt's decision to wage undeclared war on Germany had an impact on two crucial decisions made by Hitler. The first of these was the German declaration of war on the United States on 11 December 1941. The introduction of lend-lease had already convinced Hitler that the Soviet Union needed to be defeated quickly, before American resources could be thrown into the fray on the Allied side. The more US naval forces intervened to protect British shipping, the more Hitler began to fear that unless he could unleash the full force of his submarine fleet against them, the Battle of the Atlantic would be lost, and his attempt to cut off essential supplies of food, arms and raw materials from the British Isles would fail. Yet he continued to hesitate until the Japanese bombed the US Pacific naval base at Pearl Harbor on 7 December 1941. This was, Hitler said, a 'deliverance'. 'We can't lose the war,' was his response. On 11 December, the formal declaration of war on the United States was made.

The German declaration of war freed Roosevelt from his dilemma. Now the United States could enter the conflict openly and without any reservation or holding back. Kershaw asks, was this a megalomaniacal act of folly on Hitler's part? No, is his answer: war with the United States was inevitable anyway, and the Japanese aggression would tie up American resources in the Pacific, allowing Germany to win the war in Europe before the full might of the US military was brought to bear on the Anglo-Soviet side. Even had Hitler not issued his declaration, the escalating submarine war in the Atlantic would have brought America in sooner rather than later. Hitler's decision, therefore, was not fateful after all – a verdict that, while convincing enough as an argument, rather undermines its inclusion in a book titled *Fateful Choices*.

The second decision prompted, at least to some extent, by America's growing involvement in the war, was, however, truly fateful: Hitler's decision to exterminate the Jews of Europe. In a sense, says Kershaw, there was no decision that could be 'traced to a single order on a specific day'. Certainly, explicit orders have survived from Hitler ordering the mass killing of Polish intellectuals and the ethnic cleansing of Jews from the areas of Poland incorporated into Germany after the German invasion of September 1939. In 1941 Hitler's orders were less explicit, but according to Kershaw, the wide powers he gave to SS chief Heinrich Himmler, to 'pacify' the newly conquered areas and kill Soviet political commissars and Jews who posed a security threat, were decisive. By early August 1941 Himmler's SS *Einsatzgruppen* (Task Forces) and police units were indiscriminately massacring Jewish men, women and children in vast numbers, in a process of which Hitler was kept well informed.

In October 1941 the Nazi authorities began the eastward deportation of Jews from Berlin, Prague, Vienna and other Central European cities, sending them to ghettos into which vast numbers of Polish and East European Jews had already been forced, living in rapidly deteriorating conditions. Meanwhile, the shooting of Jews by the Task Forces and police units reached new heights. Himmler began to try to resolve the situation by using poison gas as a quicker method of murdering people in large numbers: first in mobile vans, then through the construction of stationary facilities in extermination camps, beginning with Belzec in November 1941. To this degree, at any rate, the pace of events was beginning to force the Nazi leadership to make a fundamental decision and coordinate the programme of killing in an orderly way – hence the decision to call a conference of the leading administrative agencies involved, at the Berlin suburb of Wannsee, in November 1941, postponed to January 1942 because of the declaration of war on the United States.

Speaking privately to Nazi leaders the day after the declaration of war on America, Hitler made it clear that 'the world war is here. The annihilation of the Jews must be the necessary consequence.' Reporting the speech to his underlings a few days later, the Governor-General of Poland, Hans Frank, was brutally explicit: 'We must destroy the Jews wherever we find them.' There were 3.5 million in his area alone. 'We can't shoot these 3.5 million Jews,' he said; 'we can't poison them, but we must be able to take steps that will somehow lead to success in extermination.' The decision had clearly been made, and it had been made by Hitler.

It is surprising, given the structure of this book, that in explaining Hitler's invasion of Russia, Kershaw does not give more prominence to Roosevelt's decision to bring about the de facto entry of the United States into the war. Through the summer and fall of 1941, Hitler repeatedly referred to what he saw as a malign worldwide Jewish conspiracy driving Roosevelt into an unholy alliance with Churchill and Stalin to bring about the destruction of Germany. All three statesmen, he believed, were under Jewish influence; and his private statements were backed up by anti-American propaganda pumped out by Goebbels's Propaganda Ministry in Berlin. Here is a link that Kershaw might have made more of.

As it turns out, therefore, not all the decisions analysed in this book were fateful, and not all of them were, strictly speaking, decisions. But they were all connected in one way or another, and there is no doubt that together they helped determine the course of the war. Of course, one could easily pick alternative choices to the ten analysed in this book, from British Prime Minister Neville Chamberlain's declaration of war on Germany in September 1939 to Hitler's refusal to let the German Ninth Army withdraw from Stalingrad at the end of 1942, from Churchill's order to bomb German cities the following year to the various decisions made by the key conspirators in the German Resistance's plot to kill Hitler in 1944, and so on. In the end, Kershaw does not really bother to argue for the fundamental importance of the period from May 1940 to November 1941 in shaping the course of the war; he knows that history isn't as simple as that. The way, indeed, would seem open for him to write a sequel, or even two sequels, to this book, covering the years 1942–3 and 1944–5. They would be well worth reading.

Such books, focusing on decision-making by wartime leaders, would seem at first sight to be far removed from the kind of social history in which Ian Kershaw began his career. But in some ways this contrast is deceptive. Kershaw nods in the direction of the individual in history: the 'fateful choices' of Mussolini, Churchill, Hitler, Stalin and the rest, he says, 'were directly determined by the sort of individuals they happened to be. At the same time, though,' he goes on, 'they were not made in a vacuum as arbitrary whims of personality. They were choices made under preconditions and under external constraints.' One cannot help feeling that the personalities of the men who made the choices do not really interest Kershaw very much. In the end, then, this book is less about the fateful choices they made than about the factors that constrained them. That is precisely what lifts it out of the rut of ordinary military and diplomatic history and puts it into a class of its own.

19. ENGINEERS OF VICTORY

D ifferent kinds of historians have tended to emphasise different reasons for the Allies' defeat of the Axis powers in the Second World War. The more traditional military historians put the stress on the varying qualities of leadership on the two sides, the inspiration provided by Churchill and Roosevelt and, in a very different way, Stalin, contrasting with the remoteness of Hirohito or the unbalanced decision-making and growing withdrawal of Hitler from public life during the war. Generalship counted for a great deal in this view, too, brilliant German military figures like Rommel, Guderian or Manstein hamstrung by Hitler's constant meddling and rigid insistence on outright victory or total defeat, and outmanoeuvred by the likes of Zhukov, or Montgomery, or Patton, all given free rein by their political bosses to pursue their own tactics in the light of the military situation of the moment.

Economic historians, naturally, have pointed to the huge disparity in resources between the two sides, with the Allies outproducing the Axis powers many times over in arms and ammunition, while Japan ran out of food and Germany ran out of fuel. More recently, as the records of the secret services during the war have become available, 'intelligence historians' have made the case for the turning of the tide through vital breakthroughs in gathering information, decrypting enemy ciphers and mounting elaborate exercises in deceit and deception. Many historians have sought to identify vital 'turning points' in the conflict, from Ian Kershaw's 'fateful decisions' taken by the leaders of the belligerent powers, to Philip Bell's *Twelve Turning Points of the Second World War* (2011). On a broader basis, Richard Overy, whose writings have encompassed both military and economic history, canvassed a variety of reasons *Why the Allies Won*, to quote the title of his 1995 book, and came to the conclusion that 'The Allies won the Second World War because they turned their economic strength into effective fighting power, and turned the moral energies of their people into an effective will to win.'

Like Overy, Paul Kennedy is an historian who has always tried to see war and international relations in the round. His book *Engineers of Victory: The Problem Solvers Who Turned the Tide in the Second World War* (2013) is sceptical of some of the more exaggerated claims made by partisans of one approach or the other. The idea that 'intelligence breakthroughs changed the course of the struggle are, he suggests, unprovable unless they are assessed in a broader context. The list of intelligence failures in the war, he points out, is a long one, from the French ignorance of the German advance through the Ardennes in 1940 to the American blindness in the face of the planned Japanese attack on Pearl Harbor. Top commanders sometimes refused to believe intelligence reports; famously, when an ex-Communist German soldier crossed the lines the night before Operation Barbarossa to warn Stalin that an invasion was coming, the Soviet dictator had him shot for spreading false rumours.

Kennedy might have added, too, that the Ultra decrypts, through which British intelligence officers at Bletchley Park were able to monitor German radio traffic and warn the troops on the ground where the next attack was coming from, were hamstrung by the fear that too obvious a redeployment might alert the Germans to the fact that their plans had become known in advance; thus in May 1941, although the commander of the British troops on the island of Crete had been told by Bletchley Park where the forthcoming German airborne invasion forces were going to land, he was forbidden to deploy his men there in case the Germans smelled a rat, thus nullifying any advantage intelligence might have provided him. By contrast, Kennedy argues, the intelligence 'breakthroughs that had provable battlefield victories that shortened the course of the war ... are on a short-order menu'. Most obvious was the Battle of Midway, where intelligence located the enemy carriers while being able to hide the location of the US forces; perhaps the Royal Navy's destruction of the Italian fleet in the Mediterranean falls into the same category; maybe, too, the sinking of the German battlecruiser *Scharnhorst* in December 1943. Otherwise, intelligence, he argues, was generally only one factor among many, and usually not the most important, though in the course of his book he mentions many other major intelligence contributions, undermining his own argument at many points.

What did make the difference, then, according to Kennedy? He points to a number of broad factors influencing the course taken by the war. The most obvious of these was the disparity in resources and productive capacity between the Axis powers and the Allies. If anything, this was even greater than Kennedy concedes; thus, far from achieving 'productive superiority by 1943–44', the Allies already had it in 1940, even before the USA entered the war, with the Soviets producing, for example, 21,000 combat aircraft and the British 15,000 to Germany's 10,000; in 1941 Britain and the USA between them made more than twice as many combat aircraft as Germany and Japan combined. And far from it being the case that it was only the Allies who learned from their mistakes and improved their weapons systems and production methods, it was the Germans who managed to do this most impressively, when Albert Speer, building on his predecessors' foundations, boosted military manufacturing to its highest rate in 1944, with new products like the Tiger and Panther tanks.

Yet in the end this made little difference. The disparity in resources was recognised early on by thinking German generals like Fritz Todt, who told Hitler the war was lost for this very reason at the beginning of 1942. 'The war in North Africa,' lamented General Erwin Rommel after his defeat, 'was decided by the weight of Anglo-American *matériel*.' And it wasn't just productive capacity that the Axis lacked;

time and again its forces were defeated because they ran out of fuel; Paulus could not break clear of his encirclement by the Red Army at Stalingrad, even had he defied Hitler and tried to, because his tanks and lorries didn't have enough fuel to make the distance, and there were many other instances of this kind. Throughout the war, Germany never had more than a million tons of oil reserves, while Britain had ten million in 1942 and more than twenty million two years later. German attempts to conquer the oilfields of the Caucasus and the Middle East came to nothing, as did IG Farben's massive investments in the production of synthetic fuel.

Yet Kennedy is right to criticise 'the crude economic determinist explanation of the war's outcome'. Germany, Italy and Japan all dissipated their resources by fighting on too many fronts at the same time (prime examples of Kennedy's concept of imperial 'overreach', a concept he developed a quarter of a century ago in his classic book *The Rise and Fall of the Great Powers* (1987)). However, while the Soviet Union was able to concentrate almost exclusively on defeating the Nazi invader, the British and Americans also faced the problems posed by waging a war on many different fronts. Kennedy suggests that the British experience of running a global empire stood them in good stead here, but more importantly, he says, 'the British leaders *knew* they were overstretched', especially after the defeat of their forces in Greece and Crete, Tobruk and Singapore and their reverses in the Battle of the Atlantic, all at the low point of the war for them, in 1941–2, even with the participation of forces from many different parts of the empire; so they made every effort to compensate for this by developing new technologies to reduce losses.

It is these technologies and their deployment that form the central focus of Kennedy's engrossing book. He divides his material into five chapters. In the first, 'how to get convoys safely across the Atlantic', he begins in 1942, when Allied merchant fleets bringing supplies to Britain lost 7.8 million tons, most of them sunk by German submarines. Allied technologists overcame this difficult situation by developing long-range bombers that could accompany the convoys across the Atlantic; centrimetric radar to locate the U-boats, which usually had to travel on the surface because they lacked the air-conditioning needed to stay underwater for long periods of time; the Hedgehog mortar, with which convoy escorts could destroy the enemy submarines; and effective and better organised convoy support groups, including small aircraft carriers, that could stalk and eliminate the German 'wolf-packs'. He downplays the role of intelligence, here as elsewhere, but a significant role in the losses of 1942 was played by the Germans' ability to decode Allied radio transmissions while blocking attempts by Allied cryptographers to decipher their own; the Allied success in reversing this situation in December 1942 was surely a significant turning point in the conflict, enabling convoys to reroute away from the pursuing submarines and locate the U-boats by their radio traffic as well as by spotting them on the surface.

Kennedy turns from this oft-told story to deal with the question: 'How to win command of the air'. By the time the Allied bombers had increased their range and got better at finding their targets than they were to begin with, it was 1943, when mass raids on Hamburg and the Ruhr caused huge damage not only to German industry but also to German morale. It was a mistake to switch to far-off Berlin as a target, where Allied navigational aids were ineffective, short-range fighter planes could not accompany the bombers and the Germans had time to organise their defences. The bomber crews suffered heavy losses, and the campaign was scaled down. The solution was found in the P-51 Mustang, a long-range fighter with an American body and a British Rolls-Royce engine. The new fighter escorts were effective in protecting the bombers, whose range itself also increased; the Allies achieved command of the skies, and the last eighteen months of the war saw increasingly devastating raids that crippled German industry and further depressed German morale. Many historians have told this story before, and Kennedy adds little that is new, but his analysis is clear and convincing all the same.

From this familiar story, Kennedy moves on to recount how the Allies learned 'how to stop a Blitzkrieg', or, in other words, how to defeat the German tactic of combining air, armour and infantry in an all-out assault. The answer lay in preparing in-depth defences well in advance, as happened at El Alamein and Kursk. Here Kennedy is on rather shaky ground, having failed to consult Karl-Heinz Frieser's groundbreaking series of studies of the *Blitzkrieg*, culminating in his dramatic reinterpretation of Kursk, in which, he calculates, 760 German tanks were lost, not 1,600 as Kennedy claims, 170,000 troops were counted missing, dead or wounded, not 50,000, and – vital but not mentioned in Kennedy's book – 524 combat aircraft were lost. Once again, while it was important that the Soviets learned how to counter the German tactics and use intelligence, aerial supremacy, technology and logistics to turn the tide, the disparity in resources was vital, for while the Red Army's losses were far greater than the Wehrmacht's, they could also be made good far more easily.

In explaining 'how to seize an enemy-held shore', the book examines in particular the Normandy landings, in the light of previous amphibious disasters such as the attack on Gallipoli in the First World War. The Allies learned the importance of landing away from well-defended areas, and of securing command of air and sea in advance. It was also vital to maintain strict secrecy about the invasion plans, as the Allies did not, disastrously, before the landings at Salerno in September 1943 or Anzio in January 1944. All these conditions were present for the Normandy landings in June 1944, along with the elaborate deception measures that sent most of the German defensive forces somewhere else and made the Germans expect the invasion at a different time; another triumph of intelligence. The key, however, says Kennedy, following most other historians of D-Day, was meticulous planning and a smoothly functioning system of command and control, to which one might add, again, an overwhelming superiority in men and *matériel*.

In his last substantive chapter, Kennedy addresses another familiar topic when he considers 'how to defeat the "tyranny of distance"'. If the Japanese overreached themselves in the vastness of the areas they conquered in 1941–2, they also posed real problems for the Allied forces when they began to try and roll them back. China was too far from the

American mainland to be viable as a base for the counter-offensive, and the topography of Burma was unsuitable. It had to be done across the Pacific. The development of fast aircraft carrier groups, the production of long-range B-29 bombers flying at 30,000 feet, out of range of enemy fighters and anti-aircraft guns, the deployment of fast and manoeuvrable fighter planes such as the Hellcat, and the skill and experience in amphibious warfare of the US Marine Corps, gave the US forces supremacy at sea and in the air and enabled them to push back the Japanese until in the final phase they began to devastate Japan's towns and cities, bringing the war to an end with the atomic bombs dropped on Hiroshima and Nagasaki. American submarines decimated the Japanese fleet with new and improved torpedoes, while the huge, lumbering Japanese submarines were easily spotted and destroyed, and no effective attempt was made to protect Japanese shipping, resulting in a devastating collapse in supplies for the population on the Japanese islands and the occupying forces across the Pacific.

Kennedy's claim that the Allies won not least because they possessed a 'culture of encouragement' or 'culture of innovation' is central to his argument. He provides examples of the technological improvements and inventions that improved the Allied war effort, but the Third Reich was equally effective in devising and developing new weapons and technologies, from the V-2 rocket to the jet fighter, from the fast, battery-equipped, air-conditioned submarine to the 'Waterfall' ground-to-air missile. German science and technology was second to none in its capacity to innovate. It is perfectly true to say, as Kennedy does, that these technologies could not be deployed effectively because Germany had lost command of the sea and air by the time they were put on to the production lines, so factories and transport facilities were repeatedly put out of action. In the end, however, the decisive impact was made not by the Allies' superior ability to solve military and logistical problems through technology, but by their massive superiority in resources and, crucially, the way in which they were able to concentrate them where it mattered.

Thus – as is well known – the Germans' decision-making structures were chaotic and ineffective in the economic sphere. As in so many other aspects of administration, Hitler's preferred approach was to appoint different people to do the same thing, in the belief that the person who came out on top in the Darwinian struggle for institutional supremacy would be the most ruthless and the most efficient. This proved to be a grave disadvantage during the war, when not even Speer could centralise production of key weapons effectively. There were rival teams working on different kinds of rockets, and even on different kinds of atomic bomb, and resources were dissipated on a whole range of projects, many of them with no real future, instead of being concentrated on one or two. Matters were made worse by Hitler's continual wavering and changing of priorities. The Messerschmitt Me262, a twin-engined combat aircraft, was ready for production in July 1943, for instance, but Hitler first went against his advisers' plea for it to be equipped as a fighter (it would have been very damaging to Allied bombers over Germany) and ordered it to be built as a bomber (where it would have had little real effect), then banned all discussion of it because he took others' attempts to change his mind as challenges to his authority.

This leads on to a wider question about the role of leadership during the war. Kennedy recognises, of course, that 'the men at the top made a difference'. Hitler's claim to be the 'Greatest Field Commander of All Time' (*Grösster Feldherr aller Zeiten*, abbreviated ironically by some of his subordinates as *Gröfaz*) was accepted by many after his initial triumph over military conventionality in the defeat of France in 1940, but it was increasingly questioned by his generals as time went on. It was Hitler, notably, who divided the German forces on the Eastern Front in the late autumn of 1941, taking troops away from the assault on Moscow and diverting the impetus of the invasion to the Caucasus. But this was not, as Kennedy implies, an act of folly: Hitler considered it a priority to occupy the grain-growing regions of Ukraine and take over the Crimea to stop the Soviets from using it as a base for air raids on the Romanian oilfields, on which Germany depended so heavily, and there was something to be said for this view.

Kennedy says that 'the Wehrmacht leadership . . . had, ironically forgotten Clausewitz's stress upon the importance of focusing upon the enemy's *Schwerpunkte* (centres of gravity, or key points)' in going along with this decision, but in fact they had not; the general commanding Army Group Centre, Fedor von Bock, was bitterly opposed to the division of German forces, remarking to the Chief of the Army General Staff, Franz Halder, that 'the turn away towards the south is a sideshow'. 'I don't want to capture Moscow,' he protested, in the light of constant War Directives from Hitler warning that the capture of Moscow was not a top priority: 'I want to destroy the enemy army, and the mass of this army is standing in front of me!' The weakening of his forces by diverting many of them away to the south meant that 'a question-mark is placed over the execution of the main operation, namely the destruction of the Russian armed forces before the winter'.

Neither man's calculations were particularly rational. Both seemed to expect that the Soviet Union would crumble easily into anarchy and chaos, Bock because Prussian military doctrine had taught him that an enemy could be defeated by a single knockout blow, Hitler because he considered the Soviet Union as a ramshackle state held together only by the terror of a Jewish–Bolshevik clique. In fact, following a series of stunning victories in the south, Hitler transferred large quantities of men and *matériel* back to Bock, who launched a further assault in October, taking some 673,000 prisoners and advancing further towards Moscow. But the Soviet military leadership had rethought its tactics, Stalin had managed to inspire the will to resist and the Soviet spy Richard Sorge in Tokyo had convinced him that the Japanese were not going to attack Russia, enabling him to transfer 400,000 experienced troops to the Moscow front. The Soviet Union did not collapse; its resources were so deep that a single knockout blow was simply not possible; and Bock's army was halted before the gates of Moscow and pushed back into a defensive position where many of the men froze to death because they had only been issued with summer uniforms, expecting to win months earlier, before winter set in.

The exchange called into question the rationality of the entire Axis war effort. For in the end, success and failure in any war have to be measured by the aims with which the belligerents enter it, and these aims have to be realistic to stand any chance of success. Japan's initial aims, though ambitious, were relatively limited: the establishment of a 'Greater Asian Co-Prosperity Sphere' or in other words a Japanese economic empire that would harness the resources of a large area of East Asia and the Pacific in a situation where oil and other supplies had been cut off by the US embargo imposed in July 1941. It might have been possible to secure this against retaliation from the already over-stretched British Empire, whose easy defeat presaged its subsequent dissolution after the war. But it was wholly unrealistic to think that the USA would meekly stand aside after Pearl Harbor and negotiate a peace settlement that would leave the bulk of the Co-Prosperity Sphere in Japanese hands. Moreover, the brutal and sadistic behaviour of the Japanese conquerors in the areas they occupied doomed any idea of 'Co-Prosperity' from the outset. The Japanese invited total war by their behaviour, and they got it; it was a war they could never hope to win.

Hitler's war aims were boundless, expressing an even greater degree of illusion about his country's ability to achieve them than the Japanese harboured about theirs. The Nazis believed above all in the supremacy of willpower; their triumph of their own will over Germany would be followed by a similar triumph over the feeble and degenerate nations of the west, and the primitive and backward Slavic societies of the east. Victory would be followed by a racial reordering of Europe, with thirty to forty-five million Slavs exterminated to make way for German farm-ers, and then the resources of a Nazi-dominated Europe would be mobilised for a new confrontation with the USA. Here, too, the ruth-less and exploitative behaviour of the Germans in the occupied countries ensured that the resources of Europe rapidly dwindled, as the subject economies plunged rapidly towards exhaustion and collapse.

So it is pointless to speak, as Kennedy does, of 'the folly of the cruel Nazi treatment of the Ukrainians and other ethnic groups within Stalin's loathed empire' – such treatment was built into the Nazis' war aims.

Similarly, it would be missing the point to lament the diversion of German resources into the extermination of the Jews. This was a racial war, in which the extermination of six million European Jews, not dealt with at all in this book because it did not seem to belong to the normal arsenal of military strategy, was a paramount war aim, to be extended ultimately from Europe to America itself, from where, Hitler supposed, the world conspiracy against Germany was being orchestrated.

Struggle, conflict, aggression and violence were central to Nazi ideology, which envisaged endless war as the only way of keeping the 'Aryan' race supreme. In the face of irrationality of this order, it is rather beside the point to suggest, as Kennedy does, that the Germans might have won the war, or to claim that without the contribution of this or that logistical, organisational or technological innovation, 'victory would remain out of grasp'. Defeat was pre-programmed for the Axis by the very nature of its war aims, not just by the means through which the Axis powers sought to achieve them. Like every book that treats the Second World War as a whole as a rational conflict along the lines of the Seven Years War or the Franco-Prussian War or the American Civil War, which were fought for well-defined ends that either side might have achieved, *Engineers of Victory* is fundamentally misconceived from the outset.

Despite its opening claims, this book isn't really about technologies but tackles its themes on a much wider basis. There have been many excellent books published recently about the Second World War, but they have focused overwhelmingly on the experience of the war, on what it was like to be a soldier at Stalingrad, a sailor at Midway, a civilian in the Blitz. This book stands out because, unlike them, it tries to think through the history of the war, to answer big questions, and to advance reasoned and carefully argued propositions about its course and its outcome. Unfortunately, very little of what it has to say is new, and the detailed case studies it presents have been covered well in many other books on the war.

20. THE FOOD OF WAR

The Four Horsemen of the Apocalypse – pestilence, war, famine and death – have always ridden together. Throughout history, war has brought death not only in battle but also from starvation and disease. In pre-industrial conflicts, marching armies trampled crops, seized food supplies, took young farmhands away from the fields into military service and starved out cities under siege. Large groups of soldiers, travelling over great distances and living together cheek-by-jowl in makeshift and unhygienic conditions, spread epidemics, causing further suffering.

In the Thirty Years' War, from 1618 to 1648, up to half of the population of Germany is estimated to have died from this deadly combination of causes. The First World War was the first international conflict in which more troops were killed by enemy action than by disease. In the same conflict, more than half a million Germans died from malnutrition as a result of an Allied blockade of Germany's overseas food supplies. Epidemics have rarely been a weapon of war, not least because they have a habit of spreading without regard to which side their victims are fighting for. But starving out the enemy always has.

The combatant nations of the First World War learned through logistical error and terrible suffering the importance of securing adequate food supplies in a prolonged armed conflict. Not least as a result of this experience, as Lizzie Collingham shows in her superb new study *The Taste of War* (2012), these same nations went to considerable lengths to keep their armies and civilian populations alive and well fed during the Second World War. For Germany and in particular its leader, Adolf Hitler, the memory of mass malnutrition and starvation during the earlier conflict was an ever-present trauma. From early in his political life, Hitler wanted to conquer 'living space' for Germany in Eastern Europe and draw on the huge grain resources of Ukraine to feed the German armed forces. The Nazis had no intention of repeating the mistake of the First World War, when rationing had been introduced too late to save the situation. Indeed, although Collingham claims that rationing was introduced in Germany in August 1939, it had already been in place for two years before that. Already by the mid-1930s, military and arms industry conscription, the requisitioning of huge tracts of agricultural land for military purposes and the imposition of foreign exchange controls to curb food imports had led to a dramatic fall in food production and a concomitant rise in food prices. In 1936 prices were frozen, and on 1 January 1937 rationing was introduced for butter, margarine and fat; consumption of coffee and citrus fruit was restricted early in 1939. The German economy was on a war footing long before the war itself began.

Hitler managed to keep people at home in Germany reasonably well fed until the later stages of the war. Collingham reckons that around 40 per cent of the bread and meat eaten by the armed forces and civilians in the Reich was produced in the occupied territories or by labourers deported from these countries to work on German farms. Her claim that 'in Germany the population only began to experience hunger *after* May 1945', however, rests on too easy an acceptance of postwar memories, when many Germans blamed the Allied occupation for failing to feed them. Food supplies in Germany in fact were already beginning to break down in the autumn of 1944, as the armed forces lost control over Eastern Europe with the westward advance of the Red Army, and road and rail communications within Germany were being severely disrupted by Allied bombing. The Nazi regime cut domestic bread rations from 12,450 grams for the month of May 1944 to 9,700 for August, 8,900 for December and 3,600 for April 1945.

Nobody could live on what they were officially allowed to buy; a huge black market, run by escaped foreign workers, emerged, wild gangs engaged in regular shootouts with the Gestapo. Diseases like tuberculosis, boosted by malnutrition and debilitation, rose sharply in incidence in 1944. And, indeed, Collingham concedes that there were 'worsening food shortages in Germany's cities until, in the last months before the Allied victory, the supply system broke down'.

If food shortages were bad in Germany, they were catastrophic in Eastern Europe. Germany, as Collingham notes, 'exported wartime hunger to the countries it occupied'. Beginning with a 'hunger plan' hatched by the leading civil servant in the Food Ministry, Herbert Backe, and expanding in scope and ambition into the General Plan for the East, devised at the behest of SS chief Heinrich Himmler, Nazi food policy envisaged the deliberate starvation of between thirty and forty-five million Slavs (Collingham's claim of 100 million seems exaggerated), its effects to be accelerated by denying them access to medical care. When Germany invaded the Soviet Union in June 1941, cities like Kharkov, bombed and blasted by air attacks and house-to-house fighting, were left without basic facilities such as water, sewerage, gas and electricity. The infrastructure was destroyed. The occupying German forces banned civilians from entering or leaving the city. The retreating Soviet forces had already implemented a scorched-earth policy, denying the incoming Germans food by burning or ruining all the warehouses stockpiled with grain, corn, flour and vegetables. Half the population was evacuated; those who remained were condemned by the Soviets as traitors. 'There are no stores,' wrote a contemporary living in the city, 'no markets, no shops of any kind . . . The town is void of eatables like a desert.' By the end of 1942 a third of the remaining 450,000 inhabitants were dead, almost all of them from starvation. In Leningrad (present-day St Petersburg), besieged for more than two years by German forces under orders to starve the city out rather than take it by storm, with all the heavy military losses that would imply, at least a million people died of starvation, and there were widespread reports of people eating dead bodies in their desperation to stay alive.

The mass murder of 'useless eaters' began as early as September 1939, as the invading Germans crammed Poland's Jews into insanitary and overcrowded ghettos, where they were forced to live on what were literally starvation rations. In the Warsaw Ghetto one observer saw only 'nightmare figures, ghosts of former human beings' suffering from 'emaciation and sickliness'. Desperate inhabitants fought over scraps, losing all human dignity. Thousands died every week; altogether as many as 100,000 starved to death, according to Collingham, though many of the dead had in fact succumbed to diseases such as typhus that were a consequence more of lack of public hygiene than lack of food. Worse was to come. Germany's invasion of the Soviet Union was followed by massive victories and the capture of millions of prisoners of war, who were herded into makeshift enclosures in the open and left to starve to death. Cases of cannibalism were reported here, too. Collingham says that 2.35 million died, but this is an underestimate: the generally agreed figure is as high as 3.3 million.

The invasion and war in general had an enormous impact on the Soviet Union. Collingham estimates that a third of all people world-wide who died during the war lived in the Soviet Union. Fully 15 per cent of the Soviet population did not survive the war – eighty-five people for every Briton or American dead. Around nine million Red Army combatants were killed, a reflection not least of Stalin's callous disregard for life as he forced his generals time and again to throw their troops into the fray. In Moscow in 1942, after the German assault had been turned back, it was said that 'the sight of men and women falling dead of starvation on [the] streets became too commonplace to attract crowds'. The disruption of communications caused by the German invasion meant that troop rations, meagre at the best of times, could be interrupted for days on end. Red Army soldiers became expert foragers, digging up crops, stealing peasants' honey and pota-toes, requisitioning animals and killing them to eat. Some would make a stew of boiled nettles or pine needles to ward off scurvy.

Not only peasants but also town-dwellers suffered. The entire econ-omy was geared ruthlessly to war production. Civilian production virtually collapsed. This happened not least because everything, including the growing of crops, animal husbandry, and food distribution, was entirely state-run. Nevertheless, the regime squeezed the agricultural sector into supplying munitions and armaments workers and their families – the overwhelming majority of the population – with food, and above all with bread, handed out in factories rather than in distribution centres to ensure it went to sustain the war production effort directly by feeding the workers first. People marginal to war production – the elderly, the sick, the disabled, the very young – were denied the basics of existence and died. Overall perhaps as many as three million Soviet citizens perished from starvation during the war, though this figure is difficult to square with Collingham's claim that the total number of civilian dead in the Soviet Union was as high as twenty million.

The United States, worried about the Soviets' ability to survive under such conditions, shipped huge quantities of food under the lend-lease agreement. An American officer who accompanied one shipment was shocked by the sight of groups of 'starved wretches' who gathered on the quayside where shipments were being unloaded, to scoop up and eat on the spot 'raw meat, scraps or steaming chicken guts thrown out with the [American] ships' galley garbage'. But however bad life may have been under the Soviet regime, it was far worse under German occupation. Death awaited Red Army soldiers who surrendered, so they fought on. Hunger did not destroy morale. The Soviet Union was 'fighting on empty' but it continued to fight, ultimately all the way to victory. The German submarine fleet's attempt to stop American supplies from reaching the northern seaports of the Soviet Union scored some successes, but ultimately it succumbed to the Allied convoy system, the superiority, in the end, of Allied intelligence and decrypting ability, and the inadequacies of the U-boat fleet. And the situation slowly improved: by 1943 the Soviet Union was receiving more lend-lease food than Britain.

Yet it was not just the Germans who used food as a weapon and tried to deny it to their enemies. The drive for self-sufficiency bolstered by the capture of food-producing areas abroad was part of Japanese military thinking as well. Manchuria, already occupied in the 1930s, was seen as ripe for settlement by Japanese farmers, coercing the existing Chinese and Korean peasants into selling their land cheaply. But the settlement plan was not a success, and Japan's heavy reliance on imported food meant that when the war in the East began at the end of 1941, supplies were quickly cut off by the Allies, just as conscription and a drastic fall in the deep-sea fishing catch caused a fall in domestic Japanese agricultural output.

Japanese forces abroad depended almost entirely on food supplies from the occupied areas. But just as the harshness of German occupation policy in Europe alienated food producers and caused a fall in production, so, too, the Japanese massacres of Chinese farmers, particularly in the rice-growing areas of Malaya, combined with the conscription of farm labour for road and railway building and the imposition of a huge indemnity on the Chinese population in southern Burma, left the remaining peasants unwilling to work and determined to hide their produce from the conquerors.

Compounding the disaster, the Japanese tried to introduce regional self-sufficiency in a region where food supplies depended crucially on inter-regional trade. The American blockade established in 1943 administered the *coup de grâce* to the Asian rice trade, with American submarines sinking increasing quantities of Japanese shipping. Malnutrition became starvation; starvation became famine. In Manila the price of rice increased tenfold between 1941 and the middle of 1943; by the end of 1944 it was forty times more; by the middle of 1945 it had increased fourfold again. Chaos and mismanagement were more to blame for this situation than any deliberate policy of starvation on the part of the Japanese. But, like the Germans, the Japanese prioritised their own survival over that of those they ruled.

Collingham explains that the Japanese high command began the war in the belief that the 'Japanese army [could] . . . continue fighting without food, if they had strong morale'. But hunger often saps morale and undermines the fighting spirit, as the Japanese troops were to discover; and in the Asian theatre of war there was no threat of annihilation by the enemy to keep them going, as there was for the Red Army in Europe. As Collingham notes: 'During the course of its war with China and America the Japanese military went from being one of the best-fed armed forces in the world to a state of miserable starvation.' Over the decades nutritional experts had devised an innovative and highly effective dietary regime involving non-Japanese food as well as the basic staple of rice (mixed with barley to provide vitamin B). But the disruptive effects of the war with China and then the American blockade forced a halving of the military food ration; and this was still twice as much as the food ration normally allowed to Japanese civilians.

As American submarines disrupted supply lines, Japanese soldiers on the Pacific islands were particularly badly affected, with 15,000 starving to death on Guadalcanal alone. The survivors who surrendered were emaciated, suffering from scurvy, 'thin as thread', as their commander noted. Ninety per cent of the 158,000 Japanese troops in New Guinea died of starvation and tropical diseases, and there were widespread reports that they were killing and eating some of the prisoners they took. In the Philippines 400,000 out of nearly half a million Japanese troops starved to death. The American blockade proved a highly effective weapon. On the other side of the globe, the Germans harboured hopes that similar measures would be able to starve out the British. The story of the Battle of the Atlantic, when German submarines sought to cut off supply lines from North America to the United Kingdom, has been told many times, but usually from the naval angle; Collingham gives it a fresh look by focusing on what the ships carried rather than on how they got it across the ocean. More than half the calories consumed by the British were contained in imported food, but administrative confusion, a prewar depression in the shipbuilding industry and the diversion of the fastest merchant ships to war uses such as carrying troops all created severe bottlenecks in the food supply within two years of the outbreak of the war, if not earlier.

By the winter of 1942–3, the U-boat menace had aggravated the situation. Around 860,000 tons of shipping were lost in November 1942 alone, amounting to 9 per cent of food shipments to Britain. Further problems were caused by the diversion of resources to supply the Allied landings in North Africa. 'The country never realized how nearly we were brought to disaster by the submarine peril,' noted the wartime Minister of Food, Lord Woolton, in his memoirs. Yet improvisation usually got food to the right places when supplies failed to arrive. The British did not starve.

It was a different story across the far-flung territories of Britain's overseas empire. The British Middle East Supply Centre successfully reorganised trade and agriculture in the region to ensure that people continued to be fed despite the arrival of large numbers of British troops. Similar efforts were not undertaken elsewhere, however. In the absence of rationing or price controls such as had been imposed in Britain, rising demand caused by the need to buy up supplies for British troops fuelled inflation, which soon put many foodstuffs out of reach of the poor in parts of the empire. Food supplies were cut off by wartime activity – some African colonies, for example, had depended heavily on imported rice from Burma and other British territories in the Far East, now no longer available because of the Japanese invasion of those countries. A drought in East Africa made things worse and famine ensued, spreading beyond British territories to claim 300,000 lives in Rwanda alone. Isolated island territories such as Mauritius were particularly vulnerable, and their inhabitants began to suffer severe malnutrition.

Worst of all was the situation in Bengal. The complacent and inefficient colonial administration in India did nothing to curb inflation, speculation and hoarding, even when Burma fell to the Japanese, depriving the subcontinent of 15 per cent of its rice supply. Provincial governments in India reacted by banning the export of food to other provinces, strangling the machinery of trade in food in what one food controller called an outbreak of 'insane provincial protectionism'. The winter rice harvest of 1942 failed because of a fungal disease that spread rapidly in unusually warm and humid weather. No measures were taken to impose rationing or force hoarders to disgorge supplies, for fear of provoking political dissent in the economic elites who were benefiting financially from the situation.

Churchill ordered a 60 per cent cut in military and civilian shipping to the Indian Ocean, commenting that Indians should not take food supplies that could be used by the mother country. Thus Britain as well as Germany exported food shortages to its empire. Even if this was not, as with Germany's empire in eastern Europe, the product of a deliberate policy of starvation, the result was much the same: famine victims poured into Calcutta in the summer of 1943 – a vast, slow, dispirited, noiseless army of apathetic skeletons, as one observer described them. As many as three million people may have died from starvation and from diseases, such as cholera, associated with the movements of large numbers of people across the country.

The government imposed strict censorship to stop news of the famine from spreading, and it was only when Viscount Wavell was appointed viceroy of India in September 1943 that decisive action was taken. Worried about morale among the Indian troops charged with the recapture of Burma, Wavell overrode the disastrous policy of regional protectionism and introduced an effective system of rationing and distribution. Even so, Wavell had to overcome considerable resistance from Churchill and the government in London. Surprisingly, perhaps, the memory of the famine played almost no part in the Congress Party's demand for Indian independence after the war; most of its leaders were in prison and did not witness the severity of the disaster. And the Indian elites who backed independence had been partly responsible for the famine themselves, as they had occupied prominent positions in provincial administrations during the war, above all in Bengal, where the famine was concentrated.

Meanwhile, other parts of the British Empire were mobilised to increase food production for the war effort. Australia doubled the amount of land devoted to vegetable farming and supplied vast quantities of dried and canned foodstuffs to the American forces in the

Pacific. The United States itself had such enormous surpluses of food that it was able to provide a rich diet to the Pacific islands when it won them back from the Japanese. 'We fed the Japanese,' one Tuvaluan islander put it; 'the Americans fed us.' GIs, sailors and marines poured into the islands, spending liberally and fuelling a rapid rise in prosperity. Yet as the conflict subsided, there was hunger everywhere, especially in the defeated nations. By the end of the war, indeed, food production in Europe as a whole had fallen to 36 per cent of its prewar levels.

The desperate situation in the Soviet Union was made worse by the failure of the harvest in 1946. A year later perhaps two million Soviet citizens had died from starvation and associated diseases; in many places rationing remained in place well into the 1950s. The Americans viewed deprivation in Germany as a punishment for the crimes of Nazism, and stopped food relief from entering the country until they realised that a discontented and depressed population might become nostalgic about Hitler or could succumb to the lure of Communism, as Stalin, even at the cost of his own population's survival, sought to gain support in satellite states and the Soviet zone of occupied Germany by pouring in food. Only gradually, as the world economy recovered and then began to boom, did the situation improve.

Examining in detail the role played by food in the greatest of all political conflicts, the Second World War, was a brilliant idea on Collingham's part. *The Taste of War* is breathtaking in its breadth and scope, global in coverage and yet anchored in detailed research. Despite the inevitable mistakes and inaccuracies of detail, which should be corrected in the paperback reprint, this is a book that anyone interested in the role played by control of food supplies in the war will want to read. Much of the material is fresh and compelling, and many of the individual vignettes, anecdotes and quotations are heartrendingly moving in their depiction of the immensity of the suffering many people had to endure.

Yet by looking everywhere for the impact of the 'battle for food', Collingham's book has an inbuilt tendency to downplay other aspects

of the conflict. Often this involves picking out one side in a controversial area simply because it supports the argument that food supplies
were of crucial historical importance. For example, the sharp acceler-
ation of Germany's mass murder of Jews in the late spring and early
summer of 1942 was justified by some German officials as necessary
because of the critical position of food supplies to the German forces
and civilian population at the time. Yet it is possible that the officials
were simply providing what seemed to them to be a convenient military rationalisation for an ideologically motivated policy. After all,
there is evidence that senior SS officers had already decided in the
autumn of 1941 that Europe's Jews were to be taken to the east: the
first large-scale gassing facilities began to be constructed in October
and November of that year; the Wannsee Conference, held early in
1942 after several weeks' postponement, already envisaged the ultimate extermination of the world's Jews.

It would be unfortunate if readers only took away from this impressive book the belief that the battle for food 'shaped the events of World
War II', to quote the promotional copy, or that 'access to food drove
both Nazi Germany and imperial Japan to occupation'. Other, more
significant factors were involved. *The Taste of War* is a book, then, that
has to be read in conjunction with other histories of the war; it views
the conflict from one angle only, and the war needs to be seen in the
round.

21. DEFEAT OUT OF VICTORY

On 22 June 1941, at 3.15 in the morning, the largest invasion force ever assembled crossed into the Soviet Union from the west to begin Operation Barbarossa, the campaign to conquer Eastern Europe. Three million German troops, another half a million soldiers from allied countries such as Hungary and Romania, 3,600 tanks, 600,000 motor vehicles, 7,000 artillery pieces and 2,700 combat aircraft opened the assault. As bombs rained down on Soviet cities and airfields, the Germans advanced up to fifty kilometres a day, taking the opposing Red Army forces by surprise, killing and capturing huge numbers of Soviet soldiers. Confused and disoriented, the Red Army virtually collapsed. Retreat was made difficult by the Germans' destruction of roads, railways and communications behind the Soviet front. By 3 July, the Chief of the German Army General Staff was noting in his diary that 'the campaign against Russia has been won in 14 days', a view echoed triumphantly by Hitler and his entourage. By 11 July, German tanks had broken through to the outskirts of Kiev, capital of Ukraine. The euphoria in Hitler's field headquarters was unbounded.

Hitler and the Nazi leadership in Germany regarded the Soviet Union as a fragile, artificial entity, consisting of a vast mass of dull peasants oppressed by a small clique of Jewish Communists. One good push and the whole edifice would collapse. As with so many aspects of Nazi ideology, this was so remote from reality that it seems justified to call it a fantasy. In fact the Soviet Union did not collapse. Stalin – who, ironically, was himself deeply antisemitic – rallied after an initial moment of panic, and called upon the Soviet people to resist in a famous radio broadcast on 3 July. Abandoning for the moment the rhetoric of Soviet Communism, he declared the defence of the motherland against the Germans to be a 'Great Patriotic War'. Realising what fate lay in store for them if they surrendered to the Germans, and conscious of the fact that they would be shot by the Soviet secret police if they showed the slightest sign of hesitation, Stalin's troops rallied behind their leader.

The Germans' looting of food supplies and destruction of Soviet towns and villages reminded the Soviet soldiers of what they were fighting for. Their families would surely perish if the Germans won. Fresh reserves of men and munitions were available in quantities the Germans could not even guess at: five million reservists were mobilised within a few days of the invasion, and nearly ten million more were soon preparing to fight. Military equipment was momentarily harder to come by, since Soviet war industries were being relocated out of harm's way east of the Ural mountains in an operation of such magnitude and complexity that it could not be completed until the end of November. The restructuring of the Red Army command and reorientation of battle tactics that Stalin realised were necessary would not be completed until several months had passed. Nevertheless, within a few weeks the Red Army had begun to fight back.

Well before the end of July, German officers and troops were complaining in their diaries and letters home that the Russians' will to resist did not seem to have been broken. German troops were exhausted after weeks of rapid forced marches over huge distances and constant combat along the way. Losses amounted to more than 200,000 by the end of the month. The advance began to slow, hampered by stretched communications, poor roads and the absence of a railway network of the necessary density to transport large quantities of men, fuel and equipment around at speed (the Germans were forced to rely on horses, of which more than 600,000 were involved in the campaign). On 30 July, the Army Supreme Command ordered a temporary halt to the invasion to recover, regroup and resupply.

The division of the advancing German forces into three Army Groups – North, Centre and South – partly dictated by the vastness of the terrain to be traversed, partly by the need to skirt the huge and virtually impenetrable obstacle of the Pripet Marshes – together with the heavy losses it had sustained, and the continual arrival at the front of new Soviet reserves, made it look increasingly less likely that the enemy could be eliminated by a single knockout blow.

While the advance stalled, Hitler and his generals debated what to do next. It had become obvious that the dissipation of German military strength was hampering the drive for victory. The weight of the campaign had to be concentrated into one of the three main Army Groups. The generals favoured strengthening Army Group Centre for a rapid advance on Moscow, where they believed the main enemy force to be located. There it could be destroyed, they thought, bringing an instant, Clausewitzian total victory. But Hitler refused. Instead, he strengthened Army Group South, taking away men and resources from Army Group Centre in order to make it ready for the assault on Kiev. Still expecting the edifice of Soviet command to collapse, he did not think the assault on Stalin's capital city should be the highest military priority. So he stuck to his original plan to concentrate on acquiring the food supplies and industrial resources of Ukraine. After that, Army Group South would push on towards the Caucasus, with its oilfields, so badly needed by the petrol-starved German tanks, assault guns and transport vehicles, while Army Group Centre would resume the march on Moscow. Overawed by Hitler, whom they held to be the architect of the previous year's rapid conquest of Western Europe, in a situation where many of them had entertained serious doubts about the wisdom of attacking through the Ardennes, the generals felt unable to gainsay their leader.

On 21 August 1941 the decision was finally taken and soon the German forces began to encircle Kiev, with General Heinz Guderian's panzers from Army Group Centre approaching from the north-east, and Field-Marshal Gerd von Rundstedt moving tanks across the River

Dnieper to the south; on 15 September 1941 the various German forces joined up. The city was surrounded, with four Soviet armies encircled. Well before this, Chief of the Soviet General Staff Georgy Zhukov had urged the abandonment of the city by the Soviet forces in order to avoid disaster. But Stalin overruled him, and indeed dismissed him from his post on 29 July. The commander on the spot, Marshal Budennyi, backed Zhukov and was also fired, being replaced by the more pliant Marshal Timoshenko.

Like Hitler, Stalin regarded retreat as a sign of cowardice, or, worse, treachery. Kiev in particular held a huge symbolic importance for him as the capital of Russia in the Middle Ages and the main city in Ukraine. The local party boss, Nikita Khrushchev, who was to become leader of the Soviet Union after Stalin's death, urged him to stand firm, perhaps sensing that this was what Stalin wanted to hear. The loss of Kiev, Stalin thought, would demoralise the defenders of Leningrad, besieged by the Germans in the north, and open the way for the Germans to take Moscow. It would also send the wrong message to the Western Allies, whom he was trying to persuade to open a second front by invading France. So he ordered his generals to hold the city. The decision was fatal. Replying to the order to 'stand fast', the chief of staff of the Soviet South-Western Army Group, General Tupikov, said bluntly: 'This is the beginning, as you know, of catastrophe – a matter of a couple of days.' Stalin dismissed his remark as 'panicky'.

The German advance was met with fierce resistance and repeated counter-attacks. 'The Russians' behaviour in action is simply incomprehensible', wrote one German soldier: 'They are incredibly stubborn, and refuse to budge even under the most powerful gunfire.' Another German account spoke of the dead bodies of Russian soldiers as a 'carpet' stretching for miles. The Soviet troops knew that their only chance of survival lay in breaking through the German lines, and threw themselves at the advancing forces with astonishing recklessness, resulting in 'such losses', as a German account reported, 'that one wonders how they can find the courage and the men to keep coming on'. Unwilling to take prisoners, they shot any Germans they managed to capture, often venting their anger, fear and frustration on them in hor-rifying acts of vengeance. The Germans replied in kind. On another part of the front, German troops came across the bodies of over a hundred of their comrades, hung by their hands from trees, their feet doused with petrol and set alight, a method of slow killing known among the Germans as 'Stalin's socks'. Following the discovery, 4,000 Red Army prisoners of war were summarily shot by German firing squads.

Around Kiev, German planes pounded Soviet positions and com-munications, German panzers and infantry fought their way relentlessly forward and the Red Army forces were steadily pushed back until the Germans finally took the citadel on 19 September 1941. The sheer scale of the victory was unprecedented. The Germans calculated that they had taken 665,000 prisoners along with staggering quantities of tanks, guns and equipment. In his detailed narrative and assessment of the campaign, *Kiev 1941: Hitler's Battle for Supremacy in the East* (2012), David Stahel reckons this is an exaggeration or even a propagandistic 'manipulation of the facts'. Still, there was no doubting the total defeat of the Red Army. At the end, its morale had finally collapsed. One local man, observing a group of captured Red Army soldiers, reported them complaining about Stalin and his henchmen: 'They want us to die for them – no, we are not as stupid as they think.' Lice-ridden, hungry, des-perate, with rags round their feet replacing broken and worn-out boots, they were susceptible to the blandishments of the Germans, who dropped or posted leaflets or broadcast with loudspeakers across the lines promising bread and cigarettes to anyone who surrendered. So demoralised were the Soviet troops that many gave themselves up in droves, despite the widespread knowledge of what had happened previously to huge numbers of Soviet prisoners of war taken by the Germans.

As soon as the Germans had taken up their quarters in the city, the Soviet secret police detonated numerous bombs they had planted around the major public buildings and offices, killing two hundred Germans including two staff colonels, while the explosions set off fires that raged uncontrollably, fanned by high winds and encouraged by

Molotov cocktails thrown surreptitiously by Soviet agents. With water supplies largely out of action, it took five days to bring the fires under control. Outraged, the German occupiers, believing after years of Nazi indoctrination that the Bolsheviks and their agents were part of a world Jewish conspiracy to destroy them, blamed the city's Jews, and on 29 September rounded up 34,000 of them, men, women and children, took them to the nearby ravine of Babi Yar, and over a period of two days shot them all, in the largest single antisemitic mass extermination of the war to date. Already, SS Task Forces were roaming the countryside rounding up and shooting tens of thousands of other Jews. Within a few weeks, the gas chambers would start implementing what the Nazis were already calling 'the Final Solution of the Jewish Question in Europe'.

Kiev was a large city with 815,000 inhabitants, around half of whom had already fled the advancing German armies. For the remainder, life under German rule became increasingly impossible. The Germans quickly banned the supply of food to the city from the surrounding countryside. 'Kiev must starve,' agricultural experts told confidential planning meetings, in order for the resources of Ukraine to be devoted to feeding German troops and civilians. Soon people were reduced to eating pancakes made from ground potato peel, or bread made from animal fodder. People were 'emaciated or swollen from hunger', as one observer reported, and were roaming the streets in search of food. It was, reported Anatoly Kuznetzov, author of the classic novel *Babi Yar*, 'a city of beggars'. By October 1943 there were only 295,000 people left in the city. Scores of thousands had died from malnutrition and associated diseases. 'First they finished off the Yids', people were recorded as saying, 'but they . . . exterminate us every day by the dozen, they're destroying us in a slow death.' Hitler had originally ordered the city to be razed to the ground, and was reportedly angry that he had been disobeyed; but the slow death of Kiev was in fact the future he had envisaged for all Russian cities in the wake of conquest, to make way some time in the not too distant future for waves of German settlers as the 'Slav' population died out.

In sheer scale at least, the Battle of Kiev was the greatest German victory of the war. Propaganda Minister Joseph Goebbels lost no time in trumpeting it as a stunning triumph for German arms and a vindication of Hitler's change of strategy on the Eastern Front. Morale at home, dampened by the slow progress of the German advance over the previous few weeks, improved dramatically, but only because, as the SS reported, many people now expected the 'final collapse of the Soviet regime' and the 'end of the war against Russia' in 'four to six weeks'. 'Kiev,' Stahel concurs, 'was uniquely Hitler's triumph.' His strategy had been bitterly opposed by his senior generals before the event. But he had been aided and abetted by the intransigence of Stalin, whose dismissal of his own senior generals and insistence on defence at all costs made a major contribution to the German victory. The two dictators, however, drew the opposite conclusion from the outcome of the battle. While Stalin belatedly recognised that it would in future be wise to leave matters largely to his generals, Hitler saw his triumph as a vindication of his own strategic genius, brushing his generals aside with ever-growing, ever more thinly veiled contempt.

Yet, as Stahel notes, the victory was Pyrrhic, the triumph illusory. Immediately after the capture of Kiev, the German forces drove on to Moscow. But it was already too late. Throughout the summer, the paucity of rail links to the combat zone had meant that the Germans had had to use the dusty unmade Russian roads for most of their transports; huge dust clouds rose from the rumbling tanks and lorries and marching columns of men, clogging up engines and making it difficult to breathe. The autumn rains came early in 1941, with rainfall in Ukraine by 11 September already the worst since 1874. 'Such is war on the steppes of Ukraine,' noted one eyewitness: 'dust, mud, dust, mud.' 'The "black earth" of Ukraine,' Rundstedt reported, 'could be turned into mud by ten minutes' rain, stopping all movement until it dried.' In mid-October another officer noticed 'a continual line of sinking, bogged down, broken-down motor vehicles' on the roads, 'hopelessly stuck fast'. The advance on Moscow was called to a halt for three weeks.

Zhukov, restored to favour after the vindication of his dire warnings about Kiev, seized the opportunity to bring up fresh reserves and reorganise Moscow's defence. On 11 November the onset of winter made the ground hard enough for the Germans to resume their advance. But soon it was snowing, and the German troops, who had not been issued with winter clothing because Hitler and the generals had expected to win the war by the autumn, began to suffer frostbite in temperatures as low as minus 40 degrees Celsius; some even froze to death. The better-equipped Red Army counter-attacked and brought the advance to a halt. The consternation at this defeat caused several German generals to suffer breakdowns; Hitler took the opportunity to reshape the army command, blaming his officers for the debacle. After the war, the surviving generals riposted by claiming they could have taken Moscow had German forces not been diverted to Kiev, thus causing a fatal delay of several weeks in the advance. But Zhukov pointed out, not unreasonably, that the existence of several Soviet armies in the Kiev area would have exposed the German flank to attacks that he certainly would have ordered them to undertake on German forces moving towards Moscow.

The weather was not the only problem. Every German victory was bought at a price the German armies could ill afford. By 16 September they had lost almost half a million men since the invasion. In some divisions the casualty rate stood at nearly 17 per cent. Guderian's Panzer Group 2 had lost a total of 32,000 men. In September alone, during and immediately after the Battle of Kiev, the German forces in the east suffered more than 50,000 fatalities. Replacements took time to train and bring up, and German combat units were already below strength when the battle for Moscow began. This meant that commanders had to ask those who remained to fight and march even harder than before. Not surprisingly, they became increasingly battle-weary. Growing attacks from Soviet partisans in the rear only added to their woes. The tired, exhausted, lice-ridden, sick and freezing soldiers who faced Zhukov's troops before Moscow in December 1941 were very different from the optimistic, dashing men who had entered the Soviet Union six months before.

Just as bad was the strain the continual fighting, and major operations such as the Battle of Kiev, placed on German supplies. Stukas and other combat aircraft caused considerable damage in the battle, but planes were being shot down and crews killed or captured. Conditions on field airstrips in the east were so bad that while 246 single-engine fighters were damaged in action on the Eastern Front in 1941, no fewer than 813 were damaged in non-combat-related activities. Fourteen per cent of aircrew were lost every month. The situation on the ground was, if anything, even worse. General Model's 3rd Panzer Division, beginning the invasion with a force of just under 200 tanks, had only ten in operation by the middle of September. As Guderian concluded: 'These figures show how badly the troops needed a rest and a period for maintenance.'

German war production and recruitment could not keep pace with losses on this scale over a long period. By contrast, the Soviet economy was outperforming the German in every respect, producing twice the number of combat aircraft and three times the number of tanks. At the beginning of February 1942 Hitler's Minister of Armaments, Fritz Todt, was warning that Germany could not hope to keep pace even with the Soviet Union, let alone with all the British Empire and the USA as well. Each of these three enemy powers was outproducing Germany: together their economic strength was unmatchable. And the Soviet Union's resources in manpower were virtually inexhaustible, especially once the bombing of Pearl Harbor and its aftermath focused the attention of the Japanese on the war with the USA and so allowed Stalin to bring huge reinforcements across from the Pacific theatre to engage in the defence of Moscow.

The year 1942 would see further German victories. But they were to be short-lived. The writing was already on the wall. Indeed, Stahel argues, it had already been there at the beginning of August 1941, when Operation Barbarossa had been brought to its first temporary halt. The whole campaign depended on a quick victory, bringing the Soviet Union to its knees in a few weeks, just as had happened with Germany's swift victories in the west, over France, Belgium, Holland,

Denmark and Norway the previous year. But the *Blitzkrieg* tactics that had worked by pinning up Germany's western enemies against the North Sea and the English Channel could not work in the limitless expanse of the Eastern European steppe. Small and medium-sized West European powers were one thing; conquering the might of the Soviet Union, increasingly helped by supplies convoyed from the USA, was an entirely different proposition.

The story of the Battle of Kiev has been told many times, but seldom in such detail as it is in David Stahel's book. Relying mainly on German sources, he brings new evidence to bear on the conflict with the official war diaries of German divisions, as well as making good use of published editions of the private field-post letters and diaries of German soldiers of all ranks. This is emphatically a military history, replete with complex (and not always easily decipherable) maps of troop movements and dispositions, technical terms, titles and abbreviations and full names for all the troop units involved. Some of this impedes readability (particularly irritating is the use of Roman numerals, as in 'the XXXXVII Panzer Corps'), but, overall, Stahel conveys extremely complex military action with exemplary clarity.

Unlike more traditional military historians, he is acutely aware of the wider context of the action, from Hitler's overall aims for the war to the importance of logistics for the outcome; from the murderous racism and ruthless pragmatism with which the German leaders, military as well as political, condemned so many Soviet civilians to starve and so many Jewish inhabitants of the area to a terrible death, to the postwar disputes among historians and retired generals over Hitler's strategy; from the conditions troops had to face in the Ukrainian and Russian autumn and winter to the basic realities of the economic foundations of the German war effort, foundations which, he argues convincingly if not entirely originally, were starting to crumble almost from the moment when Operation Barbarossa was launched.

His realism refreshingly prevents him from following traditional military historians' often over-positive and simplistic descriptions of 'great' generals and 'decisive' battles. Kiev was, as he correctly notes, only part of a much wider conflict, and the impression, so enthusiastically conveyed by Hitler and his Propaganda Minister Joseph Goebbels, that it was a decisive step in the conquest of the Soviet Union, was in reality no more than an illusion. Privately, Goebbels was far less optimistic than he told his tame press to be about the outcome of the war. Already in mid-September 1941, on the eve of the capture of Kiev, he was noting in his diary that the war in the east was not going to end as quickly as Hitler had originally supposed. The *Blitzkrieg* had become a war of resources. 'After it has become known that the campaign in the east cannot be brought to an end in the time we had actually expected to do so, the people should also be made aware of what difficulties we confront … It now depends on who can endure this the longest … Indeed, we are now fighting with our backs against the wall.'

22. DECLINE AND FALL

Why did the Germans keep on fighting to the bitter end in 1945, long after it was clear to almost everybody that the war was lost? From the catastrophic defeat of the Sixth Army at Stalingrad early in 1943, through the devastating Allied bombing raids on Hamburg in the summer of 1943, reports on popular opinion filed by secret agents of the Nazi regime record a growing belief that Germany was going to lose. So why did Germans not rise up and force the regime to sue for peace? Towards the end of the First World War, recognition that the war was lost led senior generals to the negotiating table. Not so in 1944–5. Why not?

Most wars between states in the modern age, according to Ian Kershaw's *The End: Hitler's Germany 1944–45* (2011), end with an agreed peace as soon as one side concedes defeat. It is possible to think of major exceptions to this rule, from Napoleon's France in 1814 to Saddam Hussein's Iraq two centuries later. Sometimes, too, there is regime change before peace is concluded, as in the Franco-Prussian War or the First World War. Still, the determination of the Germans to go down fighting in the Second World War demands explanation – all the more so, since the death and destruction they suffered increased hugely in the final months. In his new book, Kershaw, who began his career as a historian of Nazi Germany with pioneering work on German popular opinion in the Third Reich returns to his original focus of interest and tries to find an answer to the perplexing question of Germany's failure to surrender through a close study of popular opinion in the final phase of the war.

The first and most obvious reason lies, it is clear, in the nature of the Nazi regime itself. The Third Reich was not a normal state. It was not even a normal dictatorship, if there is such a thing. From the start of his career, Hitler was possessed with a Social Darwinist view of the world that saw relations between states as the expression of a struggle for supremacy between races. There was no compromise: either Germany would achieve global hegemony or it would go under. His war aims were neither rational nor limited. As the military situation deteriorated, he insisted with ever greater vehemence that the struggle had to continue. In the final months, he became increasingly divorced from reality, hoping for rescue by miracle weapons such as the V-1 and the V-2, expecting quarrels to break out between the Western Allies and the Soviet Union, or looking for a speedy end to the war after the death of President Roosevelt. A portrait of Frederick the Great, who had turned round the fortunes of Prussia after the occupation of Berlin by the Russians, provided him with intermittent hope.

Hitler has sometimes been credited, notably by the American historian Gerhard Weinberg, with exercising a degree of flexibility in his command of the German armed forces during the years of defeat and retreat, but even had this been the case, in the regime's final months it gave way to a stubborn insistence that retreat was treason, tactical withdrawal military cowardice and realism weakness of willpower. Exuding confidence in ultimate victory, he continued to move his armies around long after they had become desperate, disorganised and depleted rabbles. On occasion the mask of self-belief would slip, and he would confess that all was lost; at the end, he announced to his intimates, he would put a bullet through his brain. 'We'll not capitulate. Never. We can go down. But we'll take a world with us.' The German people, Hitler concluded, did not deserve to survive. They had failed the test of history. On 19 March 1945 he issued the infamous 'Nero order', telling his commanders to destroy everything that might fall into the hands of the advancing enemy.

But Hitler's self-destructiveness and contempt for the German people in some ways only deepen the mystery of why they fought on. Part of the answer clearly lies in the psychological power he still wielded. Whether by force of personality or habit on the part of his underlings, or as a result of prestige built up through the years of success, he continued to be able to persuade his immediate subordinates to follow him into the abyss. 'Even in the last weeks,' Kershaw notes, 'some went in to see him demoralised and disconsolate and came away with new enthusiasm and determination.' Albert Speer, for instance, whose efforts had done so much in the final three years of the war to increase arms production and keep it going in the face of Allied bombing raids, continued to serve Hitler even though he realised more clearly than most that all was lost.

Only at the very end did they begin to desert him: Hitler dismissed Göring for supposedly trying to seize power and Himmler for negotiating with the Allies behind his back. Even then, an extraordinary number chose to follow Hitler into oblivion, in a wave of suicides that has few parallels – not only Goebbels and Bormann, and later Göring, Himmler and Ley, but also senior government ministers like Rust and Thierack, 10 per cent of the army's generals, 14 per cent of air force generals, 20 per cent of the Party Gauleiters and many more further down the hierarchy. Their self-immolation was testimony to their allegiance to Hitler as well as to their belief that life was meaningless without him. Arrest and trial would confront them with their crimes and rob them of their belief that what they had done was historically necessary. Suicide, some thought, was an honourable, Roman way out, a heroic gesture that would serve Germans as an example for the future. The world of illusion was not inhabited by Hitler alone.

Under a different head of state, such as Göring or Himmler, Germany might have sued for peace well before May 1945. But the Allies had agreed at Casablanca in January 1943 to demand nothing short of unconditional surrender from Germany. The armistice in the First World War had been a costly mistake, they concluded. It had allowed the far right, not least the Nazis, to argue that the German armed forces had not been defeated militarily, but had been stabbed in the back by Jewish revolutionaries at home. There must be no possible doubt this time.

After the war, many surviving senior German officers blamed the policy of unconditional surrender for the continuation of the war. The demand, one of them said, 'welded us to a certain extent onto the Nazi regime', since it left them with no guarantees about their future. This claim, however, has been dismissed by historians as a flimsy excuse. 'Hardly any notice was taken' of the demand for unconditional surrender by the German High Command, according to one senior general, and there was no discussion of its possible military consequences. The reason the Germans fought on has to be sought, as Kershaw rightly says, in Germany itself, not in policies adopted by the Allies.

Certainly, the Allied demand for an unconditional surrender gave Nazi propagandists a useful justification for continuing their senseless resistance. The machinery of persuasion marshalled by Goebbels, the Propaganda Minister, functioned almost up to the end. Long before this came, its trumpeting of the imminent arrival of new wonder weapons that would turn the tide of the war, its ever more strident insistence that the fighting spirit of the German people would eventually prevail, its forced optimism and its exhortations to sacrifice were all falling on deaf ears. People thought the chorus of propaganda broadcasts, newspaper articles and newsreels emanating from the Propaganda Ministry sounded like the band playing on the deck of the *Titanic*. 'Wherever you go,' one junior officer wrote in his diary after Cologne fell, 'only one comment: an end to the insanity.' Almost all sources agree that morale had collapsed by the beginning of 1945. By the end of March, interrogations of soldiers captured by the Western Allies found that only 21 per cent still had faith in Hitler, a sharp fall from the 62 per cent who had professed loyalty in January.

More important perhaps in the minds of many army officers was the personal oath of allegiance to Hitler they had been obliged to take. Many subsequently gave this as a reason for their continued obedience to him. It was not necessarily a retrospective excuse. Military training and habits of obedience had been amplified by the Third Reich into a sense of loyalty to Hitler as the supreme commander of the armed forces. Certainly, neither the Allied demand for unconditional surrender nor the military oath of allegiance prevented a group of senior army officers from conspiring to overthrow Hitler in July 1944. But Colonel Stauffenberg's bomb failed to kill the dictator, and the majority of military commanders had in any case refused to join the conspiracy, either because they regarded its chances of success as small, or because they felt it was treachery to the nation at a difficult moment, or because they genuinely felt inhibited by their oath of allegiance. After the plot, Hitler and Himmler's drastic purge of the armed forces left only unquestioningly loyal officers in post. Even the relatively sensible General Gotthard Heinrici, charged with the defence of Berlin, felt it would be treason to refuse to obey Hitler's orders, though he confided to his diary that they were either meaningless or insane.

For civil servants, municipal administrators, judges and prosecutors, teachers and state employees across the country, an ingrained sense of duty ensured that they carried on doing their jobs. They continued even when their decisions could no longer be implemented, issuing paper orders that stood no chance of being put into effect, judging and condemning offenders criminalised by Nazi legal measures because that was what the law required them to do. That the law itself had been perverted by Nazism did not occur to them. They had unthinkingly adapted to the Third Reich because it had taken over the management of the state; they continued to work for it to the end because they felt it was their job to do so. The senior official in the Reich Chancellery, asked after the war why he had carried on working, could not understand the implication of the question: 'As a longstanding civil servant,' he shrugged, 'I was duty-bound in loyalty to the state.'

Characteristic of this almost complete alienation from reality was the demand presented to leading ministers on 23 February 1945, just over two months before the end, by Finance Minister Count Schwerin von Krosigk, for reductions in government expenditure and increases in taxes on property, tobacco and alcohol, utilities and other items of consumption in an attempt to cover the growing budgetary deficit. His initiative culminated in the Alice in Wonderland statement that 'it cannot be objected that essential provisions for the population are thereby being made more expensive', since 'a large part of the population has already been entirely without regular access, or with only restricted access, to water, gas and electricity for months'. Schwerin was still working on his proposals a month later, when there was scarcely any part of the country that was not under Allied occupation.

The state continued to function, yet in the final months it increasingly ceded power to the Nazi Party at every level. This was, Party activists commented, a 'time of struggle', like the old days before 1933. The treachery of the officers in Stauffenberg's failed plot left Hitler and the leaders of the Reich deeply distrustful of the old elites. Hitler's immediate subordinates, Goebbels, Himmler and Bormann, acted to move the Party, its Gauleiters and activists into the institutional space previously occupied by the state bureaucracy. New laws and regulations gave Party officials hugely extended powers over civilian life. They drafted labour, organised clean-ups after bombing raids, coordinated civil defence and mobilised the *Volkssturm*, the 'Dad's army' of civilian conscripts who were meant to spearhead last-ditch resistance to the invasion of the Reich. Ill-equipped and poorly trained, mostly without even uniforms, they were no match for the battle-hardened troops of the Allies and the Red Army, and 175,000 of them were killed in the last months of the war. They were usually led by hard-line Nazi activists, however, and provided yet another instrument by which the Party took control over the mass of the German people. One function of the *Volkssturm* was to punish backsliding and defeatism among the population. Shootings and informal courts-martial leading to the execution of 'traitors', increasingly held in public, became common in German towns in the winter of 1944–5. Kershaw provides many horrific examples of the ruthlessness with which the Party and its adherents punished backsliding. People who wanted to avoid bloodshed were strung up from lamp-posts with placards around their necks: 'I wanted to do a deal with the Bolsheviks'. 'In a house in which a white flag appears,' Himmler ordered on 3 April 1945, 'all males are to be shot.' For good measure the Gauleiter of Franconia added: 'Villages that raise white flags communally will be burnt down.'

This order does not seem to have been carried out, but there were enough middle and lower-ranking Nazis left in positions of power to institute a reign of terror that bullied the vast bulk of the civilian population into acquiescence with their senseless determination to fight on. The numerous cases of last-ditch Nazi brutality range from a local Nazi leader in Heilbronn who came across a street with white flags hanging from several houses to welcome the approaching Americans, stopped the car and ordered his men to jump out and shoot everyone in sight, to a drumhead court-martial unit under Major Erwin Helm, who arrested a sixty-year-old farmer who had made sarcastic remarks to the local *Volkssturm*, bullied the two other members of the court into condemning the man and hanged him 'from a branch of the pear tree just beneath the window of his farmhouse while insults were hurled at his horror-struck wife'.

Such fanatics behaved as they did not least because they knew that their crimes meant they had no future if Germany lost. The Nazi leaders played on this feeling; Himmler had already gathered high-ranking officials and generals at Posen and Sonthofen to tell them explicitly about the extermination of the Jews, thus bringing them into complicity with what he and they knew was regarded in the world at large as a crime. The Gauleiters did nothing that could imply weakness; they even refused to evacuate areas threatened by Red Army forces, though when it came to their own safety they were often unprepared to back up words with deeds; many, like Arthur Greiser, Gauleiter of the Wartheland, issued ringing exhortations to his people to defend to the last, then fled the scene.

Not only did Nazis shoot or hang 'shirkers', 'defeatists', 'deserters' and 'cowards', they also evacuated concentration camps and prisons lest the inmates should be liberated by the Allies, and sent them on

ill-organised, often aimless 'death marches', shooting and killing strag-
glers as they went. Hundreds of thousands died in the process; of the
715,000 camp inmates at the beginning of 1945, fewer than half were
still alive six months later. In the camps still unliberated by the Allies,
the huge numbers of starving and maltreated prisoners arriving from
other camps soon created impossible conditions in which typhus and
other diseases spread rapidly and scores of thousands died.

Terror also increased drastically in the armed forces. Tens of thousands of soldiers deserted – one estimate puts the number at a quarter
of a million even before the final months of chaos – but those who
contemplated running away knew that if they were caught by any of
the patrols waiting on Germany's streets, railway stations and arteries
of communication to ask people for their papers, they would face certain death. At least 30,000 soldiers were condemned to death for
desertion, defeatism and similar offences during the war, with around
20,000 being shot, in contrast to 150 during the First World War, only
eight of whom were executed. Middle and higher-ranking officers continued to operate courts-martial and pass death sentences even after
the war was officially over.

Fear of the regime and its servants kept many people going, but so
did fear of the enemy, above all of the Red Army, which in the final
months was blasting its way across eastern and central Germany,
raping and pillaging as it went. Goebbels's propaganda machine made
great play with incidents such as the massacre by Red Army troops
carried out in the East Prussian village of Nemmersdorf. Ordinary
Germans elsewhere reacted, according to the security police, by noting
gloomily that rape, murder and pillage was what they could expect,
given the atrocities carried out in occupied Eastern Europe by their
own troops. 'Have we not slaughtered Jews in their thousands?' a
security officer reported people in Stuttgart asking. 'The Jews are also
human beings. By acting in this way, we have shown the enemy what
they might do to us in the event of their victory.' These fears, which
turned out in large measure to be justified, were heightened by what
appeared to be widespread popular acceptance of Goebbels's

propaganda line that the Allies – Churchill, Roosevelt, Stalin – were being manipulated by a world conspiracy of Jews out for revenge on the German people. To many troops and civilians, fighting on seemed better than consigning themselves to the mercies of the Russians.

To ask that people should rise up against the regime, overthrow it and make peace with the Allies was to ask the impossible. Ordinary Germans, their towns and cities bombed to rubble, their gas, electricity and water services working only intermittently if at all, their factories and workplaces destroyed, their food and fuel supplies dwindling, had to concentrate on simply keeping themselves and their families alive. In any case, the pervasive presence of the Party and its agencies in the last months of the war meant that any kind of collective action was out of the question. What would happen was vividly illustrated by the fate of the gangs of foreign workers involved in black-marketeering in the industrial cities of the Rhineland, who fought pitched battles against the police amid the rubble and shot dead the chief of the Gestapo in Cologne; rounded up and arrested, they were publicly hanged in a mass execution as a warning to others.

Collective action higher up the ranks was just as impossible after the failure of Stauffenberg's bomb plot. Within the Nazi Party and the government, institutions capable of formulating a concerted policy that diverged from Hitler's had long since ceased to exist; the Reich cabinet hadn't met for years, and there wasn't anything resembling the Fascist Grand Council that deposed Mussolini in 1943. Hitler had arrogated all institutional power to himself: he was head of state, head of government, head of the Party, supreme commander of the armed forces, commander-in-chief of the army – in short, he was 'The Leader'. All power emanated from him; everyone in a senior position owed such power as they had to him; all knew they could prosper and survive only if they carried out his wishes and conformed to his ideological dictates.

Even though Hitler increasingly cut himself off in his underground bunker, ceased to give addresses to the people and lost the hold he had gained on them through his carefully orchestrated public broadcasts and speeches, his personal style of rule continued to control the actions of those who held power in Nazi Germany. There was, in the last months, Kershaw writes, 'charismatic rule without charisma. Hitler's mass charismatic appeal had long since dissolved, but the structures and mentalities of his charismatic rule lasted until his death in the bunker.' Correspondingly, once he had gone, the whole edifice crumbled into dust. Hitler was no longer there to fight for. Despite all Goebbels's efforts to create a resistance movement to harass the Allied occupying forces, the so-called *Werwolf*, there was no resistance worth speaking of after the end of the war.

The End is a vivid account of the last days of Hitler's Reich, with a real feel for the mentalities and situations of people caught up in a calamity which many didn't survive, and which those who did took years to overcome. The book does not, perhaps, give enough weight to the feelings of nationalism that imbued so many Germans, especially in the officer corps; it was more than a mere excuse when they claimed they were fighting for Germany, to protect German civilisation against the Bolshevik hordes. The effects of Goebbels's claim that it was not just German but European civilisation that was at stake could have been explored more deeply. Fear and hatred of the East did not begin with the Nazis. Nationalist convictions, mixed with a strong dose of contempt for 'Slavs', underpinned Nazism for many, and were vitally important to those whose Nazism was only skin-deep.

PART VI

THE POLITICS OF GENOCIDE

23. EMPIRE, RACE AND WAR

As a young man, Adolf Hitler became a devotee of the music-dramas of Richard Wagner, and spent much of his meagre income on tickets for performances of *Lohengrin* and other pseudo-medieval fantasies. Historians have spent a good deal of energy trying to trace the effects of this youthful passion on the later dictator's ideas and beliefs. But he had another enthusiasm, too, less commented on, and cheaper to pursue: the pulp novels of Karl May, set in the Wild West and featuring cowboys, mostly of German descent, like Old Shatterhand, whose name refers to the power of his punch, and Winnetou, a Native American who converts to Christianity. May became the centre of a literary scandal when it was revealed that he had a criminal record and had never been to America (he made his first visit not long before his death in 1912). But far from undermining Hitler's admiration, this only confirmed his belief that it was not necessary to go to a country in order to get to know it. Even during the Second World War, he was still recommending May's novels to his generals and ordered 200,000 copies to be printed for the troops.

For May, the Native Americans were noble savages, a view of indigenous peoples that Hitler certainly didn't share. Underlying the novels is an implicit Social Darwinism that portrays Winnetou and his culture as doomed to destruction at the hands of a superior, more powerful civilisation – May's debt to *The Last of the Mohicans* was obvious here, as in other aspects of his work. Social Darwinists and

racists of the late nineteenth and early twentieth century looked envi-
ously across the Atlantic to the United States, where millions of
European colonists had trekked westwards to form a new, prosperous
and powerful society, displacing, marginalising and killing the continent's native inhabitants in the process, until the vast majority of them
had perished from disease or starvation. Racial superiority, they
thought, destined the European settlers to mastery, just as they
doomed backward peoples like the Australian Aborigines to extinction, and if anyone protested, the Social Darwinists simply wrote them
off as unscientific and behind the times.

But if a race showed its superiority by conquering and subjugating
others, what part of the world was available for the Germans to
demonstrate their capacities? During the nineteenth century, Germans
became overseas colonisers in huge numbers, but they went to areas
that Germany did not control. (Five million emigrated to the
Americas, making up 40 per cent of all migrants between the 1840s
and the early 1890s.) Ethnic Germans in their millions lived outside
the Reich, in Austria, Bohemia, Russia, Romania and other parts of
Central and Eastern Europe, but they owed their allegiance to other
states, not to the German Empire created by Bismarck. The failure to
expand was deeply disappointing to extreme nationalists. 'Shouldn't
Germany be a queen among nations,' one colonial enthusiast asked as
early as 1879, 'ruling widely over endless territories, like the English,
the Americans and the Russians?' Increasing numbers of Germany's
ruling elite before 1914 clearly agreed, and from 1898 the Kaiser's government poured vast resources into constructing an enormous navy
that was intended to confront the British on the high seas and open
the way to the creation of a vast global empire.

The First World War put paid to such ambitions. The German fleet
failed to dent British naval dominance, and German defeat led to its
overseas colonies being mandated to other powers. But even before the
war, some nationalists had been turning to a more obvious area in
which to establish German colonial dominance: Eastern Europe.
Mark Mazower begins *Hitler's Empire* (2008), his sweeping survey of

Nazi rule in Europe, with an account of the emergence in late nineteenth-century Germany and Austria of the idea that the struggle
between races for the survival of the fittest required the creation of
Lebensraum, a 'living space' into which the Germanic race could
expand to secure its future, rather as European immigrants to the
Americas had done. Far-right nationalists regarded Poles, Russians and
other Slavs as backward and uncivilised; surely it was their destiny to
serve as helots for the German master race?

Germany's catastrophic defeat in 1918 opened the way for such radical ideas to enter the mainstream of politics. After 1933 they became
the official doctrine of the state. Throughout all the twists and turns
of Nazi foreign policy as Hitler feverishly rearmed the country in
preparation for a great European war, the ultimate goal remained the
same: the conquest of Eastern Europe and the creation of 'living space'
there for future generations of Germans. Hitler and the Nazis did not
abandon the idea of creating an overseas colonial empire, but first of
all Germany had to become a world power, and the way to this led
through Europe.

Mazower's book focuses, then, on Hitler as empire-builder. It is perhaps not as novel or unfamiliar a theme as he seems to think, but it
certainly gets its first extended, systematic, Europe-wide treatment
here. What the Nazi empire in Eastern Europe would mean in practical terms became brutally clear in the first few weeks of the war. As
Mazower shows in detail, the German conquest of Poland brought in
its wake the ruthless expulsion of hundreds of thousands of Poles from
their farms and businesses to make way for ethnic German settlers
from the east, where, they were persuaded, Stalin's rule didn't promise them a rosy future. Polish culture was crushed, thousands of
professionals and intellectuals were arrested, imprisoned and shot, and
the large Jewish population was rounded up and confined in overcrowded and insanitary ghettos while the Nazi occupiers worked out
what to do with them.

That death was what ultimately awaited these people became only
too clear with the invasion of the Soviet Union in June 1941. Hitler

waxed lyrical about the benefits of civilisation that German rule would bring. Sparkling new German cities would be created, acting as hubs for German farming communities rooted in the eastern soil and linked to one another by high-speed railway lines and motorways. The area's existing inhabitants would not be part of this brave new world. Their own cities, like Moscow and Leningrad (St Petersburg) would be left to rot, while Ukrainian and Russian peasant farmers would be thrown off the land just as their Polish counterparts had been. Planners estimated that millions would die of malnutrition and disease. SS academics fantasised about deporting scores of millions of 'racially undesirable' Slavs to Siberia, or even to Brazil. The ultimate prize then awaited Hitler. 'Once we are the masters in Europe,' he said in October 1941, 'then we will enjoy the dominant position in the world.' The new German Empire would at last be the equal of the existing empires of Britain and the United States. The final confrontation for world supremacy could begin.

For a brief moment in the summer of 1941, it seemed possible to the Nazi leadership that such dreams might become reality. France, Belgium, Holland, Denmark and Norway had been defeated the previous year and victorious German armies were sweeping all before them in the east, occupying huge swathes of territory in Ukraine, the Baltic states and Belarus, while in Southern Europe they had established control over the Balkans. Yet all this was an illusion.

It was not just that the Soviet Union, with its vast resources of manpower and materials, proved impossible to defeat. More important was the fact that the Germans had no coherent idea of how their huge new empire was to be made to serve the global purposes for which it was intended. Mazower points out the great variety of administrative arrangements under which it was governed, from collaborationist regimes like Slovakia and Vichy France through military government running alongside a surviving native civil service, as in Belgium, or a specially created German apparatus of rule, as in the Reich Commissariat of Ukraine or the Polish General Government. Some areas were incorporated directly into the Reich, including large areas of western

Poland, while others were regarded as likely to be absorbed at some future date, including the Netherlands, whose people the Nazi leadership regarded as predominantly 'Aryan'.

This huge empire had no central direction, and there was no coordination in the way it was run. The Germans never created any equivalent of the Greater East Asia Ministry through which the Japanese governed their conquests. This, Mazower argues, was partly because Hitler bypassed the civil service in favour of committed Nazi fanatics whom he could trust to construct the new Greater Germany along racial lines. As a consequence, the Nazi Party, led by 'Old Fighters' who had been members since the 1920s, and particularly by the regional leaders, the Gauleiters, gained power at the expense of the interior ministry, whose officials began to lament the absence of any centralised administration of the new territories. For his part, Hitler complained that 'among us, the conception of the monolithic state implies that everything should be directed from a centre ... The English in India do exactly the opposite.' 'There is no possibility,' he concluded, 'of ruling this huge empire from Berlin.'

Adding to the confusion was the inexorable growth of Himmler's SS, which bypassed civilian and Party administrations in pursuit of its openly proclaimed purpose of redrawing the racial map of Europe. German military and civilian administrators from Holland to Ukraine were faced with the choice of either turning a blind eye as the SS rolled in to massacre or deport the Jews under their control, or of putting their own resources at its disposal in the genocide. Dissatisfied with existing arrangements and desperate for some kind of central direction, some senior civil servants, such as the interior ministry's Wilhelm Stuckart, turned to Himmler: if there was to be a new colonial elite in the long run, then perhaps Himmler's cohorts of highly educated and efficiently organised young SS officers would provide it.

The reality remained stubbornly different. Mazower exaggerates when he claims that it was Germany's 'pre-1914 colonies that provided what little relevant administrative expertise existed in the Third Reich'. Certainly, some former colonial officials played a role, such as Viktor

Böttcher, the governor of Posen, who had helped run German Cameroon before 1914, but they were inevitably a tiny minority, given the very small size of the German colonial administration before the First World War. Administrative experience came overwhelmingly from the domestic civil service. But it found itself increasingly sidelined by Hitler's preferred representatives of 'political leadership'. Thus the chaos remained, and sharp-eyed observers continued to complain that the supposedly highly centralised Reich was in practice divided into dozens of self-willed satrapies; as one of them despairingly noted, it altogether lacked 'a functioning government'.

Mazower is on slightly safer ground when he notes that German race laws in colonies like Namibia provided a basis for similar regulations in German-dominated Europe after 1939, according to which Poles and other Slavs were subjected to harsh discrimination and – especially if they were drafted in to work in the Reich, as they were in their millions – banned by law from having sexual relationships with members of the German master race. However, recent claims by some historians that the war of annihilation conducted by German armed forces in their suppression of the Herero and Nama revolt in Namibia in 1905–6, when scores of thousands of tribesmen were driven into the desert or marooned on an island and left to starve, provided the model for Nazi policy towards the Jews, fail to convince because there is no evidence of a direct connection.

There were plenty of other models of racial discrimination for Hitler to draw on, including the US, where Native Americans were defined up to 1924 as 'nationals' but not 'citizens', or almost any colony or dependency of the British, where land was confiscated for distribution to white settlers, and Africans were drafted on to forced labour schemes. In South Africa in particular there was harsh racial oppression and the abrogation of the rights of supposedly racially inferior social groups. The major contrast here was that the Nazi empire applied such policies in Europe itself, rather than in overseas colonial territories. But there were other differences, too. By the interwar years, as Mazower points out, imperial powers generally held out the prospect of eventual self-government to colonised peoples, even if only in the distant future, and encouraged the formation of educated indigenous elites. For Hitler, however, conquered peoples like the Poles, Czechs or Russians had no such future: they were doomed to extinction to make way for the Germanic master race, and the sooner this happened the better.

In his mealtime monologues, recorded for posterity on the orders of Martin Bormann, Hitler repeatedly returned to the example of British India. 'Let's learn from the English,' he said, 'who, with two hundred and fifty thousand men in all, including fifty thousand soldiers, govern four hundred million Indians.' 'What India is for England,' he remarked on another occasion, 'the territories of Russia will be for us.' He didn't ask how the British had managed to retain their hold on the Indian subcontinent with such limited forces at their disposal; he simply assumed it was a result of their racial superiority. 'The Russian space,' he said, 'is our India. Like the English, we shall rule this empire with a handful of men.' He thought that German colonialism had failed not least because it had imported the German schoolmaster into the colonies. 'It would be a mistake to claim to educate the native. All that we could give him would be a half-knowledge – just what's needed to conduct a revolution!' In occupied Western Europe, the racial affinities assumed by the Nazis could lead to rule through existing administrative channels. But in the new empire in Eastern Europe, Germany would rule by force.

Thus any chance of co-opting nationalist groups in countries like Ukraine, where Soviet rule had caused untold misery and starvation, and where local people welcomed the invading German troops as liberators with traditional gifts of bread and salt, was firmly rejected despite the advocacy of men like the Nazi ideologue Alfred Rosenberg, who ran the largely powerless Reich Ministry for the Occupied Eastern Territories. Mazower discusses in detail the alternative proposals put forward by Rosenberg and others for ruling the east. A Baltic German driven by hatred of Communism, Rosenberg thought of the Germans as liberators of the oppressed masses from the curse of

Stalinism. He urged the creation of independent states purged of their Communist administrations, and warned that 'the conquered territory as a whole must not be treated as the object of exploitation'. But Hitler, and even more Himmler, were dismissive of the idea that 'subhumans' like the Ukrainians could have any racial affinity with the Germans: they were Slavs, to be used and then discarded once they had served their purpose. The result, as one of Rosenberg's aides pointed out in February 1944, was that the German occupiers had, 'within a year, chased into the woods and swamps, as partisans, a people which was absolutely pro-German and had jubilantly greeted us as their liberator'.

The brutal and murderous policies that achieved this result stood in sharp contrast to the relatively mild policies imposed in Western Europe. Following the defeat of France in 1940, Nazi planners came up with the idea of a 'New Order in Europe', in which the French and other Western European economies would be mobilised in a wider sphere of economic cooperation to rival the huge economic blocs of the US and the British Empire. Throughout the summer and autumn of 1941, following Hitler's declaration that the German economy could not survive on the basis of 'autarky' or self-sufficiency, economists and planners engaged in detailed discussions about European economic integration in the service of Germany's global ambitions, while big firms like IG Farben envisioned the creation of Pan-European cartels as their contribution to the realisation of this ambition. 'We are not alone in Europe,' the Reich Economics Ministry warned in October 1940, 'and we cannot run an economy with subjugated nations.'

Mazower perhaps dismisses these elaborate discussions a little too brusquely when he remarks that the Nazi vision of a new European order 'disappeared almost as soon as it arose'. But he is right to point out that the practical effects of such discussions were both limited and short-lived. Well before the end of 1940, Hitler and Goebbels were insisting that all that mattered was Germany, and that the rest of Europe should be exploited as far as possible in the interests of the

German war effort. The Reich may not have imposed financial reparations on France and the other defeated nations but it slapped on 'occupation costs', fixed exchange rates to give German troops and administrators purchasing power that Frenchmen or Belgians couldn't hope to match, and it ruined transportation systems by shipping railway engines and rolling stock back to Germany. In the end, the wealthy industrial regions of Western Europe contributed far less to the German war effort than Berlin had hoped.

In some of his most interesting and original pages, Mazower suggests that the very ruthlessness and brutality of the German empire in Europe served to discredit the idea of world empires run by self-proclaimed racial overlords. The triumphant resurgence of nationalist resistance movements in the second half of the war did not stop at the boundaries of Europe. The victorious powers in 1945 were not imperialist, as in 1918, but anti-imperialist: the US and the Soviet Union. And in the imperial metropoles, doubts about the legitimacy of imperial domination grew apace. Mazower quotes George Orwell: 'What meaning would there be,' he wrote, 'in bringing down Hitler's system in order to stabilise something that is far bigger and in its different way just as bad?'

The age of imperialism ended in 1945. The idea that eventually triumphed in Europe was a modified version of the 'New Order', which economists like Ludwig Erhard, the future West German chancellor, had spent so much futile intellectual energy discussing in the early 1940s. Some of these men re-emerged after the war to take a role (mostly behind the scenes) in putting together the first building blocks of European union. 'No political order,' Mazower writes, 'begins from nothing.' But the new Europeans believed that economic cooperation could no longer be a propagandistic fig leaf for one nation's exploitative intentions. Nor could the idea of a Pan-European economic sphere be built in opposition to the interests of the United States. Along with imperialism, the idea of a world divided between vast economic empires competing with one another for survival and domination had disappeared as well.

Hitler's empire disappeared as quickly as it was created, the shortest-lived of all imperial creations, and the last. Mark Mazower has written an absorbing and thought-provoking account of its rise and demise. By placing it in the global context of empire, he makes us see it afresh, and that is a considerable achievement. Paradoxically, perhaps, it makes us view the older European empires in a relatively favourable light. Growing up over decades, even centuries, they had remained in existence only through a complex nexus of collaboration, compromise and accommodation. Racist they may have been, murderous sometimes, even on occasion exterminatory, but none of them was created or sustained on the basis of such a narrow or exploitative nationalism as animated the Nazi empire.

24. WAS THE 'FINAL SOLUTION' UNIQUE?

When Hitler attempted what he called 'the Final Solution of the Jewish Question in Europe' through the systematic murder of some six million Jews, he seemed to many to be doing something without precedent or parallel in history. So appalling was this crime that some commentators have argued that it is illegitimate to compare it with anything else. Yet unless we compare it to other events, we cannot establish its uniqueness. Comparison doesn't mean simply drawing out similarities, it also means isolating differences and weighing up the two. Moreover, there's an obvious problem if we deny any kind of comparability of an event like the Nazi extermination of the Jews in Europe. If it can't be legitimately compared to any other historical process or event, and it is indeed utterly unique, then it cannot be repeated in any form, and thus the slogan 'never again' – often uttered when attempts are made to draw lessons for the present and future from these terrible events – is meaningless, since the 'Final Solution' has no relevance to anything else and no lessons to teach us in the present day. Positing a categorical uniqueness takes it in my view into the realms of theology, and while this may be legitimate or rewarding for theologians, the historian has to approach it in the same way as any other large-scale historical phenomenon, which means asking basic, comparative questions and trying to answer them at the level of secular rationality.

An obvious comparative starting point presents itself with the invasion of Poland, in September 1939. Very quickly, the conquerors began systematically to suppress the language and culture of the defeated Poles. Polish libraries and cultural institutions were closed, Polish monuments, memorials and street signs were destroyed. Half a million Poles were arrested and confined in labour camps and prisons, where many of them were brutally maltreated and killed. Some 20,000 officers and alleged Polish nationalists were shot. Up to one and a half million members of the Polish cultural and intellectual elite were arrested and in 1940 they were taken out of the country in unheated cattle trucks; a third of them did not survive the privations of the journey.

This human tragedy was the consequence not of the German invasion of western and central Poland, but the result of the Soviet conquest of Poland's eastern provinces. The parallels with the policies of Nazi Germany were obvious, and from the point of view of the victims, it is equally obvious that it was not easy to distinguish between the two occupations. Nevertheless, differences there were. The Soviet Union's aim in occupied Poland was to carry out a social revolution along the lines already achieved by Lenin and Stalin in Russia. The eastern part of the country was incorporated into the Soviet system on the basis of a rigged plebiscite. The occupation authorities nationalised the property of the Polish elite, in particular, of course, banking and industrial firms. They broke up the larger landed estates of the Polish nobility and distributed them amongst the mostly non-Polish small peasants, and they incited the Ukrainian and Belarussian lower classes who constituted the majority of the population in this part of Poland to stage violent uprisings against the Polish elites. Thus the Poles were not attacked on racial but on class grounds, in a clear parallel to the murderous 'red terror' carried out in Russia itself in 1918, immediately after the Bolshevik Revolution.

Moreover, those whom the Soviet occupiers regarded as members of the bourgeois-reactionary nationalist elites were deported not away from Soviet territory but deep into its interior, indicating that the purpose of the deportation, however brutally it was conducted, was not the complete elimination of a national minority but its political neutralisation and if possible indeed its conversion to Communism – goals recognisable in the other deportations carried out by Stalin later in the war as well. In this sense, indeed, the deported groups were not separated from the rest of the Soviet population but shared its fate and its sufferings. In a formal, constitutional sense, the Soviet conquest of eastern Poland brought with it the introduction of equal political rights for all adults irrespective of their ethnicity. For many Jews, that meant liberation from the antisemitic discrimination practised by the prewar regime of the Polish colonels.

Nevertheless, of course, there is no doubting the murderous nature of the Soviet takeover of eastern Poland. It was in fact only one of a number of mass murders and brutal population transfers carried out on Stalin's orders. From September 1941 onwards the Soviet secret police deported more than 1,200,000 ethnic Germans from Ukraine, the Volga region and several Soviet cities to Siberia under notably harsh conditions; 175,000 of them did not survive the experience. Half a million members of various other ethnic minorities from the Caucasus followed them into Siberian exile. And as the German armies advanced, the Soviet secret police systematically murdered alleged nationalists and counter-revolutionaries locked up in Soviet prisons that lay in their path; 100,000 prisoners were shot, bayoneted to death or blown up with hand-grenades in prisons in the western Ukraine alone. All of this was done in the name of Soviet military security; the suspicious Stalin considered all these people a security threat.

For all the violence meted out to the unfortunate deportees, this was not an attempt to exterminate entire peoples. In one case, however, it has been argued that Stalin did indeed carry out a genocidal programme of mass murder deliberately targeting a single ethnic group. This was the case of the Ukrainian famine of the early 1930s, which some Ukrainian groups now want to be given equal status with the Holocaust. In 2006 the Ukrainian parliament debated a law making it illegal to deny that the Ukrainian famine was a genocide. The law was not passed. Ukrainian immigrant associations in Canada and the USA now use the term *Holodomor*, meaning murder by famine. A Holodomor remembrance day is held every year in Ukraine and by Ukrainian communities elsewhere, and museums and memorials have begun to be built devoted to its memory.

There are widespread claims, including by Victor Yushchenko, President of Ukraine at the time that the 2006 law was introduced, that the total of deaths reached ten million, thus exceeding the number of Jews killed by the Nazis. In 2003 twenty-five countries at the United Nations, including Russia and the USA, issued a statement noting the seventieth anniversary of the famine and putting the number of victims at seven to ten million. Ukrainian groups have campaigned in Canada to have the Holodomor given equal status to the Holocaust in the new Museum of Human Rights. The Ukrainian Canadian Civil Rights Association sent out a postcard with a picture of a pig, taken from Orwell's *Animal Farm*, with the words: 'All galleries are equal, but some galleries are more equal than others.' Branding supporters of the Holocaust gallery in the Museum of Human Rights as pigs was clearly intended to be particularly offensive to those Jews who featured among the gallery's supporters. Critics of the UCCRA pointed out that it failed to mention either the role of Ukrainian nationalists in providing auxiliaries and helpers in the administration of death camps such as Treblinka, or the fact that 9,000 Ukrainian SS men emigrated to Canada at the end of the Second World War, doubtless affecting the way that Ukrainian-Canadian organisations have approached these sensitive and emotive issues.

The figure of seven to ten million deaths is clearly intended to rank the Holodomor above the Holocaust. Is it plausible? Robert Conquest, in his pioneering book *Harvest of Sorrow*, the first to bring the famine to general attention, put the number at five million. Demographic historians such as Stephen Wheatcroft estimate deaths at three million. Recently opened Soviet archives record a death toll of 1.8 million, but in addition there were over a million deaths from typhus, a disease spread by the human body louse and common in poor, unhygienic and overcrowded situations; there were, one should note, many comparable deaths from typhus in Nazi concentration camps during the war, and of course malnutrition makes people less able to resist such epidemics. Finding a reliable figure is extremely difficult, but the figure of three million seems the most plausible. Were these deaths deliberately inflicted by Stalin? There is plenty of evidence to show that although the harvests of the early 1930s were not particularly bad, and could under normal conditions have fed the population, the Soviet authorities seized grain from the farmers, refused to provide food aid to the starving, banned people from leaving affected areas and even deported some to places where there was no food. The famine was thus man-made: it was neither accidental nor natural.

Was it genocide? Around 80 per cent of the victims were Ukrainian. Yet the famine has to be seen against the background not of Russian racism but of Stalin's policy of forced industrialisation, in which he seized food from the countryside to give to the new industrial towns, and forcibly reorganised agriculture into collective farms to centralise production, achieve economies of scale and, not least, ease the collection and requisitioning of food. So much was taken that there wasn't even enough to feed livestock. Farmers who resisted were shot or deported in large numbers as 'kulaks', allegedly capitalist, market-oriented peasants and enemies of the revolution. A considerable number showed their resistance by destroying their crops and killing their livestock. Knowing that their crops would be requisitioned, peasants didn't bother to sow for the coming season.

Stalin ascribed this resistance not only to capitalist kulaks but also to Ukrainian nationalism. The Ukrainian Communist Party was purged, and in 1933 a campaign of cultural Russification was launched, not least in response to the creation of the Nazi dictatorship in Germany, since German militarism had encouraged Ukrainian nationalism during the First World War and Stalin feared a repetition. Yet these measures coincided with the scaling-down of requisitioning and arrests, and the mounting of famine relief efforts by the Soviet regime. The famine had in essence achieved its major objective, by breaking the will of independent peasants. By 1936 more than 90 per cent of peasant households had been collectivised. A quarter of a million collective farms had replaced twenty-five million small, private ones. These secured the supply of food to the industrial towns, into which no fewer than twenty-five million people moved between 1926 and 1939. In the end, therefore, the famine, while undoubtedly deliberately created, did not target Ukrainians because they were Ukrainians, nor did it attempt to kill them all without exception.

What Nazi mass murder was motivated by was from the very beginning a racist ideology that targeted victims defined by ethnicity. These groups included not only Jews but also Slavs. In the German-occupied western parts of Poland from September 1939, racial criteria were decisive in framing Nazi policy. Thus although Polish and Jewish property was confiscated without recompense, it was not nationalised; instead it was redistributed to German owners within a continuing capitalist economic system. Only the western parts of the Polish Republic were incorporated into the German Reich; the Poles and Jews who lived there were driven to the area reserved for them, the so-called General Government, run by the Nazi jurist Hans Frank. In the long run, the General Government, too, was intended to be Germanised, and here, too, the authorities started to drive out and dispossess Poles and bring ethnic German settlers in to start up German farming and small-town communities. More than a million Polish forced labourers were deported to Germany, but for purely economic, not political reasons.

These population transfers can only be fully understood, as can those carried out in Nazi-occupied Soviet territory after June 1941, in the context of the far-reaching plans of the Nazi regime for the ethnic reordering of Eastern Europe, developed above all by SS chief Heinrich Himmler, in his capacity as Reich Commissioner for the Strengthening of the German Race. Half a million ethnic Germans from east Poland, Romania, the Soviet Union and other parts of Eastern Europe were brought into German-occupied Poland as settlers, taking the place of roughly the same number of dispossessed

Polish farmers. This process had been going on for some months when the SS and its planning experts began in 1940 to develop the so-called General Plan for the East. In its final form, this envisaged that up to 85 per cent of the Polish population, 64 per cent of the Ukrainian and 75 per cent of the Belarussian, along with 85 per cent of Estonians and 50 per cent of Latvians and Lithuanians, would die of hunger and disease, deliberately deprived of medication and food. Between thirty and forty-five million Slavs from these areas and Russia itself would perish, according to the plan. The area they lived in would be settled by millions of German farmers. The eastern boundary of the Greater German Reich would be extended about a thousand kilometres. If this plan had become reality, it would have been the greatest genocide in history. As it was, a start was made when three and a third million Soviet prisoners of war were killed, mostly by deliberately letting them starve to death, along with millions more Soviet civilians – a million alone in the city of St Petersburg, known by the Soviets as Leningrad, where the Germans set up a blockade that lasted for the best part of three years, deliberately avoiding the expense in men and *matériel* that a full-scale invasion of the city would have caused them.

The General Plan for the East owed its existence to Hitler's long-harboured ambition to create German 'living space', or *Lebensraum*, in the east of Europe. This was intended not least to avoid the fate of Germany in the First World War, when some 600,000 Germans had died of hunger and associated illnesses because of the Allied blockade and the inability of German agriculture to feed the German population without importing food supplies. There was, indeed, a close connection between this general planning for a German area of domination and settlement in Eastern Europe and the more specific so-called 'Hunger Plan' that was discussed in May 1941 at a meeting between representatives of the armed forces and state secretaries from a variety of government ministries. According to the minutes of this meeting, 'umpteen million' people in the occupied eastern territories would have to die of hunger if the German troops in the field, and the civilians at home, were to remain well fed.

The extermination of European Jews by the Nazi regime has therefore to be understood in this broader context of racial reordering and genocide. At the same time, however, it would be wrong to reduce it to just one more facet of this larger process. The Jews of Poland and Eastern Europe in general were overwhelmingly poor, with little property and few assets, and lived mostly in towns. The economic advantages that their arrest, incarceration in ghettos and finally murder brought to the German Reich were small. The landed estates and properties intended for occupation by German settlers were almost exclusively owned by non-Jews. The millions of people whom the General Plan for the East envisaged murdering or allowing to perish from hunger and disease included Jews but the overwhelming majority were Slavs. Representatives of the German armed forces and bureaucrats in the Agriculture Ministry did, to be sure, justify the killing of Jews on the grounds that they consumed food without producing for the war economy and were thus 'useless eaters', to quote a phrase commonly used by the Nazis. Where Jews could be put to work for the German war economy, as in the Lódź Ghetto, they were allowed to live on. But here the conditions under which they were forced to work were deliberately made so poor that another phrase entered common bureaucratic parlance at the same time: 'extermination through labour'. Justifications for their mass murder in terms of the food supply situation or the economic interests of the Reich did not in the end reflect the central reason for the killings, even though it is possible that the extermination programme was accelerated in the late spring and early summer of 1942 because of a crisis in the food supply for Germany and its occupying forces. Even if this is the case, it still needs to be explained why the Nazis always put the Jews of Eastern Europe at the bottom of the heap when drawing up quotas for rationing, rules and regulations for work, and much else besides: below the Russians, below the Czechs, below the Ukrainians, below the Poles, even below the Gypsies.

Nazi propaganda and ideology regarded and portrayed 'Jewry', *Judentum*, the collective term for Jews, in quite different terms from those in which they represented 'Slavdom', *Slaventum*. Slavs, Poles, Czechs, Russians and so on, were subhumans who were portrayed as primitive, backward, passive and stupid, posing no threat to Germany unless they were led by clever and ruthless Jews. In themselves, Slavs were dispensable, but they did not challenge the very existence of Germany and the German race. Even in the final phase of the war, when Nazi propaganda concentrated on whipping up fear among ordinary Germans of the 'Bolshevik threat', it consistently portrayed Bolshevism and Stalinism as tools of an international Jewish conspiracy. In the end, Slavs were a regional obstacle to the extension of the German empire in Europe; Jews were a worldwide threat to the very existence of the Germans. 'The Jew', as Goebbels's propaganda machine never tired of claiming, was, unlike 'the Russian' or 'the Pole', nothing less than 'the world-enemy', the *Weltfeind*.

Here as in other areas, Nazi propagandists and ideologues drew on the experience of the First World War, or, rather, on their paranoid understanding of Germany's defeat. This was the infamous stab-in-the-back legend, according to which Jews in Germany in 1918 had exploited popular dissatisfaction with the miserable conditions under which Germans had to live, with starvation and disease rampant, and food shortages reaching unbearable levels, in order to foment a socialist revolution at home, which then overthrew the hitherto undefeated armed forces from within. In fact, the majority of German Jews were not revolutionaries at all but nationalist liberals and conservatives, well integrated into German society, and fully behind the war effort.

Nevertheless, between January 1933 and September 1939, Germans were constantly bombarded with antisemitic propaganda from every organ of the Nazi-controlled media, while the regime inexorably drove the Jews out of the German economy and society through a long series of discriminatory laws and regulations, dispossessions and assaults. The aim was to prepare Germany for a new European war by reducing and as far as possible altogether eliminating the supposed potential Jewish threat from within. Roughly half the small Jewish population of Germany left the country by the time the war began. With the invasion of Poland, however, German soldiers for the first time came face to face with a poor and downtrodden Jewish population on a large scale. Two and a half million Jews lived in Poland, almost all of them practising the Judaic religion, speaking Yiddish, dressing differently from their Polish neighbours, and altogether, as many field-post letters from German soldiers made a point of noting, looking like caricatures out of the Nazis' antisemitic newspaper *Der Stürmer*.

German soldiers and officials, ethnic German militias, and above all members of the SS Task Forces sent into Poland to provide 'security', maltreated Poles, arrested them, dispossessed them, attacked them, deported them in unheated cattle trucks, put them into camps, beat them to death, shot them and in general treated them as less than human, just as they later did the inhabitants of the other areas of Eastern Europe that they conquered. But their behaviour towards the Jews they encountered had an extra edge: soldiers stopped Jews in the street, pulled their beards out or set light to them, forced them to smear each other with excrement, assembled them in public squares and made them perform gymnastic exercises at gunpoint for hour after hour until they dropped from exhaustion; they compelled Jewish girls to clean public toilets with their blouses, they subjected all of them to ritual humiliation and public degradation in a way that they did not with Poles and other Slavs.

This sadistic behaviour towards Jews was also apparent in the two other European states which participated in the genocide largely if not entirely on their own initiative, namely Croatia and Romania. Up to 380,000 Jews were killed by Romanian forces during the war, in circumstances that even the German SS described in disapproving terms as 'sadistic'; large numbers, for example, were deliberately penned into enclosures on a state pig farm, while the Romanian fascists, the Iron Guard, put other Jews through all the stages of killing in a state slaughterhouse, ending by hanging their corpses from meat hooks. In the German puppet state of Croatia, 30,000 Jews out of a total population of 45,000 were killed by the Ustasha militia, acting under government orders; many were beaten to death with hammers and iron bars or put in concentration camps where they were deliberately infected with diseases and left to perish from malnutrition.

In Croatia, Catholic priests and especially Franciscan friars urged the militia on to kill the infidels, while in Romania the head of state Marshal Ion Antonescu justified the killings by calling the Jews the creatures of Satan. Nevertheless, the use of religious reasoning, which was almost wholly absent from Nazi antisemitism, does not mean that we are dealing with two essentially different varieties of antisemitism here, the religious and the racial. For all its religious rhetoric, Antonescu's antisemitism was in fact fundamentally racist, regarding Jews of all kinds as the force behind Communism, defining Jews for legislative purposes in racial terms, and proclaiming the need to rid Romania of its Jews in order to achieve the *racial* cleansing of society. The difference lay in the fact that, for Antonescu, the Jews were a local or at most regional problem, not the world-enemy, so that he expelled many thousands of Jews across the border to Ukraine, simply to get rid of them and drive on the racial purification of Romania. It was emphatically not the purpose of Antonescu's regime to pursue and destroy Jews wherever they were found.

Similarly in Croatia, it was the aim of the fascist Ustasha regime to purify the country of racial minorities, leaving the Croats in sole occupation: 300,000 Serbs and many thousands of Gypsies (the latter in Romania, too) were murdered alongside the Jews. In both Croatia and Romania, therefore, genocide was directed inwards. Both regimes believed in the fantasy of a world conspiracy of Jews, using the tool of international Communism, but neither went so far as to claim that the main purpose of this conspiracy was the destruction of either Croatia or Romania. In the final analysis, both antisemitisms were a subordinate aspect of a wider-ranging, virulent and extreme form of authoritarian, populist nationalism in which minorities of all kinds were to be destroyed.

For the Nazis, by contrast, the extermination of the Jews possessed a central importance. It was closely connected with the boundless war aims of the Third Reich. Hitler believed that it was only through the universal destruction of the 'world-enemy', the Jews, that Germany could gain mastery over Europe and in the long run the entire world. Romania and Croatia were, of course, only regional powers, in no position to launch a war for the domination of Europe. A substantial part of the uniqueness of the Nazi genocide of the Jews derived from the fact that Germany had been a rising world power before the First World War, a power that went through so deep and comprehensive a crisis in its political system, its society, its economy and its culture as a result of its defeat in 1918, that a significant number of Germans believed that the only answer to the question of how Germany could rise again to become a world power was an apocalyptic one. An extreme crisis demanded extreme measures to solve it. These people were, of course, always a minority, but in 1933 they came to power, and by 1939 they were beginning to put their ideas into effect.

So the reductionist attempts of some historians to portray the 'Final Solution of the Jewish Question in Europe' in terms of war-related economic rationality are not only unconvincing in their vast overestimation of the resources acquired by the German Reich by killing the Jews, they fail on a larger scale to encompass the depth and breadth of Nazi antisemitism. Not only were Jews dispossessed, arrested and deported to extermination camps in East Europe from countries such as France, Belgium, Holland, Norway, Italy, and at least in the intention Denmark, very soon after they were occupied by Nazi Germany; Hitler pressed his allies such as Hungary to deliver up their Jewish population for extermination, and Heinrich Himmler, head of the SS, even went to Finland specifically to ask the government to surrender its tiny and completely unimportant Jewish community to be taken to Auschwitz and killed. The minutes of the Wannsee Conference, held early in 1942 to coordinate measures for the killing of Europe's Jews, also listed other insignificant Jewish communities in countries yet to be conquered by Germany, such as Ireland or Iceland, marking them down for eventual extermination as well.

This obsessiveness, this desire to be comprehensive and make no exceptions, anywhere, is a major factor distinguishing the Nazis' racial war from all other racial wars in history. There have, of course, been many racial conflicts in Europe and other parts of the world both before and since the Second World War. Some of them have rightly been called genocidal. One in particular has been singled out as providing a precedent and perhaps an impulse for the Nazi murder of the Jews: the extermination of the Hereros in the German colony of South-West Africa, now Namibia, in 1905–6. Following a rebellion by the Hereros, a German military force arrived with the officially proclaimed intention of exterminating the tribe, whose people were shot, driven into the desert to starve, or incarcerated in murderous and brutal conditions in concentration camps. Sixty-five thousand out of 80,000 Hereros died. Yet the Hereros, and the other ethnic group subjected to the genocidal violence of the German troops, the Nama, were regarded by the Germans as racially inferior beings, to be cleared away to make room for German settlers. They were in no sense a global threat; they were not even seen as an overall threat to German rule in South-West Africa. If there was a parallel with Nazi racial policy, it was a parallel with Nazi policy towards the Slavs, not Nazi policy towards the Jews. In this sense, the German racial war in Eastern Europe from 1939 to 1945 was also a colonial war. Hitler, indeed, often drew parallels in his lunch- and dinner-time monologues between the annihilation of millions of Slavs envisaged in the General Plan for the East, and the annihilation of the indigenous population by European settlers in Australia or North America. The extermination of the Jews, however, cannot be understood in this way.

For Hitler, the Second World War was from the very outset a racial war, as he emphasised already in August 1939 in conversation with leading representatives of the armed forces. He regarded the eugenic improvement of the German race as an integral part of this war, just as he did the removal of the Jews from Germany and in the longer run from Europe. It was significant that when he signed the order to begin the long-planned mass killing of the mentally ill and handicapped in Germany in October 1939, he backdated the order to 1 September 1939, the first day of the war; more significant still was the fact that when, as he did on many occasions during the war, he recalled his prewar 'prophecy' that 'if international finance Jewry within Europe and without should succeed in precipitating the peoples once more into a world war, then the result will not be the Bolshevisation of the earth and with it the victory of Jewry, but the annihilation of the Jewish race in Europe', he dated it incorrectly, not to 30 January 1939, when he had actually said this, on the anniversary of his appointment as Reich Chancellor, but to 1 September 1939, the day the war began. For Hitler, in other words, the introduction of radical measures for the racial renewal of Germany, Europe and the world all began on the same day, with the launching of the new world war.

A key aspect of waging war for the Nazis was the strengthening of the so-called Aryan race and the elimination not only of the mentally ill and handicapped but also of alleged 'asocials' and criminals, indeed of everyone who was classified as 'alien to the national community'. The overwhelming majority of the 16,000 or more death sentences carried out during the Third Reich were carried out during the war years. From September 1942 onwards, some 20,000 state prison inmates incarcerated as repeat petty offenders under provisions made earlier for 'security confinement' were removed from the prisons and sent to the concentration camp at Mauthausen, where they were subjected to 'annihilation through labour'; more than a third of them were dead by the end of the year. Nazi ideology classified criminality as hereditarily determined, so that even minor offenders threatened to cause racial degeneracy if they were left alive.

This belief extended to Germany's and Europe's Gypsies as well, who were arrested in large numbers, taken to concentration camps and sent to the gas chambers of Auschwitz in their thousands. It was significant that in the classification system applied to camp inmates by the SS, the Gypsies were overwhelmingly registered as 'asocial', and made to wear the black triangle reserved mainly for vagrants, tramps, alcoholics and other deviants from Nazi behavioural norms. More than 20,000 of them died in Auschwitz alone, three-quarters from sickness and malnutrition. The SS Task Forces killed thousands in various parts of Eastern Europe, the German army shot many more in Serbia, and the Croatian and Romanian authorities placed large numbers in camps, or shot them in mass executions. Here, too, Gypsies were primarily regarded as criminals, or, as in Serbia, tools of the Jews in partisan and resistance movements. The killing of the Gypsies, however, was far less systematic than that of the Jews. Many survived, particularly if they worked in war-related industries. Between 5,000 and 15,000 remained in Germany to the end of the war, though some 2,500 of these were forcibly sterilised.

Killing Gypsies was an urgent task the Nazis set themselves in order to win the war. Even more urgent, however, was the annihilation of the Jews. Immediately after the invasion of the Soviet Union on 22 June 1941, Hitler, Goebbels and the entire Nazi propaganda apparatus unfolded an intensive antisemitic campaign that portrayed Churchill, Stalin and Roosevelt as tools of international Jewry, engaged in a world conspiracy to destroy the German race. Lasting until the end of the year, this propaganda offensive created a genocidal climate in which Nazis at many different levels of the hierarchy, particularly in the SS, encouraged personally by Himmler and his deputy Heydrich, competed with one another to carry out the extermination of Eastern Europe's Jews.

At the same time, however, it was also clear that what Hitler called 'the annihilation of the Jewish race in Europe' was indeed to be a Pan-European programme of murder. Already in September 1941, the Reich Security Head Office, Himmler's headquarters, realised that it could not be achieved by mass shootings of the kind already being carried out by SS Task Forces behind the Eastern Front. The technical experts of the so-called Action T-4, the gassing of thousands of mental hospital inmates, were now available for practical advice, since the first phase of the action, in which 70,000 mentally ill and handicapped people had been murdered, had been brought to an end by the public protest of the Catholic Bishop of Münster. It would be wrong to see a causal link here; if the T-4 action had indeed continued in the gas chambers of German mental hospitals, instead of what now happened, namely its continuation in a less conspicuous way by lethal injections and the starvation of patients, this would certainly not have prevented the use of mass gassing in the murder of the Jews.

By the end of December 1941, each of the four SS Task Forces behind the Eastern Front possessed a mobile gas chamber, in which Jewish men, women and children were murdered by carbon monoxide exhaust fumes piped into a sealed chamber at the back of a lorry. In March, May and July 1942 respectively, Belzec, Sobibor and Treblinka, the three extermination camps of the so-called Reinhard Action, under construction, of course, for several months previously, began the mass extermination of the Jewish inhabitants of Nazi-created ghettoes in Warsaw, Lódź and other Polish cities, through the pumping of motor exhaust gases into sealed rooms. From March 1942 the largest of the extermination camps, at Auschwitz-Birkenau, also came into operation, using the cyanide-based disinfectant gas Zyklon-B to kill a total of over a million Jews not just from the east but from Western and Southern Europe as well.

Poison gas had already been used in international conflicts as a weapon of war, by both sides in the First World War, by the Spanish in putting down a rebellion in Spanish Morocco and by the Italians in the conquest of Ethiopia. But all of these examples involved the use of poison gas against active combatants. In Germany as well as in England, the government's fear of gas bombs being dropped on major cities in air raids was so great that millions of gas masks were manufactured and distributed to the population. But such raids were never carried out, probably because both sides feared the escalation of the conflict that this would mean. There was no parallel, therefore, to the Nazis' use of poison gas to murder non-combatant civilians.

At the same time, however, it would not be right to reduce the uniqueness of the Nazi extermination of the Jews to the mere technical factor of the use of poison gas to carry it out. The extermination camps were only one instrument of a wider programme of killing using a variety of methods. By the time the war came to an end, the Nazis and their allies had murdered nearly six million Jews. Three million died in the gas chambers, 1.3 million were shot by SS Task Forces and police and army units, 700,000 were murdered in mobile gas vans and up to a million died as a result of deliberate starvation, of disease, and of maltreatment in the camps, the ghettos set up by the Nazis from late 1939 onwards in Eastern Europe, or in transit. No other genocide in history has included among its methods the use of poison gas in specially constructed facilities. But in identifying what was unique about the Nazi genocide of the Jews *in general, as a whole*, it is more important to specify why, rather than how. Its peculiar characteristics derived from the fact that the Nazis regarded the Jews of Europe, and indeed the world, as a deadly, universal threat to their existence, and that of Germany more generally, that had to be eliminated by any means possible, as fast as possible, and as thoroughly as possible.

Mass gassing, of course, belonged undoubtedly to the modern industrial age as did another unique feature of Nazi death camps, the exploitation of the victims' bodies for economic purposes, in the collection of gold from dental fillings, for example. It would be wrong to claim, however, that the use of technical-industrial methods implied that there was something impersonal or automatic about the Nazi murder of the Jews that set it apart as a uniquely modern form of genocide. The arrests in the ghettos, the conditions of life there and in the transit camps, the circumstances in which the victims were transported, the brutality of the police and SS men who guarded them, lacked nothing in terms of physical, face-to-face violence exercised by some human beings, the Nazi SS and police and their helpers, on others, their victims. The machinery of killing was uncomplicated, makeshift and often broke down under the strain of dealing with such huge numbers of victims, even in Auschwitz. And the unbridled violence meted out by the SS and camp orderlies to the victims on their way to the gas chamber can have left hardly any of them in any doubt about the fate that awaited them. There was nothing clinical or impersonal about the killings, nor about the motivation of the fanatical antisemites like Reinhard Heydrich and Adolf Eichmann who organised them.

The Nazi genocide of the Jews stood at the middle of a century that witnessed a variety of genocides in a variety of places. In 1915, the so-called Young Turks, nationalists who had seized power in the Ottoman Empire following its loss of 40 per cent of its territory during the Balkan Wars, launched a campaign of genocide against the Armenian Christian minority in Anatolia. There had already been pogroms and massacres, notably in 1894–6 and again in 1909, but this time the scale was much larger, serving the interests of a Pan-Turkish ideology that regarded non-Turkish minorities as agents of the enemy power, Russia, and obstacles to the revolutionary creation of a new Pan-Turkic state that would include areas at the time controlled by other powers, notably tsarist Russia. Armenians were deported from eastern Anatolia into the Syrian desert, many being killed along the way, and many more dying of thirst and starvation en route or after they arrived. Officially sponsored killing squads were formed to massacre Armenians, often accompanying the murders with horrifying atrocities. Around a million Armenians died, and between 1918 and 1923 another half a million, totalling three-quarters of the entire Armenian population of the Ottoman Empire.

Like the Jews, the Armenians specialised in trade and finance, and a large proportion of them practised a different religion from that of their persecutors. Like the Nazis, the Young Turks took as their aim the creation of an ethnically homogeneous state. Like the Nazis, they had come to power in a violent revolution. Like the Nazis, they claimed that the minority whose elimination they sought was an agent of a foreign power – in the German case, the world Jewish conspiracy, led from America, in the Turkish case, the Russians. Like the Nazis, the Young Turks aimed to invade other countries to create a new, powerful empire. As in Germany, the genocide took place in the middle of a world war. The parallels did not end there. The extreme right in the Weimar Republic, including the Nazis, regarded the killing of the Armenians, to whom they referred as 'the Jews of Turkey', in a favourable light, rightly or wrongly seeing it as the expression of a nationalist, militarist government far stronger and more determined than the feeble democracy of the Weimar Republic, something to be translated into German politics and copied rather than criticised.

At the same time, however, there were significant differences. The Armenians were geographically concentrated, in eastern Anatolia, near to the Russian border, while Germany's and even more so Europe's Jews were not. The Young Turks did not accuse the Armenians of fostering a subversive and degenerative spirit amongst the majority population as the Nazis did the Jews. The Armenians were killed overwhelmingly by deportation under murderous conditions, not in death camps or shooting pits, though shootings did indeed take place on a considerable scale. Nor were they viewed as the agents of a *world* conspiracy to undermine Turkey. Correspondingly the Turks had no intention of annihilating Armenians outside Turkey, even outside the larger Turkey that they planned. The Jews in Germany at least were not, as has sometimes been claimed in comparative studies, a low-status, deprived minority like the Armenians, but, on the contrary, a well-established, well-acculturated group, many of whom were well off and played a prominent role in national life and culture: by 1914 the Judaic religion was in decline in Germany, with intermarriage between religious Jews and Protestants reaching around 50 per cent of all Jewish marriages in a city like Hamburg, for example. The killing of the Armenians was not part of a wider programme of ethnic reordering and eugenic cleansing such as the Nazis undertook, but a nationalist campaign of ethnic cleansing directed against a particular religious, social and territorial minority, comparable to later genocidal massacres of Jews and Gypsies in Romania or Jews, Gypsies and Serbs in Croatia.

At the other end of the century, in 1994, following a brief ethnic civil war at the beginning of the decade that ended in a fragile peace brokered by Tanzania, the majority Hutu inhabitants of the African country of Rwanda mobilised to murder all the members of the Tutsi minority they could find, with machetes, guns, grenades and clubs, in a face-to-face orgy of homicidal violence. Hutu ideologues claimed the Tutsi were interlopers who had enslaved them for centuries, pastoralists who did not belong in a settled agricultural society. Radio broadcasts during the violence even urged Hutus to 'exterminate the Tutsi from the globe' and to invade neighbouring countries in order to do so. In a few weeks, at least seven out of every ten Tutsis were brutally murdered, with the death toll reaching at least 800,000. Yet for all its genocidal ideology and ambition, this, too, was a regionally limited action. What made the Nazi genocide of the Jews unique was among other things the fact that it was geographically and temporally unlimited. The Nazi vision of the future envisaged a world of endless and continuing struggle, struggle for its own sake, where one triumph would only lead on to another, greater conflict. Hitler's ultimate vision of a global conflict between a German-run Europe and the United States was already foreshadowed in his *Second Book*, written in 1928 though not published until 1961. He regarded from early on the Jews of America as Germany's implacable enemy, warning them, as he saw it, through the 1 April 1933 boycott of Jewish shops in Germany, then through his speech of 30 January 1939 and all his subsequent references to it. The Nazi conquest of Europe would therefore have most likely been the springboard for a war with America, in which a Nazi victory would have led to the extermination of America's Jews, too.

There was never any chance of this happening. But the status of 'world Jewry', *Weltjudentum* in Nazi ideology had no parallel in, say, Young Turkish concepts of Armenians, or Hutu concepts of the Tutsi. Of course, there were many genocides in the modern age, and every genocide was different. The extermination of the Native Americans or the Australian Aborigines was no less a genocide simply because it was achieved mainly by disease. Ideology is crucial here. The 'death marches' from the Nazi camps in the face of the advancing Red Army, along with the terrible final phase of the camps' existence, killed over half the 715,000 prisoners held in the camps at the beginning of 1945. The vast majority of these prisoners were not Jewish, but that does not mean the death marches were not genocidal: the SS regarded all of them as racially inferior and shot, burned or starved them to death or let them perish from disease, unlike the tens of thousands of British and other prisoners of war evacuated from their camps at the same time, who were not subjected to such treatment.

Thus although the Nazi 'Final Solution' was one genocide among many, it had features that made it stand out from all the rest as well. Unlike all the others it was bounded neither by space nor by time. It was launched not against a local or regional obstacle, but at a world-enemy seen as operating on a global scale. It was bound to an even larger plan of racial reordering and reconstruction involving further genocidal killing on an almost unimaginable scale, aimed, however, at clearing the way in a particular region – Eastern Europe – for a further struggle against the Jews and those the Nazis regarded as their puppets. It was set in motion by ideologues who saw world history in racial terms. It was, in part, carried out by industrial methods. These things all make it unique.

But its uniqueness in this sense doesn't mean we can't learn from it. We can look at extreme nationalist and racist ideologies and see from the experience of Nazi extermination when they look like spilling over into genocide and mass murder, and intervene at this point to stop them going any further. The international criminal jurisdiction created at Nuremberg was not brought into being to deal with the Nazi extermination of the Jews, but, as it becomes stronger, it can pose an increasingly powerful obstacle to outbreaks of genocidal violence, especially where they are state-sponsored, across the world. Human societies have a continuing ability, it seems, to generate ethnic hatreds, but the means to stop these escalating into genocide have become more effective in the twenty-first century above all because of the cultural memory of Nazi genocide in the second half of the twentieth.

NOTE
This essay originated in a lecture delivered (in German) at the French embassy in Berlin, at the start of an international conference on the use of poison gas as a means of mass murder in Nazi camps, and so, as a lecture, it was un-footnoted. For this revised version, published here

for the first time in English, it is perhaps useful to append a brief discussion of the literature on the various topics covered.

A good starting-point is the collection of essays edited by Alan S. Rosenbaum, *Is the Holocaust Unique: Perspectives on Comparative Genocide* (third edition, Boulder, CO, 2009), marred, however, by excessive moralising and, in places, mystification (including the argument that it is sacrilegious or immoral to engage in comparison at all). Among the most cogent contributions are Vahakn N. Dadrian, 'The Comparative Aspects of the Armenian and Jewish Cases of Genocide: A Sociohistorical Perspective' (139–74), Barbara B. Green, 'Stalinist Terror and the Question of Genocide: The Great Famine' (175–200) and Scott Straus, 'The Promise and Limits of Comparison: The Holocaust and the 1994 Genocide in Rwanda' (245–57). For a useful general introduction, see Dan Stone, *Histories of the Holocaust* (Oxford, 2010), 206–44, which raises some of the central issues of modern genocide studies in relation to the Nazi extermination of the Jews, and links them to recent studies of colonial mass murder, notably of the Hereros and, in a different way, Native Americans.

On the mass murders committed in Poland under Stalin, see Jan T. Gross, *Revolution from Abroad: The Soviet Conquest of Poland's Western Ukraine and Western Belorussia* (Princeton, NJ, 1988), and for a good comparison with the Nazis' policies in the part of Poland occupied by them, Mark Mazower, *Hitler's Empire* (London, 2008), 96–101. Richard J. Evans, *The Third Reich at War* (London, 2008), 3–47, covers the German-occupied part of the country and provides further references. Robert Conquest's classic *The Great Terror* (London, 1968) is the indispensable starting-point for a broader consideration of Stalinist mass murder. The case for treating Stalinist population transfers and mass killings as genocides is argued in Steven Rosefielde, *Red Holocaust* (London, 2009) and Norman Naimark, *Stalin's Genocides* (Princeton, 2010). On the Ukrainian famine, Robert Conquest, *Harvest of Sorrow* (London, 1986), remains the classic account. Stephen G. Wheatcroft, 'The Scale and Nature of Stalinist Repression and its Demographic Significance', *Europe-Asia*

Studies 52 (2000), 1143–59, and idem, 'Towards Explaining the Soviet Famine of 1931–33', *Food and Foodways* 12 (2004), 107–36, provide some concrete evidence of numbers; however, see also Robert Conquest, 'Comment on Wheatcroft', *Europe-Asia Studies* 51 (1999), 1479–83. The best way to follow the often acrimonious debate about the Ukrainian commemoration of the famine, both in Ukraine and elsewhere (especially in Canada) is by accessing articles on 'Holodomor' on the internet, which provide summaries of newspaper stories and polemics originally published in Ukrainian as well as in English.

The Nazis' General Plan for the East is outlined and discussed in Götz Aly and Susanne Heim, *Architects of Annihilation* (Princeton, 2003), 234–82, and German resettlement plans are covered by Robert K. Koehl's classic *RKFDV: German Resettlement and Population Policy 1939–1945* (Cambridge, MA, 1957). The Nazi treatment of the Poles, and the many atrocities committed during and after the invasion, are covered in Alexander Rossino, *Hitler Strikes Poland* (Lawrence, KS, 2003). The classic account of the 'Final Solution of the Jewish Question in Europe' is Saul Friedländer, *The Years of Extermination: The Third Reich and the Jews 1939–1945* (New York, 2007); details of antisemitic atrocities can be found in Ernst Klee et al. (eds), *'Those Were the Days': The Holocaust as Seen by the Perpetrators and Bystanders* (London, 1991); antisemitic propaganda is covered by Jeffrey Herf, *The Jewish Enemy* (London, 2006).

The subsidiary genocides of the Jews in Croatia and Romania, facilitated by the German conquest of Eastern Europe but possessing their own autonomous dynamic, are described in Jozo Tomasevich, *War and Revolution in Yugoslavia 1941–1945* (Stanford, CA, 2001), Edmond Paris, *Genocide in Satellite Croatia 1941–1945* (Chicago, 1961), and Dennis Deletant's excellent *Hitler's Forgotten Ally: Ion Antonescu and his Regime: Romania 1940–44* (London, 2006).

The argument that the Nazi extermination of the Jews was driven by economic considerations is advanced in Götz Aly, *Hitler's Beneficiaries: Plunder, Racial War, and the Nazi Welfare State* (New York, 2007), discussed in more detail in chap. 8 of the present collection.

The extermination of the Herero tribe in German South-West Africa in 1905–6 was brought to light in the first, and still the best, treatment of the subject, by Helmut Bley, *South-West Africa under German Rule* (London, 1971). Jürgen Zimmerer, 'Annihilation in Africa', *Bulletin of the German Historical Institute London* 37 (2005), 51–7, and Benjamin Madley, 'From Africa to Auschwitz', *European History Quarterly* 35 (2005), 429–64, put the case for a direct link to the Nazi extermination of the Jews; Robert Gerwarth, 'Hannah Arendt's Ghosts', *Central European History* 42 (2009), 279–300, the case against.

For the Nazi killing of the (allegedly) mentally handicapped and ill, see Henry Friedlander, *The Origins of Nazi Genocide* (Chapel Hill, NC, 1995), and repeat offenders in the prisons, Nikolaus Wachsmann, *Hitler's Prisons* (London, 2004), 284–318. The annihilation of the Gypsies is dealt with comprehensively in Guenter Lewy, *The Nazi Persecution of the Gypsies* (New York, 2000). There is no good study of the Nazi persecution of homosexuals.

The most up-to-date research on mass killing through the use of poison gas is unfortunately only available in German, in the volume in which the present essay originally appeared: Günter Morsch and Bertrand Perz (eds), *Neue Studien zu nationalsozialistischen Massentötungen durch Giftgas* (Berlin, 2011). The most useful source of information in English is the admirable Nizkor Project (accessible through its website, http://www.nizkor.org/). The 'death marches' that were carried out during the evacuation of the camps are persuasively presented as genocidal in Daniel Blatman, *The Death Marches* (Cambridge, MA, 2011).

Many recent works place the Nazi extermination of the Jews in the broader context of twentieth-century genocides. Among the most useful are Donald Bloxham and Dirk Moses (eds), *The Oxford Handbook of Genocide Studies* (Oxford, 2010), and Dan Stone (ed.), *The Historiography of Genocide* (London, 2008). Eric D. Weitz, *A Century of Genocide* (Princeton, NJ, 2003), is a solid introduction. Donald Bloxham, *The Final Solution: A Genocide* (Oxford University

Press, 2009) is representative of this overall trend. Among other genocides, the Armenian is covered by Raymond Kevorkian, *The Armenian Genocide: A Complete History*. (London, 2011) and the Rwandan by the dramatic narrative of Philip Gourevitch, *We wish to inform you that tomorrow we will be killed with our families* (London, 2000) as well as by Linda Melvern, *Conspiracy to Murder: The Rwandan Genocide* (London, 2004).

25. EUROPE'S KILLING FIELDS

'Who, after all, speaks today of the annihilation of the Armenians?' Adolf Hitler asked his generals in 1939, as he told them to 'close your hearts to pity', 'act brutally' and behave 'with the greatest harshness' in the coming war in the east. It's often assumed that in reminding them of the genocide of at least a million Armenians by the Ottoman Turks during the First World War, Hitler was referring to what he intended to do to Europe's Jews. But he was not referring to the Jews: he was referring to the Poles. 'I have sent my Death's Head units to the East,' he told the generals, 'with the order to kill without mercy men, women and children of the Polish race or language. Only in such a way will we win the living space that we need.'

Over the past couple of decades, historians have been steadily uncovering the true extent of Nazism's genocidal ambitions in Eastern Europe. A month before the invasion of the Soviet Union in June 1941, leading German military, economic and agriculture officials, following the direction indicated by Hitler and Göring, adopted a 'Hunger Plan' that prescribed the removal of food supplies from the areas shortly to be conquered, in order to feed German troops and civilians; the inhabitants of eastern Poland, Ukraine and Belarus were to be left to starve. This was soon trumped by a more ambitious plan, pursued by the SS chief, Heinrich Himmler, and officially adopted just over a year later. According to the General Plan for the East, ethnic Germans were to be settled in Germanised towns and connected to the Reich by high-speed railways and autobahns. Anywhere between thirty million and forty-five million Slavs living in the region were to be left to die, deliberately deprived of food and medical care. This was genocide on a gargantuan, almost unimaginable scale, and it was never fully carried out only because Nazi Germany was defeated in the war in the east.

As Timothy Snyder reminds us in his book *Bloodlands: Europe Between Hitler and Stalin* (2010), the Nazis made a start on this scheme of racial annihilation with the blockade of Leningrad, which led to the death of a million of its inhabitants, and the deliberate murder by starvation and disease of more than three million Red Army prisoners of war who fell into their hands during the massive encircling movements with which the Wehrmacht defeated the Soviet forces in the first months of Operation Barbarossa. Many more civilians perished in the towns, villages and country areas invaded by the Nazis in the second half of 1941. Already hundreds of thousands of Poles had been expelled from their homes, enslaved, deported to Germany or killed.

But the Nazis were by no means the only architects of the suffering that the people who lived in this part of Europe had to endure in the 1930s and 1940s. Hitler's enemy in the east, Joseph Stalin, was just as murderous in his pursuit of a Utopian programme, different though Stalinist Communism might have been from the hierarchical racist ideology of the Nazis. Some three million people, mostly Ukrainians, were sacrificed to the Bolshevik plan to collectivise agriculture in the early 1930s; three-quarters of a million Soviet citizens perished in Stalin's purges later in the decade; during the war, the transmutation of Stalin's vision from social revolution to patriotic defence of the Russian homeland led to the forcible deportation of millions more – Poles, Volga Germans, Crimean Tatars and other ethnic minorities – under conditions so appalling that hundreds of thousands died.

Altogether, Snyder reckons, some fourteen million people perished in this part of Europe in the 1930s and 1940s as a result of policies enacted by the Nazis and their allies, or the Soviet Communists and theirs. Snyder describes these countries – Poland, Belarus, Ukraine, the

Baltic states and the western fringes of Russia – as Europe's 'Blood-lands'. This was where the vast majority of Europe's Jews lived, and they also bore the brunt of the genocidal thrust of Nazi policy. Initially, Snyder argues, they were killed as useless consumers of much needed foodstuffs. But once Barbarossa got into difficulties a month after the invasion of the Soviet Union on 22 June 1941, Hitler began to see the mass murder of the Jews as an end in itself, an act of revenge against an imagined Jewish world conspiracy. At this point, Himmler's SS Task Forces began shooting Jewish women and children as well as Jewish men; and as German forces suffered their first serious reverses in the east in December, Hitler went over to an unrestrained policy of annihilation, resulting in the creation of the death camps and the murder of virtually the entire Jewish population of the 'Bloodlands'.

Both Hitler and Stalin, Snyder argues, began by trying to imple-ment unrealisable visions: respectively, the conquest of the Soviet Union and the creation of a German-occupied 'living space' in Eastern Europe; and the rapid collectivisation of agriculture, mainly in Ukraine, in order to feed an urban population created by a headlong rush into industrial modernity. Both these programmes failed: Hitler's armies were stalled in July 1941, then stopped before Moscow in December; Stalin's collectivisation met with massive resistance from the peasantry and proved impossible to implement in the short time he had allowed. Both dictators responded by blaming minorities for their failure, Hitler the Jews, Stalin above all Ukrainians, Belarussians and Poles; and both vented their anger by killing these people in their millions.

Snyder draws many other parallels between the motivation and behaviour of the two dictators in their policies of genocide and mass murder. Are they convincing? Certainly, scapegoating played a role in Stalin's terror, but so did his desire to create a new elite by eliminating the old, and his determination to modernise the country at all costs. These policies weren't confined to the collectivisation campaign in Ukraine, but were directed against the entire population of the Soviet Union. Snyder's claim that the people of Soviet Russia were far less likely to be touched by Stalin's terror than national minorities in the 'Bloodlands' doesn't stand up to scrutiny. The starvation policy of the early 1930s was directed not specifically against Ukrainians but against kulaks, allegedly well-off peasants, who included many inhabitants of Soviet Russia – and Ukrainian peasants were themselves incited by Stalin's political police to kill the more prosperous Don Cossacks in their thousands.

Other groups, too, such as Kazakh nomads, were starved in huge numbers. Stalin's purges affected millions of Russians; the death rate of 10–15 per cent Snyder cites for the inmates of the Gulag is given by Robert Conquest in his classic *The Great Terror* (1968) as a minimum, exceeded many times over in some years; citing official Soviet documents, Anne Appelbaum has recorded that a total of 2,750,000 people died in the camps and exile settlements under Stalin, again most likely an underestimate. The vast majority of these, as of the more than twenty-eight million Soviet citizens subjected to forced labour in Stalin's time, were Russians. Snyder's relentless focus on Poland, Belarus, Ukraine and to a lesser extent the Baltic states, and the large claims he makes for the victimisation of their inhabitants, sidelines the fate of the millions of Russians who died at Stalin's hands.

A historian of East-Central Europe, Snyder hasn't really mastered the voluminous literature on Hitler's Germany. This leads him into error in a number of places. He wrongly claims, for example, that Hitler surprised his conservative allies in 1933 by calling a snap election (the calling of elections had been part of the original coalition deal); that Hitler dissolved the Reichstag at this point (it was not Hitler, but Hindenburg, as president, who did this); that the 'Aryanisation' of Jewish property in Germany began on a substantial scale only in 1938 (it began immediately, in 1933); that the 'Reinhard' extermination camps were shut down in 1944, when they were actually closed the previous year because they had done their job of killing the Jewish inhabitants of the Polish ghettoes to make way for new arrivals from the west, and not because, as Snyder states, the Red Army was approaching; that people received 'a sentence to the concentration camp Belsen' (they did not; Belsen was not a concentration camp to which people were sentenced but a holding facility, or *Aufenthaltslager*, which gained its notoriety at the end of the war when it was overwhelmed by thousands of evacuees from other camps); and so on and so forth.

Much more seriously, Snyder's assertion that the launching of the 'Final Solution of the Jewish Question in Europe' was the outcome of Hitler's rage and frustration at not being able to win the war against the Soviet Union does not stand up to scrutiny; though there were impassioned debates within the German leadership in late July, August and September 1941 about the best way to defeat the Soviet Union, based on the realisation among some senior generals that it was proving more difficult than they had expected, nobody, least of all Hitler, felt that the German advance had ground to a halt, let alone been defeated. Hundreds of thousands of prisoners continued to be taken by the German armies (and left to starve to death), major cities like Kiev continued to fall, and Hitler continued to think that the war in the east would soon be won. 'Never before,' he declared on 8 November 1941, 'has a giant empire been smashed and struck down in a shorter time than Soviet Russia.' At one point Snyder himself concedes that it is perfectly possible that Hitler was prompted to give the order for the killing of the Jews in a moment of euphoria at the scale and rapidity of German victories rather than in a mood of despair brought on by German failures.

It was not until the Red Army fought the Germans to a standstill before Moscow and then forced them to retreat to defensible lines for the winter, that Hitler conceded that Barbarossa had gone wrong and looked for scapegoats; but the people he blamed were the generals, not the Jews. Relying on an article written in the 1990s by the German historian Christian Gerlach, Snyder asserts that it was at this moment that Hitler took the decision to annihilate Europe's Jews, in fulfilment of his 'prophecy' of January 1939 that if the Jews started a world war, they would be the ones who would die. But while there is certainly evidence that he informed his satraps that the Jews would be killed, this does not amount to a decision. In his argument that the decision to kill the Jews was taken on 12 December 1941, Gerlach pointed to the entry of the US into the war the day before as the trigger, not the Red Army's success in pushing back the Wehrmacht from the gates of Moscow (that didn't begin until 16 December). In any case, few historians have accepted Gerlach's claim, and he subsequently distanced himself from it.

Snyder portrays the Nazi decision-making process as far more clear-cut than most historians now think it was. The search for a single moment in which the Final Solution was decided on has long since been abandoned in favour of a more sophisticated understanding of a process that was driven from above by a ceaseless barrage of anti-semitic propaganda emanating from Hitler and Goebbels, beginning immediately after the invasion of the Soviet Union and continuing unabated until the end of the year; and implemented by Himmler, his deputy Heydrich and their agents on the ground in a relatively haphazard manner, though one that was always aimed at the goal of total annihilation.

It was not just events in the east, but also in the west, that directed Hitler's attention to his 'prophecy' and intensified his drive to see it fulfilled. June 1941 witnessed not just the beginning of the titanic war between the Third Reich and the Soviet Union, but also the beginnings of the American entry into the conflict, with a sharp increase in military supplies shipped from the US to Britain and then the Soviet Union, followed by the signing of the Atlantic Charter in August. In mid-August, Hitler was telling Goebbels that the Jews of America would eventually be made to pay just as the Jews of Europe's east were already being made to pay, and, by the beginning of October, Heydrich was telling people that all the Jews of Europe would be 'evacuated' to the east.

It was the comprehensive European, even global scale of the Nazis' intentions towards the Jews that marked out the genocide from other mass exterminations of the period, or indeed any period. By addressing Nazi antisemitism almost entirely in the context of Hitler's plans for Eastern Europe, and drawing rhetorical parallels with the mass murders carried out on Stalin's orders in the same area, Snyder distracts attention from what was unique about the extermination of the Jews. That uniqueness consisted not only in the scale of its ambition, but also in the depth of the hatred and fear that drove it on. There was something peculiarly sadistic in the Nazis' desire not just to torture, maim and kill the Jews, but also to humiliate them in public, in a violent spirit of revenge for imagined crimes against Germany, notably the mythical 'stab-in-the-back' that had supposedly brought about German defeat in 1918. The Slavs, in the end, were for the Nazis a regional obstacle to be removed; the Jews were a 'world-enemy' to be ground into the dust.

By focusing exclusively on what he calls the 'Bloodlands', Snyder also demeans, trivialises or ignores the suffering of the many other Europeans who were unfortunate enough to fall into Nazi hands. Thus the eight million foreigners working in the Reich in the latter stages of the war were not all 'from the East' as Snyder claims – one and a quarter million of them were French, more than half a million were Italian and nearly half a million were Belgian or Dutch. The killing of up to 200,000 mentally handicapped and sick Germans by Nazi doctors gets a brief paragraph in *Bloodlands*; the hundreds of thousands of German and Western European Jews who were murdered are dismissed in a little more than a page; sites of mass murder that lie outside Snyder's 'Bloodlands' and where the killings were not perpetrated by the Nazis or the Soviets are dealt with in equally perfunctory fashion. The 300,000 Serbs slaughtered by the Croatian government, and further afield, the tens of thousands of Spanish Republican prisoners executed by the Francoists and the hundreds of thousands more confined in brutal labour camps after the end of the Civil War, or the Gypsies killed in large numbers not just by the Germans but also by the Croatians and Romanians – all of these get barely a mention or no mention at all. Yet they were also victims of the mass murders visited upon 'Europe between Hitler and Stalin'.

These omissions expose another serious weakness of *Bloodlands*:

Snyder isn't interested in examining anything outside what he calls the Bloodlands. What he really wants to do is to tell us about the sufferings of the people who lived in the area he knows most about. Assuming we know nothing about any of this, he bludgeons us with facts and figures about atrocities and mass murders until we're reeling from it all. The prose style in which he conveys his facts doesn't help: the endless succession of short sentences hits us like a series of blows from a cudgel until eventually brain-death sets in. The same phrases and formulations are repeated over and over again in an almost incantatory fashion, as if Snyder doesn't want us to think critically about what he's telling us, just to feel the pain he's describing.

Yet his constant drawing of abstract rhetorical parallels and contrasts, and above all his obsession with statistics, counting with an implausible exactness the numbers of the deported and dead, make it difficult to do this. As if he realises the dehumanising effect of his approach, Snyder at various points inserts short accounts of some of those who fell victim to the murderous policies pursued by the two dictators. Some of these accounts are given at the beginning of the book without the victims' names being mentioned; then, in a cheap rhetorical trick, in the opening paragraph of the final chapter, entitled 'Humanity', he restores their identity to them by giving us their names. But merely naming them does not restore their humanity.

For that to happen, we would need to know much more about them than can be conveyed in a single paragraph at either end of the book, a paragraph that covers no fewer than five individual victims. They remain essentially without human contours, as do all those whose fate is mentioned in this book: just names, no more. As a result the insertion of their stories into the narrative seems merely gratuitous. 'The Nazi and Soviet regimes turned people into numbers,' Snyder says at the end of the book: 'It is for us as humanists to turn the numbers back into people.' But for all the self-congratulation exhibited in this portentous exhortation, and in the sentimentality with which he briefly recounts the stories of individual victims, he fails in this task. To succeed, he would have needed to explore the lives of his emblematic victims in far more detail, using diaries, letters, personal testimonies, on the model of Saul Friedländer's deeply moving account of Nazi Germany and the Jews in *The Years of Extermination* (2007).

Equally anonymous are the men who planned and executed the atrocities. Snyder shows no interest in their character or motivation, in what turned them into torturers, or in what was the driving force of mass murder in both the Nazi and Soviet cases. And the book gives us no sense at all of the 'Bloodlands' as a region; its physical, social and cultural features are nowhere described; it, too, has no real identity here. That's because it's an entirely artificial construct – a label for the location of mass murder, nothing more.

Snyder claims that his purpose in describing 'all of the major killing policies in their common European historical setting' was 'to introduce to European history its central event'. But he has not described all the major killing policies and they did not all have a common setting. And to assert that they are the central event in the whole of European history is rhetorical overkill, to say the least. A number of other historians have written recently, and more perceptively, about this same topic, from Richard Overy in *The Dictators* (2004) to Robert Gellately in *Lenin, Stalin and Hitler* (2007) – some, like Norman Davies in *Europe at War 1939–45* (2006), from a similar perspective to Snyder's own. Despite the widespread misapplication of Hitler's statement about the Armenians, few claims advanced in Snyder's book are less plausible nowadays than the assertion that 'beyond Poland, the extent of Polish suffering is underappreciated'. In fact, we know about the events Snyder describes already, despite his repeated assertions that we don't. What we need is not to be told yet again the facts about mass murder, but to understand why it took place and how people could carry it out, and in this task Snyder's book is of no use. Instead, it forms part of a post-Cold War narrative that homogenises the history of mass murder by equating Hitler's policies with those of Stalin.

PART VII

AFTERMATH

26. THE OTHER HORROR

At the end of the Second World War, between twelve and four-teen million people, ethnic Germans, were forcibly expelled from Eastern Europe, or, if they had already fled, were prevented from going back to their homes. Many of them were simply bundled on to cattle trucks of the sort previously used to take Europe's Jews to their fate in the gas chambers of Auschwitz and Treblinka, and sent west-ward to Germany without food, water or adequate winter clothing. Others were detained in appalling conditions in concentration camps for weeks, suffering from disease, starvation and maltreatment, before they were brutally pushed out to the west. Long lines trudged towards Germany, with the weak succumbing to hypothermia and malnutri-tion. Altogether probably half a million and perhaps as many as a million perished in what was the largest action of what later came to be known as 'ethnic cleansing' in history.

This massive act of expulsion and forced migration is still largely unknown outside the countries most closely affected by it. The story appears in standard histories of Germany and Europe in the twentieth century as little more than a footnote. Calling it to public attention questions the widespread popular understanding of the Second World War as a wholly good fight by the Allies against the evil of Nazism and German aggression. Unfortunately, history is seldom as simple as that. Until recently, few historians troubled to investigate the expulsions in any depth, and what writing there was on the topic was bedevilled by

one-sided narratives of German suffering or Polish or Czech self-jus-
tification. But since the fall of Communism and the opening of the
archives in these countries, serious and reasonably objective historical
research by a new generation of younger historians less affected than
their predecessors by national or ethnic prejudice has begun to appear.
R. M. Douglas's *Orderly and Humane: The Expulsion of the Germans
after the Second World War* (2012) draws on this recent work and incor-
porates archival research in Germany, Poland and the Czech Republic as
well as the files of the International Committee of the Red Cross, the UN
Relief and Rehabilitation Administration and the records of the British
and American governments. It is a major achievement: for the first time
it puts the whole subject on to a scholarly footing.

The expulsions, as Douglas points out, were no mere act of mass
revenge carried out by peoples of Eastern Europe who had suffered
under the Nazi jackboot. On the contrary, they were ordered by the
Allies, and planned long before the war came to an end. The mis-
treatment of ethnic minorities before and during the First World War
in the Habsburg and Ottoman empires had led not just to a determination in the international community to guarantee their rights, but
more importantly to a decision to cut through the problem by creating unitary national states. As the tsarist empire, itself no mean
oppressor of minorities such as the Poles, fell apart, the Western Allies
found meaning in the continuing conflict by declaring one of its objectives to be the realisation of the democratic principle of 'national
self-determination'.

At the Paris Peace Conference in 1919, however, the seemingly
simple and obvious idea that every nation should have the democratic
right to elect its own government foundered on the intractable realities
of centuries-old patterns of ethnic and religious diversity in East-Central
Europe, and ran up against the requirements of security and viability
for the new states created out of the wreckage of the old. Almost every
one of them contained substantial national minorities. Naturally the
peacemakers did their best to incorporate guarantees of minority rights
into the settlement, but these proved impossible to enforce.

A case in point was the German-speaking minority in Czecho-slovakia – three million people who made up nearly a quarter of the new Republic's total population. The historic borders of the Kingdom of Bohemia included these people, and without them the new state would have lacked vital industries and defensible borders. Czech nationalism, already very passionate before 1914, was too strong a force to admit the German-speaking minority to equal rights, though liberal Czech politicians did their best to limit discrimination. And when Eduard Beneš took over as president in 1935, a new, harder note of Czech nationalism was heard, sparking a new radicalism among the German minority, who soon flocked to support the Sudeten German Party of Konrad Henlein. By 1937 this had become a Nazi front, dedicated to subverting the integrity of the Republic and opening it to German invasion and occupation.

During the wars, Beneš pushed aside the Sudeten German Social Democrats, led by Wenzel Jaksch, whose advocacy of a multinational postwar state was effectively suppressed. Jaksch is something of a hero to Douglas, though it has to be said that the amount of support he commanded among Sudeten Germans by 1939 had shrunk to an almost irreducible minimum, and it is doubtful whether his policy would have commanded much support among them even later on, after the war. Beneš convinced the Western Allies that the continued presence of a large German minority in Czechoslovakia would saddle the state with a million or more 'young, incorrigible Nazis' who would be a major potential source of destabilisation. 'National minorities,' he declared in 1942, 'are always – and in Central Europe especially – a real thorn in the side of individual nations. This is especially true if they are German minorities.' He won further sympathy for this point after the German destruction of the town of Lidice and the murder of most of its inhabitants as a reprisal for the assassination of Reinhard Heydrich in 1942. By the middle of that year, the British government had accepted the principle of the transfer of German-speaking minorities out of Eastern Europe, a principle strongly supported by the Labour Party that came to power in 1945.

Hitler's exploitation of the grievances of national minorities also extended to Poland, which before 1918 had been divided between Russia, Germany and Austria. The interwar Polish state included a Ukrainian population amounting to 14 per cent of the whole, along with a 2.3 per cent minority of German-speakers, who suffered increasing discrimination by the Polish nationalist regime. These had also been used by Hitler as a 'fifth column' of subversives whose oppression, cynically exaggerated by Nazi propaganda, provided the excuse for invasion in 1939. All this made the presence of recalcitrant national minorities seem a permanent threat to the peace and integrity of national states in the retrospective vision of Allied planners for the postwar European order.

Hitler also planned to create an ethnically homogenous Germany by expelling the Jews, and then, during the war, clearing out the bulk of the 'Slavic' population to make way for German settlers, extending the borders of the Third Reich eastwards by a thousand kilometres in pursuit of the racist idea expressed in the slogan 'one people, one empire, one leader' (*Ein Volk, Ein Reich, Ein Führer*). As part of Nazi policy even before the invasion of the Soviet Union in June 1941, hundreds of thousands of Poles were thrown out of their farms and businesses without compensation to make way for a potential half-million or more ethnic Germans brought 'home to the Reich' from Eastern Europe and the Baltic states under the Nazi–Soviet Pact of August 1939, along with a quarter of a million more from Hungary and Romania.

Increasingly exposed to attacks by Polish or Communist partisans, the settlers began to flee westwards in large numbers as Soviet forces advanced towards the end of the war, following ethnic Germans who had fled the Black Sea region, Ukraine, Romania and Yugoslavia in 1943–4 to escape the retribution of the Red Army. Germans in the annexed Czech lands, conquered by the Americans only at the very end of the war, did not have time to flee, and most of them in any case did not see the necessity. As Douglas notes, they entirely failed to understand that their occupation of confiscated property and their privileged status under Nazi rule where non-Germans were discriminated against, expropriated, starved and terrorised, 'had traumatized and radicalized the societies of which they were a part'.

The chaos and violence that had accompanied previous twentieth-century forced population transfers, notably between Greece and Turkey in the early 1920s, should have sent a warning signal to the Allied politicians who now set about organising the removal of ethnic Germans from East-Central Europe. But it did not. Douglas describes in detail how policy was made on the hoof and constantly revised as negotiations about Europe's postwar boundaries evolved. Warnings of the suffering that the transfers would entail were brushed aside by politicians anxious not to seem soft on the Germans, or alternatively dismissed by them as unduly pessimistic. Only a few commentators, such as George Orwell, warned that an 'enormous crime' was about to be committed, 'equivalent to transplanting the entire population of Australia'. Nobody listened.

Very late in the day, towards the end of 1944, it became clear that Stalin would hang on to the territory in eastern Poland he had annexed in 1939 under the terms of the Nazi–Soviet Pact, and that there was no alternative to compensating the postwar Polish state with the territories to the west, in Silesia and up to the rivers Oder and Neisse, that had been part of Prussia and later Germany for years, decades or even centuries. The Red Army was in occupation and Stalin held all the trump cards. All the Allies could do at the Potsdam Conference in July 1945 was to ratify a *fait accompli*.

Already, millions of ethnic Germans had fled the onrushing Red Army, whose soldiers raped, looted and killed German civilians as they went. The situation was made more desperate still by Stalin's own expulsion of Poles from the areas annexed by the Soviet Union, which now became overwhelmingly Ukrainian in ethnic composition. Forced out to the west, the Poles had nowhere to go except, in the view of the new Polish authorities, to areas inhabited by the remaining ethnic Germans. Neither the Czech government-in-exile nor the Polish authorities backed by Stalin had made any coherent plans for the expulsions. But in the late spring and summer of 1945 they both sent in troops, police and militia to initiate a process that, in Douglas's view, has been misunderstood as a series of spontaneous acts of revenge by local inhabitants but in reality was centrally planned and directed.

True, there was a brief wave of popular violence against Germans after SS units had continued fighting to the very end of the war, and in a few instances afterwards – but even this was in many cases instigated by police or militia, as in the case of Brno, where at least 300 ethnic Germans were killed at Kaunitz College in May and June 1945, Germans were publicly tortured to death on a sports field, and 28,000 were rounded up and taken on a 'death march' to the Austrian border, where they were dumped in a series of makeshift camps without proper supplies or sanitation. Shocked witnesses compared such events to the atrocities of the Nazis, and a few politicians urged restraint, but no concrete action was taken to control the violence.

Even though Brno, as Douglas notes, was exceptional in the extremism of its violence, politicians such as Ludvík Svoboda, Minister of Defence in the Czech government and later the country's president, called for 'the complete expulsion from Czechoslovakia of all Germans, even those so-called anti-Fascists, to safeguard us from the formation of a new fifth column'. With encouragement of this kind, local authorities acted on their own initiative, sometimes helped by the Red Army or the Czechoslovak armed forces. Germans had to wear a white square on their chest, labelled *N* for *Nemec* (German), echoing the yellow badge and star or 'J' that Jews had been forced to wear by the Nazis, but the process of identifying them was frequently arbitrary and involved the offloading of many local rivalries and resentments.

Whole towns and villages with a mainly or wholly German population were emptied and their inhabitants forced out of the country. In Poland, where the German occupation had been far harsher, such reprisals were, perhaps surprisingly, far less common, and Polish troops even protected German women from the Red Army as it swept through the country, its troops indiscriminately raping any women they found, especially if they were German. Far more violent was the expulsion of ethnic Germans from Yugoslavia and Romania, though endemic corruption in the latter country meant that it was possible to bribe officials to allow a casual Romanian passer-by to take one's place on the transport to Germany.

In many cases, the expellees were not pushed out directly but spent a period of some weeks or months in internment camps, where the authorities had begun to place them already well before the end of the war. Some of these were improvised, while others had already been used as camps by the Nazis. These included the concentration camps at Majdanek and Theresienstadt, and indeed Auschwitz, where a gap of less than two weeks separated liberation by the Red Army from the influx of the first ethnic German inmates. There was soon a vast network of these detention centres: ninety-six in Yugoslavia alone, for example. Around a quarter of a million ethnic Germans were imprisoned in camps in Czechoslovakia. Often the inmates were used on forced labour schemes to make good the devastation caused by the war. Conditions in the camps were atrocious, with poor supplies and hygiene, sadistic beatings, torture, disease, malnutrition and murder. In the camp at Lambinowice, in Poland, some 6,500 inmates had died by the time it was closed in 1946, many of them arbitrarily shot on the orders of the commandant.

Camp administrations were massively corrupt, with commandants selling the labour of the inmates to nearby businesses or taking bribes in return for safe conduct to the border. Often, camp commandants and guards explicitly tried to replicate the conditions of the German camps in which they themselves had been held. Not even in the German camps, however, had sexual exploitation and sexual violence, rape and the sadistic sexual abuse of female inmates been committed on the scale that Douglas documents for Czech and Polish camps. British and other Allied journalists and officials who tried to publicise this dire situation had no impact on politicians anxious not to be seen to be soft on the Germans. Czech and Polish crowds demonstrated publicly in support of detention. Only a handful of the camp commandants and guards were ever brought to justice.

In no country was there any serious resistance to any of this on the part of the Germans, most of whom were old people, women and children, the vast majority of the young adult men having been killed or taken prisoner in the war. By midsummer, more than 5,000 Germans were arriving every day in Berlin from Czechoslovakia on trains filled with the dead and dying, the sick and starving. More than half a million arrived in July alone. More came by road, thrown out of their homes and robbed of their possessions under blows, curses and the threat of death. These expulsions and the accompanying chaos and violence caused widespread shock and outrage among Western observers in Berlin, and helped to persuade the Allies at the Potsdam Conference to sanction further expulsions only on the condition that they were 'orderly and humane'.

On 20 November 1945, it was agreed that the Soviet Zone of Occupation of Germany would take 2,750,000 Germans from Poland and Czechoslovakia, the American zone 2,250,000 from Czechoslovakia and Hungary, the British zone 1,500,000 from Poland, and the French one 150,000 Sudeten Germans, and that the expulsions would be done gradually, in stages, to be completed in July 1946. This agreement undermined the position of State Department officials who wanted the American government to condemn the expulsions. In 1945–6 Washington still gave priority to punishing the Germans for the crimes of Nazism. Still, the agreement promised to mark a transition from the 'wild expulsions' of 1944–5 to a phase where they would be carried out in a more centralised, more controlled, and therefore more rational manner.

Yet the 'organized expulsions' of 1946–7, as Douglas notes, 'defied the efforts of the countries involved to impose any kind of order on the process'. Deporting millions of people in the space of a few months and with minimal resources devoted to the operation was a recipe for chaos. The Allied Combined Repatriation Executive achieved a great deal despite these hindrances, laying down rules and regulations to ensure safe passage, stop the spread of epidemic disease and arrange proper reception facilities. But the expelling countries were in a rush to rid themselves of unwanted minorities before the Allies called a halt to the deportations, so these conditions were frequently disregarded. The expulsions degenerated into a shambles, with huge numbers of sick, malnourished and debilitated elderly expellees arriving poorly clad and without food or supplies, and trains disgorging corpses or people so ill they had to be taken straight to hospital, to the disgust of many of the receiving Allied officials.

Often the deportees' baggage had been impounded or stolen at the point of embarkation. Corruption was rife, with confiscated equipment being sold to the next trainload of deportees, and bribes to Polish officials getting deportees transported in better conditions, granted exemption from luggage restrictions, or moved to a place at the head of the queue. 'Anti-fascists' were deported along with the supposedly dangerous majority, and Zionist groups took the opportunity to supply money and fake documents in order to get Jews classified as Germans and removed from Poland to Germany on their way to Palestine. Fit young males were frequently kept behind for labour service. But these were a small minority, and the sheer scale of the deportations overwhelmed the authorities, not least as Hungary, though officially a former enemy state, jumped on the expulsionist bandwagon, too.

By 1947, American officials were complaining about the chaos and warning that it was time to stop regarding 'occupied Germany as a waste-paper basket with a limitless capacity for the unwanted waste of the world'. Germany had its own massive problems of reconstruction, with towns and cities devastated by Allied bombing during the war, inadequate supplies of food and fuel, rampant inflation under the influence of a flourishing black market and widespread malnutrition and high rates of disease and mortality amongst the German population, especially during the hard winter of 1946–7. Millions of expellees were severely exacerbating these problems and diverting scarce resources from their solution at a time when the Western Allies were beginning to worry about the appeal of Communism to the beleaguered Germans and starting to think that it was more important to rebuild Germany's economy and society rather than to continue to punish its people for the crimes of Nazism.

Many Allied officials were outraged at the terrible conditions the deportees had to endure in the camps and on the transit trains. And with the rapid deepening of anti-Communist sentiments in the United States as the Cold War took hold on policy and opinion and East-Central Europe fell under Stalinist dictatorships imposed by the Soviet Union, the expellees came to be defined, as the head of the US Displaced Persons Commission declared, not as potential 'fifth columnists' but as 'oppressed victims of a Godless dictatorship'.

The expulsions left a gaping hole in the societies from which so many millions had been so hurriedly removed. Farmland was left abandoned, houses unoccupied, and there were even (as the London *Times* correspondent reported on a tour of the Sudetenland in the summer of 1947) 'whole villages without an inhabitant'. In one Czech district, twenty-two villages out of a total of twenty-nine were allowed to fall derelict, and in many areas farmland was converted to forest. The deserted areas descended into looting, banditry, violence and crime. The Czech and Polish governments lost control of the redistribution of confiscated German properties, and government ministers often took over German villas for their own private occupation. Often the same people became rich, as *The Economist* magazine noted in July 1946, 'by looting the property first of murdered Jews and then of expelled Germans'. Red Army troops looted and plundered as well, and gunfights were reported between units squabbling over abandoned German property. As settlers gradually came in, the inducements they were offered by their governments proved insufficient, and the evacuated areas became bywords for agricultural poverty and industrial decay.

Astonishingly, however, the millions of ethnic German expellees, far from becoming a disruptive element in postwar West German society, integrated seamlessly into it within a few years. Of course the vast majority were angry and resentful and desperate to return to their former homes, and the pressure group they founded, the *Bund der Heimatvertriebenen und Entrechteten* (literally the League of People Driven from their Homes and Deprived of their Rights) soon began to exert an influence in West German politics. But West German Chancellor Konrad Adenauer cleverly took the wind from its sails by raising a new tax, the so-called *Lastenausgleich*, to compensate the expellees for their losses, setting up a special Ministry to deal with them, and giving them eligibility for social insurance.

In foreign policy Adenauer vociferously demanded the return of the territories annexed by Germany's eastern neighbours and insisted on the expellees' right of return. He realised that these demands were unrealistic, but he persisted with them because he knew they won him the expellees' political support. Massive propaganda underlining their sufferings helped create a feeling of sympathy among West Germans and aided integration. Above all, however, the so-called 'economic miracle' in West Germany gave them, in little more than a decade, a much better material life than they had ever enjoyed before. Initially housed in camps, they were given help by the churches (whose role is underestimated by Douglas) and by the state, and benefited from the massive programme of home building. By the early 1960s their unemployment rate had fallen to little more than the average in West Germany as a whole.

Yet the expulsions left a legacy of bitterness and resentment that endures to the present day. Douglas rightly dismisses claims that they were carried out humanely, or that they were justified because the expellees were themselves guilty of atrocities against the occupied populations of Eastern Europe under Nazism, or that they were inevitable consequences of mass popular hatred against Germans triggered by the brutality of Nazi rule. On the contrary, they were the product of political machinations and government policies that could have been prevented or reversed. Carefully avoiding the use of the voluminous and self-evidently biased materials produced by expellee organisations and indeed by the Adenauer government, he uses Polish, Czech and

Allied sources to drive home his argument with conviction. 'Expulsions,' he concludes, 'are not practicable unless they are carried out quickly; and if they are carried out quickly, they cannot be carried out humanely.'

Recent proposals for the creation of 'ethnically homogeneous' populations in Bosnia, Serbia and Croatia, for example, are recipes, says Douglas, for a repeat of the disaster that befell Central Europe at the end of the Second World War. And though he does not say so, a lesson of this book is surely that the principle of national self-determination proclaimed at Versailles in 1919 led to untold suffering in Europe during the following thirty years – suffering that underlines the need for all states and societies to be tolerant of ethnic, religious and other minorities rather than trying to expel, convert or suppress them. This important, powerful and moving book should be on the desk of every international policy-maker as well as every historian of twentieth-century Europe. Characterised by assured scholarship, cool objectivity and convincing detail, it is also a passionate plea for tolerance and fairness in a multicultural world.

27. URBAN UTOPIAS

In 1941, the architect Hans Stosberg drew up ambitious plans for a new model town to be constructed on the latest lines, with monumental public buildings grouped around a central square and leafy boulevards branching off a central avenue leading to the factory complex that would provide the bulk of the work for a population eventually estimated at 80,000. There were to be twelve schools, six kindergartens, twenty sports fields, swimming pools, offices, banks, shops, and a number of satellite settlements, each also constructed around a central square and equipped with similar public buildings and modern amenities. The whole conglomeration was to form an 'urban landscape', divided into cell-shaped districts each forming its own sub-community within the overall structure of the town. Houses, or 'people's dwellings' as they were called, were to be supplied with central heating, garages, gas cookers, laundries and vegetable gardens. The old idea of a city as a concentration of densely populated buildings packed into a townscape of narrow streets and winding alleyways was to be superseded by the modern concept of a spread-out complex of roads and buildings that merged seamlessly into the natural environment. Funds duly poured in from the government and businesses vied for a favoured place in the new urban landscape. To celebrate the start of construction, Stosberg had special greetings cards made for the New Year in 1942, which he sent out to friends, colleagues and acquaintances. The words below the picture proudly announced: 'Birth of the new German town of Auschwitz'.

Stosberg proclaimed in January 1943 that his purpose in building the town was 'to provide German people with an expanse of soil that can become a stretch of home earth for their children and themselves'. Recently incorporated into Hitler's Reich, Auschwitz and the surrounding area had been inhabited by an inconvenient mixture of Poles and Jews before Stosberg began his project. Some 5,000 Jews were arrested and deported to the ghettos of Sosnowitz and Bendzin and, no doubt, in due course, murdered. The employees of the IG Farben chemicals factory that was to provide work for the Germans coming into the town lined the streets to see them go. The Poles – 90 per cent of the remaining 7,600 inhabitants – were examined and if they showed no physical signs of being racially German, such as blond hair or a long skull, they were dispossessed and deported, too. By October 1943 an initial population of 600 Reich Germans had expanded tenfold.

But the countrified urban idyll they had been promised did not materialise. Construction was slow, the water supply and sewage disposal system did not work properly, conditions were insanitary and there was the repeated irritation of the sweetish smell of burning flesh wafting over from the nearby extermination camp at Auschwitz-Birkenau. But on the whole, relations between the townspeople, the ever-expanding IG Farben factory and the SS cohorts who ran the nearby camp, remained cordial. In March 1943, the camp SS officers even invited the settlers to a 'communal feast followed by entertainments in the afternoon'. While the forced labourers in the IG Farben camp at nearby Monowitz and the two camps at Auschwitz were succumbing to diseases caused by malnutrition, lice-borne spotted fever, beatings, shootings and gassings, 200 of the German inhabitants of the new town celebrated the New Year in 1943 at the Ratshof pub on the town square, eating their way through goose liver, blue carp in aspic, roast hare roulade and pancakes, washed down with numerous bottles of German sparkling wine.

Auschwitz was in many ways the model of what Nazi town planners looked forward to in the postwar world, above all in the German east:

a new urban landscape inhabited by ethnic Germans, who managed vast factory enterprises worked by forced labour from Slavs and other supposedly inferior racial groups, bordered by extermination facilities designed to deal with the expendable, the hostile and the racially alien. Part of the purpose of dividing the new town into small community cells was also to make it easier for the Nazi regime to control the population through locally based officials such as the so-called 'Block Wardens', at least according to one later critic of the concept. It was not only the grandiose public buildings to which he was referring when Hitler himself remarked, 'our buildings are built to reinforce our authority'.

The new model settlement of Auschwitz offered more than living space and employment to Germans and opportunities for the assertion of authority and control to the Nazi Party. Its spread-out design meant it would be less vulnerable than conventional cityscapes to attacks from the air. Thousands of Germans flocked to the area from Hamburg, Essen, Cologne and other cities damaged by the strategic bombing offensive in 1943. Ever since the First World War, the widespread belief that cities would be totally annihilated by aerial bombardment in the next major European conflict had inspired architects and city planners to think of how to build cities that would be less vulnerable to attack from above. 'The war of the future', declared one German architect in 1934, marked 'the death sentence for cities in their present-day form'. The answer lay in the 'intermeshing of cities with the surrounding countryside'. The modernist French architect Le Corbusier claimed in similar fashion that 'fear of aerial torpedoes' would lead to 'the complete transformation of cities, through their demolition and reconstruction'. 'Ideally,' wrote a German air raid protection official, 'cities should be rebuilt from scratch.'

With the massive destruction wrought on so many of Europe's cities by the bombing offensives of the Second World War, many town planners saw their opportunity to put their ideas into effect. 'The city of the last century,' said the German architect Konstanty Gutschow on 2 February 1944, 'spread out in a never-ending, uninterrupted sea of houses, the object of our impotent rage as urban planners, has now been overtaken by its dreadful fate.' It was not only German town planners who descended on Europe's devastated cities like vultures on a half-eaten corpse. The Polish Jan Chmielewski, looking at the ruins of Warsaw after his escape from the Majdanek concentration camp, expressed his 'relief' after having been compelled over the previous decades to witness 'chaotic growth ... devoid of any planning'. The City Architect of Coventry saw the destruction of the city by German bombers as 'an opportunity to be grasped with both hands'. Lewis Mumford, a leading American critic of urbanism, even complained in 1942 that 'the demolition that is taking place through the war has not yet gone far enough', and urged society to 'continue to do, in a more deliberate and rational fashion, what the bombs have done'.

In *A Blessing in Disguise*, a lavishly illustrated volume published to accompany a major exhibition held in Hamburg in August and September 2013, a number of architectural historians have come together to explore the relationship between aerial warfare and town planning in Europe during the 1930s and 1940s. The many maps and plans reprinted in colour in the book, a high proportion of them never previously published, testify to the enthusiasm with which planners went about their work. Their utopian schemes stood, of course, in a long tradition of planning in the wake of urban catastrophe, the most famous example being Sir Christopher Wren's plans for the reconstruction of London following the Great Fire of 1666. Fully aware of this tradition, the authors have included a lengthy contribution on the city of Hamburg, Germany's second-largest after Berlin, which was heavily damaged in its own Great Fire in 1842, putting postwar reconstruction into a deep historical context. The task of rebuilding was entrusted to an Englishman familiar with Wren's plans, the engineer William Lindley, who spoke German, and was at the time managing the construction of one of Germany's earliest railway lines, close by the damaged city.

Narrow streets were broadened, partly to give any future fire diminished opportunity to spread, and new streets were cut through the remains of many old alleyways. A second catastrophe hit Hamburg half a century later in the form of a cholera epidemic that killed some 10,000 people in the space of six weeks, the only city in Western Europe to be seriously affected by the disease at this late stage in cholera's history. The epidemic itself had been partly caused by the displacement of 20,000 harbour workers and their families to make way for new warehouses on the waterfront in the 1880s, who (contrary to the authors' claims) were not 'relocated' but were simply thrown out of their dwellings, causing massive overcrowding elsewhere and facilitating the rapid spread of the epidemic when it arrived in 1892. 'Slum clearance' on a comparable scale followed on from the epidemic but, again contrary to the authors' assertions, this was not because the houses and tenements in question were unhealthy (though they were), but because their inhabitants had taken the lead in a massive dock strike four years later, in 1896: this was the moment when the redevelopment began, not 1892, after the epidemic. 'Slum clearance' was seldom purely altruistic; political calculation often weighed heavily in the decision to undertake it.

The alleged centres of crime and left-wing radicalism in Hamburg's 'Alley Quarters' continued to be cleared during the following decades, to make way for large and ugly office blocks (the ugliest of all being the much-praised eyesore of the *Chilehaus*), reflecting a more general change in urban spatial structures in the late nineteenth and early twentieth centuries. Housing was moving out of city centres, which were being taken over by commercial buildings. Planners sought to take advantage of this process; business interests trumped them. In Germany, however, the planners saw their opportunity with the coming of the Third Reich. Hamburg was once more to be remoulded, this time as the Nazi state's gateway to the world. Its area expanded in size by the incorporation of outlying towns and villages in 1937, the city was intended to host some of Hitler's most grandiose construction projects, including a new regional headquarters for the Nazi Party housed in a skyscraper taller than the Empire State Building and a suspension bridge over the River Elbe longer than the Golden Gate ('the greatest bridge in the world', as Hitler called it). A parade ground would provide the opportunity for 100,000 people to gather to hear the Führer speak, and the whole redesigned city would be ringed by a grand new autobahn.

The plan was put into law in 1939 but never came to anything. The ground was too soft for the skyscraper, and work on the bridge came to a halt because of the war. Other, no less ambitious plans for the city envisaged the introduction of more green spaces (replacing working-class districts where former Communists and Social Democrats, diehard opponents of Nazism, lived), the rationalisation of the transport system and the disaggregation of the population into low-density urban cells. The planners were still at work in May 1945, drawing lines across their maps just as Hitler was moving non-existent armies across his, in the final, catastrophic stage of the war.

By this time, not much was left of Hamburg, which had been subjected to some of the most destructive raids of the war in July and August 1943. Thirty-five million cubic metres of rubble had to be cleared away (in the much larger capital, Berlin, the quantity was fifty-five). Planners like Fritz Schumacher reiterated their old idea of a city broken up into semi-rural community cells. In Marseilles, indeed, this idea had already been at least partially put into effect during the war, shortly after the Germans invaded the Free Zone of France in November 1942. The Nazis abominated the colourful mixture of races they found in the narrow alleyways and tenements of the area immediately north of the Vieux Port. It was a 'pigsty', and it was demolished at the beginning of 1943 on the orders of Heinrich Himmler. Four thousand Jews were deported to Auschwitz and the other inhabitants of the district expelled. To justify this drastic action, the Germans claimed they were adhering to a prewar urban plan drawn up by the French architect Eugène Beaudouin. In this case, destruction from the air proved unnecessary. New boulevards, highways and modern buildings replaced the picturesque squalor of the ancient settlement, much to the subsequent regret of those who eventually moved back in. A quarter formerly teeming with life had lost its soul.

Doubtless something like this would have happened in many European cities had the planners got their way. Yet for most European cities, the main priority after the war was to build housing for the people made homeless by bombing raids. If possible, ruins were patched up where they stood. Cheap housing was thrown up too rapidly to take account of long-term planning. Property rights frequently obstructed plans for the reconfiguration of streets and squares. More importantly, many Europeans felt the need to restore normality by rebuilding cities as they had been before the war. 'We cannot be reconciled to the destruction of our architectural heritage,' declared a senior Warsaw official in 1946: 'We will rebuild it from the foundations up to hand down to later generations.' The city centre of Frankfurt was rebuilt as it had stood, including new half-timbered houses on the Römerberg made to look just like the ones destroyed by the bombs. Some cities, like Rotterdam, were reconstructed on a new plan, but where planning utopias came into being, the results were not always popular. The town centre of the planned new town of Cumbernauld, near Glasgow, was voted the worst building in Britain in 2005, when the town's inhabitants expressed a strong desire to see it demolished. The book reproduces many of the soulless planning grids of the postwar era, with box-like dwellings arranged in neat rows on either side of broad motorways, separated by what Mrs Thatcher subsequently dismissed as 'windswept piazzas'.

Particular depths were plumbed by the Soviet Union, where ruined cities like Stalingrad (later renamed Volgograd) were provided with grand neo-classical public buildings arranged around a central square celebrating the heroism of the Red Army and the Soviet people during the war, while the bulk of the population were tucked away in wooden, plaster or slab-concrete barracks in the suburbs. Reconstruction officials envisaged the building of half a million square metres of residential space a year, less than a third of which was to be equipped with running water or sewage disposal facilities, and only 30 per cent of which was divided into apartments. All designs were standardised under the 'unified state management of architecture'.

Standardisation might lower costs, but it did not make for anything more than the most basic kind of housing provision; the results can still be seen all over East-Central Europe, in constructions like the hideous apartment blocks that disfigure the outskirts of Bratislava or the cheaply built housing thrown up so hastily in former East German cities like Leipzig or Dresden.

In the city of Königsberg, the capital of East Prussia, raids by the RAF at the end of August 1944 generated a firestorm that incinerated a large part of the city. A lengthy siege by the Red Army completed the destruction, and at the end of the war fewer than twelve in a hundred of the city's buildings were still left standing. Forty-two thousand of Königsberg's inhabitants had been killed, and most of the rest had fled or been evacuated. The victorious Soviet regime deported the remaining Germans, razed most of the surviving buildings to the ground and renamed the city Kaliningrad (after the Soviet head of state), incorporating it into the USSR and Russianising it completely. Gradually a new Soviet city emerged, dominated by a thirty-storey 'House of the Soviets' surrounded by broad avenues lined with widely spaced multi-storey buildings. Planning here was designed not least to erase all traces of Königsberg's Prussian past, but it produced something 'a lot more like the "dreams" of wartime and prewar planners than most reconstructed cities of Western Europe'. At the centre, where there had been cobbled streets and quaint old buildings, there was an almost total absence of buildings, creating an alienating, anomic effect on anyone who stood there.

In Western Europe, monstrosities such as the Tour Montparnasse in Paris were intended to express a new spirit of optimism and progressivism after the disasters of the war. A similar spirit of optimism animated the 150 reports aimed at building on the ruins of bombed-out towns and cities in the United Kingdom with the 'City of Tomorrow' published between 1940 and 1952. A New Jerusalem, it was proclaimed, would rise on the ashes of the ruined cities of the past. The Blitz, as Julian Huxley remarked, was 'a planner's windfall'. In their plans for London, Ernö Goldfinger and E. J. Carter declared their aim was to give the capital 'order and efficiency and beauty and spacious-ness'. This would inevitably require further destruction: 'The blitz has cleared some sites and we must clear many more,' they warned ominously.

But as Raymond Postgate and G. D. H. Cole, two Labour Party intellectuals, complained in 1946, it had already become clear that anything that required compulsory purchase 'would be strenuously resisted by vested interests'. Ambitious plans for postwar Plymouth, sweeping away the confused street layouts of the damaged city and replacing them with tidy geometric patterns, similarly ran into the sands. The *Plan for Plymouth* proposed to relocate well-known structures away from the city centre because 'in a scheme of this mag-nitude ... some of the important buildings will interfere with the proposals'. But people wanted them to stay. The planners came up against popular opinion, and lost. 'The well-known English capacity for compromise will triumph,' one planner gloomily forecast, 'and we shall get a modern city dressed in "mediaeval" trappings: a city with a modernised street system incongruously lined with mock "medi-aeval" façades. There can be no doubt,' he concluded, 'that this is the kind of future city which is envisaged by many citizens.' He was right.

Yet such compromises often had to give way not merely to vested interests but also to the rapacity of postwar capitalism. In Germany, the materialism of the economic miracle led to the cancerous prolif-eration of massive department stores, each one built on exactly the same lines in whichever town or city it appeared in, so that a multi-storey Horten shop would be instantly recognisable by its silver-grey lattice façade, and its rivals Karstadt or Kaufhof by their own unique brand of design as well. These weren't merely put up on bomb sites, either: the medieval centre of the city of Konstanz, for example, undamaged by bombs because, the legend goes, the mayor during the war had the lights left on so the bombers would think it was in neutral Switzerland a few hundred yards away across the border, was disfig-ured by a huge department store planted down in the middle of the ancient townscape. In London, Frankfurt and other business centres, planners were unable to resist the Manhattanisation of cityscapes pushed forward by global capitalism. Only in a very few places, where there was no existing city, like Patrick Geddes's Tel Aviv, could urban planning be counted a success; where existing cities had to be rebuilt, the planners in the end were pushed aside by more powerful forces.

Defying all the best intentions of the planners, the motor car proved impossible to contain within urban confines, and towards the end of the century the public began to turn to public transport again. In Britain, the mass closure of railway lines in the wake of the Beeching Reports in the 1960s proved in retrospect to have been a colossal error. Conservation movements secured the preservation of older buildings such as St Pancras Station in London, following the demolition of its Victorian near-neighbour at Euston and its replacement with the grim, gloomy concrete sheds of today. Urban planning utopias have never been popular except with political elites. Peter Willmott and Michael Young, in their *Family and Kinship in East London*, published in 1957, painted a dire picture of community warmth in the old East End giving way to anomie and alienation in the new town to which bombed-out families were forced to move. In the end, the destruction of European cities in the war did not prove a blessing in disguise. The planners might complain about 'the disorder of the cities' with their 'great mess of houses and factories', and politicians polemicise 'against provincialism, against the worship of the old', but most people liked it that way.

The planners whose work is analysed and illustrated in *A Blessing in Disguise* were utopians, men who shared the radicalism and revolutionary ideals of the modernist age. But they were also in many significant ways part of a wider anti-urban movement, first thoroughly documented in Klaus Bergmann's book *Agrarromantik und Grossstadtfeindschaft* (Agrarian Romanticism and Hostility to the Big City, published in 1970 but unfortunately not referenced in this book). Many of them wanted to make the city more like the country. Had they been given their head, they would have done far more

damage than Sir Arthur Harris's bombers did to towns and cities in
Germany. The 'sustainable city' on which planning now focuses bears
some resemblance to the 'urban landscape' dreamed of by planners in
the 1930s and 1940s; yet its purposes are more modest and more realistic. Planning is needed if only to stop rampant and uncontrolled
urban development. A city such as Istanbul, where growth has gone
unchecked, has hardly a green space to offer its inhabitants, except in
a thin strip along the shores of the Bosphorus. No wonder people
there protested against the loss of the last of its parks.

On the whole, therefore, this book might be read as a critique of the
utopian modernist planners like Le Corbusier or Fritz Schumacher.
But it's hard for the reader to extract any consistent argument from its
pages. This is partly because the authors often ramble on at inordinate
length, repeat themselves, digress, and get stuck on side issues. There
is a virtual obsession, for instance, with Schumacher, whose name will
be known to very few non-German readers. And those readers will be
taken aback by the execrable standard of much of the English. We are
told, for instance, that the Nazis in Hamburg planned a 'belowground
railway' that 'provided connectivity', while residences were 'repurposed
as office buildings'. The Elbe was to be crossed by a 'suspended bridge'
with 'a new marked-out route for the bridge' provided by a 'tread road',
all this based on a 'new plan for the destroyed Hamburg'. The editing
is sloppy, too: D. H. Lawrence, for instance, is referred to simply as
'D.H.'! Thomas Sharp becomes at one point Dennis Sharp, planners
are said to warn people of 'the inevibility of progress', and Prussia is
confused with Russia, with the ludicrous result that the map on page
213 is said to illustrate 'former territory of Hamburg, now incorporated into Russia', which was hundreds of miles away, the other side of
Poland. Far more serious than these often comic slips, however, is the
fact that *Stadtlandschaft* (urban landscape, denoting the merger of
town and country in the new ruralised city) is repeatedly translated as
'regional city' thus depriving it of its obvious meaning by assimilating
it to the obscure term used in the USA by Lewis Mumford to describe
his own particular urban idea. This is all very unfortunate, for the

editors and authors have produced a highly instructive volume with some arresting contemporary quotes and a very large number of beautifully reproduced illustrations. Perhaps it would be best just to look at the pictures and give up the struggle to read the text.

28. ART IN TIME OF WAR

The looting of artefacts and cultural objects in times of war and violent political upheaval continues to arouse international concern in the twenty-first century just as it did in the twentieth. The plunder of archaeological sites in Egypt during the 'Arab Spring' (after they were abruptly abandoned by teams of archaeologists who were understandably concerned about their personal safety) is only the latest example. In Afghanistan and Iraq, too, war in the early twenty-first century was followed by the wholesale looting of museums and other sites, and it was not long before plundered objects began to find their way into collections in the West.

What can be done about the trade in looted art? How has society dealt with it in the past and how should it deal with it now? The history of this practice goes back far indeed, beginning perhaps with Jason and the Argonauts looting the Golden Fleece; and it continued with the Romans' habit of looting art from conquered cities in order to parade it through the streets of Rome in the ceremonial procession of the Roman triumph before putting it on show in the Forum. Cultural looting on a grand scale, with the stolen objects appropriated for public exhibition in the conqueror's capital, was in the ancient world an act of state designed to advertise the supremacy of the victor and underline the humiliation of the defeated. Here, these displays said, was a great power whose generals could beat rich and well-resourced rival powers; they advertised both to the victorious state's own citizens the rewards that could be gained from military conquest and to the rest of the world the inadvisability of coming into conflict with a state of such power and magnificence.

In Byzantium, the Hippodrome was adorned with looted art, and during the Fourth Crusade in 1204 the city itself was in turn looted by the crusaders, with large amounts of cultural booty taken back to Venice to adorn the Basilica of St Mark – most notably, of course, the four gilded horses of the Apocalypse which can be seen in the city today. During the Thirty Years War, Swedish troops looted book collections across Europe to stock the university library at Uppsala. In other examples, such as the sack of Magdeburg in 1631, when the army of the Catholic Holy Roman emperor massacred the inhabitants of the rebellious Protestant town, wanton destruction as well as the theft of riches was carried out by individual soldiers for their own personal enrichment. Magdeburg, in fact, caused widespread shock and dismay across Europe; while early modern lawyers such as Grotius conceded that, provided a war was being fought for a just cause, any property seized from the enemy became the property of the individual or state that took it, they also urged moderation and insisted that soldiers needed the express permission of their commanding officer before engaging in looting of any kind.

Private looting indeed has always gone on side by side with state-sponsored spoliation, but it has also aroused more disapproval. Most notorious of all was Thomas Bruce, seventh Earl of Elgin, British ambassador to the Ottoman court. He obtained permission from the sultan to take away old pieces of stone – the decorative frieze – from the Parthenon in Athens, then under Turkish rule, which he and his team did with such enthusiasm – and carelessness, breaking a number of the sculptures in the process – that several shiploads returned with them to Britain, where he intended to use them to decorate his home.

These are only the best known of a vast series of acquisitions of ancient archaeological remains in the nineteenth century, many of which were taken from territory occupied by the Ottoman Empire by purchase or agreement with the Ottoman authorities, often achieved through the use of bribery. Even at the time, Elgin's action ran into widespread criticism, in England as well as from the nascent Greek independence movement – supported by Lord Byron with some of his most biting satirical verses. Defenders of such acquisitions argued above all that they would not be safe if they remained *in situ*, since local people were already quarrying many of these sites for building materials; critics argued that the remains were far more seriously damaged by those who took them to pieces in order to carry off the most valuable parts.

Elgin's actions reflected his belief that educated Englishmen were the true heirs of classical civilisation, whose legacy permeated the minds of educated elites across Europe. This influence was nowhere greater than in revolutionary France, where Napoleon's victorious armies began concluding a series of treaties with conquered states across Europe, notably the Treaty of Tolentino, signed by the Pope in 1797, that allowed them to appropriate artworks to stock the Louvre Museum, founded in 1793. The loot carried off to Paris from all over Italy included the four horses of the Apocalypse from St Mark's in Venice and scores of ancient Greek statues, which entered the city in a Roman-style triumphal procession, accompanied by banners that read: 'Greece relinquished them, Rome lost them, their fate has changed twice, it will never change again'. They were joined in the procession by Renaissance paintings, live camels and lions, and the entire papal archive. All this underlined the claim of Paris to be the new Rome. Only the French, so the proclamation went, were civilised enough to appreciate such treasures. During the French invasion of Egypt in 1798, large quantities of antiquities were collected by a team of 167 scientists, scholars and artists shipped over to Africa by Napoleon. When he was defeated, the British claimed the collection – including the famous Rosetta stone – as booty themselves, validated by the Treaty of Alexandria, and put it in the British Museum, where it remains. No one seems to have objected.

Spoils (or the decision as to what to do with them) still went to the winner, and after Napoleon's defeat at the Battle of Waterloo, the

Prussians took back the artworks and cultural objects stolen from them by force. However, at this point, attitudes were already beginning to change. The Duke of Wellington, commander of the Allied armies, resisting pleas from Britain's Prince Regent to purchase some of the finer pieces for the royal collection, decided to arrange for the rest to be returned to the 'countries from which,' he wrote, 'contrary to the practice of civilised warfare, they had been torn during the disastrous period of the French Revolution and the tyranny of Bonaparte'. 'The same feelings which induce the people of France to wish to retain the pictures and statues of other nations,' he added, 'would naturally induce other nations to wish, now that success is on their side, that the property should be returned to their rightful owners.' In addition, he noted, returning it would underline to the French the scale and finality of their defeat, while keeping it in Paris might encourage them to believe that they were still the rightful masters of Europe.

In the event, only just over half of the looted objects were returned; the rest had been sent out to provincial museums in France, beyond the knowledge of the occupying Allied armies. These events sparked widespread debate across Europe. Paradoxically, they led to a new determination by European states to found or expand museums and to send out expeditions to acquire ancient cultural artifacts, following the lead of Napoleon rather than that of Wellington. This new development, among others, led, for example, to the acquisition of the Elgin Marbles by the British Museum in 1816. Nevertheless, Wellington's disapproval of military plunder did find an increasing number of supporters as the nineteenth century progressed. The duke himself thought that plunder distracted the troops from the military operations at hand and alienated the local population, which, as his experience in expelling Napoleon's forces from Spain had shown, it was very important to keep on one's side (at the time, Wellington had won over the locals by keeping his soldiers well disciplined, and in return, *guerrilleros* had fought alongside the British and the Portuguese).

This latter consideration played a significant role in the American Civil War, in which the Union wanted to avoid lasting damage to universities, museums and their collections in the South and so ordered that 'Classical works of art, libraries, scientific collections, or precious instruments, such as astronomical telescopes, as well as hospitals, must be secured against all avoidable injury, even when they are contained in fortified places whilst besieged or bombarded.' This was the first formal recognition that cultural property was different from other kinds of property and formed the basis for subsequent international declarations on the issue.

The rise of the nation-state brought with it a growing consciousness of the need to preserve the national heritage. The idea that the looting of cultural objects in wartime should be outlawed thus gained strength. European nations began to catalogue and protect their own artifacts and valuables, and to take steps to preserve what was increasingly regarded as the common European cultural heritage, above all in Greece and Italy. Even the destruction and looting of the Chinese emperor's Summer Palace in the Second Opium War in 1860 aroused widespread criticism in Europe. In 1874, the Brussels Declaration on the laws and customs of war outlawed the destruction of enemy property unless it was militarily required. These principles were elaborated at the first Hague Conference in 1899 and enshrined in the Hague Convention of 1907, to which Germany was a signatory (a significant point in view of events later in the twentieth century).

The Hague Convention explicitly banned what it called 'pillage' and declared that an occupying country must act as the trustee of the property and possessions of the defeated state and its citizens. The problem was, however, that modern artillery warfare, high-explosive shells and the sheer mass and weight of the military hardware then available made indiscriminate bombardment of towns and cities far more likely than ever before. Meanwhile, the advent of democracy and mass nationalism had begun to transform the nature of warfare into a conflict not between professional armies but between whole nations and peoples, in which attacking the civilian population by means of economic blockade or, indeed, bombardment from the ground or air was becoming tacitly accepted, even though with the state of military technology at the time, accurate pinpointing of targets to avoid cultural monuments was more or less impossible.

In the First World War, zeppelins bombed London, and German and Austro-Hungarian shelling destroyed the Serbian National Museum in Belgrade. It proved impossible to stop actions such as the destruction of the Catholic University of Leuven's library by the German army in 1914 along with sundry other, less famous monuments. On the other hand, actual looting, and in particular the theft or removal of works of art, was carried out on a fairly limited scale during the First World War, at least in comparison to what came after. The stalemate on the Western Front ensured that there was little opportunity for the occupying Germans to acquire works of art illicitly – Paris was well beyond the German zone, for instance – and few examples seem to be known of theft on the more mobile Eastern Front. The Hague Convention, signed so recently, still commanded some respect.

Not for long. The Second World War saw the plunder, looting and spoliation of cultural objects in Europe to a degree that dwarfed anything seen even in the French revolutionary and Napoleonic periods. The First World War may not have witnessed much state-sponsored theft, but the upheaval of the conflict opened up a new world of expropriation on a general scale. The Bolshevik Revolution in Russia was followed by the wholesale confiscation of private property. And in Germany, the Nazis believed they had a right to take what their enemies – notably the trade unions and the socialists – owned, without compensation, which they did as soon as they came to power, following this with the stage-by-stage expropriation of the property of Germany's Jews. In the struggle of all against all that Social Darwinism (at least in the version the Nazis believed in) preached, might was right, and the defeated had no rights either to property or even ultimately to life.

In practice, of course, such beliefs legitimised not only formal practices of looting and expropriation by the Nazi Party and the German state but also random yet very widespread acts of individual theft, blackmail and extortion by ordinary Party members, lower state officials, low-ranking stormtroopers and, during the war, members of the armed forces. Not surprisingly, the Third Reich soon became a byword for corruption. A few leading Nazis used their newly acquired fortunes to start building up large collections of art, both personal and institutional. Hermann Göring, for instance, owned ten houses, castles and hunting lodges, all provided and maintained at the taxpayers' expense. In all these locations, and particularly in his vast and ever-expanding principal hunting lodge at Carinhall, named after his deceased first wife, Göring wanted to display artworks, tapestries, paintings, sculptures and much else besides to emphasise his status as the Reich's second man.

By contrast, the Reich's first man, Adolf Hitler, made a point of avoiding ostentatious displays of personal wealth, preferring instead to accumulate an art collection for public use. Hitler had long planned to turn his hometown of Linz, in Austria, into the cultural capital of the new Reich, even drawing sketches for the new public buildings and museums he hoped to construct there. Berlin, too, had to have art museums suitable for its new status as 'Germania', the coming capital of the world. In 1939, Hitler engaged the services of an art historian, Hans Posse, a museum director in Dresden, to build the collection he needed for this purpose. Posse was provided with almost limitless funds, and by the middle of the war he was acquiring art objects (at manipulated prices and in defiance of individual countries' laws) from all over German-occupied Europe, amassing an almost incredible total of more than 8,000 by the time of his death.

In March 1938, the Nazis invaded Austria. While German soldiers and Austrian Nazis broke into the homes of Jews, stealing whatever they wanted, or stopped Jewish women on the streets and divested them on the spot of their fur coats and jewellery, the SS and Gestapo made straight for the homes of Vienna's most prominent Jewish families with orders to confiscate the contents. Top of the list were the

Rothschilds, whose collections were confiscated and then put up for auction to meet alleged tax liabilities – a common practice in the 1930s, made easier by 1939 through the imposition of special taxes and levies on German and Austrian Jews. Further regulations required Jewish emigrants to leave their assets behind if they emigrated, for appropriation by the Reich. After the conquest of France in 1940, too, the property of citizens who had fled the country also fell to the German Reich; the same applied eventually to all Jews deported from every occupied country in Europe to Auschwitz and other extermination camps in the east.

Looting was also widespread in countries inhabited by people the Nazis regarded as 'subhuman'. German culture to the Nazi mind was intrinsically superior to that of others, and inferior races were capable neither of sustaining their own heritage nor of properly safeguarding the products of other cultures. Thus, German cultural artefacts had to be repatriated. Such beliefs were reminiscent of the French view, under Napoleon, that only France had the right to safeguard European culture, but, of course, the Nazis took this credo much further, gave it a racial twist and applied it in an extreme version of the nationalist ideology of the nineteenth century to their own alleged heritage rather than that of the Classical world.

Following the German takeover in March 1939 of what remained of the Czech state after the Munich Agreement of the previous September, the invaders began confiscating objects without compensation from both public and private collections, including not only allegedly German items from the Czech National Museum and the library of Charles University in Prague but also from the palaces of the Habsburg, Schwarzenberg and Lobkowitz families. However, Hitler's treatment of Czechoslovakia was relatively mild compared to that meted out to the Poles, whose country he invaded in September 1939. Hitler vowed to wipe Polish culture and identity off the face of the earth. The German invaders carried off large quantities of cultural booty. Country houses along the invasion route were ransacked, and pressure was applied to their aristocratic owners to reveal the whereabouts of hidden treasures. On 16 December 1939, the German authorities ordered the compulsory registration of all artworks and cultural objects dating from before 1850, together with jewellery, musical instruments, coins, books, furniture and more from the same period, in the parts of Poland annexed to the Reich. These were duly confiscated, along with the vast majority of Polish property in these areas. The orders in effect constituted a licence to Germans to loot what they wanted.

Nazi legal expert Hans Frank ruled the remainder of Poland, decorating his headquarters with stolen artworks and shipping trophies back to his home in Bavaria (when American troops arrived there in 1945, they found a Rembrandt, a Leonardo, a fourteenth-century Madonna from Kraków, and looted vestments and chalices from Polish churches). Quarrels broke out as Hermann Göring tried to obtain pictures for himself, with Hans Frank objecting to the removal of prize finds from his headquarters. Perhaps this was not such a bad idea, however, since Frank had no idea how to display or preserve Old Masters, and was once reprimanded by Nazi art historian Kajetan Mühlmann for hanging a painting by Leonardo da Vinci above a radiator.

This process of looting and expropriation was repeated on an even-larger scale when Germany invaded the Soviet Union on 22 June 1941. Among the most famous of these items was the celebrated Amber Room given to Peter the Great by King Friedrich Wilhelm I of Prussia and subsequently augmented by further gifts from his successor. The Soviets had taken away all the furniture and movable items but left the amber panelling in place, and the room, installed in the Catherine Palace in the town of Pushkin, was dismantled and returned to Königsberg in East Prussia where it was put on display; most of it was in all likelihood destroyed in the battle for Königsberg at the end of the war (any items remaining in storage will by now have crumbled into dust). The Soviets, of course, had removed many cultural treasures out of reach of the invading armies. There were no great private collections left in the Soviet Union, since all had been confiscated by the Communist state, and the Germans never managed to conquer Moscow or St Petersburg; but much still remained to be looted. Two hundred and seventy-nine paintings were carried off from Kharkov, then the third largest city in the Soviet Union and the most populous the Nazis captured. Heinrich Himmler requisitioned considerable quantities to decorate and furnish his planned SS headquarters at Wewelsburg.

The scale of looting and expropriation practised by the Germans between 1938 and 1945 was thus unprecedented – and its legacy carried on far beyond the Nazi defeat. The Bolsheviks, who had used Communist ideology to justify the mass confiscation of private property after 1917, were not unfamiliar with the practice, and the Nazis' atrocities gave the opportunity, or excuse, for similar acts of plunder (both official and individual) by the incoming Red Army in the later stages of the war. In their hasty retreat, the Germans were forced to leave behind numerous collections, like others across Europe by this time placed for safekeeping in cellars, mines and other hiding places away from the heat of battle and the destructiveness of bombing raids. Soviet art recovery units roamed the countryside searching for these hoards, and those they succeeded in finding were carried off to a special repository in Moscow. One and a half million cultural objects were eventually returned to East Germany with the establishment of the German Democratic Republic as an ally, or client state, of the Soviet Union after 1949.

But a good deal went astray. The mayor of the north-west German town of Bremen, for example, had sent the city's art collection for safekeeping to a castle not far from Berlin, where Red Army troops found it. Arriving to inspect the collection, Viktor Baldin, a Russian architect enlisted in the Red Army, found the valuable works scattered around the countryside and did his best to recover them, in one case trading a Russian soldier a pair of boots for an etching by Albrecht Dürer. While Baldin kept the hundreds of drawings he had found, waiting for an opportunity to return his hoard to Bremen, other items from the same collection began to turn up on the art market at intervals; one dealer gave a Berlin woman 150 marks and a pound of coffee in return for a Cranach shortly after the war.

Eventually, when Mikhail Gorbachev inaugurated a more liberal regime in Russia, Baldin was able to petition the government to start negotiations for the collection's return. The Bremen City Council offered a panel from the Amber Room taken by a German soldier who had been employed in packing it away, and a small number of other items were handed over, but this was not enough, and the Russians asked why they should give back looted art to Germany when so many of their own cultural treasures had disappeared or been destroyed as a result of the actions of the invading Nazi armies. Indeed, in 1998 the Russian Duma declared all the looted art state property, requiring an act of parliament to return it to the Germans. Controversy continues to rage in Russian political circles, and, in the meantime, the bulk of the collection remains in the Hermitage; 1,500 items from the Bremen state museum are still reckoned to be missing.

In the chaos and destruction of the last months of the war, many valuable cultural objects of all kinds were lost or destroyed. The Western Allies, not least as the result of pressure on the military authorities by concerned art experts in Britain and the United States, were acutely aware of the need to preserve the cultural heritage of Europe in the final phase of fighting – even before the D-Day landings in 1944. Eisenhower's supreme headquarters established a Monuments, Fine Arts and Archives section, or MFAA, charged with locating and safeguarding cultural objects and preventing looting by Allied troops. US officials everywhere began compiling lists of stolen art to prevent Nazis from keeping the works hidden and profiting on the art market once the memory of the war had faded, MFAA units followed the army into liberated towns, scoured castles and mines, and began storing artworks preparatory to returning them to their original owners.

Artworks found in concealed locations in Germany were stored at the Munich Central Collecting Point. A major operation soon began to return the works. Lorries and trains carried thousands of paintings, drawings, sculptures, altarpieces and other objects across Europe back to their places of origin. The collecting points were finally closed down in 1951, when the remaining objects were handed over to a West

German agency, which returned another million finds to their owners, three-quarters of them outside Germany, over the next ten years. The rest, some 3,500 lots, were then distributed to German museums and other institutions from which they could, and can still, be claimed on presentation of the proper documentation. Inevitably, a large number of pieces remained unaccounted for – at least 20,000 of them according to one estimate. Most of these are small items – silver, jewellery, crockery and the like – or paintings and drawings by minor artists that are obscure enough to have escaped the attention of art experts. It may not have been simple to conceal well-known paintings by celebrated artists, but such items as these were far easier to hide away until the opportunity presented itself to bring them to sale. During the 1950s, art dealers were not particularly concerned about the provenance of the items they were asked to put up for auction: most of their effort went into establishing their authenticity. Large numbers of artworks were brought on to the market by people who had acquired them in a variety of dubious ways during the war, and then sold them on to institutions that in many cases bought them without knowing where they had come from.

Following the return of so much looted art to its owners in the aftermath of the war, the number of restitution actions and claims fell sharply during the 1950s. Furthermore, time limits on legal claims to the return of stolen goods existed, and still exist, in almost all European countries (Germany, thirty years; England, six years). Only two countries in Europe do not have such legislation: Poland, because of the sheer scale of the spoliation to which Polish collections were subjected during the war, and Greece, because of the Elgin Marbles. In essence, it became very difficult for former owners to obtain legal redress against the misappropriation of their possessions during a war that ended as long ago as 1945. The interest in restitution more or less died in the face of all these obstacles.

Then, in 1989–90, came the fall of the Berlin Wall and the collapse of Communism. As court cases for the restitution of houses and businesses seized by the Communists from 1949 onwards grew in number, compensation actions for loss and damage caused by the Nazi regime were launched, especially by former slave labourers. In the United States, and to some extent elsewhere as well, historical memory of the Nazi extermination of the Jews moved to the mainstream of national culture, with memorial museums being founded in many cities, and increased attention in the mass media, reaching perhaps a high point with Steven Spielberg's film *Schindler's List*. The 1990s saw the renewal of war-crimes trials in some countries (although few in number and not all successful). And Eastern European archives were opened for investigation, allowing many missing works to be traced.

Thus the art world reawakened to the problem of looted art after decades of treating it as a low priority. In December 1998, the new tone was set by the Washington Conference on Holocaust-Era Assets, hosted by the US Department of State with over forty national governments and numerous NGOs invited. The meeting built on the experience of the previous year's international conference set up to deal with the question of Nazi gold, including that taken from the dental fillings of extermination camp victims, much of which had found its way into the vaults of Swiss banks by the end of the war. The 1998 conference demanded the identification of all art confiscated by the Nazis, with a view to restoring it to its former owners on moral grounds even if they were not entitled to it legally. The commitments forged at the Washington Conference were followed up by similar agreements made by art gallery and museum directors. There have been resolutions by international bodies such as the Council of Europe to similar effect. In this climate, the chances of claimants successfully securing the return of looted art were dramatically increased.

Considering the favourable environment for looted art's return, many expected museums and galleries in the UK and elsewhere to be inundated with claims. But this has not happened. In many cases, the trail has gone cold, and evidence is almost by definition hard to obtain since the cases in which claims were clear were often settled in the immediate aftermath of the war. Often the original owners are dead, and sometimes their heirs had been killed by the Nazis as well. Entire families perished in very large numbers in Auschwitz and the other death camps, and while institutions, museums and galleries possessed the knowledge, the resources and the evidence to mount actions to try and regain what they had lost, the same was seldom true of individuals. So only a small fraction of the artworks identified by museums and other bodies as of uncertain provenance during the years 1933 to 1945 have actually attracted claims. The UK Spoliation Advisory Panel set up in 2000 by the Department for Culture, Media and Sport has dealt with little more than one case a year since then, though the steady trickle of claims shows no sign of drying up. In view of this trend, other countries such as the United States have been reluctant to follow suit and set up similar public bodies.

What is the future of preservation and restitution, then? As far as art taken from one country by another is concerned, as a general principle there is clearly a clash between any nation's need to preserve and display its own cultural heritage and the global community's need to learn about other cultures through universal museums like the Metropolitan or the British Museum. The way forward is surely to accept the validity of the universal museum, but to make exceptions where an object has been stolen relatively recently, or where it is of overwhelming cultural and historical importance to the nation or region from which it has been, whether legally or illicitly, removed.

In the process of righting the wrongs of the past, it is clearly not possible to achieve anything like adequate restitution on a global scale. The major thrust of the restitution effort has been directed towards reparation for the crimes committed by the Nazis, not least because the survivors and their immediate heirs are still among us. As Michael Marrus remarked in his recent study, *Some Measure of Justice* (2009), 'the Holocaust restitution campaign arose in highly unusual circumstances, unlikely to be replicated and unlikely therefore to affect other campaigns for justice for historic wrongs'. In the end, as he says:

Restitution is more about the present than about the past: it speaks to the survivors who are still among us ... to the society at large for which such issues may be said to matter ... and to a world in which injustice and wrongdoing are still too common – but for which, at the very least, we should have mechanisms available, when the carnage ends, to seek some measure of justice.

While there is a sincere and to some degree effective worldwide effort to restore art looted in the Nazi period, however, the international community has been signally unsuccessful in preventing looting and destruction from occurring during and immediately after new military conflicts. While there is now a mass of international legislation in place to preserve cultural artifacts in times of war, it is still very difficult to enforce it effectively. International intervention in conflicts like the Balkan wars of the 1990s is obviously difficult to organise and slow to implement. By the time it takes place, it may be too late. In the wake of the disintegration of Yugoslavia, Serbian forces deliberately shelled the public library in Sarajevo in an attempt to obliterate the cultural and historical memory of Bosnia, while Croatian gunners knocked down the historic and symbolic bridge at Mostar and vandalised Serbian Orthodox churches in the places they conquered.

In the chaos following the invasion of Iraq by US and allied troops in the early twenty-first century, the motivation for looting and destruction was not cultural genocide but private gain, coupled with military indifference. As the reporter Robert Fisk noted:

I was among the first to enter the looted Baghdad archaeological museum, crunching my way through piles of smashed Babylonian pots and broken Greek statues. I watched the Islamic library of Baghdad consumed by fire – fourteenth- and fifteenth-century Korans embraced by flames so bright that it hurt my eyes to look into the inferno. And I have spent days trudging through the looters' pits and tunnels of Samaria, vast cities dug up, their precious remains smashed open – thousands upon thousands of magnificent clay jars, their necks as graceful as a herons, all broken open for gold or hurled to one side as the hunters burrowed ever deeper for ever older treasures.

As Fisk explains: 'Of 4,000 artefacts discovered by 2005 from the 15,000 objects looted from the Baghdad Museum two years earlier, a thousand were found in the United States ... 600 in Italy', many of them pillaged by order from private collectors and their agents. Greed, he noted, had been globalised. It is hard to resist the comparison with 1945, when the careful preparations made by the MFAA ensured that Europe's cultural heritage was largely preserved and its looted assets returned to their rightful owners.

It is vital to learn the lessons of the Second World War and put effective arrangements in place in advance of future fighting to rescue and restore cultural objects and prevent looting. Such arrangements were not made in Iraq in 2003, and the devastation was vast. The international community cannot prevent looting and destruction in the course of civil unrest, but it can take steps to minimise it in cases of inter-state conflicts. Above all, the art and museum world needs to be more vigilant in monitoring the trade in looted goods in the wake of conflicts such as those in Iraq or Afghanistan, and law enforcement agencies need to step in with sanctions against those who encourage – or benefit – from it. In a globalised world, every state has, as the Hague Convention urged more than a century ago, a duty to act as the trustee of the culture of all nations, not just its own. This is one of many reasons why the memory of Nazi Germany and its crimes remains alive, and will rightly continue to do so for the foreseeable future.

ACKNOWLEDGEMENTS

The author is grateful to Dr Victoria Harris for her assistance in putting this volume together. Author and publisher are grateful for permission to reprint the following articles:

1. 'Spot and Sink'. Review of David Stevenson, *With Our Backs to the Wall. Victory and Defeat in 1918* (Penguin/Allen Lane, 2011), in *London Review of Books* 33/24 (15 December 2011), 31–2.

2. 'Gruesomeness is my Policy'. Review of Sebastian Conrad, *German Colonialism: A Short History* (Cambridge University Press, 2011), in *London Review of Books* 34/3 (9 February 2012), 35–7.

3. 'The Scramble for Europe'. Review of Shelley Baranowski, *Nazi Empire: German Colonialism and Imperialism from Bismarck to Hitler* (Cambridge University Press, 2010), in *London Review of Books* 33/4 (3 February 2011), 17–19.

4. 'The Life and Death of a Capital'. Review of Thomas Friedrich, *Hitler's Berlin: Abused City* (Yale University Press, 2012), in *The Book: An Online Review at The New Republic* (27 September 2012).

5. 'Social Outsiders in German History: From the Sixteenth Century to 1933', in Robert Gellately and Nathan Stoltzfus (eds), *Social Outsiders in Nazi Germany* (Princeton University Press, 2001), 20–44.

6. 'Coercion and Consent in Nazi Germany', *Proceedings of the British Academy* 151 (2006), 53–81, published by Oxford University Press.

7. 'How Willing Were They?' Review of Peter Fritzsche, *Life and Death in the Third Reich*, (Harvard University Press, 2008) in *New York Review of Books* LV/11 (26 June 2008), 59–61; 'All Hailed: The Meaning of the Hitler Salute'. Review of *The Hitler Salute: On the*

Meaning of a Gesture, by Tilman Allert, translated from the German by Jefferson Chase (Metropolitan Books, April 2008) in *The New York Sun*, 16 April 2008; 'Parasites of Plunder?' Review of Götz Aly, *Hitler's Beneficiaries: Plunder, Racial War, and the Nazi Welfare State* (Metropolitan Books, 2007), in *The Nation*, 284/2 (8/15 January 2007), 23–8.

8. 'Thank you, Dr Morell'. Review of *Was Hitler Ill? A Final Diagnosis*, by Hans-Joachim Neumann and Henrik Eberle, translated by Nick Somer (Polity Press, 2013), in *London Review of Books*, 35/4 (21 February 2013), 37.

9. 'Adolf and Eva'. Review of Heike B. Görtemaker, *Eva Braun: Life with Hitler* (Knopf, 2011) in *The National Interest* 115 (Sept./Oct. 2011), 76–86.

10. 'Prophet in a Tuxedo'. Review of *Walther Rathenau. Weimar's Fallen Statesman*, by Shulamit Volkov (Yale University Press, 30 April 2012) in *London Review of Books*, 34/22 (22 November 2012), 20–2.

11. 'Immoral Rearmament'. Review of Adam Tooze, *The Wages of Destruction: The Making and Breaking of the Nazi Economy* (Viking, 2006), in *New York Review of Books* LIV/20 (20 December 2007), 76–81.

12. 'Autoerotisch'. Review of Bernhard Rieger, *The People's Car: A Global History of the Volkswagen Beetle* (Harvard University Press, 2013), in *London Review of Books* 35/17 (12 September, 2013), 35–7.

13. 'Nothing They Wouldn't Do'. Review of Harold James, *Krupp: A History of the Legendary German Firm* (Princeton University Press, 2012), in *London Review of Books* 34/12 (21 June 2012), 21–4.

14. 'Tainted Money?', *Times Higher Education* (16 March 2011), 41–4; see also correspondence in *THE* (14 April 2011), 38. An Exchange: 'Toepfer and the Holocaust', *Standpoint* 35 (November 2011), 16–17; revised, with additional material.

15. 'Kisses for the Duce'. Review of Christopher Duggan, *Fascist Voices: An Intimate History of Mussolini's Italy* (Bodley Head, 2012), and Paul Corner, *The Fascist Party and Popular Opinion in Mussolini's Italy* (Oxford University Press, 2012), in *London Review of Books* 35/3 (7 February 2013), 6–8.

16. 'The Mistakes'. Review of Zara Steiner, *The Triumph of the Dark:*

European International History 1933–1939 (Oxford University Press, 2011), in *The Book: An Online Review at The New Republic* (1 September 2001).

17. 'The German Foreign Office and the Nazi Past', *Neue Politische Literatur* 56 (2011), 165–83.

18. 'Why It Happened the Way It Did'. Review of Ian Kershaw, *Fateful Choices: Ten Decisions That Changed the World, 1940–1941* (Penguin Press, 2007), in *The Nation* 284/22 (4 June 2007), 29–34.

19. 'Engineers of Victory'. Review of Paul Kennedy, *Engineers of Victory: The Problem Solvers Who Turned the Tide in the Second World War* (Random House, 2013), *New York Review of Books* LX/19 (5 December, 2013), 50–4.

20. 'Food Fights'. Review of Lizzie Collingham, *The Taste of War* (Penguin Press, 2012) in *The Nation* (16 April 2012), 27–32.

21. 'Defeat Out of Victory'. Review of David Stahel, *Kiev 1941: Hitler's Battle for Supremacy in the East* (Cambridge University Press, 2012) in *The Book: An Online Review at the New Republic*, 26 April 2012.

22. 'Into Dust'. Review of Ian Kershaw, *The End. Hitler's Germany 1944–45* (Allen Lane/Penguin, 2011), in *London Review of Books* 33/17 (8 September 2011), 11–13.

23. 'Let's Learn from the English'. Review of Mark Mazower, *Hitler's Empire* (Penguin/Allen Lane, 2008), in *London Review of Books* 30/18 (25 September 2008), 25–6.

24. 'Wie einzigartig war die Ermordung der Juden durch die Nationalsozialisten?', in Günter Morsch and Bertrand Perz (eds), *Neue Studien zu nationalsozialistischen Massentötungen durch Giftgas: Historische Bedeutung, technische Entwicklung, revisionistische Leugnung* (Metropol Verlag, 2011), 1–10 [revised and extended English-language version; published here for the first time].

25. 'Who remembers the Poles?'. Review of Tim Snyder, *Bloodlands: Europe between Hitler and Stalin* (Bodley Head, 2010), in *London Review of Books* 32/21 (November 2010), 21–2.

26. 'The Other Horror.' Review of R. M. Douglas, *Orderly and Humane: The Expulsion of the Germans After the Second World War* (Yale University Press, 2012), in *The Book: An Online Review at The New Republic*, 25 June 2012.

27. 'Disorderly Cities'. Review of Jörn Düwel and Niels Gutschow (eds),

A Blessing in Disguise: War and Town Planning in Europe, 1939–45 (DOM, 2013), in *London Review of Books* 35/23 (5 December 2013), 27–9.

28. 'Art in Time of War', *The National Interest* 113 (May/June, 2011), 16–26.

NOTES

CHAPTER 6. SOCIAL OUTSIDERS

1 For a useful overview, see Michael Burleigh and Wolfgang Wippermann, *The Racial State: Germany, 1933–1945* (Cambridge, 1991); the authors' general approach to the subject is discussed at the end of this chapter. A useful local collection was produced in 1986 by the Projektgruppe fur die vergessenen Opfer des NS-Regimes: Klaus Frahm et al. (eds), *Verachtet-Verfolgt-Vernichtet: zu den 'vergessenen' Opfem des NS-Regimes* (Hamburg, 1986).

2 Ulrich Herbert, *A History of Foreign Labor in Germany, 1880–1980* (Ann Arbor, MI, 1990), is the most useful overview; the broader question of German attitudes towards the Slavs is beyond the scope of the present chapter.

3 Richard van Dülmen, 'Der infame Mensch: Unehrliche Arbeit und soziale Ausgrenzung in der Frühen Neuzeit', in idem (ed.), *Arbeit, Frömmigkeit, und Eigensinn: Studien zur historischen Kulturforschung* (Frankfurt am Main, 1990), 106–40.

4 Wolfgang von Hippel, *Armut, Unterschichten, Randgruppen in der Frühen Neuzeit* (Munich, 1995), 32–43.

5 Richard J. Evans, *Rituals of Retribution: Capital Punishment in Germany, 1600–1987* (Oxford, 1996), 193–201.

6 Ibid., 56–64; see also Jutta Nowosadtko, *Scharfrichter und Abdecker: Der Alltag zweier 'unehrlicher Beruf' in der Frühen Neuzeit* (Paderborn, 1994); Gisela Wilbertz, *Scharfrichter und Abdecker im Hochstift Osnabrück: Untersuchungen zur Sozialgeschichte zweier 'unehrlicher' Berufe im nordwestdeutschen Raum vom 16. bis zum 19. Jahrhmdert* (Osnabrück, 1979).

7 Evans, *Rituals*, 122–3; Hippel, *Armut*, 96–101; Isabel V. Hull, *Sexuality, State, and Civil Society in Germany, 1700–1815* (Ithaca, NY, 1996), 349–50.

8   Evans, *Rituals*, 372–83.

9   K. Bott-Bodenhausen (ed.), *Sinti in der Grafschaft Lippe: Studien zur Geschichte der 'Zigeuner' im 18. Jahrhundert* (Munich, 1988); H. Lemmermann, *Zigeuner und Scherenschleifer im Emsland* (Sögel, 1986).

10 H. C. Erik Midelfort, *Mad Princes of Renaissance Germany* (Charlottesville, VA, 1994), 60–70.

11 Carsten Küther, *Menschen auf der Strasse: Vagierende Unterschichten in Bayern, Franken und Schwaben in der zweiten Hälfte des 18. Jahrhunderts* (Göttingen, 1983); idem, *Räuber und Gauner in Deutschland: Das organisierte Bandenwesen im 18. und frühen Jahrhundert* (Göttingen, 1976); Uwe Danker, *Räuberbanden im Alten Retch um 1700: Ein Beitrag zur Geschichte von Herrschaft und Kriminalität in der Frühen Neuzeit* (Frankfurt am Main, 1988).

12 The best coverage of this process is still that of Klaus Saul, 'Der Staat und die "Mächte des Umsturzes": Ein Beitrag zu den Methoden antisozialistischer Repression und Agitation vom Scheitern des Sozialistengesetzes bis zur Jahrhundertwende', *Archiv für Sozialgeschichte* 12 (1972), 293–350; and Alex Hall, '"By Other Means": The Legal Struggle against the SPD in Wilhelmine Germany', *Historical Journal* 17 (1974), 365–80. For the Weimar years, see the classic by Heinrich Hannover and Elisabeth Hannover-Druck, *Politische Justiz, 1918–1933* (Frankfurt am Main, 1966).

13 Jürgen Scheffler, 'Die Vagabundenfrage: Arbeit statt Almosen: Herbergen zur Heimat, Wanderarbeitsstätten, und Arbeiterkolonien', in *Wohnsitz: Nirgemdwo. vom Lebem und Überleben auf der Strasse*, Michael Haerdter (ed.) (Berlin, 1982), 59–70.

14 See Richard J. Evans, *Death in Hamburg: Society and Politics in the Cholera Years, 1830–1910* (Oxford, 1987), 99–100, for a brief description of the Elberfeld system; for police policy toward Gypsies in this period, see Michael Zimmermann, *Verfolgt, vertrieen, vernichtet: Die nationalsozialistische Vernichtungspolitik gegen Sinti und Roma* (Essen, 1989).

15 See Richard J. Evans, *Tales from the German Underworld: Crime and Punishment in the Nineteenth Century* (London, 1998), 166–212.

16 Dirk Blasius, *Der verwaltete Wahnsim: Eine Sozialgeschichte des Irrenhauses* (Frankfurt am Main, 1980); see also idem, '*Einfache Seelenstörung*': *Geschichte der deutschen Psychiatrie, 1800–1945* (Frankfurt am Main, 1994).

17 For one such example from shortly before the First World War, see Evans, *Rituals*, 477–84.

18 Anon. (ed.), *Eldorado: Homosexuelle Frauen und Männer in Berlin 1850 bis 1950. Geschichte, Alltag, und Kulttw* (Berlin, 1984); Magnus Hirschfeld, *Berlins drittes Geschlecht* (Berlin, 1905).

19 H. Stümke, *Homosexuelle in Deutschland: Eine politische Geschichte* (Munich, 1989); Angelika Kopecny, *Fahrende und Vagabunden: Ihre Geschichte, Überlebensküinste, Zeichen, und Strassen* (Berlin, 1980).

20 J. S. Hohmann, *Verfolgte ohne Heimat: Geschichte der Zigeuner in Deutschland* (Frankfurt am Main, 1990).

21 Martin Broszat, *Zweihundert Jahre deutsche Polenpolitik* (Frankfurt am Main, 1972), is still the best overview of the Polish question. For imprisonment, see Evans, *Tales from the German Underworld*, esp. 61–4.

22 Michel Foucault, *Discipline and Punish: The Birth of the Prison* (London, 1975).

23 See Daniel Pick, *Faces of Degeneration: A European Disorder, c. 1848–c. 1918* (Cambridge, 1989).

24 Evans, *Death in Hamburg*, 528–39; and Ute Frevert, *Krankheit als politisches Problem: Soziale Unterschichten in Preussen zwischen medizinischer Polizei und staatlicher Sozialversicherumg* (Göttingen, 1984).

25 Richard F. Wetzell, 'The Medicalization of Criminal Law Reform in Imperial Germany', in *Institutions of Confinement: Hospitals, Asylums, and Prisons in Western Europe and North America, 1500–1950*, Norbert Finzsch and Robert Jütte (eds) (Cambridge, 1996), 275–83.

26 Evans, *Rituals*, 434–45.

27 Henry Friedlander, *The Origins of Nazi Genocide: From Euthanasia to the Final Solution* (Chapel Hill, NC, 1995), 9; for prostitutes, see Evans, *Tales from the German Underworld*, 209, citing Kurt Schneider, *Studien über Persönlichkeit und Schicksal eingeschriebener Prostituierter* (Berlin, 1921), a work based on research carried out before the First World War.

28 Detlef Garbe, *Zwischen Widerstand und Martyrium: Die Zeugen Jehovas im 'Dritten Reich'* (Munich, 1982), 45–6.

29 Hans von Hentig, *Über den Zusammenhang zwischen dem kosmischen, biologischen, und sozialen Ursachen der Revolution* (Tübingen, 1920).

30 Michael Burleigh, *Death and Deliverance: 'Euthanasia' in Germany 1900–1945* (Cambridge, 1994), chap. 1.

31 Wolfgang Ayass, *'Asoziale' im Nationalsozialismus* (Stuttgart, 1995), 13–18. See also Klaus Scherer, *'Asoziale' im Dritter Reich* (Münster, 1990).

32 Nikolaus Wachsmann, *Hitler's Prisons: Legal Terror in Nazi Germany* (London, 2004), chap. 1.

33 Joachim S. Hohmann, *Robert Ritter und die Erben der Kriminalbiologie: 'Zigeunerforschung' im Nationalsozialismus und in Westdeutschland im Zeichen des Rassismus* (Bern, 1991); Burleigh and Wippermann, *The Racial State*, 113–17; Rainer Hehemann, *Die 'Bekämpfumg des Zigeunerunwesens' im Wilhelminischen Deutschland und in der Weimarer Republik 1871–1933* (Frankfurt am Main, 1987).

34 Günter Grau (ed.), *Homosexualität in der NS-Zeit: Dokumente einer Diskriminierung und Verfolgung* (Frankfurt am Main, 1993); Burkhard Jellonnek, *Homosexuelle unter dem Hakenkreuz: Die Verfolgung von Homosexuellen im Dritten Reich* (Paderborn, 1990), 37–50; Richard Plant, *The Pink Triangle: The Nazi War against Homosexuals* (New York, 1986).

35 Garbe, *Zwischen Widerstand und Martyrium*, chap. 1.

36 See Stümke, *Homosexuelle in Deutschland*, for details.

37 Künstlerhaus Bethanien (ed.), *Wohnsitz: Nirgendwo. vom Leben und vom Überleben auf der Strasse* (Berlin, 1982), 179–232.

38 Burleigh and Wippermann, *The Racial State*, 128–30; Sally Marks, 'Black Watch on the Rhine: A Study in Propaganda, Prejudice, and Prurience', *European Studies Review* 13 (1983), 297–334; Gisela Lebeltzer, 'Die "Schwarze Schmach": Vorurteile-Propaganda-Mythos', *Geschichte und Gesellschaft* 11 (1985), 37–58; Reiner Pommerin, 'Sterilisierung der Rheinlandbastarde': Das Schicksal einer farbigen deutschen Minderheit 1918–1937* (Düsseldorf, 1979).

39 Wolfgang Ayass, 'Vagrants and Beggars in Hitler's Reich', in *The German Underworld: Deviants and Outcasts in German History*, Richard J. Evans (ed.) (London, 1988), 210–37; Detlev Peukert, 'The Lost Generation: Youth Unemployment at the End of the Weimar Republic', in Richard J. Evans and Dick Geary (eds), *The German Unemployed: Experiences and Consequences of Mass Unemployment from the Weimar Republic to the Third Reich* (London, 1987), 172–93; Eve Rosenhaft, 'Organising the "Lumpenproletariat": Cliques and Communists in Berlin during the Weimar Republic', in Richard J. Evans (ed.), *The German Working Class, 1888–1933: The Politics of Everyday Life* (London, 1982), 174–219.

40 Lynn Abrams, 'Prostitutes in Imperial Germany, 1870–1918: Working Girls or Social Outcasts?' in Evans (ed.), *The German Underworld*, 189–209; Pommerin, *Sterilisierung der· Rheinlandbastarde*; and, for examples of the arbitrariness of diagnosis, Evans, *Rituals*, 526–36.

41 Karl Heinz Roth, ed., *Erfassung zur Vernichtung: Von der Sozialhygiene zum 'Gesetz über Sterbehilfe'* (Berlin, 1984).

42 Preamble to a never promulgated law of 1944 on the treatment of 'com-

munity aliens', quoted in Norbert Frei, *Der Führerstaat: Nationalsozialistische Herrschaft, 1933 bis 1945* (Munich, 1987), 202–8.

43 Detlev Peukert, 'The Genesis of the "Final Solution" from the Spirit of Science', in Thomas Childers and Jane Caplan (eds.), *Reevaluating the Third Reich* (New York, 1993), 234–52.

44 For these various arguments, criticised here, see Burleigh and Wippermann, *The Racial State*, 2.

CHAPTER 7. COERCION AND CONSENT

1 Karl Dietrich Bracher, *The German Dictatorship: The Origins, Structure and Consequences of National Socialism* (New York, 1970); Tim Mason, 'Intention and Explanation: A Current Controversy about the Interpretation of National Socialism', in Gerhard Hirschfeld and Lothar Kettenacker (eds), *The 'Führer State': Myth and Reality* (Stuttgart, 1981), 23–40.

2 Useful historiographical surveys include Ian Kershaw, *The Nazi Dictatorship: Problems and Perspectives of Interpretation* (fourth edition, London, 2000), and John Hiden and John Farquharson, *Explaining Hitler's Germany: Historians and the Third Reich* (second edition, London, 1989); classic studies include Franz Neumann, *Behemoth: The Structure and Practice of National Socialism 1933–1944* (New York, second edition, 1944); Martin Broszat, *Der Staat Hitlers: Grundlegung und Entwicklung seiner inneren Verfassung* (Munich, 1969); idem, et al. (eds), *Bayern in der NS-Zeit* (6 vols, Munich, 1977–83); Jeremy Noakes, 'The Oldenburg Crucifix Struggle of November 1936: A Case Study of Opposition in the Third Reich', in Peter D. Stachura (ed.), *The Shaping of the Nazi State* (London, 1983), 210–33; Tim Mason, *Social Policy in the Third Reich: The Working Class and the 'National Community'* (Providence, RI, 1993, first published in German in 1977). For the *Sopade* reports, see Klaus Behnken (ed.), *Deutschland-Berichte der Sozialdemokratischen Partei Deutschlands (Sopade) 1934–1940* (7 vols, Frankfurt am Main, 1980).

3 Klaus-Michael Mallmann and Gerhard Paul, 'Omniscient, Omnipotent, Omnipresent? Gestapo, Society and Resistance', in David F. Crew (ed.), *Nazism and German Society 1933–1945* (London, 1994), 166–96, at 174–7; Reinhard Mann, *Protest und Kontrolle im Dritten Reich: Nationalsozialistische Herrschaft im Alltag einer rheinischen Grossstadt* (Frankfurt am Main, 1987), 292; more generally, Robert Gellately, 'Die Gestapo und die deutsche Gesellschaft: Zur Entstehung einer

selbstüberwachenden Gesellschaft', in Detlef Schmiechen-Ackermann (ed.), *Anpassung, Verweigerung, Widerstand: Soziale Milieus, Politische Kultur und der Widerstand gegen den Nationalsozialismus in Deutschland im regionalen Vergleich* (Berlin, 1997), 109–21.

4   Eric A. Johnson and Karl-Heinz Reuband, *What We Knew: Terror, Mass Murder, and Everyday Life in Nazi Germany: An Oral History* (Cambridge, MA, 2005), 329–33 and jacket flap text; Robert Gellately, *Backing Hitler: Consent and Coercion in Nazi Germany* (Oxford, 2001), 14–16; Hans-Ulrich Wehler, *Deutsche Gesellschaftsgeschichte*, IV: *Vom Beginn des ersten Weltkrieges bis zur Gründung der beiden deutschen Staaten 1914–1949* (Munich, 2003), 614, 652.

5   Götz Aly, *Hitler's Beneficiaries: Plunder, Racial War, and the Nazi Welfare State* (translated by Jefferson Chase, New York, 2007), 28.

6   Wehler, *Gesellschaftsgeschichte*, IV, 675–6 (the section is entitled 'Die Konsensbasis von Führerdiktatur und Bevölkerung').

7   Bill Niven, *Facing the Nazi Past: United Germany and the Legacy of the Third Reich* (London, 2002), provides a balanced assessment.

8   Robert Gellately, 'Social Outsiders and the Consolidation of Hitler's Dictatorship, 1933–1939', in Neil Gregor (ed.), *Nazism, War and Genocide: Essays in Honour of Jeremy Noakes* (Exeter, 2005), 56–74, at 58 (also quoting Wehler, op. cit., 676); and idem, *Backing Hitler*, 257; Frank Bajohr, 'Die Zustimmungsdiktatur: Grundzüge nationalsozialistischer Herrschaft in Hamburg', in *Hamburg im 'Dritten Reich'*, herausgegeben von der Forschungsstelle für Zeitgeschichte in Hamburg (Göttingen, 2005), 69–131.

9   Wehler, *Gesellschaftsgeschichte*, IV, 380.

10   Gellately, 'Social Outsiders', 58.

11   For these arguments, see Richard J. Evans, *The Coming of the Third Reich* (London, 2003), 451–6, with further references; also Norbert Frei, 'Machtergreifung': Anmerkungen zu einem historischen Begriff', *Vierteljahrshefte für Zeitgeschichte* 31 (1983), 136–45; and Bracher, *The German Dictatorship*, 246–50.

12   Gellately, 'Social Outsiders', 58–60; November 1932 election results summarised in Evans, *The Coming*, 299, and analysed authoritatively in Jürgen W. Falter, *Hitlers Wähler* (Munich, 1991), esp. 34–8.

13   Gellately, 'Social Outsiders', 58 ('far fewer members of the SPD were "persecuted" in any way', i.e. compared to the Communists); Gellately's use of the inverted commas to distance himself from the term 'persecuted' suggests in any case that the persecution was largely a figment of the victims' imagination.

14　These and many other, similar incidents, are detailed in Evans, *The Coming*, 320, 341, 347, 360–1; for a good regional study, see Richard Bessel, *Political Violence and the Rise of Nazism; The Storm Troopers in Eastern Germany 1933–1934* (London, 1984).

15　Evans, *The Coming*, 341. Numerous documented examples of violence against Social Democrats and others (including, especially, Jews) were provided in the *Brown Book of the Hitler Terror and the Burning of the Reichstag* (London, 1933, ed. World Committee for the Victims of German Fascism, President Einstein). The *Brown Book* was not reliable on the Reichstag fire.

16　Dick Geary, 'Working-Class Identities in the Third Reich', in Gregor (ed.), *Nazism*, 42–55; Rüdiger Hachtmann, 'Bürgertum, Revolution, Diktatur – zum vierten Band von Hans-Ulrich Wehlers "Gesellschaftsgeschichte"', *Sozial. Geschichte* 19 (2004), 60–87, at 80; Geoff Eley, 'Hitler's Silent Majority? Conformity and Resistance under the Third Reich', *Michigan Quarterly Review* 42 (2003), 389–425 and 555–9.

17　Details in Evans, *The Coming*, 322–3, 363–6; also Martin Broszat, 'The Concentration Camps 1933–1945', in Helmut Krausnick et al., *Anatomy of the SS State* (London, 1968), 397–496, 409–11; more generally Günther Lewy, *The Catholic Church and Nazi Germany* (New York, 1964), 45–79.

18　Evans, *The Coming*, 367–74. The best account of the enforced dissolution of the non-Nazi political parties and the accompanying violence is still the heavily documented collection edited by Erich Matthias and Rudolf Morsey, *Das Ende der Parteien 1933: Darstellungen und Dokumente* (Düsseldorf, 1960), in which Friedrich Freiherr Hiller von Gaertingen's account of the Nationalists (the DNVP), on pp, 541–642, is particularly valuable.

19　Richard J. Evans, *The Third Reich in Power* (London, 2005), 31–6, with further references. For a well-documented narrative, see Heinz Höhne, *Mordsache Röhm: Hitlers Durchbruch zur Alleinherrschaft 1933–1934* (Reinbek, 1984).

20　Richard Bessel, 'The Nazi Capture of Power', *Journal of Contemporary History* 39 (2004), 169–88, at 182 (my italics).

21　Wehler, *Gesellschaftsgeschichte*, IV, 676; Hachtmann, 'Bürgertum', 80.

22　Gellately, 'Social Outsiders', 63–4.

23　Aly, *Hitler's Beneficiaries*, 29.

24　Johnson and Reuband, *What We Knew*, 354.

25　Ernst Fraenkel, *The Dual State: Law and Justice in National Socialism* (New York, 1941).

26 Ulrich Herbert, Karin Orth and Christoph Dieckmann, 'Die national-solzialistischen Konzantrationslager: Geschichte, Erinnerung, Forschung', in idem (eds), *Die nationalsozialistischen Konzentrationslager* (2 vols, Frankfurt am Main, 2002), I, 17–42, at 26.

27 Evans, *The Third Reich in Power*, 67–75; Richard J. Evans, *Rituals of Retribution: Capital Punishment in Germany 1600–1987* (Oxford, 1996), 620–45; Nikolaus Wachsmann, *Hitler's Prisons: Legal Terror in Nazi Germany* (New Haven, CT, 2004), esp. 165–83; Gerhard Fieberg (ed.), *Im Namen des deutschen Volkes: Justiz und Nationalsozialismus* (Cologne, 1989), 68. For the early camps, see Jane Caplan, 'Political Detention and the Origin of the Concentration Camps in Nazi Germany, 1933–1935/6', in Gregor (ed.), *Nazism*, 22–41.

28 Evans, *The Third Reich in Power*, 79, 85–7.

29 William Sheridan Allen, *The Nazi Seizure of Power: The Experience of a Single German Town, 1922–1945* (2nd ed., New York, 1984), 218–32.

30 Evans, *The Third Reich in Power*, 244–7.

31 The classic study of coercion on the shop floor is Mason, *Social Policy*, 266–74.

32 Detlef Schmiechen-Ackermann, 'Der "Blockwart": Die unteren Parteifunktionäre im nationalsozialistischen Terror- und Überwachungsapparat', *Vierteljahrshefte für Zeitgeschichte* 48 (2000), 575–602.

33 Dieter Nelles, 'Organisation des Terrors im Nationalsozialismus', *Sozialwissenschaftliche Literatur-Rundschau* 25 (2002), 5–28; Evans, *The Third Reich in Power*, 114–18, 272, 276, 485–6.

34 Johnson and Reuband, *What We Knew*, 359–60.

35 Otmar Jung, *Plebiszit und Diktatur: Die Volksabstimmungen der Nationalsozialisten: Die Fälle 'Austritt aus dem Völkerbund' (1933), 'Staatsoberhaupt' (1934) und 'Anschluss Österreichs' (1938)* (Tübingen, 1995); Theodor Eschenburg, 'Streiflichter zur Geschichte der Wahlen im Dritten Reich', *Vierteljahrshefte für Zeitgeschichte* 3 (1955), 311–8; Evans, *The Third Reich in Power*, 109–13.

36 For detailed evidence, see Evans, *The Third Reich in Power*, 109–13.

37 Johnson and Reuband, *What We Knew*, jacket flap copy.

38 Evans, *The Third Reich in Power*, 585–7.

39 Johnson and Reuband, *What We Knew*, 332, 335.

40 Ibid., 335.

41 Ibid., 325–45.

42 Claire Hall, 'An Army of Spies? The Gestapo Spy Network 1933–45', *Journal of Contemporary History*, 44 (2009), 247–65.

43 Bernward Dörner, 'NS-Herrschaft und Denunziation: Anmerkungen zu Defiziten in der Denunziationsforschung', *Historical Social Research* 26 (2001), 55–69; Werner Röhr, 'Über die Initiative zur terroristischen Gewalt der Gestapo – Fragen und Einwände zu Gerhard Paul', in Werner Röhr and Brigitte Berlekamp (eds), *Terror, Herrschaft und Alltag im Nationalsozialismus: Probleme der Sozialgeschichte des deutschen Faschismus* (Münster, 1995), 211–24; Gerhard Hetzer, 'Die Industriestadt Augsburg: Eine Sozialgeschichte der Arbeiteropposition', in Broszat et al. (eds), *Bayern*, IV, 1–234; Gisela Diewald-Kerkmann, *Politische Denunziation im NS-Regime oder die kleine Macht der 'Volksgenossen'* (Bonn, 1995); Evans, *The Third Reich in Power*, 96–118.

44 Gellately, 'Social Outsiders', 59.

45 Allen, *The Nazi Seizure of Power*, 218–32.

46 Evans, *The Third Reich in Power*, 37–8.

47 Ian Kershaw, *Popular Opinion and Political Dissent in the Third Reich: Bavaria, 1933–1945* (Oxford, 1983).

48 Goebbels's speech of 15 March 1933 in David Welch (ed.), *The Third Reich: Politics and Propaganda* (second edition, London, 2002), 173–4; on the effects of propaganda more generally, see the judicious assessment by Ian Kershaw, 'How Effective Was Nazi Propaganda?', in David Welch (ed.), *Nazi Propaganda: The Power and the Limitations* (London, 1983), 180–203.

49 Hetzer, 'Die Industriestadt Augsburg', 146–50; Schmiechen-Ackermann, 'Der "Blockwart"'; Evans, *The Third Reich in Power*, 22; Evans, *The Coming of the Third Reich*, 383.

50 Thus the arguments in Omer Bartov, *The Eastern Front 1941–1945: German Troops and the Barbarization of Warfare* (London, 1985); and idem, *Hitler's Army* (Oxford, 1991), dating these processes from the invasion of the Soviet Union onwards.

51 Richard J. Evans, *The Third Reich at War* (London, 2007), chap. 1, for details.

52 Dick Geary, 'Working-Class Identities in the Third Reich', in Gregor (ed.), *Nazism*, 42–55, at 52.

53 Peter Longerich, *'Davon haben wir nichts gewusst!': Die Deutschen und die Judenverfolgung 1933–1945* (Berlin, 2006), 313–29.

54 Gregor, 'Nazism', 20.

55 Mason, 'Intention and Explanation', 229, quoted in ibid.

56 Bessel, 'The Nazi Capture of Power', op. cit., 183.

CHAPTER 17. NAZIS AND DIPLOMATS

1   Donald M. McKale, *Curt Prüfer: German Diplomat from the Kaiser to Hitler* (Kent, OH, 1987).

2   Ibid., 179–87.

3   Donald M. McKale (ed.), *Rewriting History. The Original and Revised World War II Diaries of Curt Prüfer, Nazi Diplomat* (Kent, OH, 1988), 116. The diaries are now held in the Hoover Institution, Stanford, California.

4   Ibid., 132.

5   Ibid., 151.

6   Ibid., 226–7.

7   Ibid., 114–15.

8   Cited in McKale, *Prüfer* (footnote 1), 61.

9   Ibid., 100–1, 175–6.

10 McKale, *Rewriting History* (footnote 3), 74.

11 Ibid., 11, 151.

12 Ibid., 113, 225.

13 Auswärtiges Amt (ed.), *Auswärtige Politik heute* (Bonn, 1979).

14 Eckart Conze, Norbert Frei, Peter Hayes and Moshe Zimmermann (eds), *Das Amt und die Vergangenheit: Deutsche Diplomaten im Dritten Reich und in der Bundesrepublik* (Munich, 2010), 10, 583–5.

15 Jan Friedmann and Klaus Wiegrefe, 'Angriff auf die "Mumien"', *Der Spiegel* 43 (2010), 36–8; 'Fischers Gedenkpraxis', *Frankfurter Allgemeine Zeitung*, 10 February 2005.

16 *Das Amt*, 16.

17 Jan Friedmann and Klaus Wiegrefe, 'Verbrecherische Organisation', in *Der Spiegel* 43 (2010), 40–50.

18 See the links in 'Pressespiegel zur Debatte um das Auswärtige Amt und seine Vergangenheit: Ausgewählte Artikel und Interviews', zusammengestellt von Georg Koch/Matthias Speidel/Christian Mentel, URL: <http://www.zeitgeschichte-online.de/site/40209125/default.aspx> [accessed 13 May 2011].

19 Friedmann and Wiegrefe, 'Angriff' (footnote 15), 38.

20 Rainer Blasius, 'Schnellbrief und Braunbuch', *Frankfurter Allgemeine Zeitung*, 13 January 2011.

21 Christopher Browning, *The Final Solution and the German Foreign Office: A Study of Referat D III der Abteilung Deutschland 1940–1943* (New York and London, 1978).

22 Hans-Jürgen Döscher, *Das Auswärtige Amt im Dritten Reich: Diplomatie*

im Schatten der 'Endlösung' (Berlin, 1987); idem, *SS und Auswärtiges Amt im Dritten Reich: Diplomatie im Schatten der 'Endlösung'* (Frankfurt am Main and Berlin, 1991); idem, *Verschworene Gesellschaft: Das Auswärtige Amt unter Adenauer zwischen Neubeginn und Kontinuität* (Berlin, 1995); idem, *Seilschaften: Die verdrängte Vergangenheit des Auswärtigen Amts* (Berlin, 2005).

23   See, for example, Stefan Troebst, 'Rezension zu: Eckart Conze, Norbert Frei, Peter Hayes and Moshe Zimmermann (eds), *Das Amt und die Vergangenheit: Deutsche Diplomaten im Dritten Reich und in der Bundesrepublik* (Munich, 2010)', in *H-Soz-u-Kult*, 15.02.2011, URL: <http://hsozkurt.geschichte. hu-berlin.de/rezensionen/2011-1-108> [accessed 13 May 2011].

24   Hans Mommsen, 'Das ganze Ausmaß der Verstrickung', *Frankfurter Rundschau*, 16 November 2010; idem, 'Vergebene Chancen, "Das Amt" hat methodische Mängel', *Süddeutsche Zeitung*, 27 December 2010; Johannes Hürter, 'Das Auswärtige Amt, die NS-Diktatur und der Holocaust: Kritische Bemerkungen zu einem Kommissionsbericht', *Vierteljahrshefte für Zeitgeschichte* 59 (2011), 167–92. See also Klaus Wiegrefe, 'Historiker zerpflückt Bestseller', *Der Spiegel*-online, 1 April 2011, URL: <http://www.spiegel.de/politik/deutschland/ 0,1518,754558,00.html> [accessed 12 May, 2011]. The editors have recently published a response to Hürter's review: 'Zauberwort Differenzierung', *Frankfurter Rundschau*, 3 May 2011.

25   Mommsen, 'Vergebene Chancen' (footnote 24); for Ulrich Herbert's comments on Mommsen's remark see, 'Am Ende nur noch Opfer. Interview mit Ulrich Herbert', *die tageszeitung*, 8 December 2010.

26   Peter Hayes, *Industry and Ideology: IG Farben in the Nazi Era* (Cambridge, 1987); idem, *From Cooperation to Complicity: Degussa in the Third Reich* (Cambridge , 2004); Norbert Frei, among numerous publications perhaps most relevantly, idem, et al., *Flick, Der Konzern, die Familie, die Macht* (Munich 2009); Eckart Conze, *Die Suche nach Sicherheit: Eine Geschichte der Bundesrepublik Deutschland von 1949 bis in die Gegenwart* (Munich, 2009). Moshe Zimmermann's research expertise is in the nineteenth century though he has published overviews of German-Jewish history.

27   Alan Posener, 'Das ist eine Kampagne: Das Münchener Institut für Zeitgeschichte greift den Bestseller Das Amt und die Vergangenheit an', *Die Welt*, 4 April 2011. See also the joint statement of the editors in *Süddeutsche Zeitung*, 10 December 2010.

28   Daniel Koerfer, interviewed in *Frankfurter Allgemeine Sonntagszeitung*,

28 November 2010; see also Blasius (footnote 20). Ulrich Herbert comments on Koerfer in 'Am Ende nur noch Opfer' (footnote 25).

29   Lars Lüdicke, *Griff nach der Weltherrschaft: Die Außenpolitik des Dritten Reiches 1933–1945* (Berlin, 2009).

30   *Das Amt*, 72.

31   Ibid., 51.

32   Ibid., 128.

33   Ibid., 141.

34   Jan-Erik Schulte, *Zwangsarbeit und Vernichtung: Das Wirtschaftsimperium der SS: Oswald Pohl und das SS-Wirtschaftsverwaltungshauptamt 1933–1945* (Paderborn, 2001).

35   *Das Amt*, 138, 152–3.

36   Ibid., 123.

37   Ibid., 29.

38   Saul Friedländer, *Nazi Germany and the Jews: The Years of Persecution 1933–39* (London, 1997), 19.

39   *Das Amt*, 101.

40   Ibid., 147; Ian Kershaw, *Hitler 1889–1936: Hubris* (London, 1998), 562–9 (the Foreign Office is mentioned only as reporting on the 20 August meeting).

41   *Das Amt*, 400–1.

42   Hürter, 'Das Auswärtige Amt' (footnote 24), 174–5. There is a brief treatment of the role of the German embassy in Warsaw in the run-up to the war (p. 223) but not much more.

43   Jochen Böhler, *Auftakt zum Vernichtungskrieg: Die Wehrmacht in Polen 1939* (Frankfurt am Main, 2006).

44   *Das Amt*, 161–71.

45   Ibid., 200–20.

46   Ibid., 221–86 and 227–94.

47   Ibid., 254–7.

48   Christopher Browning, *The Origins of the Final Solution* (Lincoln, NB, 2004), 323–5.

49   Peter Longerich, *Holocaust: The Nazi Persecution and Murder of the Jews* (Oxford, 2010), 265–6.

50   Döscher, *Das Auswärtige Amt* (footnote 22), 255.

51   *Das Amt*, 167–99, 171–85 respectively.

52   Ibid., 293.

53   Ibid., 295–316.

54   Ibid., 321–42.

55   Ibid., 342–62.

56 Astrid Eckert, *Kampf um die Akten: Die Westallüerten und die Rückgabe von deutschem Archivgut nach dem Zweiten Weltkrieg* (Stuttgart, 2004); *Das Amt*, 375–401.

57 Including Annette Weinke, *Eine Gesellschaft ermittelt gegen sich selbst: Die Geschichte der Zentralen Stelle Ludwigsburg 1958–2008* (Darmstadt, 2008); *Die Nürnberger Prozesse* (Munich, 2006); and *Die Verfolgung von NS-Tätern im geteilten Deutschland: Vergangenheitsbewältigungen 1949–1969 oder: Eine deutsch-deutsche Beziehungsgeschichte im Kalten Krieg* (Paderborn, 2002); *Das Amt*, 401–35.

58 *Das Amt*, 431–2, 435–48.

59 Ibid., 448–88.

60 Ibid., 201.

61 Browning, *The Origins* (footnote 48), 303, 307, 324, 326, 368, 414.

62 Gerald Reitlinger, *The Final Solution* (New York, 1953).

63 *Das Amt*, 588–95.

64 Ibid., 489–532.

65 Ibid., 533–58.

66 Ibid., 558–69.

67 Ibid., 616.

68 Ibid., 11.

69 Tim Mason, 'Intention and Explanation: A Current Controversy about the Interpretation of National Socialism', in Gerhard Hirschfeld and Lothar Kettenacker (eds), *The 'Führer State': Myth and Reality: Studies on the Structure and Politics of the Third Reich* (Stuttgart, 1981), 23–40, at 40.

INDEX

943.086 EVA Evans
Evans, Richard J.
Third Reich in history and memory, The

DATE DUE			
6/9/15			
6/22/15			
8/07/15			
5/10/18